Christmas '98.

Bought in othBoy cShop
29-11-2007   NED

"A lot of nonsense"
$\frac{0}{10}$ "Dont waste your life reading this"
"Drivel":

Signed
A.R. Tillery
6·12-2023
11·40pm.

An Age of Innocence

Irish Culture 1930-1960

In Memoriam
P. F. 1905-1974

AN AGE OF INNOCENCE
Irish Culture 1930-1960

BRIAN FALLON

Gill & Macmillan

Gill & Macmillan Ltd
Goldenbridge
Dublin 8
with associated companies throughout the world

© Brian Fallon 1998
0 7171 2461 4

Index compiled by Gloria Greenwood
Print origination by Andy Gilsenan, Dublin
Printed by MPG Books Limited, UK

This book is typeset in Berkeley 10.5/12.

A catalogue record for this book is available from the British Library.

5 4 3 2 1

CONTENTS

Chapter 1

IN PERSPECTIVE

The thirty years dealt with in this book (I do not write 'covered in this book', because genuine, detailed coverage would require several volumes) were far more than a mere period of transition. Of course they were that as well – transition from the Literary Revival dominated by Yeats, AE, George Moore and other founding fathers to a generation of writers which was largely self-contained and did not necessarily look to London as its centre; transition from a largely peasant society and the remnants of the Anglo-Irish Ascendancy to a country largely dominated by the newly emerging Catholic bourgeoisie; and politically, transition from dominion status inside the British Empire to a republic.

Though it is often depicted as a time almost entirely dominated by ruralism and back-to-the-land philosophies, many people – including young women – were deserting the countryside and the small farms; and while peasant values were paid lip service by politicians and others, in practice the Irish were already on the way to becoming what Seán O'Faolain has called 'a nation of urbanised peasants'. There was a powerful nostalgia for the old country ways and the simple, frugal country life, yet while many members of the new middle class may have looked back emotionally on their rural upbringing, they were still glad enough to live in the towns or in new, charmless Dublin suburbs. They might hang on their parlour wall a calendar reproduction of a Paul Henry West of Ireland landscape with the inevitable thatched cottage, turf rick and small blue lake, but they had no real intention of going back to such a life, and their chief ambition was to ensure that their children got a good education and climbed the ladder in whatever professions they might choose.

Seen in this context, it becomes plain that it was not an era of regression, but rather of deep social and cultural change which led – sometimes by odd or circuitous routes – to the Irish society of today. It was also one of deep divisions, social, political, intellectual and ideological. Today we tend to see those thirty years in a kind of levelling monochrome, though Ireland was actually in constant flux and many crucial intellectual debates were fought out which have largely made us what we are today, for better or worse – or for neither. The newborn Ireland was grappling, sometimes hesitantly and sometimes ineptly, with its role or place in the modern era. Yet for a long time now the tendency has been to see it as dominated by insularity, defensive-minded nationalism, the Church, censorship, a retreat from the outer world. This attitude has fossilised into a kind of dogma, which a surprising number of people – including some well-informed ones – refuse to criticise or reconsider. In the words of Louis MacNeice: 'Man's deference to any logic of black-and-white, of all-or-nothing, is probably due to his basic illogicality; he just cannot cope with the world in colour. He refuses to distinguish conditions from causes.'

The tendency to rebel against the recent past, or even to reject it altogether, seems to be a recurrent trait of nations, cultures and even entire generations, almost a part of the in-built rhythm of things. It often has a basis of sound sense, and it is also a natural, even healthy instinct; each generation has to clear the decks for its own battles, to jettison what has suddenly become oppressive, restricting, or simply anachronistic, and to stamp its own particular image on its age. Children, as Zola once told George Moore, devour their fathers (with the extra meaning, in this case, that his former disciple had turned against him).

It is only quite recently, to quote one relevant historico-cultural parallel, that England has been able to look at and re-evaluate the entire Victorian Age with some degree of objectivity. Victorian revivalists such as John Betjeman were widely regarded for a long time as partly jokers, partly self-indulgent eccentrics. Hatred of the Victorians remained almost obsessive for decades, and in retrospect the reason is only too obvious – the Victorian Age was so powerful, so domineering and so strong in its apparent certainties that it weighed on the immediately succeeding age like an immense, musty pall. All those eminent Victorians – bearded, patriarchal, puritanical, some of them muscular Christians and others high-minded agnostics preaching Duty and Progress and the virtues of unstinting hard work and moral self-improvement – were like so many Freudian father-figures who had to be exorcised from the collective consciousness for the sake of attaining some degree of self-belief. A radical break with the immediate past and its tyrannous system of hereditary values was urgently needed, so that a new generation could raise its head and open its lungs, breathe new air and find room for its own individuality, its own creativity and moral ethos – or even, as in the case of the Twenties, the relative lack of one.

This was done, however, at the huge cost of denigrating and putting virtually under ban one of the greatest epochs in British (and European) history. The sustained orgy of literary, cultural and social iconoclasm which followed was in many ways a disaster, disrupting organic continuity, distorting history, propagating myths, anti-myths and misunderstandings, and even (on a purely physical level) levelling or vandalising many fine buildings and works of art because they did not conform to the dictates of twentieth-century Modernism.

How much more intelligent, and more constructive, it is to come to terms creatively with the past than to amputate it like a diseased limb, or put it under interdict! We are likely to find ourselves in the position of the self-conscious moderniser who, having thrown out his ancestral furniture and paintings or sold them off for a knockdown price, finds inside a few years that these have now become valuable, respected antiques and that he himself is much the poorer, financially as well as culturally. After all, at the risk of labouring the obvious, the past has produced us, and when we deny it we deny our own immediate ancestry, and even an essential part of ourselves.

In Ireland's present intellectual climate, the demonisation – there is hardly any other suitable word for it – of the thirty-odd years dealt with in this book is still almost automatic and unquestioning, amounting to what used to be called a conditioned reflex. For one thing, it was an age in which the authority of the Catholic Church was rarely questioned seriously by the great majority – and today there is a reaction against that Church which is often as uncritical and simplistic as the worst dogmas and shibboleths of forty years ago. Unthinking clericalism has simply given way to unthinking anti-clericalism; the coin has been flipped to come down heads instead of tails – but it remains the same well-worn coin. Yet Irish Catholicism cannot be summed up in the puritanical zealotry of Archbishop John Charles McQuaid or the moral nosey-parkerism of the Legion of Mary.

Secondly, it is still regarded as an era of almost monomaniac nationalism, while just now Ireland is obsessed with creating a cosmopolitan, internationalist image of itself, in line with what it sees as its formal entry into European status. This politico-cultural motif is not new, of course – it is a recurrent one in Irish history and has been debated numerous times since independence – but at no time previously was it so vocal and aggressive as it is today. Yet is not a large part of this frenzied internationalism at heart inverted provincialism, the product of an unsure, partly-fledged culture lacking the courage to be wholeheartedly itself? Where once we looked to and deferred to Britain in so many fields, we now look to the EU to tell us what we should be thinking and doing.

And thirdly, the period is seen in intellectual terms as the age of literary censorship and intellectual repression, when Irish writers were either silenced and curbed at home, or else forced to live and write abroad. There has been for years a widespread belief that after the golden age of the Literary Revival or Renaissance, Irish literature and art regressed almost to provincial level, while the surviving major figures emigrated to more grateful climes, like swallows before the coming of winter. According to this view, which is particularly strong in English and American academic circles but is also widely accepted at home, Ireland became too narrow and puritanical a context for any writer or artist or thinker of the first rank to develop his or her full potential in it, or at least to endure the Irish way of life without constant friction.

It goes without saying that all these accusations have a solid core of truth; the historical evidence is sometimes overwhelming, and it has been spelt out *ad nauseam*. Yet the case for the prosecution is often partial, selective, even one-sided, arousing the suspicion that it is anxious to secure a conviction at all costs and is even prepared to shut out almost any evidence that does not support its viewpoint absolutely. There appears to be a definite, preconceived, *a priori* agenda at work here, a psychological need to paint the present in even brighter colours by correspondingly blackening the past – a kind of historical chiaroscuro, you might almost say. Underlying it is a basic emotional insecurity, almost a kind of moralistic hysteria, as though our era can only find reassurance for the validity of its stances and convictions by abusing those of the age immediately before it. This, however, is a facile and obvious intellectual trick which proves more against the accuser than the accused. In the words of Yeats: 'They must, to keep their certainty, accuse / All who are different of a base intent.' An age of genuine enlightenment would not show such intolerance of a preceding age whose main crime was to think and feel differently from it.

Historically, we know by now that few epochs are divisible into simple black and white, though some on first examination may seem outwardly a uniform grey; the past, like the present, is many-sided and often contradictory. Speaking on the broadest and most basic level, let any reasonably well-informed person take a quick bird's-eye survey of American history in this century, both cultural and socio-political, and he/she will come across many dark or opaque areas in the recent past of the world's leading superpower, now the arbiter of many or most of our contemporary values. To list a few almost at random: the refusal to allow the theory of evolution to be taught in schools in the Biblical-minded Southern states, the Saccho and Vanzetti case with its blatant miscarriage of justice, the defacing of Diego Rivera's (admittedly Communist-inspired) murals in New York, the McCarthy years during which so many gifted and able people were humiliated and even the great Einstein was attacked as being un-American, the barbarous treatment meted out to Ezra Pound in old age because of a few foolish broadcasts he had made on behalf of Mussolini . . . All these are unanswerable historical facts, yet we all know equally well that they are only part of the many-coloured picture and that it would be just as easy to list outstanding examples of American liberalism and intellectual freedom.

To pursue this type of national analogy further, British literary journalists for decades have aired their views on Irish censorship without, apparently, considering the frequent fatuities of their own. Yet it was Britain and America which banned Joyce's *Ulysses* for some years, whereas his native country never did – in spite of a widespread belief that Joyce's writings were not only prohibited by the Irish Censorship Board, but by the Papal Index as well (equally untrue). As for the treatment given to D. H. Lawrence, it surpasses in sheer sustained hostility that meted out to any Irish writer past or present. Not only were certain novels of his

banned, and his exhibition of paintings forcibly closed by the police, but he himself
was harried and humiliated by officialdom as an immoral and subversive influence
until he left England for ever, in a mood of complete hostility and disillusion. The
public attacks on the sculptor Epstein went on for many years, and were
accompanied by the vandalisation of some of his best-known public works (in Paris
as well as in England, incidentally). And the virtual ostracism of P. G. Wodehouse –
probably at that time the best-loved writer in the English-speaking world – for some
ill-judged, but innocuous and totally non-political wartime broadcasts he made
from Germany while interned there as an alien, does not make pretty reading. Yet
again, to look on the positive side, no country has greater respect than Britain for
the privileges of free speech, and for the rights of the individual.

Or take even France, often spoken of as the heartland of Europe's intellectual
freedom; yet it too has its shadowy areas. The novelist Colette, after her death in
1954, was denied Catholic burial rites by the then Archbishop of Paris – an incident
which moved Graham Greene to write an open letter of protest to the Church
authorities. If a similar incident had occurred in Ireland, it is only too easy to guess
at the angry or caustic headlines which would have appeared almost automatically
in the foreign press, and the familiar half-humorous, half-moralistic condemnations
of such a typically Irish example of clerical bigotry and philistinism.

More recently Sweden, not so long ago regarded as the European showpiece of
liberal democracy, damaged its international prestige by the mistreatment of
probably its leading figure in the arts, the film director Ingmar Bergman. Accused
of tax evasion, he was publicly arrested and humiliated in a manner better suited to
an embezzler of state funds or a crooked businessman who had cheated and bribed
his way to ill fame. Bergman would have been fully justified if he and his company
had left Sweden. Fortunately for Sweden he did not do so, and the matter was
eventually sorted out, but the incident was a salutary lesson in how bureaucratic
intolerance and philistinism can lurk behind the facade of democratic consensus –
that is to say, public conformity – in even the most developed modern states.

The examples I have quoted are not listed here merely to prove that if the Irish
kettle is black with soot, then so are most of the pots and pans of other Western
nations, individually or collectively. That would be a childish ploy and would prove
very little except what is already sufficiently known – that the most enlightened
countries are capable periodically of intolerance and folly. I have chosen them in
order to demonstrate that no country, big or small, backward or progressive, has a
monopoly of censorship and philistinism; they are aspects of human nature which
are always likely to recur, though in differing forms, and there will always be
sincere, well-meaning yet blinkered people who support them for what they believe
are valid, or at least adequate, reasons. Anybody who believes that we are now living
in a new era of tolerance and international understanding – whether political,
ideological or artistic – knows little of the realities of human nature and history, not
to mention economics. We live in an era of permissiveness, that is all, and this

permissiveness dominates our accepted codes of behaviour largely because it is underwritten by massive commercial and other interests.

Censorship today takes many other forms than the old sexual taboos, and it has weapons and methods vastly more subtle and powerful than the blundering asininities of the Censorship of Publications Board in this country a generation ago. The pressures exerted by political interests, by commercial forces, by official ideologies, by such vocal pressure groups as the radical wing of feminism (which few publishers can risk offending), by the various conformities of our age, and by that curious but all-pervasive phenomenon called Political Correctness, are powerful and constant. Political Correctness indeed appears to be the official cant of our time – the contemporary equivalent of Victorian hypocrisy, or of the socio-religious conformity of a large section of the Irish public forty or fifty years ago.

As the Kerry writer Bryan MacMahon wrote in his autobiographical book *The Master*: 'I consider the greatest mistake any commentator can make is to pass judgment on "then" in the context of "now". To do so is to ignore the prevailing atmosphere of a particular era and hold it up to unjust scrutiny or ridicule by applying to it standards that now prevail in a completely altered set of circumstances.'

O f all the reiterated charges brought against what might be called, very broadly and not very accurately, the Ireland of de Valera, probably the most prominent is that of so-called isolationism. According to this intellectual and political assessment, Ireland (or at least the Free State) withdrew voluntarily from the congress of other European nations into a kind of chauvinist self-sufficiency, ringing itself with tariff walls and with literary and intellectual censorship. In effect, it opted out of international politics and culture and chose instead to cultivate its own garden, or rather to dig its own patch of bog.

Politically, this does not hold water. It could be argued that from the Civil War onwards, Ireland was in a state of shock or prolonged convalescence; it also had to find its feet as an entirely new national entity, to define itself and its aims as a state, and to build up almost overnight a new machinery of government and civil administration. It was also, by Western European standards, a very poor country and according to Tom Garvin's 1922 *The Birth of Irish Democracy*, the devastation of the Civil War had left a bill of £50 million, an enormous sum for those days, which had to be met as a priority. Later, de Valera's refusal – largely justified in principle, but clumsily carried out – to suspend payment of the land annuities to Britain backfired into the costly and damaging Economic War; this was resolved after a few years, but then came the thorny issue of the Irish ports.

Politically, economically and diplomatically, Ireland seemed to totter from one crisis to another – although, of course, the Thirties was a troubled decade almost everywhere, with Communism and Fascism growing in strength, the old liberal democracy under threat, American capitalism in crisis, and the worldwide Great Slump throwing millions out of work and sowing the seeds of social unrest and revolution. Europe as a whole was living on its nerves, and it would have been strange, even unnatural, if Ireland had not reflected the social and ideological strains and conflicts of the time, though in its own idiosyncratic way. Finally, of course, came the second World War and the furore over Irish neutrality, an argument which has been carried on over fifty years. I discuss that issue in a later chapter, but the chief point to be made about it here is that the myth of isolationism largely stems from it. The State's decision to stay out of the fighting – or, more accurately and realistically, not to allow British or American troops to garrison it – has not been forgiven. The Anglo-American world felt betrayed, and accordingly it has taken its revenge over decades.

As Bernard Share put it cogently in a special supplement to *The Irish Times* of 8 May 1985, dealing with the years of the so-called Emergency:

> *The assessment that Ireland through remaining neutral had cut herself off from all informing outside influences and thus drifted into a brackish backwater was one that was widely canvassed outside the country by those who saw in that neutrality a political or human betrayal. The British, who still in 1939 regarded the Irish Free State for all practical purposes as integral to what continued to be described as the 'British' Isles (a denotation still valued for its ambiguity), were particularly attracted to this view, and since what the rest of the world learnt about Ireland it learnt almost exclusively from British sources, it was a view which acquired widespread currency.*

> *Thus the currency was to fan out into history of a small, selfishly inward-looking community deliberately cutting itself off from 'germinating' ideas – a suggestion rarely, if ever, encountered in the case of, say, neutral Sweden or neutral Switzerland. It is a concept that has only recently met with any serious challenge.*

Perhaps Bernard Share places a little too much emphasis on British opinion and too little on that of the United States, which increasingly emerges from the history of the later Thirties as already, in effect, the Big Brother of what later became the Atlantic Alliance; otherwise his thesis seems to me not only sound but acute. President Roosevelt was, by temperament and background, extremely close to British views and sentiments, as well as being temperamentally rather anti-Irish, and this was enhanced by the reports showered on him by the American Ambassador in Dublin, David Gray – a militant Wasp, a distant relative of the President, and a man who was despised and detested by most of the Irish intelligentsia. Gray mixed mainly with, and listened to, people of a 'West British' background, who told him what in any case he wanted to hear – that Ireland should go into the war at once, more or less as a British satellite. In the eyes of these people, as Share says, 'to be cut off from Britain ideologically, and therefore culturally, was to be cut off from much of the world that mattered.' It is even said that the then English Ambassador to Dublin, Sir John Maffey (later Lord Rugby), was playing cricket in a (Protestant) public school on the outskirts of the city when he was told of the fall of France. As he bent to take off his pads, he remarked comfortably that such a decadent country as France could really expect no better fate.

The war, of course, cut Ireland off from Continental Europe anyway, even though various foreign embassies and legations (including, to Anglo-American fury, the German one) remained open in Dublin. In spite of wartime censorship, however, communications with Britain remained surprisingly open; many Irish people crossed the Channel to work there during the war, thousands more fought in the British armed forces or served with the merchant marine, and English newspapers and magazines still achieved entry, though not in the same numbers as before. Irish newspapers themselves, though harshly censored by the Government as part of its neutral face, relied heavily on English reports and agencies for their limited coverage of external events. Above all, however, the various wavelengths of the British Broadcasting Corporation dominated radio listening ('the wireless', as it was called) and poor Radio Éireann, in comparison, was merely a country cousin or poor relation.

Cultural contacts with Britain continued in a muted way; the poet John Betjeman came to Dublin as a kind of cultural ambassador (some even said, as a spy) and Elizabeth Bowen travelled to and fro between the two countries. She too was in touch with British Intelligence, as she admitted herself later, though to call her a spy would be a distortion; she acted mainly out of reasons of conscience.[1] Betjeman until his return to England in the summer of 1943 encouraged cultural exchanges between Ireland and Britain insofar as wartime conditions allowed; he brought English celebrities to Dublin, encouraged London editors to publish work by Irish writers including Patrick Kavanagh, and struck up friendships (partly diplomatic, partly genuine) with writers-intellectuals such as Frank O'Connor, Seán O'Faolain and Frank Gallagher – who gave him personal access to de Valera. Betjeman even managed to smuggle English films into the country through his diplomatic mailbag.[2] Other distinguished immigrants included Erwin Schrödinger, the great nuclear physicist, who was brought to Dublin by de Valera; and a number of English painters, a handful of them genuinely gifted, settled in Ireland, some temporarily and others for good (the general opinion was that they came to escape war service, a sensible decision for an artist). Distinguished musicians came sometimes, and even some well-known actors. Review copies of English-published books managed to struggle through, often printed on wartime paper which looked like crushed straw.

From all this it would seem that our isolation was – to state the obvious again – probably much less than that of most Continental nations, who were either forcibly occupied by Germany or had, themselves, rigid censorship and press controls, imposed by their ruling regimes. Switzerland and Sweden had liberal governments, but both were in highly vulnerable situations and so had to tread warily. Spain was recovering from its devastating Civil War and Franco, after some early flirtation with the Axis Powers, followed a policy not unlike de Valera's. In retrospect, Ireland's neutrality was not a glorious episode in its history, but neither was it a shameful one. It was not in any real sense an ideological stance; it was dominated by survival values and by pressing internal problems – including the IRA – and in my opinion de Valera had little choice but to act as he did. That it ultimately helped rather than hindered the Allied war effort seems nowadays to be increasingly admitted and recognised, and few dispute any longer that it was essentially pro-Ally, though without spelling out the fact.

As for the pre-war years, political isolation scarcely applies in any real sense to them either. Ireland took a creditable role in the League of Nations, with de Valera prominent, and at the time of the Danzig crisis in 1939 which proved the initial flashpoint of war, the League's commissioner there was a distinguished Irishman, Seán Lester. In the post-war years we joined the United Nations as soon as Soviet hostility allowed us, in 1955, and here again the Irish record was a good one, as a recent book on the subject sets out.[3] We also played some part in reshaping the British Commonwealth of Nations into something more modern and democratic than its original, quasi-imperialist character, a fact which has been noted by a distinguished historian, the late Dr Nicholas Mansergh.[4] Much has been made of Irish tariff barriers, but trade wars and tariff wars were a commonplace of the pre-war period and were a feature of its economic climate: they were a direct result of worldwide economic ignorance and consequent economic failure. What is now called autarchy was a policy which made sense to some shrewd brains at the time, and in the eyes of most people it seemed preferable to pay one's way – or at least attempt to do so – rather than run up massive trade deficits or gigantic national debts. In any case, in Ireland's case tariffs were used originally as a *pro tem* device, a kind of crutch to be employed until our infant industries learned to walk. (As has recently been pointed out by Professor Tom Garvin, by the late Thirties de Valera had largely abandoned his policy of making Ireland overwhelmingly a country of small farms, and, in the face of a good deal of internal hostility, was making strong efforts to industrialise it.[5])

In the cultural field, of course (which is what this book is primarily about), literary censorship offers a ready handle to grasp for those who uphold the isolationist argument. Just how deeply it damaged intellectual life, or how much deprivation it created both for writers and readers, is not an easy question to answer – in fact it is probably unanswerable, at least in the case of the private reader. Yet it should be remembered that censored books were only a fraction of the number which entered the country and were sold at bookshops or borrowed from circulating libraries. (This point has been emphasised by Brian Inglis, among others.[6]) Censorship, though often excessively stupid and puritanical, never actually attempted to set up an intellectual inquisition or to control ideas, as was done or at least attempted in totalitarian countries. Books and magazines were banned on two basic grounds – that they were 'indecent or obscene' or that they advocated contraception and abortion. (They could also be banned for exploiting violence and crime, though there was relatively little effort made to curb violence in the popular cinema.[7]) Since these criteria were often applied rigidly and unimaginatively, as has usually been the case with bureaucratic censorship through the ages, many important modern writers joined the *non legenda* lists and a number of eminent native ones suffered along with the rest. Ideas and opinions, however, were not censored as a rule and Marxist and anti-clerical writings often circulated freely, as did books and articles which were sometimes bitterly hostile to almost all things Irish.

Irish publishing was always a relatively limited enterprise (except in the field of school books and certain other specialised areas) so English importations flooded the market, censors or no censors. The bread-and-butter fare of the small circulating libraries which existed in most Irish towns was likely to include numerous thrillers, Westerns, popular love stories, the writings of P. G. Wodehouse, books by Baroness Orczy, Zane Grey, Jeffrey Farnol, Monica Dickens, Mazo de la Roche and their like, along with some popular biographies and memoirs; virtually the only Irish writer who could compete on this popular level was the romantic novelist Maurice Walsh. The Carnegie Libraries generally had a wider and better selection; indeed many Irish people were introduced to 'serious reading' through these. Books for children, too, were overwhelmingly English-produced. The paperback revolution had not yet arrived, though a handful of Penguin Books were available and this imprint made a rapidly increasing impact in the years after the war, when Penguins could be bought even in the newspaper shops of small towns.

British magazines, covering a huge range of interests and tastes, could be seen in rows on the counter of any newspaper shop (the now-vanished *Picture Post*, for example, had a big Irish circulation). English comic papers were sold in thousands every week to Irish schoolchildren, ranging from the elementary comic-strip kind catering for primary-school children to ones which printed serial stories aimed at young teenagers. Virtually the only native answer to these was *Ireland's Own*. Though the Irish national newspapers had and kept a firm home readership, this did not prevent English ones from winning a large share of the market, particularly on Sundays; these Sunday papers ranged from quality ones such as the *Observer* to popular scandal sheets. Literary magazines such as Cyril Connolly's *Horizon* were bought and read by the Irish literati, while during the Fifties the *New Statesman* became almost a public badge for those who wanted to pass as being well-informed. From the late Forties, too, the *Listener* and the *Spectator* were virtually compulsory reading for such people. The post-war wave of Americanisation brought in the *New Yorker* – to which leading Irish fiction-writers contributed, including Mary Lavin, Frank O'Connor and Benedict Kiely – while on a rather lower level, *Time* magazine began to appear prominently on the news-stands, and even *Colliers* and the *Saturday Evening Post* for a time became domestic reading, though they were never available in large supply.

Above all, however, this Anglo-American domination of popular taste was exercised through the cinema, which was overwhelmingly the popular art of the times – even small villages sometimes had their own shabby little picture-houses. 'The films' (Orson Welles, during his stay in Dublin in the 1930s, noted that the latter word was generally pronounced as a disyllable – fill-ums) provided the imaginative escape-hatch or fantasy land of the poor, the favourite relaxation (along with ballroom dancing) of the middle and lower-middle classes, and a home-from-home for the mating rituals of courting couples. The films they watched were almost entirely British and American, which in many ways supplied young people with what we should now call role-models – much as the Pop Culture does today. They also helped to bolster the huge popularity of Anglo-American popular music, much or most of which was commercial ephemera and banality (the word 'muzak' was not yet current). The dance halls were full of the aural wallpaper of Tin Pan Alley, while the radio filled middle-class homes with it; it was sung or played at parties and hummed in offices, homes and even school corridors.

When all this is taken into account, the accepted picture of a culturally chauvinistic statelet shutting its doors (and windows) on international currents turns out, in several respects, to be almost the reverse of the truth. Instead, Ireland, badly in need of a developing national culture of her own, was hopelessly out-gunned by external forces – mainly commercial – over which her leaders had little control, and few institutions or public bodies knew how to combat these forces effectively. Well-meaning but backward-looking people might call Jazz 'jungle music', and Radio Éireann for a while held out against it, yet that did not stop the young from buying or listening to jazz records. If officialdom was hostile to swing music and the like, it was a simple matter to switch to the BBC Home Service and listen to Henry Hall. The clergy might storm from their pulpits on Sundays against the 'pagan' English yellow press, yet in nearby streets – sometimes, even, just outside the church gates – those same newspapers were on sale and doing a brisk trade. As for the popular cinema, it was of course subject to censorship, but in no way could it be banned; it was a source of state revenue, and arguably it kept young people out of worse places, such as pubs. Above all, the mass of people wanted and liked it, and it provided family entertainment of a relatively sanitised and innocuous kind. Hollywood itself had its own home censors in the Hays Office, and there were also vigilance bodies like the League of Decency to make it toe the line. In any case, the Hollywood moguls themselves had by now discovered the value of this family-dominated market with its hatred of anything questioning or disturbing, let alone shocking, and they knew very well where and how their bread was buttered. Hollywood, in effect, had become its own censor.

Against all these massed commercial phalanxes, the efforts of bodies such as the Gaelic League were largely powerless. Ireland had no film industry of its own, and in spite of occasional pioneering efforts from men such as Denis Johnston, it did not succeed in developing one (though after the war an increasing number of English and American films were made in Ireland). In one field alone the nativists triumphed – sport, where the Gaelic Athletic Association fought hard and usually successfully against the encroachment of 'foreign games'. It did not, of course, succeed in banning soccer and rugby, but soccer was largely confined to certain – usually urban – areas, while rugby remained largely the game of the public schools and the universities. By contrast, Gaelic football and hurling were played by the rural masses and by many city-dwellers as well, and Radio Éireann and most of the national newspapers gave them wide coverage and a kind of semi-official encouragement. This development had begun long before the Thirties, of course; but with the advent of Fianna Fáil to power, the GAA had more friends than ever in high places.

So if many pronouncements and denunciations of the time do read or sound today like cultural isolationism (again that word!), the people who made them were not necessarily all embattled or semi-ignorant provincials. After all, numbers of them had fought or at least hoped for a self-ruling Ireland with a lifestyle and culture of its own, instead of which they were being offered something that in several respects seemed more like a Mid-Western American state. Even AE (George Russell), a thorough cosmopolitan, had complained periodically about the advance of Americanisation in his own lifetime, and after his death it accelerated steadily and reached a crescendo in the years immediately after the second World War. And leaving Americanisation aside, there remained a great deal of the old colonial reliance upon Britain – which was probably inevitable, since whatever nationalist-minded people might say, London was still unanswerably the cultural as well as the political capital of the British Isles. The best Irish writers (including Yeats, AE himself, and most of the better-known novelists) depended on English publishers to bring out their work, though the Cuala Press for some decades provided a valuable service to the younger Irish poets. This had both a positive and negative side, since the judicious encouragement and support of discerning English publishing houses did much for the careers of some leading Irish writers – one might evidence not only the relationship between O'Casey and Harold Macmillan, but the wise criticism and backing which the young Seán O'Faolain received from Edward Garnett.[8] (Similarly, in the post-war years many Irish writers were grateful for the outlets given to them by the *New Yorker* magazine.) Against that, the London literary establishment was generally more sympathetic towards writers in the Anglo-Irish tradition (MacNeice, Elizabeth Bowen, Molly Keane etc.) than it was to those with a Catholic and nationalist colouring. As Irish literature in general became progressively less 'Anglo', English readers and critics generally felt less kinship with it.

Unfortunately, attempts to stem the flood-tide of commercial modernism were often naïve, homespun and ill-advised. The Irish-language lobby might insist on compulsory Gaelic in schools, but the teaching of it was poor and ultra-academic, there were too few skilled native speakers to go around, and the parents themselves, while often quite happy to support the language policy in theory, in practice scarcely tried to make Irish take root in the only power base from which it could ultimately have been revived – the family home. A modern literature in the Irish language was slow to develop and in spite of the Blasket Island school of writers, arguably it only arrived at maturity in the post-war era, with the emergence of writers such as Máirtín Ó Cadhain and Seán Ó Ríordáin. Irish music, like Irish dancing, too often meant the Clandillon type of céilidh band with its jigging fairground beat and basic three-four time; purely on musical grounds alone, jazz was distinctly preferable. Seán Ó Riada, who transformed our idea of Irish traditional music, only began to emerge as a national figure at the end of the Fifties and his later career does not belong inside the span of this book.

So far I have tended to stress the negative element, but there were many positive developments too, and many seeds of future growth were planted. Radio Éireann committed itself seriously to furthering a taste for classical music and was eventually responsible for the creation of a national symphony orchestra. The Gate Theatre, which had been founded in 1928 but whose most creative years were probably in the Thirties, gave a new impetus to writers, actors and producers at a time when the Abbey appeared to have lost its original spirit of adventure and was becoming an institution rather than a creative force. In 1943, in the darkest days of the war, a small nucleus of dedicated people founded the Irish Exhibition of Living Art, which became an annual forum for Irish Modernism and threw up a talented new generation of painters and sculptors. Meanwhile, Jack Yeats was painting the masterpieces of his 'third period', pictures which were probably more advanced than those of any artist in contemporary Britain and the equal of the great figures of the School of Paris. And in 1955 a young Irish painter, Louis le Brocquy, achieved European fame by winning a prize at the Venice Biennale.

In 1940 *The Bell* magazine was founded, a landmark in the literary and intellectual history of modern Ireland, with Seán O'Faolain as its editor until Peadar O'Donnell succeeded him, in 1946. David Marcus founded *Irish Writing* with the assistance of Terence Smith, and in 1949 John Ryan's *Envoy* began its vigorous but too-short life. All these were major literary magazines, and Ryan also gave space to the visual arts; meanwhile Seumas O'Sullivan's much-loved *Dublin Magazine*, founded back in 1924, managed to run until 1958. There has been nothing to compare seriously with this quartet since, even allowing for the obvious eclipse of the literary magazine as a genre.

The great age of the Irish short story, during which O'Connor, O'Faolain, Liam O'Flaherty and others earned international reputations, lies largely within the period under discussion; and although O'Flaherty's very finest stories were mostly written in the Twenties, it was in the Thirties that he produced *Famine*. This work towers over his other novels – the novelist John Broderick even claimed it to be the greatest Irish novel and forecast that it would be regarded as such when Joyce would have been relegated to the universities. Leaving Joyce himself out of the reckoning, that is possibly as close as the decade came to producing a genuinely great novel, apart from Flann O'Brien's brilliant but (in my opinion) somehow faintly juvenile and perhaps over-praised *At Swim-Two-Birds*, though Kate O'Brien, Elizabeth Bowen, Brinsley MacNamara, and Francis MacManus were all active and productive, and so was the young Beckett. Much of the finest poetry of Austin Clarke, Patrick Kavanagh, Padraic Fallon, F. R. Higgins, John Hewitt, belongs also to these three decades, and the same is true of Louis MacNeice, assuming that we are justified – as we surely are – in including him as an Irish rather than an English poet. Arguably, like Yeats, he is both, but MacNeice's essential Irishness is now increasingly recognised.[9] Or alternatively, might we say he is both Irish and international?

The 1940s and early Fifties saw the golden years of Myles na Gopaleen's unique 'Cruiskeen Lawn' column in *The Irish Times*, which (as some critics claim) may have damaged his development as a novelist but has left a series of comic vignettes and Swiftian comments which no other Irish writer, and very few writers outside Ireland for that matter, have managed to equal. On a very different plane, this decade also saw courageous efforts by Austin Clarke, Donagh MacDonagh and certain others to bring verse plays successfully to the stage, and so continue the legacy of Yeats. The development of the Irish verse play after Yeats is relatively neglected by contemporary critics and academics, who seem bemused or mesmerised by the achievement of Beckett to the exclusion of virtually all others. Yet MacDonagh's *Happy as Larry*, for instance, achieved a New York production in 1948 with set designs by no less a figure than the great sculptor Alexander Calder, and it was also printed in a widely distributed Penguin paperback along with verse plays by T. S. Eliot, Christopher Fry and Charles Williams. A number of Padraic Fallon's radio plays were performed (sometimes with elaborate musical scores) on the BBC Third Programme during the 1950s and were also translated into German for broadcasting from Hamburg radio.

It is true that the National Museum was relatively neglected and that the National Gallery of Ireland was starved of funding until the establishment of the Shaw Bequest enabled it to buy new pictures; both institutions were the subject of much debate in the national press and elsewhere, but this produced little official action until years later. Against that, the setting up of the Dublin Institute for Advanced Studies in 1940 was a landmark of its kind, and it was largely due to de Valera's initiative that Erwin Schrödinger was attracted to Ireland and took up a post in the institute. From Dublin Schrödinger carried on a remarkable correspondence with his friend and former colleague Albert Einstein,[10] and some of the lectures he delivered during his years in Ireland contained a number of his finest insights.

Another landmark was the establishment of the Irish Folklore Commission in 1935 under the directorship of Séamus Ó Duilearga, which eventually grew to be a massive archive of written, oral and visual material, attracting scholars from all over the world. And in 1950 the New York-born mining engineer, millionaire, philanthropist and art collector, Sir Alfred Chester Beatty, gave to the National Gallery a remarkable collection of French paintings which included works by Millet and Corot. However, Beatty went one better when he moved his residence to Dublin and in 1953 built the special library building named after him, to house his unique collection of Oriental art-works, books and manuscripts. Left in trust to the Irish nation, it became a magnet for all interested in Oriental studies and remains one of the greatest cultural assets which Ireland has ever possessed. As a gesture of thanks, Beatty was not only made a freeman of Dublin, but became the first ever honorary Irish citizen; and when he died at Monte Carlo in 1968, in his nineties, his body was taken to Ireland for burial in Glasnevin.

It seems unnecessary, and even insulting, to adopt a defensive or apologetic tone for such a cultural period. Undoubtedly it produced its full quota of stupidity, hysteria and myopia, but so has our own epoch – as Nietzsche has remarked, epochs are almost always mad, though individuals rarely are. The stupidities of certain public men are too often quoted – sometimes out of context – while the quality of sharp, vigorous and sometimes acidulous intelligence which also characterised it is almost forgotten, or else misunderstood. For instance, would a Myles na Gopaleen be possible today? Personally I doubt it, since the present wave of litigiousness has threatened to geld the Irish national press, yet he was read then almost daily by thousands and his mentality and comic-ironic tone are far more typical of his milieu than some recent commentators appear to think.

Undoubtedly there is a specific intellectual malaise underlying this milieu, a sense of frustration which was partly the outcome of disappointed (and perhaps exaggerated) hopes for what independence might achieve, partly an exasperation created by censorship, by economic failure (Ireland, it should be stressed over and over again, was a poor country) and lack of opportunity; and by native muddle and an inbred oddity and eccentricity which seemed to be woven into the texture of Irish life. The economic and other failures undoubtedly helped to breed a pessimism which strengthened the Irish intellectual's innate tendency towards self-doubt and self-questioning, so that much of the writing and thinking of the whole period, or periods, has an introspective, almost navel-gazing quality. This bitter-sweet quality is found too among French and Austro-German writers and intellectuals, and is woven into Russian literary history, but it is largely foreign to the Anglo-Saxon races who do not quite comprehend the love-hate relationship which usually lies behind it. Great aspirations, little room . . . . The Irish passion for self-criticism and even self-denigration has given hostages to people today who are eager to indict an entire age in order to fulfil certain intellectual agenda of their own. Dublin literary life was often ridden by feuds, factions, rivalries and quarrels, and the Irish at best are not a verbally charitable people; yet these quarrels also sharpened men's wits, verbally as well as socially, and accentuated the sharp, cerebral, sometimes openly malicious mentality so typical of this period, and which intelligent outsiders often mistook for cynicism or *schadenfreude*.

This apparent Irish bitchery occasionally shocked or alienated English observers (who appear to have accepted the po-faced malice of Bloomsbury without comment, or even the rampant malice which characterised Cyril Connolly's circle). Yet Harold Macmillan, whose firm published Yeats among others, once remarked: 'I don't attempt to keep pace with the quarrels of my Irish authors. They are bosom friends when I meet them on one occasion. A few months later, the same people are deadly enemies. I keep outside it all.' Dr Johnson's dictum about the Irish never speaking well of one another has been quoted *ad nauseam*, and even *post nauseam*, in this connection. Perhaps, too, the famed Dublin wit was never quite as witty as people believed or wanted to believe, the conversation never quite so pointed and swift-moving as memories made it, and very often Irish literary men were curiously lame and disappointing speakers in public. What did exist, quite unarguably, was a real feeling for words, a love of language for its own sake – a quality the intelligentsia shared, though in a very different way and at a very different level, with both the Dublin working-man and the farm labourer in his muddy boots. This quality still existed when I was in my late twenties, but I usually listen in vain for it today.

Those who approach the whole milieu expecting to find a continuation of the patrician wit of Wilde, or the social nuance of George Moore, inevitably are disappointed and disillusioned. Much of the humour was four-square, the wit was often inbred, and the social setting often either homespun rural, or humdrum small-town. English commentators in particular, who had always equated Anglo-Irish society with the 'civilised' aspect of Irish life, sometimes felt that everything had been delivered over to priests, peasants and gunmen turned politicians. That, in essence, is the attitude which J. B. Morton (better known as 'Beachcomber', and a firm friend to Ireland) found among the British upper classes.[11] Irish neutrality in 1940-45, of course, confirmed them in their views. Nevertheless, as sensitive an observer as Louis MacNeice, in his autobiographical *The Strings are False*, speaks affectionately of Dublin in 1939 but remarks scathingly: 'The potboy priests and the birds of prey were still the dominant cast; the petty bureaucracy continued powerful and petty . . .' And in the brilliant 'Autumn Journal' of the previous year he is equally damning:

> *Let the children fumble their sums*
> * In a half-dead language;*
> *Let the censor be busy with the books,*
> * Pull down the Georgian slums.*
> *Let the games be played in Gaelic.*

> *Let them grow sugar-beet; let them build*
>   *A factory in every hamlet;*
> *Let them pigeon-hole the souls of the killed*
>   *Into sheep and goats, patriots and traitors.*

Similarly the Irish-American novelist James T. Farrell, visiting Ireland in 1938, thought that power was 'in the hands of the gombeen men and the reverend clerics . . . There is a killing insularity here.'[12] That these phenomena might be the cruder, negative aspects of a new society with an innate vitality was commonly overlooked by middle-class intellectuals of leftist views. Other writers such as the Welsh poet R. S. Thomas, who also visited Ireland in the same 'Year of Munich,' reacted warmly and almost ecstatically to the landscape (particularly in the West), to the hospitality and, above all, to a certain intangible aura of what can only be called spiritual life.[13]

But perhaps the most macabre tribute of all to Irish spirituality was paid by the Frenchman Antonin Artaud, founder of the so-called Theatre of Cruelty and an intermittent drug addict. He came to Ireland in 1937 with the intention of returning to it an ancient wooden cane given to him by the wife of a Dutch painter, who claimed that it had once belonged to St Patrick. After leaving a trail of unpaid bills, sending threatening 'spells' by post to people in Paris, and being arrested at least once for vagrancy, Artaud was deported from Cobh as an 'undesirable' and on his return to France was taken in a straitjacket to the first of a series of psychiatric hospitals, where he remained for eight years. No Irish writer seems to have interested himself or herself in his case, and the fact that Ireland had on its soil a prophet of avant-garde theatre appears to have passed quite unnoticed.[14]

Chapter 2

BEGGING THE QUESTION

Certain stereotypes, distortions and misunderstandings have become so embedded in many people's view of the post-1930 years, that it might be appropriate to list some of the more prominent here in relatively condensed form, with (I hope) considered answers. In certain cases, fuller discussion or refutation is offered in subsequent chapters.

1. That the triune objective of an Ireland Gaelic, Catholic and nationalist became an obsession of the new State and its various cultural establishments, overriding more pressing economic or social questions and sometimes even the wishes of the majority.

– This is so simplistic that it deserves, in turn, no more than a simplistic refutation. Though the language question was always prominent in public and private debate, less money and energy was spent on teaching and reviving Irish than is often claimed. Many, if not most, politicians and public servants paid it lip service and little more. Both the Free State Government and de Valera's 1932 Government had many more immediate problems on their hands, political, social and economic. Neither was the revival of Irish tied in closely with religious issues: a handful of individual priests apart, the Catholic Church certainly set no public example by its use. Even the commitment of the Department of Education is open to some question, whatever it might have professed in public.

As for Catholicism, the overwhelming majority of people in the South were practising Catholics who naturally expected a Catholic ethos to permeate public and private life. This was simple demographic fact. The famous clause in the 1937 Constitution (now abolished), recognising the 'special position' of the Catholic Church as the religion of the great majority of Irish citizens, was little more than a *de jure* definition of what already existed *de facto*. Clergy, however, were generally not encouraged to enter political life or even political debate. There was no Irish equivalent to Monsignor Ignaz Seipel in Austria, who became his country's Chancellor for some years – much less any figure resembling the infamous Monsignor Tisza in Slovakia, who helped to pave the way for Hitler's take-over of his country. Those who still talk somewhat wildly about a 'Catholic theocracy' are guilty of a misuse of language; Ireland was a Western European democracy with a Catholic outlook, not an equivalent to Iran under the Ayatollah Khomeini.

As Liam de Paor and others have pointed out, twentieth-century Irish society shows in many ways its hybrid ancestry and mixed origins. De Paor's definition is surely the best and most objective; he describes modern Ireland as 'an overwhelmingly Catholic state formed, or mainly formed, socially, culturally, and above all politically in a Protestant mould'.[1] To which could be added the definition by another historian/intellectual, Desmond Williams: 'The law, in historical origins, was English; the principle of a written Constitution was American; the moral and religious content was Christian.'[2]

Finally, Irish nationalism is/was inseparable from economic issues, since many of its roots were in social injustice and deprivation, and the so-called War of Independence had many of the trademarks of an agrarian war. While not underrating the genuine political idealism of many nationalists, without this economic spur they probably would not have achieved enough popular support to create a new state. But in any case it is obvious that Irish nationalism had many facets and gradations, from the heirs of John Redmond and the Home Rulers to out-and-out IRA extremists. The republican tradition inherited a legacy of clerical dislike and distrust which it took de Valera some years to dispel. To package it with Gaelicism and Catholicism – not to say clericalism – does not hold up to analysis. They are three separate entities which sometimes run parallel, occasionally converge, but only rarely or temporarily merge into one.

Far from economic issues being ignored, they were a virtual obsession. For instance, Dr Alfred O'Rahilly, the intellectual spokesman (at least in his own eyes) of the Catholic Right, wrote and polemicised constantly about his economic theories. Dáil and Senate debates on ways of improving the national economy sometimes reached heights or depths of invective, while some of the senior clergy (e.g. Bishop Lucey of Cork) showed a strong socio-economic awareness, however wrong-headed their proposed solutions might be. Many academic intellectuals had their own nostra to propound, and at times even the writers joined in like true successors of AE. Salvador de Madariaga, for instance, in writing about the Irish, noted: 'They have all learned a tremendous amount of political economy, which increases their spleen and melancholy.'[3]

2. That there was an unbalanced emphasis on rural life at the expense of urban values, both in social policies and in cultural life.

– Since Ireland was overwhelmingly an agricultural country, it was to be expected that farming policies and land distribution would rank high on any government agendum. The strength of the nationwide land hunger is difficult to grasp today, although it is only a generation since it ceased to be a national passion; its central role in Irish rural life is attested to in many plays and novels.[4] It is quite untrue, however, that industry was correspondingly neglected,[5] even if many projects in this field proved to be ill-judged or a disappointment. A certain rural ethos – or even rural mystique – throughout the country was natural and unavoidable, but it did not dominate matters in the cultural field as is so often claimed. It is in any case unrealistic, and even presumptuous, to demand of Irish writing that it should reflect an industrial or big-city ethos which did not exist. Successive attempts since the late Forties – and even since the Thirties – to bring it into line with the dominant Anglo-American urban tone have ignored this fairly obvious fact. This school of thought is again very vocal today, despite the fact that Dublin (which is the only part of Ireland whose existence it appears to recognise) is obviously not an international metropolis like New York or London. Admittedly, however, its excesses are no worse than those of many romantic ruralists of fifty years ago, and arguably one convention has begot the other.

Even in the theatre, the Abbey tradition of rural farce was not allowed to get out of hand. Some of the Abbey's most successful writers, indeed, were quite the reverse of rural. The Protestant lineage of Big House writing also continued through Lennox Robinson, Elizabeth Bowen, M. J. Farrell and various others, while many of the best plays, novels and stories written before and after the second World War dealt with small-town rather than rural life – an area of Irish society which had, and has, its own autonomy. Dublin produced its unique demotic school of writing from O'Casey down to Brendan Behan and James Plunkett. There were regular, and cyclical, anti-rural reactions, one of whose leading exponents was Brian O'Nolan/Myles na Gopaleen. In fact, the conventions of Irish rural writing were frequently guyed and parodied – a tradition going back to the parodies of Synge written by H. A. Morrow decades before, which gave birth to the routine joke about 'the mist that does be on the bog'. And the typical Irish writer/intellectual of the period – caustic, cynical, hard-bitten and complex, able to quote his Baudelaire fluently though usually with a poor French accent – certainly did not conform to any rural stereotype. In fact, he probably had a wider culture, and a deeper and more innate European-ness, than his equivalent today. (This, sadly, appears to be true of the Continent as well; in spite of the obvious achievements of the EU, the 'good Europeans', and great patrician liberals such as Ortega y Gasset or Salvador de Madariaga or Count Harry Kessler, seem to be more and more a relic of the past. Ravaged and disillusioned by two world wars, Europe looks in danger of becoming intellectually provincialised. The apparent cultural sterility of contemporary France, for instance, is a thoroughly alarming phenomenon.)

3. That Irish writing, and the visual arts, retreated into relative provincialism and lacked contact with European developments.

– As I write in a later chapter, many of the Irish intelligentsia looked to France, more than to Britain, for cultural leadership and example. Inevitably, the second World War cut off contacts with Continental Europe, but these were rapidly re-established after 1945. Brendan Behan was only one among many Irish men and women to rediscover Paris in the post-war years; Beckett was already there. The influence of French writers and intellectuals on Irish writing of the 1940s was considerable. Existentialist philosophy, for instance, became very *courant* in Dublin during the 1950s.

During the 1930s, Peadar O'Donnell and Kate O'Brien both wrote informed books about Republican Spain, while Liam O'Flaherty wrote an odd and subjective one about his visit to Soviet Russia – a work which tells us more about O'Flaherty's own strange, egocentric psychology than it does about Stalinist society.[6] A young Irish poet, Charles Donnelly, died fighting in the Spanish Civil War, whose tragic course was followed eagerly in Ireland by all classes of people. The wartime experiences of Samuel Beckett in France, and those of Francis Stuart in Germany, have become too well known to be rehearsed here. Other Irish writers were strongly influenced by modern American literature, both in prose and verse. Since the later 1950s, this influence has crowded out French and other continental models.

Irish painters, almost overwhelmingly, looked to France for their models and influences. This tradition went back to the nineteenth century and only ended with the eclipse of French art internationally in the Sixties. The Irish Exhibition of Living Art, established in 1943, was permeated by French influences. Neither were the visual arts in general provincialised, though there were plenty of provincial practitioners among them; Jack Yeats, indisputably Ireland's greatest painter, created his finest and most original works in the Forties.

4. Sexual puritanism and repression permeated both private and public life, preventing writers from exploring and expressing this crucial area of modern life.

– There is more weight in this charge than in any of the previous ones, though just how badly Irish writing was affected is something which cannot be proven or measured. (Nor can it seriously be claimed that sexual liberation has produced much good writing in contemporary Irish literature, whatever claims may be made for Edna O'Brien and other fashionably daring middlebrows.) However, sexual puritanism had existed for at least two previous generations; historically, it is usually traced to the generation which grew up after the Famine. Many of its real roots were economic and social rather than religious or moral. In some ways, it was a belated version of Victorianism and was concerned with social respectability above all else.

The Irish clergy, in common with a large number of equally naïve lay people, appear to have assumed that the Irish race – or at least its female half – was gifted with some inborn, quasi-mystical quality of sexual chastity, which it was their special mission to tend and watch over like a sacred flame. Recent decades have shown this up for the self-deceiving nonsense it always was, and even a cursory look at previous centuries should have given them a saner perspective on the matter. Like the Welsh and the Scots, the Irish tend temperamentally to veer between extremes of puritanism and licence, and there is no reason to think that the pendulum of sexual behaviour will cease swinging to and fro as it always has done.

However, we are still seeing the previous age largely through the perspective of the sexual permissiveness which emerged in the Sixties – which, of course, was itself a reaction against it. What are sometimes regarded as peculiarly Irish sexual taboos were common to many or most countries at the time, though usually to a less extreme – or eccentric – degree. A glance at English writing of the Thirties, for instance, will show how strait-laced most of it was compared with today, and the treatment of D. H. Lawrence in his lifetime is a proof that sexual censorship was certainly not confined to Ireland. In America, Mae West was briefly jailed for obscenity and the extremes of film censorship there sometimes outdid Evelyn Waugh in sheer comic absurdity. 'Dirty books' were almost a universal obsession of the decades between the two world wars, when many responsible people – not necessarily prudes or bigots – worried about the possible exploitation of the new mass literacy by unscrupulous publishing interests. (The spread of pornographic or violent videos today offers some sort of parallel.)

War, always a social and moral solvent, helped considerably to loosen sexual mores and conventions in Britain during the 1940s. In Ireland, which escaped or evaded this process, British permissiveness was widely viewed as modernist decadence, but though the clergy, and many older people generally, fought a rearguard action against the contagion spreading across the Irish Sea, they could not man and maintain moral barriers against it for long, any more than modern Irish governments have succeeded in keeping out drugs. However, this fear – or rather, moral panic – may at least partly explain the spasmodic attempts at a renewed severity of censorship during the Fifties, before it petered out in the following decade.

5. That enforced emigration stunted the growth of Irish literature after its inspiring beginnings under Yeats, Synge, George Moore etc. Joyce is the most obvious case, but there are also O'Casey, Beckett and many more illustrious examples.

– The list of Irish literary emigrés is a distinguished one: it includes Moore, Joyce, Shaw, Beckett, James Stephens, AE, O'Casey, as well as many lesser names. Of these, however, only AE and Beckett emigrated in the period under review and their reasons for doing so had little in common. AE was at the end of his active career, lonely since the death of his wife and needing new horizons; he only lived for a few years after his departure, and even during these he returned to Ireland for painting trips in Donegal. Beckett, certainly, found 1930s Ireland increasingly provincial and antipathetic, but it is probable that he would have found Edwardian Dublin equally or even more so, as his master Joyce did. Both belonged to a specific type of Irish intellectual – the cerebral, latinised, rather scholastic one, who is drawn traditionally to France, Italy or sometimes Spain. Beckett was also, of course, a Protestant and a graduate of Trinity College, but there were many people with a similar background who did not see any reason to emigrate. Beckett was Beckett – an odd individualist, who cannot be quoted as a typical case.

O'Casey had made many enemies in Dublin and, as an emotional Marxist, he was soon at odds with most of what the new Ireland stood for. In any case, his finest plays had already been written and acclaimed before he left the country; when he learned of the rejection of *The Silver Tassie*, he was already in England. The long periods spent by Frank O'Connor and Seán O'Faolain in America cannot be regarded as deliberate, lifelong exile. Though both suffered under the literary censorship, they always maintained a considerable readership in their homeland, as well as a strong footing there. In spite of persistent attempts to portray them as outsiders or even intellectual martyrs, both were tough, ambitious, ultra-professional men of letters, resourceful and resilient, with an ability to thrive or at least keep afloat in almost any situation.

The tradition of literary, artistic and intellectual emigration from Ireland is an old one, which continues today. Sheridan, Burke, Shaw, Wilde, Thomas Moore, Lady Morgan, are all cases in point. There need be no special mystique about it – ambitious and talented people usually head for centres where they can earn fame or fortune, or both. Dublin, even at the height of the Literary Revival, could never offer either the financial rewards or the wider horizons for which such people naturally yearn. In any case, to pinpoint literary censorship as the prime motive for the self-exile of a heterogeneous group of writers is to exaggerate its power and importance. There were plenty of others who suffered equally under censorship, but they preferred to carry on the battle against philistinism on home ground. Austin Clarke is one example, and he lived to see his work acclaimed in old age and the obscurantists vanish into the shadows. Good writers, after all, are made of more durable stuff than censors and vocal humbugs.

The charge that intellectual and artistic life was stunted in its development during the Thirties, Forties and Fifties seems to fly in the face of the facts. The work of the Gate Theatre, the foundation of the Irish Exhibition of Living Art in 1943, the considerable achievements of a new school or schools of Irish historians symbolised by the founding of 'Irish Historical Studies' by Robin Dudley Edwards and Theo Mooney in 1938, the impressive record of Gaelic scholarship, the forum offered to all shades of opinion by the flourishing national press, the existence of several major literary journals, the new outlet offered to writers (including Austin Clarke, Padraic Fallon, Brendan Behan and James Plunkett) by Irish radio, the official patronage offered to folk music and folk culture generally, are all obvious and undeniable facts. And can a national literature which included O'Flaherty, O'Connor, O'Faolain, Kate O'Brien, Benedict Kiely, Francis MacManus, Flann O'Brien, Mary Lavin in prose, and Clarke, Kavanagh, Fallon, Higgins, Patrick MacDonogh, Denis Devlin, Blanaid Salkeld, etc, in verse, really be accounted as stunted and provincial? It is true that several of these writers did not earn reputations outside Ireland, but what is surely significant is that they are still read at home. 'Internationalism' is not the sole measure of a country's literature and art, nor are the writers who are acclaimed internationally necessarily the best of their time. (How the reputations of certain

Nobel Prize winners – Galsworthy, Benavente, Mauriac, Pearl Buck, Sinclair Lewis – have shrunk since their deaths!)

It is true that no major new writer for the theatre emerged if we except Beckett, though for a time Denis Johnston was believed in many quarters to be the new Messiah of the Irish theatre. His later plays, however, were generally disappointing. T. C. Murray, M. J. Molloy, Paul Vincent Carroll, Donagh MacDonagh all had their followings for a time, but their reputations have shrunk. It is far from certain, however, that their works will not be revived; some of their plays thoroughly merit it.

Louis MacNeice lies outside the immediate scope of this argument, since he was a Northern Irish Protestant, educated in England, whose career was largely anchored in the London literary world of his time. Though he had friends in the South and often visited Dublin, he found its Catholic/nationalist ambience foreign and even hostile. It is now clear, however, that MacNeice could never forget or deny his own Irishness and was at heart an emotionally divided man, as his poetry shows. His later poems, such as the 'Donegal Triptych', show an increasing *rapprochement* with Ireland as a whole, and while we may allow him dual literary citizenship like Yeats, MacNeice remains ineluctably an Irish poet with, in many respects, a quite un-English mentality. The case of Elizabeth Bowen is rather similar in several respects, except that she had a tough practicality and worldliness which MacNeice generally lacked, and which allowed her to enjoy the best of both worlds, in Ireland and Britain.

John Hewitt, the most considerable Ulster-born poet after MacNeice, is a different case from either. He was a self-consciously regional writer, who deliberately resisted most of the fashionable stances of the time and cultivated his own, emphatically Northern tone of voice. He was, however, always respected in Dublin.

6. That an unbalanced hatred of England and things English dominated the period, producing a myopic and distorted viewpoint, as well as driving Ireland further into isolation.

– In intellectual matters, and in other fields too, it is important to distinguish separatism from embittered hostility. Leaving aside mere harp-and-shamrock patriots for whom the Lion and the Unicorn were traditionally hated symbols, the urgent need for national self-definition invariably led to a rejection of the colonial Anglicisation which had dominated Irish culture in the nineteenth century. There was not, however, any serious rejection of English literature (which of course continued to be very widely read and was taught in schools) though there was a widespread recognition that the intellectual and literary essence of Irishness, however hard to define, needed its own independent voice. It was generally felt that Ireland must develop its own independent literature in the English language, as America had already done. There was nothing particularly negative or isolationist about this form of cultural nationalism; it has its parallels in many other European countries since the mid nineteenth century. Hungary, Finland, the Czechs are all instances – though most of them succeeded where Ireland failed, in reviving or retaining their ancient languages. Closer to home, and closer in time, Scotland as late as the 1930s produced a literary renaissance of sorts dominated by the anglophobe poet Hugh MacDiarmid, while Wales produced something similar under the inspiration of Saunders Lewis. All these are classic examples of nations rejecting, in the interests of their own cultural survival or at least self-rediscovery, the dominance of powerful neighbours. The words 'Sinn Féin' have been regularly mis-translated as 'Ourselves Alone'. In fact they mean simply 'We Ourselves', and both politically and culturally, all the Irish really asked for was the right to be Irish, rather than to be British at second-hand – although clouds of rant, rhetoric and sheer chauvinism very often darkened what was basically a simple issue.

There was, undoubtedly, a good deal of suspicion and resentment shown towards England and things English, particularly by minor politicians, hack journalists, and a certain type of civil servant and national-school teacher; but such an outlook was despised and berated by the Irish intelligentsia in general. It is easy to cull, from the newspaper reports of the period, public examples of a certain troglodytic mentality, such as the statement made by a Dublin city councillor during the 1940s that he was opposed to a monument being erected to the composer John Field because his music had 'nothing Irish about it'. Such a mind-set was not uncommon, but it was scarcely representative of anything more than its own stupidity. It would be equally easy to compile a list of similar pronouncements from newspapers in the American Middle West – or, for that matter, from the Beaverbrook press of barely a generation ago, with its tone of almost lunatic populism and imperial sabre-rattling. The British popular press has almost habitually been hostile to Ireland and things Irish, and this mentality naturally bred its mirror-image across the water.

And finally, it should be remembered that Britain in the 1930s meant something very different from what it did in the post-war years. It was still an empire, with its full share of inherited imperial arrogance and racial superiority, though even then these were being steadily eroded. Ireland, by comparison, felt itself to be rather like a small boat in the path of a huge oncoming ocean liner. Anti-Englishness was often, in fact, no more than anti-imperialism, which is why so many Irish people rather enjoyed, in a spirit of bravado, pulling the lion's tail on occasion.[7] But from 1945 onwards, Britain became the 'progressive' country, a welfare state with a relatively liberal-leftist outlook, while Ireland in the same period fell behind in social policies and other fields, as de Valera and his once-revolutionary generation began to lose their grip, their energy and possibly their self-belief. It is to this factor that much of the frustration and bitterness of the Fifties must be traced; yet that decade, in my opinion, was also the turning point or transition between one age and the modern one.

Chapter 3

A Disinherited Culture

Historical alibis have been overused and even grossly abused for many of Ireland's failures and shortcomings; the 'most distressful country' has not, examined objectively, a more lamentable history than Poland or Hungary or the small Baltic countries. Yet the fact remains that while other nations have suffered the official suppression of their national identities and languages, including most of those already named as well as Finland, Bohemia (now the Czech Republic), and Catalonia, nevertheless in certain vital respects their break with the past probably was never quite as traumatic as was Ireland's. The Irish were virtually disinherited from their ancient culture, or 'dispossessed' as Thomas Kinsella chooses to put it.

This, of course, is what Irish schoolchildren used to learn from their early teens, and it became a repetitive theme-song for a certain school of embittered nationalism. At least thirty years ago, Irish people decided that they had heard that particular tune too often and that the theme of Ireland's wrongs should now be put in cold storage for an indefinite period. Yet culturally it is not a myth. It is sober fact which can no more be ignored than the Industrial Revolution can in understanding the forces which shaped contemporary Britain. One need not be a cultural nationalist, or even a nationalist at all, to appreciate the intellectual and linguistic schizophrenia, the lack of continuity and development, the loss of self-belief and self-definition, that such an historical break implies. This was compounded by religious persecution – admittedly also a commonplace in European and world history.

Religion was another essential badge of identity, and though here the loss has largely been made good, the Irish language has neither survived in strength nor has it been revived, except on paper. Gaelic literature and culture, among the oldest in Europe, dwindled into little more than a folk tradition, just as Irish Catholicism had been largely dispossessed and became more and more the creed of the uneducated and the semi-ignorant. In the words of a contemporary historian, D. George Boyce, 'membership of the Church of Ireland was a necessary card for admission to any role in public life and polite society . . . . Protestantism, progressiveness, Britishness, liberty of conscience and a superior outlook were its hallmarks. Its best advocate was Jonathan Swift . . .'[1] That, certainly, is how it saw itself and there was no place for Counter-Reformation Catholicism under the same roof.

Outside this Protestant elite, Ireland at the start of the nineteenth century was virtually a *tabula rasa* culturally and had to start again more or less from the beginning. It took nearly a century to nurture a new national literature which was English in vocabulary but recognisably Irish in sensibility and outlook; and while there has been a reasonably flourishing literature in Irish in the past half-century, the revival of the spoken language appears to have more or less been written off, both officially and by popular consensus. The loss cannot be exaggerated – an entire racial psyche had lost its tongue and natural outlet. As for religion, arguably Irish Catholicism has only come of age since Vatican II which, historically, may prove to have been too late for its own good, or even its own survival, though a revival in the next generation is not to be ruled out. At present Irish society, disillusioned and angry with a clergy which previously it had irrationally idealised and had deferred to blindly and uncritically, seems more likely to throw religion to the four winds than to take the more constructive, intelligent option of rethinking and regenerating it. As for the clergy themselves, they seem incapable of coping intellectually or emotionally with a situation for which, obviously, no contingency plans ever existed.

The current national mood, boosted by some decades of Revisionism, might be defined something like this: The past is dead, and we have had far too much of it thrust on us anyway. Irish cannot, realistically, be revived even as a minority language. The Celtic Twilight is remote from contemporary culture, and the old rural Ireland is dying fast. Instead of listening to the seanachaí, Irish people now look at television; instead of hearing stories about the Children of Lir or Cuchulain, they want to read about pop stars and listen to their music. Nationalism is out of date, the world is becoming a global village, and what moved Irish people seventy years ago is largely irrelevant to the twenty-first century. Religion has lost its hold, traditional family life is dissolving under new pressures and strains, marriage nowadays is optional at most, ancestral values no longer have any validity or even meaning for the new generation. A new, cosmopolitan urban culture has replaced the Old Folk Ways everywhere. We must cut our losses and live in the present, a present which is dynamic and exciting. In a short time a new, internationally-oriented society will evolve and Ireland will exist only as part of a far greater whole offering a vast new range of possibilities. In short, the world is opening up so wide and so fast that we must make sure we are not left behind once again, bogged down in our tribal, inward-looking past. So throw the old fetishes and shibboleths – what is left of them – out on the scrap heap, and instead face contemporary reality, face the future!

This is probably the gist of popular and even informed sentiment today, mirrored by the media and by a variety of political, cultural and other institutions. It is, however, based largely on a presupposition which time and time again has proved to be false, or at least misleading – the belief that what is 'going strong' at the moment will continue to do so, and is likely to get even stronger as its momentum increases. But the historical evidence suggests that successive ages tend to react against one another, rather than advance with mathematical regularity; history seemingly moves in cycles rather than in straight lines. There is no proof that today's values will be the values of tomorrow – in fact, it is a fairly safe prediction that they will not be. (That they will not be those of yesterday either seems reasonably certain.)

It might be pointed out that there is a basic difference between being tied to the past and coming to terms with the past – in other words, understanding it and learning from it. By doing so, we may learn at least some degree of self-definition and a certain sense of continuity. There is certainly a great deal to be said for Ireland moving out of the nightmare and frustrations of history into a new national maturity and self-confidence. But has this really happened? Growing economic prosperity, technological advances, an upgraded educational system, a footing in the new Europe – these are all important gains. But the losses are considerable too: an inner confusion as to precisely where we are heading and what we ultimately want, an unresolved identity crisis which has been papered over repeatedly by the jargon of career academics and the evasive rhetoric of politicians, the abandonment of many previously cherished national and cultural aspirations, galloping Americanisation (often naïvely and misleadingly termed 'internationalism') and – above all – a virtual capitulation to the Pop Culture, to consumerism and the omnipresent Fast Food values. There also seems to me (but not to me alone, by any means) to have been a serious loss of literacy, in the higher sense – though this appears to be a European problem generally, or even a universal one. It is doubtful if in at least two centuries the written word has been so devalued as it has been in the closing years of the twentieth. And it is by the written word, after all, that Ireland made its strongest mark on the modern world. Apart from the august exception of Jack Yeats, our visual art, our architecture and our serious music have never made a comparable impact.

I am not alone in believing that much of our national schizophrenia, and of the irregular, stop-go, disconnected character of Irish culture in the past two hundred years, have their roots in the loss of the Irish language. This disinheritance, to use no stronger term, continues to haunt certain Irish writers, particularly the poets, in spite of the strenuous efforts of many recent critics, academics and literary journalists to devalue the Celtic tradition and steer us more and more into the so-called 'international' currents of contemporary Anglo-American writing. For instance, Thomas Kinsella has brilliantly analysed the plight of the Irish poet in his book The Dual Tradition,[2] as well as translating 'The Táin', while Seamus Heaney has shown an equivalent awareness of the importance of the Gaelic tradition, both in his translations from the Irish and in his own verse. (It may be pointed out that both these writers are themselves close to modern American literature and have been considerably influenced by it, but they have not allowed it to swallow their individuality. Unlike many other writers, they refuse to dwindle to a speck on some Mid-Western university campus.) When Ireland's two leading contemporary poets – one of them a Nobel Prize winner – take such a stance, perhaps those who talk so glibly about ditching Ireland's cultural past might rethink their position a little. Far from the language issue dying away, it seems that it has come back into the forefront of our literary consciousness and refuses to be exorcised. To state the obvious once again, ignoring it will not make it go away.

The problem is that culturally the Irish are both a very old nation and a very recent one – a 'dual tradition' in the most literal sense. This is far from being an original view, of course; it has been stated many times and in many differing contexts. As things stand, the Gaelic literature of a thousand years is as inaccessible to the ordinary reader as 'Beowulf' is to the average, reasonably literate Englishman; what we (like the rest of the world) call Irish literature is only a century and a half old, and it only gained a European dimension with the Literary Renaissance dominated by Yeats. Moore, Mangan and Ferguson in the nineteenth century scarcely add up to a coherent national tradition, in spite of Moore's European fame – which no longer exists, nor does his literary influence. And equally, Ireland is also a new country, which explains its frequent gaucherie and naïvete, the curious difficulty it has shown at times in coming to terms with novel or challenging ideas, its occasional signs of stunted or delayed development, its tendency to pound the obvious to pulp and to acclaim as novel and daring what is often old hat in most other Western countries. Various scapegoats have been produced for this seemingly arrested growth – apart, that is, from the language factor I have discussed, but which many commentators prefer to ignore, or at least to discount.

The Church is now the most favoured target, but it is surely the case that for several generations Irish Catholicism represented the country at large and that the one shaped the other. To distinguish between priests and people seems to me arbitrary and even false. Another favourite scapegoat is the isolationism already mentioned, but as I have tried to show, this is to a great extent a myth. Even if Ireland had chosen to isolate itself politically and socially from the modern world, it could not realistically have done so – the ineluctable realities of international politics, international economics, etc. would have crushed its defences as the German panzers crushed Poland and France. As for cultural isolation, it would never have been feasible or even possible in an age of developing mass media, modern communication systems, and the rapid conquest of the old barriers of space and time.

Perhaps in certain respects the best parallel is not with Britain or France or Germany – all of them major European countries who, whatever they have suffered by wars and revolutions, were able to develop their cultural and intellectual traditions with a good deal of continuity. A closer parallel with Ireland's development lies west across the Atlantic. That grand old American man of letters,

Malcolm Cowley, in an essay called 'The Revolt against Gentility',[3] sketches out a rather similar situation in his own country, starting with the award of the Nobel Prize for Literature to the novelist Sinclair Lewis in 1930 – which, of course, happens also to be the year in which this book begins. Cowley does not claim that Lewis is/was one of the giants of American literature, but he shows him to have been a man and writer fully equal to the occasion, and with the wit and presence of mind to speak for the best elements in his huge, still relatively raw country. The secretary of the Swedish Academy, Erik Axel Karlfeldt (incidentally, a magnificent poet in his own right and the only man to be awarded the Nobel Prize posthumously) said in his speech of welcome: 'Sinclair Lewis is an American. He writes the new language – American – as one of the representatives of a hundred and twenty million souls. He asks us to consider that this nation is not yet finished or melted down; that it is still in the turbulent years of adolescence. The new great American literature has started with national self-criticism. It is a sign of good health.'

When Lewis came to make his acceptance speech two days later, he was answering not only Karlfeldt but an attack on himself which had been given publicity in American newspapers. Dr Henry van Dyke, a member of the American Academy of Arts and Letters, a former Princeton professor and also a former Presbyterian minister, had denounced as an insult to America the award to a man who had scoffed so much at American institutions and the American way of life. Lewis replied: 'Most of us – not readers alone but even writers – are still afraid of any literature which is not a glorification of everything American, a glorification of our faults as well as our virtues . . . We still more revere the writers for the popular magazines who in a hearty and edifying chorus chant that the America of a hundred and twenty million population is still as simple, as pastoral, as it was when she had but forty million . . . that, in fine, America has gone through the revolutionary change from rustic colony to world empire without having in the least altered the bucolic and puritanic simplicity of Uncle Sam.'

How relevant some of this is to Ireland will be obvious at once, and it is tempting to put Dr Alfred O'Rahilly, or indeed any other learned obscurantist of his kind, in the role of an Irish Henry van Dyke. The latter's attack on Lewis is an almost exact parallel to the attacks by conservative spokesmen on Seán O'Faolain, Kate O'Brien and other prominent fiction writers in the years between the two world wars – a process which goes at least as far back as the famous (or infamous) sequence of events triggered off by the publication of Brinsley MacNamara's novel *The Valley of the Squinting Windows* in 1918. In many ways, Irish rural society of the time must have resembled the equally rustic and raw American Mid-West (which nevertheless fed the very different talents of Willa Cather and Hamlyn Garland). It was also equally sensitive about any literary attempts to portray it in a hard, modern light, as is so often the way with rather backward and unsophisticated communities which feel their respectability impugned.

Much more of what Lewis said on that occasion has a relevance to other literatures besides America's. If the Nobel Prize had gone instead to Theodore Dreiser, he said, 'respectable scholars would complain that in Mr Dreiser's world, men and women are often sinful and despairing, instead of being forever sunny and full of song and virtue, as befits authentic Americans. And had you chosen Mr Eugene O'Neill . . . you would have been reminded that he has done something far worse than scoffing – he has seen life as not to be neatly arranged in the study of a scholar but as a terrifying, magnificent and often quite horrible thing . . . that Miss Willa Cather, for all the homely virtue of her novels concerning the peasants of Nebraska, has in her novel *A Lost Lady* been so untrue to America's patent and perpetual and possibly tedious virtuousness as to picture an abandoned woman who remains, nevertheless, uncannily charming even to the virtuous, in a story without any moral; that Mr Henry Mencken is the worst of all scoffers; that Mr Sherwood Anderson viciously errs in considering sex as important a force in life as fishing . . . and that Mr Ernest Hemingway is not only too young but, far worse, uses language which should be unknown to gentlemen; that he acknowledges drunkenness as one of man's eternal ways to happiness . . .'

Where the parallel does not extend, obviously, is to the relative self-confidence and wealth of American and Irish society during this period. America was the richest and most powerful nation in the world, while Ireland was one of the smallest, weakest and poorest. It was to take the newborn nation many years to exorcise an inherited feeling of being looked down upon, of being the poor relation of the entire English-speaking world. Blundering from ancestral semi-poverty into middle-classness, caught up in the *embourgeoisement* of a largely peasant society, Irish people had little firm ground under their feet and, in many respects, were a typical post-colonial society in search of new, stable patterns of living. One of the few things they could still call their own was their religion, and quite understandably they clung to it fiercely.

T he first decade of Irish independence saw power largely in the hands of decent, conservative, rather old-fashioned (though not reactionary) politicians much of whose support came from the Catholic upper bourgeoisie, the lawyers, doctors, strong farmers, businessmen, and big shopkeepers, along with a smattering of the Anglo-Irish landowning and manufacturing class – a number of whom had found some sort of makeshift power base in the new Senate. To a large extent, this society still modelled itself on the old Dublin Castle and Vice-Regal days, and there was much stress on the wearing of top hats and frock coats and on appearances at prestige social events and race meetings. It was against such a social background that Yeats, Gogarty and men such as

Thomas Bodkin moved, and the Dublin Arts Club – very fashionable at the time, and as much a social institution as an artistic one – represented it in minuscule, though with rather more stress on the Anglo-Irish and Protestant aspect.[4] Very broadly, this Government represented a bourgeoisie which was moderately nationalist, law-abiding and constitutional, very Catholic in a special late-Victorian way, socially and culturally rather conservative, and highly class-conscious. In the words of Liam de Paor, for some time previously this class, 'which gained legitimacy from its judicious waving of the green flag on appropriate occasions, stood by, ready to take over from the Protestant middle class in the greater part of the island.'[5] Anglo-Ireland, with its political power base gone, either gave half-hearted support to this *arriviste* regime or, in the words of Brian Inglis,[6] pretended that nothing had happened and tried to go on as before. And in practice, enough remained of the traditional Irish Protestant world to give it some reassurance – the Horse Show,[7] the hunt balls, Trinity College, the great monolith of Guinness's Brewery, such of the Big Houses as had survived both the Civil War and slow economic decay, *The Irish Times*, the Kildare Street Club, the recognised Protestant educational institutions such as the High School, St Columba's School and (for girls) Alexandra College, the Bank of Ireland, the Shelbourne Hotel, a still flourishing though rather inbred social life . . . To an extent the Catholic upper-middle class based its social code of behaviour on this world, whose self-assurance it sometimes secretly or openly envied; and in any case it had no other or better models at hand.

It is, of course, almost insuperably difficult to distinguish between Protestant Ireland and Anglo-Ireland (that is, unless we accept Brendan Behan's definition of an Anglo-Irishman as 'a Protestant with a horse'). Obviously, in many areas they were one and the same. The Protestant business and professional class, however, was a good deal tougher, more resilient and more realistic than most of the decaying horsey gentry, and was also shrewder generally in coming to terms with the new dispensation. In the arts, the most obvious example was Yeats, who practised spiritualism, claimed to believe in fairies and even tried his hand at magic, yet inherited the hard head and managerial bent of his Protestant ancestors. Yeats belonged socially and culturally almost as much in London as in Dublin, though he had vigorously thrown in his lot with the new State and served – effectively, it seems, in spite of some statements to the contrary – in the Irish Senate and in other public or semi-public roles. He came to lay great stress on his Anglo-Irishness and on his intellectual kinship with Swift and Berkeley and Burke, and in the Senate and elsewhere he sometimes aligned himself with landowning Protestants and with prestigious businessmen such as Andrew Jameson the whiskey distiller. Plainly Yeats saw himself as a bridge between Catholic and Protestant Ireland and as a reconciler between them and their contrasting traditions, but ineluctably he belonged more to the second than to the first. His own ancestry included Dublin merchants, clergymen and small landowners and he was thoroughly at home in places such as the Kildare Street Club (Yeats had always liked clubs, particularly if they were exclusive). He liked to think that his outlook was aristocratic, and so it was in the intellectual and aesthetic fields, but in the everyday world he often looked and sounded like a traditional, upper-middle-class Dublin Protestant snob. (The wife of one leading Abbey actor habitually referred to him as 'that lump of pomp up in Merrion Square'.)

As Louis MacNeice shrewdly remarked, 'Yeats had for a long time regarded the essential Ireland as incarnate in the country gentry and the peasantry, his ideal society being static and indeed being based upon caste. The Irish "Troubles", however, evoked in him an admiration, even an envy, for the dynamic revolutionary.'[8] This admiration was soon transformed, after the horrors and destruction of the Civil War, into genuine respect for politicians of the new order such as Kevin O'Higgins, who had crushed the militant republicans and paid for it with his life. What MacNeice seemingly omits, however, is any reference to the growth of the new Irish middle class. Yeats had largely grown up in a society where at least the upper stratum of this class was predominantly Protestant, but even before independence had arrived he had noted ominously the encroaching power of a new Catholic one, exemplified by William Martin Murphy, whom he regarded as grasping, uncultivated, narrow, and in short had all or most of the disagreeable characteristics of the nouveau riche.[9] He had clashed head-on with this class in the *Playboy* and Lane Pictures controversies, which had inspired his famous gibes about 'Paudeen's pence' and 'greasy tills'. Earlier, in his eyes, this class had played a prominent role in pulling down one of Yeats's heroes, Parnell.

What he had scarcely foreseen, however, was the imminent rise of yet another class, the petit-bourgeoisie recruited mainly from the small towns and the urbanising peasantry, and whose values were to become increasingly vocal and even dominant in the next quarter-century. It was almost as if Christy Mahon or the colourful, devious, earthy peasants of the Somerville and Ross stories had moved into concrete-built suburban housing estates and had become small shopkeepers, minor civil servants, businessmen, bank clerks, publicans and chemists. 'Folk' Ireland was breaking up – though much of it survived in certain areas, mainly in the West – as the *embourgeoisement* already mentioned continued to gather impetus. It was a phenomenon very similar to the emergence of the lace-curtain Irish in America – except that in that vast country they were very much a minority, and one with limited political power or social prestige, while in Ireland this levelling, collective mentality infiltrated into almost every field of activity. The nation was witnessing the very twentieth-century phenomenon of populism – although the word did not come into vogue until many years later.

There could only have been one strong social corrective or counterbalance to this new philistinism, at once levelling and ambitiously genteel, and that was precisely what Ireland did not possess – a thoroughly secure, cultured, liberal upper-middle class such as exists or existed in the major European countries, a group able to make its influence felt in the chambers of power. There were, of course, individuals and even whole families who answered to this description, but there was no coherent social group which did so. It is a hiatus or imbalance which largely remains to this day, although what has come to be called 'Dublin 4' presumably now sees itself as playing such a role in national life. Perhaps such a class can only emerge against a background of moderate wealth, educational privilege, inherited culture and an inbred self-belief and capability. Perhaps it also needs a tradition of socio-political stability and parliamentary rule, but Ireland had just gone through the throes of revolution and civil war, and traditional class patterns had mostly been shaken or overturned. As for parliamentary rule, it was a recent growth and excepting a handful of exceptional people, the level of administrative talent and of public debate in both the Dáil and the Senate was uninspiring (in fact the general quality of public speaking in Ireland, a country which had once prided itself on its eloquence and its respect for oratory, was to decline miserably in the next fifty years and still shows little obvious signs of recovery).[10]

The rise of populism seems to me to be one of the dominant realities of Irish life in this century, yet so far as I know no leading historian has discussed it in depth as such. This worldwide phenomenon has been variously called the Tyranny of the Majority and the Rise of the Common Man, though the term 'populism' has now become intellectually respectable. In essence, it might be defined as a levelling, mass-mind mentality, communal, simplistic, sentimental, lacking in taste, knowledge or self-criticism, though often earthily shrewd and with an eye to its own profit. It resents privilege, sophistication, complexity, elitism, and virtually all that it does not understand, which tends to be a great deal – though it has proved itself well able to cope with modern technology. It also rather dislikes eloquence in the traditional sense and any too-obvious display of intellect or culture, since in its eyes these are mostly displays of elitist snobbery designed to elevate a few people and make the majority feel small. (Incidentally, this phenomenon of modern Mass Man has been magnificently analysed by the great Spanish philosopher Ortega y Gasset, in his book *The Revolt of the Masses*.)

Ireland, in the first part of the century, was an obvious breeding-ground for this mentality, given the vacuum left by its history, the lack of intellectual or cultural content in Irish Catholicism as practised by the majority, the inherited absence of taste or style in everyday life, the aforementioned lack of a strong, self-sufficient, liberal haute-bourgeoisie, and the long-standing alienation of the mass of the people from the ruling Protestant minority. Inevitably, in its origins it was closely tied to the powerful, almost subliminal forces of land hunger and land agitation, perhaps the most potent of all socio-economic factors behind the revolution headed by Collins and de Valera. Both of these remarkable men came from small farms, and neither ever quite lost the emotional values and reactions instilled in them by being the children of smallholders. In that, they were typical of thousands of other Irish people over two generations.

When de Valera and his Fianna Fáil Party won an overwhelming majority in the general election of 1932, fear and revulsion gripped a large section of the upper and middle classes. The landowners and big farmers feared for their land, since agrarian reform and distribution was one of Dev's main policy planks; the clergy – some of whom had opposed him from public platforms during the election campaign – feared republicanism which they had denounced for more than a century; the 'West Brits' feared social levelling and increased taxation, even some form of socialism, and so did many of the more privileged Catholic bourgeoisie. The land-hungry wild men, it was widely assumed, had finally come to power and would overthrow, or at least subvert, the established social order, based largely on property, law and order, class structures, parliamentarianism, and the Church. De Valera, who later became in many eyes a conservative statesman, was at this stage widely regarded as a kind of Fidel Castro figure, an agrarian revolutionary and the leader of landless and potentially lawless men. After all, it was less than a decade since the gun had finally been holstered in Irish politics – in fact, it was a mere five years since Kevin O'Higgins had been shot down.

Of course, Dev turned out to be very little of the bogeyman figure which conservatives had feared. There was a great deal of land distribution, a rather rudimentary attempt at social welfare,[11] and a remarkable rural housing drive which, inside a short space of time, virtually replaced the old hovels and bohauns with slate-roofed cottages. There were many new schemes and projects hatched, some of which were practical and some visionary, while others were never tried (one of Dev's crazier ideas was to improve native honey-making by importing Egyptian bees, large and vicious insects which proved so troublesome that they had to be destroyed en masse). The Anglo-Irish landowning and business elements in the Senate had their power broken, and they were ruthlessly ejected while Dev overhauled the Upper House on a 'vocational' basis. By refusing to pay the land annuities to Britain, he triggered off the Economic War which recoiled on him, deprived Irish farmers of markets and for a time lost him much of his support. Eventually the dispute was resolved, and Chamberlain – who, unlike his successor Churchill, was usually well-intentioned towards Ireland – allowed Dev to negotiate the treaty about the Irish ports which was one of the great coups of his career.

Dev also came to terms with the Church which had previously excommunicated him and his followers, though – contrary to what has often been said and written – his 1937 Constitution did not actually make Catholicism the State religion, and while a strong Catholic he was never a 'priest's man'. Undoubtedly the former revolutionary had become respectable and generally acceptable, even to many of the Anglo-Irish, so that Ireland's hard-won parliamentary democracy was strengthened rather than weakened; the Blueshirts were thwarted and discredited, and Ireland (as has been mentioned already) won some credit internationally for its work in the League of Nations.

This is social and political history, or course, not cultural, but since they are all closely intertwined it is relevant here. Dev had led a party of real or potential revolutionaries into constitutional, parliamentary politics and had made them bury the gun – with the exception of the IRA, which eventually was outlawed. The country, in any case, yearned for peace and the rule of law, as it had done for nearly two decades, so Dev had read the times shrewdly; but this pacification had its negative side too. Like so many revolutionaries before and since, the gunmen (or at least those with wives and families) soon became almost narrowly respectable and even conformist, hanging up lace curtains in their turn, going to mass on Sunday and rearing their children to be God-fearing and – when possible – property-owning, or at least with money in the bank. The Grocer's Republic was already in sight, and an unaesthetic and uninspiring affair it was, even an unspiritual one – though, typically, it tended to pride itself on precisely its spirituality. Sunday mass-going became the main measure of a man's soul.

So along with the populist urge already described, national conformity received another powerful motivation – the desire for internal peace and quiet and for the consolidation of whatever social and economic advances had been achieved. So far as the times allowed, Irish society settled – at least outwardly – into some kind of consensus based on a general need or yearning to get on with the humdrum demands of everyday living. It was this mood which disaffected intellectuals such as Seán O'Faolain – who had fought with the Republicans in the Civil War, like his friend Frank O'Connor – regarded as mediocrity and stagnation, an ideological sell-out and a betrayal of revolutionary hopes.[12] AE, too, mourned the post-revolutionary loss of ideals and beliefs, though he thought that it would be temporary only. Meanwhile, Europe continued to drift nearer to war, under the horrified gaze and agonised predictions of intellectuals and literary men who were already divided among themselves over the Civil War in Spain. Soon they were to be equally divided over the question of Ireland's wartime neutrality, a subject which will be dealt with at some length in a later chapter.

Chapter 4

YEATS CENTRE STAGE

In 1931 Edmund Wilson published his seminal book *Axel's Castle*, which he subtitled *A study in the imaginative literature of 1870-1930*. Its main thesis, or rather linking thread, was the influence of French Symbolism on the writers whom he considered key figures of the modern age: Yeats, Valéry, Eliot, Proust, Joyce, Gertrude Stein. As a kind of coda, there is a chapter 'Axel and Rimbaud', linking Villiers de l'Isle-Adam's famous (and seemingly unactable) drama, which gives the book its title, with Rimbaud and ultimately with what was then the modern age.

It may be difficult today to understood just why Gertrude Stein's contemporaries took her at her own evaluation of herself as a great modern experimentalist and innovator; already, her famous prose style seems for the most part to be simplistic twaddle. Otherwise, the book is not only acute but also highly prescient. Wilson was well ahead of English (or Irish) critics in his insights and he put his finger on the main creative currents of the previous decades and also looked daringly into the future. Today, more than sixty years after the book was written, many or most of his arguments and evaluations are still perfectly valid, as well as highly relevant. It is a proof of how valuable and even exhilarating can be the clarifying perspectives of a great critic.

Wilson virtually begins with Yeats, though curiously enough the essay on him does not mention either Yeats's visit to Paul Verlaine in Paris in 1894 or the fact that the poet in company with Maud Gonne (who spoke excellent French) went to a performance of *Axel's Castle* around the same time. Both were crucial events in Yeats's development, and it can be safely presumed that Wilson knew about them even if he chose not to mention them. Yeats was a notoriously poor linguist, partly the result of natural incapacity and partly of an inadequate early education; he relied heavily on his friend Arthur Symons to act as a filter for developments in contemporary French literature. Yet he seems to have possessed the kind of insight into language – particularly poetic language – which most of the great poets have displayed, and also an instinctive sense (what Ezra Pound has called 'the vital sense') of just where and how the pulse of literature was beating. Though he was already accepted in London literary circles and had proved energetic and adroit in making his career there, he was wholly receptive to these vitalising new currents flowing from France. He himself admits the influence on his early work of Mallarmé, whom he approached through Symons's translations, and Wilson draws a fascinating parallel between a relatively late Yeats poem, 'On a Picture of a Black Centaur' and Mallarmé's sonnet beginning 'Le vierge, le vivace et le bel aujourd'hui'.

Wilson is also the first eminent critic, so far as I know, to chart the work of Yeats in three distinct periods and to show how his language grew steadily in dynamism and flexibility and even absorbed the kind of colloquial speech he had shunned in his youth. He goes so far as to give a reasonably sympathetic analysis of *A Vision*, a book which many modern Yeats admirers and commentators shy away from as an oddity or aberration in his development, and generally rather an embarrassment. In his final chapter, Wilson rejects the prediction of certain people (including Valéry himself) that Symbolism as a literary movement or source has become obsolete; on the contrary, he believes that its legacy will be absorbed into Modernism, though in a diffused and even underground fashion, and that its achievements in creating a poetic-imagistic rather than a prose logic for language are permanent and valid. (This prophecy seems to me to have been borne out completely, for Irish as well as for Anglo-American and European poetry.)

All this, of course, relates mainly to the poet's youth, although he never abandoned Symbolism, which nourished him in his old age as it had inspired him in his twenties. At the start of the 1930s, Yeats was an awesome figure for younger writers and even for many of his English contemporaries. His Nobel Prize, his career which stretched back into the early eighteen-nineties, his role as a founding father of modern Irish literature, his international standing, his central position in the Abbey Theatre which gave him great power over the careers of ambitious young playwrights and even their elders, his sometimes vatic pronouncements, the power of his personality and his deliberately cultivated aristocratic hauteur, were both impressive and distancing. From his youth Yeats had dressed and acted the part of a poet, so that even in his early London days his friend Richard Rowley, the Northern Irish writer, had heard a couple of cockneys discussing the poet's appearance and deciding that 'e must be a hactor'. His height and bearing, the carriage of his head and his bardic white hair, his carefully chosen clothes and even the occasional look of absent-mindedness which also seems to have been at least partly cultivated, made him noticeable wherever he went. His ceremonious manners, especially when he appeared in public, added to this hieratic impression and Yeats himself was never more flattered than when he heard that members of the Swedish Royal Family, whom he met at his Nobel Prize presentation in Stockholm in 1924, considered that he had 'the manners of a courtier'.

E. R. Dodds, poet, classical scholar and lifelong friend of Louis MacNeice, called him 'no mere rhymester, but a Vates, a poet in the full, ancient, arrogant meaning of the word', and noted that he seemed like the bearer of a mystery, 'the mystery of words, which alone is good'.[1] The young Kate O'Brien thought him a magnificent and imposing figure as she watched him walk along St Stephen's Green – just as she had been awed by the sight of Maud Gonne, nearly six feet tall, out walking with her Irish wolfhound at her side. As probably the most famous living Irishman apart from Shaw, Yeats was already part of the daily mythology of Dublin, a celebrity whose private life was a source of fascinated gossip and speculation, though Yeats maintained a regal reserve with all except a small cenâcle of close friends and followers. After the long, hopeless years of courting Maud, he had married a much younger Englishwoman, Georgina Hyde-Lees, who had made him the best of wives and was a firm, tactful barrier between him and the regiments of people who laid siege to him. First in the house in Merrion Square, then later at Riversfield in Rathfarnham, he held court to favoured visitors and admirers and to his own circle which included Oliver St John Gogarty, Lennox Robinson and F. R. Higgins.

The younger generation of writers, particularly the poets, was fully aware of Yeats's towering stature, and while most of them enormously admired him his immense reputation and personal formality often inhibited or overwhelmed them. He was not, in any case, a clubbable man in the usual sense, and certainly not a pubbable one – an important factor in Dublin, where the literary pubs were increasingly becoming centres of sociability, intellectual interchange and gossip, whether amiable or bitchy. Yeats himself had a notoriously catty side, which is frequently revealed in his letters but was also an essential part of his conversation when he relaxed among his intimates and listened to their sometimes malicious talk. Few could administer a snub more devastatingly, and he was also a master of boardroom tactics, who knew how to outmanoeuvre those who obstructed him on the Abbey Board and elsewhere. The once gauche, inhibited young man had become highly formidable and worldly, showing an energy and grasp of practical affairs which may have been a legacy of the businesslike Pollexfens on his mother's side but may also – bypassing his much-loved but Micawberish father – have been part of his male ancestry. Nobody took liberties with him, and very few people outside his immediate family were allowed to call him by his Christian name. ('There is no fool can call me friend.') Even his devoted sisters, who ran the Cuala Press, sometimes found his behaviour towards them domineering and almost dictatorial. Yeats in his way was fond of power and even of manipulation, and he generally contrived to exercise close control over virtually all areas of his day-to-day activities – which, during his term as a senator, had included chairing the commission to create a national coinage.

Meanwhile, those younger writers who found the courage to approach him rarely broke through his self-created barriers – and in any case, it was often said around Dublin that Gogarty, Lennox Robinson and Higgins had the skills of seasoned courtiers in keeping potential rivals away from the vicinity of the throne. Austin Clarke, who approached Yeats with the project of writing his biography, was treated coolly and abandoned the plan (Clarke's experiences with Yeats were generally unhappy; he was excluded from Yeats's *Oxford Book of Modern Verse* and a play he submitted to the Abbey Theatre was rejected.) When he related this to the essayist Robert Lynd in London, the usually gentle Lynd remarked dryly that if he had been a duchess with a coronet his reception would have been very different. Francis Stuart admitted years later that he always found Yeats's company a strain, his conversation lacking in ease or lightness, and his humour contrived and ponderous.[2] The young Padraic Fallon thought him 'psychologically unapproachable', though he also noticed that Yeats at close quarters revealed behind his glasses 'the eye of a cattle-jobber'. When Frank O'Connor, whose translations from Irish poetry Yeats admired, claimed in his biographical writings (published when Yeats was long dead) a degree of friendship and even intimacy with the poet, few people in Dublin believed him; it was alleged that he was parading a non-existent friendship, and Austin Clarke, reviewing one of these books for *The Irish Times*, openly expressed his scepticism.[3] In particular, protégés of AE (George Russell) were likely to be cold-shouldered and Yeats habitually referred to them as 'AE's canaries'. Yet Higgins had originally been one of these discoveries, so had James Stephens, and O'Connor had also been encouraged by him. At his most top-loftical, Yeats had once said to his old friend Russell: 'For you the personal, for me the aesthetic', yet the *Oxford Book of Modern Verse* directly refutes this, since it is full of favouritisms and strange choices which baffled contemporary critics. His Olympian pose of objectivity had many chinks in it and as Mary Colum and others remarked, many or most of his swans turned out to be geese.

Another writer consistently snubbed was the poet Monk Gibbon, who claimed to be related personally to the Yeats family, but antagonised WBY by his verbosity and by arguing with him in conversation – a dangerous thing to do. He revenged himself by publishing in 1959 his book *The Masterpiece and the Man*, which is probably the most unflattering picture of the poet since George Moore's *Hail and Farewell* trilogy, though at the same time Gibbon was almost painfully aware of Yeats's greatness. He noted his dislike of argument and contradiction, his frequent rudeness or coldness towards AE, his ruthless way of dealing with those who had occasionally crossed or become troublesome to him, such as Clarke, Seumas O'Sullivan and Thomas Bodkin. The dominant impression he received was one of 'hauteur, irascibility and a proud detachment . . . One could never penetrate his defences. They were the work of a lifetime.' Gibbon observed that Yeats enjoyed Gogarty's 'well-rehearsed dirty stories', and at one of the poet's famous Monday evenings he was rather shocked by the bawdiness of the conversation, dominated again by Gogarty and Higgins. Yeats in old age was increasingly preoccupied – obsessed, some people said – with sex, and the self-consciously Rabelaisian tone which Higgins sometimes cultivated was grist to his mill; I suspect, and I am not alone in this, that the 'Crazy Jane' poems show Higgins's fingerprints quite strongly. Yet allowing that disappointed vanity explains much of Gibbon's negativity (he too was excluded from the *Oxford Book*, something which he never forgave) he does paint from life a *grand seigneur* of literature, whose self-created carapace had grown to be an integral part of him, and whose formidable egoism placed a magic circle between himself and other men. The Mask, Yeats's lifelong obsession, had become the man, and it was as hieratic as the golden mask of Mycenae.

Yet even his huge prestige and world reputation did not place Yeats beyond denigration and personal attacks. When he was appointed to the Senate, for instance, D. P. Moran's *Leader* magazine had denounced the choice of 'this minor West British poet' and remarked after his controversial speech on divorce: 'Mr Yeats has divorced Kathleen Ni Houlihan and formed an alliance with Dolly Brae.' He was still suspect to a large sector of Catholic opinion, while even many people of his own Protestant background must have regarded him as a nationalist and renegade who had sold them out to the enemy. Others regarded him merely as an ambitious poseur and secret careerist, with a hunger for power, self-aggrandisement and manipulation. Yet Yeats himself under the Olympian manner he affected, or rather had grown into, seems often to have felt wounded or isolated in 'this blind, bitter land' and the 'unmannerly town' of Dublin, where issues so quickly became personalised and rancour against individuals was the rule rather than the exception. Yet like his models, Parnell and Standish O'Grady, he had schooled himself from youth to stand above and apart from the mob and cast a cold eye. (It is remarkable, incidentally, how often Yeatsian commentators advert to the image of a proud horseman, head in the air, an image which occurs also in his own epitaph for himself. It is also noticeable how many people thought that in old age he resembled a hawk or an eagle, and in fact both horses and heraldic birds are a feature of his poetry from first to last.[4])

This anti-populist stance was shared by others in his circle, including Gogarty who cultivated what he called *eutrephilia*, well-bred arrogance, as a defensive weapon against the 'dirty little Firbolgs' who seemed to be encroaching more on the national life every day. (This stance, incidentally, was shared and applauded by an unlikely ally, Gogarty's friend the Scots Communist poet Hugh MacDiarmid.)[5] Inevitably at this stage the issue of the poet's alleged Fascism comes up once more, yet Yeats seems to have seen through General O'Duffy's comic-opera brand of politics quite quickly and to have realised that, far from being an expression of the aristocratic spirit, it was essentially mob-oriented and intellectually null and void. This dalliance with the Radical Right was as much a feature of the time as its polar opposite, conversion to Communism or at least socialism. The reaction of other sensitive writers and thinkers, including Eliot and Pound in their very different ways, against the often mindless levelling and spiritual vulgarity of commercial mass democracy has acquired a bad smell today, largely because of Pound's ill-judged association with Mussolini (whom he apparently regarded as a new type of Renaissance man, a sort of Federigo de Montefeltre reborn) and because it sometimes showed an ugly streak of anti-Semitism. Yet it went far deeper than a mere flirtation with the aristocratic Old Right or the new populist one; it was a deep and genuine fear, shared by Central European writers such as Rilke and Karl Kraus, that the West's spiritual and artistic patrimony was under threat from a new barbarism. Pound himself recalls in his book *A Guide to Kulchur* a conversation he had with Yeats in Italy, in which he propounded the idea that the intellectuals and the Catholic Church should now enter into an intellectual and cultural alliance against Babbitt (Sinclair Lewis's personification of small-town philistinism). Yeats answered testily: 'But CONfound it, in my country the Church IS Babbitt!'

Since the 1920s Yeats had suffered a good deal of ill-health, aggravated by overwork, and during the Thirties he underwent the Steinach operation and also suffered from heart trouble and nephritis. The Tower at Ballylee had been given up in 1929, and Yeats in the last years of his life spent an increasing amount of time on the Continent seeking sunshine and rest, as well as visiting London regularly as he had always done. His relations with his English contemporaries do not appear to have been particularly close, though John Masefield, the Poet Laureate, retained a special feeling for him and came to Dublin in 1935 for the celebration in honour of the older poet's seventieth birthday. The gentle Walter de la Mare seems to have felt inhibited by his presence and though he himself wrote much about fairies and folk legends, he was partly bored and partly mystified whenever Yeats, at some social gathering, launched into one of his typical monologues about the occult.[6] In 1931 Yeats wrote to Rabindranath Tagore, whose poetry he had known for many years and included in his *Oxford Book*, on the occasion of the Indian writer's seventieth birthday celebrations: 'I am still your loyal student and admirer. Your poems, as you know, came to me as a great excitement; and of recent years I have found wisdom or beauty, or both, in your prose.'[7] He had, however, lost touch personally with Tagore years before. Perhaps most of Yeats's relatively few close friendships were formed early in life, Lady Gregory being the most obvious example; but in any case he simply was not a warm or bonhomous man. His painter-brother Jack, by contrast, was loved by many and liked by virtually everyone he met, even though his personality was without ostentation and he never ranked among the great Dublin wits and conversationalists. People who came in contact with him sensed, almost at once, a humanity and humour which reached out to all sorts and conditions of men and women, without pose or pretence.

WB's friendship with Gogarty had a firm basis in the fact that they had been fellow-senators, that they were each of them men who favoured the upper reaches of society, and that Gogarty was both a poet and a public personality, as well as being an acclaimed raconteur and wit, a man of action, and physically brave – all qualities which Yeats respected and some of which he envied. The friendship with Higgins probably had an element of calculation in it, whether conscious or unconscious; for the older man Higgins was a bridge with the younger generation of poets, he was a potential ally on the Abbey board, and he was a self-conscious spokesman for the folk Ireland which Yeats had always praised even if he scarcely knew it at first hand. Seán O'Faolain called it 'an attraction of opposites'. Yet though

Higgins revered Yeats as an artist and was often in awe of him as a man, he was not a mere follower or lackey; he occasionally opposed him on Abbey Theatre matters and had a mind of his own on most things.

As for gentlemanly, cultured Lennox Robinson, he was by this stage largely a spent force and a discreet though confirmed tippler who, on social evenings at Merrion Square or Rathfarnham, apparently did little more than sit in a corner, sip his drink and contribute occasional polite noises or giggles. Robinson's creative years were already behind him, so were his best years as an Abbey producer and administrator, yet Yeats's virtual sidelining of him in the theatre, in complicity with Ernest Blythe, still seems unduly cold-blooded and duplicitous. Once again, the ruthlessness of his business ancestors showed itself. Blythe, who himself was a cunning manoeuvrer with years of hard political experience behind him, has recorded that when he joined the board he was visited at his home by two other directors, Higgins and the novelist-playwright Brinsley MacNamara, who proposed that the three of them should act together. Scenting danger or difficulties, Blythe declined to give such an undertaking. 'They said that I obviously had no idea of his (Yeats's) craftiness, of the complexity of his mind, or of his capacity for using people for his own ends. I was taken aback by the vehemence of their talk.'

Yet Blythe, at least by his own account, was also genuinely impressed by Yeats in action in the boardroom. 'I think he dominated the board because he had clear, well-considered views on practically every issue that might arise, because he argued every point equably and sensibly and because his prestige and air of lofty detachment gave his views authority. He never allowed anything to deter him from doing what he thought was necessary for the good of the theatre, or to rush him into precipitate action.'[8]

Apart from his central role in the Abbey, probably Yeats's greatest contribution to Irish cultural life in an institutional sense was the founding of the Irish Academy of Letters in 1932. This was inaugurated at the Peacock Theatre, with Bernard Shaw as president and Yeats as vice-president. Its initial members were AE, Edith Somerville (Violet Martin, her writing partner, was long dead), James Stephens, Padraic Colum, Lennox Robinson, Seumas O'Sullivan, T. C. Murray, St John Ervine, Forrest Reid, Brinsley MacNamara, Austin Clarke, F. R. Higgins, Liam O'Flaherty, Gogarty, Frank O'Connor, Peadar O'Donnell, Francis Stuart and Seán O'Faolain. This was an obviously impressive phalanx, carefully selected to show the collective strength of contemporary Irish literature, though some formidable names were missing. James Joyce, Douglas Hyde, George Moore (who simply ignored the letter of invitation signed jointly by Yeats and Shaw) and Seán O'Casey all declined membership, along with Stephen McKenna the translator of Plotinus, Daniel Corkery and Lord Dunsany. Hyde's reason for refusing was the same as Corkery's — writers in the Irish language should be included; McKenna declined 'out of modesty'. As for Lady Gregory, she had died at Coole some months before.

Though the Academy had been largely his brainchild and he was a powerful figure at its early meetings, it marked the stage at which the direction of Irish writing effectively slid more and more from Yeats's hands into those of a younger generation. He remained a force in its councils, but ill health, advancing age and absence abroad meant that he could no longer steer or manipulate proceedings in his old masterful style. In any case, times and taste were unalterably changing and the new prose realists, chiefly O'Connor and O'Faolain, were already challenging the whole basis of the Literary Revival as it had taken shape in previous decades. With Moore now settled in London and sworn never to return (in any case, he was eighty years old and died the following year, 1933), Lady Gregory dead and Hyde no longer a literary force, the founding figures of the Irish Renaissance were passing out of contemporary life and into literary history. For the next two decades at least, prose and polemics, rather than poetry or drama, were to dominate Irish writing; it was to prove the golden age of the Irish short story, of outstanding literary magazines and great polemical journalism, but no real successor to Yeats himself arose, even if Ireland still produced some admirable poets. The Abbey, lacking a new Synge or a new O'Casey, was to go into slow but steady decline, though perhaps less so than it has become fashionable to say (in a later chapter, I attempt an examination of this generally accepted view). Certainly the poetical theatre which Yeats had fought to create became instead a realist theatre, but then was it not always that in reality?

The chief reason for the foundation of the Academy was to create a respected and powerful official body which would fight the censorship of books, an increasingly menacing development since the Censorship of Publications Act had become law in 1929. Yeats himself had prophesied earlier that though much had already been fought for and achieved, the most difficult period for Irish writers might now lie immediately ahead. Once again, things had passed from glorious revolution/innovation, with all its aspirations, hopes, idealism and atmosphere of common self-sacrifice, into a post-revolutionary situation, in which the new conservatism was hardening and striking back. That prude, gossip-diarist and dedicated chronicler of theatre first nights, Joseph Holloway, wrote that the Academy's 'sole aim seemingly is to do away with the Censors and give all a free hand to flood the Free State with filth. I call the new venture the Irish Academy of Litters.' As things turned out, the Academy achieved relatively little in its battles against the censors, and in practice did not do a great deal more than give prizes and awards, as well as organising occasional festive dinners in honour of respected literary figures – including Edith Somerville, by then an old woman whose books were quite out of fashion, and who had been embittered by the murder of her brother Boyle by the Cork IRA in 1936.

In 1936 appeared Yeats's famous, or infamous, *Oxford Book of Modern Verse*, which drew fire from many English critics; Desmond McCarthy said that it was a 'book of strange choices and strange omissions', while Sir Arthur Quiller-Couch, the

F. R. Leavis of his day, was said to have 'snorted with rage' at any mention of it. Others complained that it was primarily an Irish anthology and even Yeats's first biographer, Joseph Hone, admitted that it showed 'a partiality to friends of the moment and to old friends'. Gogarty was allowed twelve pages, almost double the space given to Ezra Pound, although today Gogarty's verse has vanished from most anthologies. Dorothy Wellesley, Yeats's titled mistress (she was, in fact, Duchess of Wellington), was given thirteen pages though she, too, is almost forgotten today, outside biographies of her poet-lover. Louis MacNeice, rather surprisingly, was allotted eight pages; Higgins, O'Connor (with translations from the Irish), Joseph Campbell, Thomas McGreevy, James Stephens, Synge, Colum, AE, were all represented, sometimes generously. Even Lady Gregory was admitted by virtue of some flat-sounding versions from the Irish. Both Austin Clarke and Patrick Kavanagh were ignored, and so, notoriously, was Wilfred Owen, by then already a posthumous cult figure with the new generation of leftist intellectuals and pacifists. In his curious and rather rambling introduction, Yeats justified his exclusion of war poets on the grounds that 'passive suffering is not a theme for poetry'.

Though Yeats had included Modernists such as Eliot, Auden, and George Barker, plainly he was increasingly out of sympathy with the mood and mode of the age. He was, as he himself proclaimed, one of 'the last Romantics', who was consciously pinning his colours to the masthead of a slowly sinking galleon; the brittle Neo-Classicism of the Twenties, and the 'socially conscious' verse of the Thirties, were both in their very different ways deeply hostile to Romanticism. Yet in spite of the many hostile reviews – or perhaps helped by all the controversy – the book was a commercial success, going into five editions by 1939, the year of Yeats's death and, of course, of the outbreak of war. Perhaps the shrewdest comment was made on it by Louis MacNeice some years later: 'Yeats, I suspect, had quite a childlike liking for simple poetry of the folk type: his selection from that kind of poetry is much better than his selections from more intellectual work. He still liked to think of poetry as coming from the people – a rural people – or at least being in form and content sympathetic to them.'[9] In these words, a whole generation gap is defined – the gap between MacNeice's own generation and that of Yeats, Masefield and de le Mare. Yet, curiously and almost contradictorily, it was also the hardness and frequent complexity of Yeats's later poetry which had helped to shape the idiom of modern verse, including MacNeice's own.

There remains the lingering suspicion that he had been a little cavalier about the whole business, that he knew anthologies of their nature were transitory, and that he did not give it quite the time or thought which such an extensive and complex subject demanded. How he coped with it at all is a question worth asking on its own; Yeats during the Thirties carried a workload which would have killed most people (and probably it helped to kill him in the end). *Words for Music Perhaps* was published in 1932, the epochal *Collected Poems* was brought out by Macmillan the next year, and in the two successive years came *Collected Plays* and *A Full Moon in March*. In 1935 appeared the last of his autobiographical writings, *Dramatis Personae*, a book which has often been underrated and which marks a new lightness and ease in his prose style (again MacNeice, one of the most acute critics of Yeats, has pointed this out). The earlier *Autobiographies* had never quite freed themselves from the mannered cadences and repetitive dying falls of Walter Pater, but in *Dramatis Personae* Yeats at last found a prose style which was both lapidary and conversational, one wholly commensurate with the strides made by his late verse. Perhaps this is, at least in part, a result of his self-immersion in Swift and Berkeley and other writers of the eighteenth century. Purely as literary history the book is also invaluable, since it describes a crucial period in Irish literature and also sets out the complex, shifting relationships between Yeats himself and George Moore, Lady Gregory and Edward Martyn, by then all of them dead.

Dublin, however, suspected that there was something more to it than mere historical retrospect. Yeats had never forgotten or forgiven Moore's treatment of him in *Hail and Farewell* and he was determined to set the record straight – from his own perspective anyway – and to show up 'that preposterous person', George Moore. Moore had described him as a 'literary fop', so in turn Yeats represented Moore as a literary buffoon and licensed jester. At times this obsession gets out of hand and tends to spoil the book. While Yeats possessed verbal edge and malice he lacked Moore's talent for the comic and burlesque, and though he was capable of the most ruthless self-analysis he was too dignified for self-mockery. A reviewer for the *Dublin Magazine* complained that it was essentially a sustained diatribe against Moore – who of course was dead and could not fight or bite back – and that overall the book lacked wit. The last charge is untrue, since large passages of *Dramatis Personae* are delightfully catty and the psychology throughout has the ring of truth, in spite of the underlying tone of self-justification. Yet Yeats, with his own death only a few years away, instead of shaking hands across the grave had chosen to pay off old scores and to scratch again at sores which for years had itched or ached. Mary Colum in her *Life and the Dream* remarks: 'If anybody injured or hurt him or someone close to him he never forgot or forgave.' The words 'someone close to him' may supply a key, since Moore had also handled Lady Gregory roughly and for Yeats she was his Fairy Godmother and, as such, always sacrosanct.

Yeats went on to revise *A Vision*, and to publish *Essays 1931 to 1936* and finally *New Poems* (1938). *Purgatory*, widely considered to be his most effective stage work, was performed at the Abbey in 1938 – it is curious and perhaps significant that it is a work in prose rather than blank verse. Most or at least many contemporary critics seem to agree that his lifelong ambition to revive poetic drama remained essentially unfulfilled, mainly no doubt because the times were against it and because Dublin audiences (and probably Irish actors too) seemingly could only cope with realism, but was it not also because, however much he tried, he simply was not a born playwright? All over Europe a reaction against stage realism was setting in, and in any case the Abbey's two leading playwrights, Synge and O'Casey, arguably had aimed at an imaginative dimension to their work which went well beyond it. In Northern Europe Expressionism had triumphed in many centres, triggered off by Strindberg and the late plays of Ibsen – a European giant of the theatre whom Yeats had almost wilfully misunderstood and misinterpreted. Expressionism was known in Dublin and the early plays of Denis Johnston were obviously influenced by it, but Yeats remained largely untouched by such developments. His knowledge of the Japanese Noh plays was at second hand and any attempt to re-create such a stylised theatre in Ireland required a training and special skills which Irish actors lacked – and besides, where was the audience for it? In his occasional experiments with ballet and musical effects, Yeats was of course well ahead of his public and in retrospect he even comes close to Lorca's plays which often move in a surreal, balletic world where drama in the traditional sense is subjugated to a kind of dreamlike-cum-poetic logic of its own.

Yet the awkward fact remains that in spite of decades of special pleading from well-meaning academics and various fringe-theatre personalities, his stage works simply do not come alive dramatically except before a small, specialised audience which is intellectually geared to them. They have never fully established themselves in the repertory of any major theatre company, after more than half a century, and even in his own lifetime performances in the Abbey usually attracted, in the words of Padraic Fallon who attended some of them as a young man, 'two rows of bored people'. The two possible exceptions are generally agreed to be *Purgatory* and *The Words on the Window Pane*, which in any case are rather apart from his main development and are not concerned with his usual mythic or quasi-metaphysical themes. His occasional attempts to write folk-dialect plays, such as *The Unicorn from the Stars*, are little more than aberrations and reinforce the old jibes against what used to be called 'Kiltartanese'.

The great question is: was he ever a playwright whose work stands on its own feet, rather than as the subsidiary activity of a great lyric poet? Or in other words, would his plays survive on their own merits if the vast prestige of his name were not attached to them? Certain respected critics, such as Vivian Mercier, have made large claims for a number of his stage works, but I suspect Robert Hogan is nearer the truth when he states flatly that Yeats's plays are essentially undramatic.[10] Hogan points to their unwieldy, static expositions, the fact that when Yeats employs spectacle he 'so formalises it that it becomes unspectacular', and – surely a rather damning criticism – that 'there are no great roles in Yeats; indeed there are almost no roles at all. An actor playing Forgael or Cuchulain has nothing to characterise. He does not have to be an actor at all – only an elocutionist.' And finally, while admitting that Yeats must have learned something at least from forty-odd years of close connection with the Abbey, he declares that he 'was never interested in theatre and knew little about it'. In support of this harsh-sounding indictment, Hogan points out: 'When Yeats did try to take a practical hand in the staging of a play, the players were usually baffled, amused or covertly contemptuous.'

In short, though a shrewd head of affairs on the Abbey board, and an upholder of literary standards when they were low on the British and Irish stage generally, he was never what would be called a professional man of the theatre, and was interested primarily in the realisation of his own poet's vision through actors and scenery. Or to put it rather differently, he wanted something from the stage which was over and above what it could give, just as a philosopher such as Plato demanded from political life something which was over and above politics in the pragmatic sense. In the essay 'A People's Theatre', which is written in the form of a letter to Lady Gregory, he declared: 'I want to create for myself an unpopular theatre and an audience like a secret society where admission is by favour and never to many.' We might almost be back in the esoteric atmosphere of the eighteen-nineties, back with *Axel's Castle* and Mallarmé.[11]

Admittedly, in recent years there has been a revival of interest in plays such as *The Herne's Egg*, which used to be considered unplayable, and a number have been revived with some degree of critical approval, but that is a very different thing from bringing them firmly into the dramatic repertory. As Padraic Fallon remarked, Yeats 'had no gift for character, much wit but no humour except irony, and the liveliness of the streets was beyond him. He was basically a literary man.'[12] The theatre seemingly does not surrender itself to those who despise it; and while Yeats no doubt was fully justified in despising the commercial London theatre of his time and the plays of Pinero and his kind, he simply could not pump enough blood into his own. That he left a certain legacy to Austin Clarke, Fallon himself (in his radio plays) and even Samuel Beckett, is accepted fact. Where he failed ultimately was in not creating anything comparable to the classics of the Elizabethan stage, the French theatre of Corneille and Racine, or the German Romantic theatre which stretches from Goethe and Schiller to Hebbel and Kleist and Grillparzer, and even into the twentieth century with Hauptmann. To bring Neo-Platonism on the stage, after all, was not entirely a new undertaking; it had been done by Shakespeare in *Love's Labour Lost*, as Ted Hughes has recently shown.[13] But dramatically Yeats was no Shakespeare or Ben Jonson, and he offered for the most part dry bones and metaphysics to an audience asking for flesh and blood. In essence, his dialogue was with himself, not with the gallery, and what he presented as dramatic characters were simply masked projections of his own inner debates and contrasting personae.

A. Norman Jeffares in his biography[14] remarks on the 'inhuman remoteness from ordinary life' in some of the very late poems, although Yeats had certainly not withdrawn from the world and his broadcast talks on the BBC marked a new level of mass communication. In August 1938 he made his last public appearance at the Abbey for *Purgatory* and shortly afterwards he wrote the long poem 'Under Ben Bulben' in which he revisits childhood scenes and even goes back to his boyhood love of Shelley. The night before he set out to winter in the Riviera, he talked in Rathfarnham with his near-neighbour F. R. Higgins, who remembered: 'After midnight we parted on the drive from his house. The head of the retiring figure, erect and challenging, gleamed through the darkness, as I looked back; while on the road before me, my thoughts were still singing with the slow, powerful accents of his chanting:

> *Irish poets, learn your trade,*
> *Sing whatever is well made.*
> *Scorn the sort now growing up,*
> *All out of shape from toe to top . . .'*[15]

That was Yeats's last night in Ireland, since he died at Roquebrune a few months later. He was writing and revising until a few days before his death on 26 January 1939. As is well known, the second World War prevented the transferral of his body back to Ireland until 1948 and his ceremonial reburial at Drumcliffe, in his beloved Sligo – a public event, given the blessing of the State. By then Higgins was seven years dead, though Austin Clarke and Louis MacNeice both attended the funeral, held in pouring rain. Yeats's widow lived on for decades and near the end of her life was visited by Ezra Pound, who was nearing the end of his own. John Montague, in a recent issue of the poetry magazine *Agenda*, has left a lively impression of her in old age, fond of a drink and a chat or argument, and giving her frank opinion that contemporary Irish writers were too staid and cautious: 'Willie loved a row.'[16]

Irish poets – and not, of course, only poets – were quick to pay tribute to what they had lost. One of the first was Austin Clarke in the *Times Literary Supplement*, who wrote that in the late poetry 'is posited the plight of the poet in modern times, whether we regard Yeats as the last of the great Romantics, a lonely thinker concerned with ultimate questions of time and the soul's circumstance, or as one who ventures to peer into the moving future.' F. R. Higgins also saw the late work as the crowning of a long career: 'He sought to rid himself of elaboration, of redundancy – through various ways. He found his new method by ballad-writing, for instance, and by writing out first in prose the substance of the verse on which he was working. He, however, succeeded mainly in his later work by the introduction of and tenacious adherence to stern theme and structure. With that success his poetry of mood gives way to his poetry of dramatic passion. It becomes hard-bitten; more Gaelic in feeling.' Both of these judgments give the lie to those who claim that the literary Ireland of the Thirties and Forties was too provincial and too obsessed with folk balladry to absorb the true measure of Yeats's later development. Even earlier, in the *Dublin Magazine* in 1934, Padraic Fallon had written: 'This period of "The Tower", "The Winding Stair", is more important, I have come to think in spite of myself, than any of his earlier periods, because in it he has come to realise intellectually an attitude that was once romantically sensuous. Himself now, unclothed, is his theme.'

It is probably true, however, that for the ordinary poetry-lover he remained in essence the author of 'The Lake Isle of Innisfree' and 'The Fiddler of Dooney'. Certainly 'Innisfree', which Yeats himself apparently came to detest, continued to haunt anthologies, both Irish and English, for many years. The public had been bewitched originally by the soft glow of the Celtic Twilight and it took a long time to educate it into liking the hard white light and sharp outlines of the Celtic Noonday. In his last dozen years of life, Yeats had travelled too far into the future for the bulk of his readers to keep pace with him.

Louis MacNeice, as a Northern Irelander educated in England, had never identified himself with literary Dublin and was antagonistic to much that it stood for, though he and Higgins were friendly across the inevitable divide created by their contrasting temperaments, backgrounds and ideals. He had come to admire the modernism of T. S. Eliot and was widely identified with the so-called school of Auden and Spender and Day-Lewis, which stood collectively for most of what Yeats had detested. Yet his book *The Poetry of W. B. Yeats*, published in 1940 and already quoted in this chapter, remains one of the best studies of its kind and testifies once again to MacNeice's stature as a critic – something which has not always been recognised. He begins it by saying: 'I had only written a little of this book when Germany invaded Poland. On that day I was in Galway. As soon as I heard on the wireless of the outbreak of war, Galway became unreal. And Yeats and his poetry became unreal also.' It must quickly have become real again, however, since MacNeice goes on to make point after valid point with an insight and objectivity exceptional for a young man writing about his seniors.

He admits frankly that his own generation was suspicious of Yeats because 'all his life (he) was a pronounced enemy of facts'. He dislikes his celebration of Big House culture, but realises that 'Ireland meant to Yeats something special. It is not Ireland as the ordinary person knows it, yet it is something distilled from that Ireland.' MacNeice admits that when he first read 'The Tower' and 'The Winding Stair' he found them 'frigid, unsympathetic', as he was then under the dominant (and fashionable) influence of Eliot. Within a few years he felt differently, perhaps because he had realised that Eliot's poetry itself was 'largely both mannerism and fantasy' and also that the 'daylight of realism was itself largely fiction'. MacNeice now appreciates that the two volumes he had originally disliked are the highest achievement of Yeats's genius. He goes on to compare his poetry with Rilke's, who at that stage was still relatively little known in the English-speaking world – though Yeats himself appears to have read some of him, or at least to have known about him.[17] Compared with the general reaction of the public school Left which was already dominant in English poetry politics, MacNeice shows himself notably open-minded and far-seeing.

Inevitably, however, reaction against the entire culture and mentality of the Twilight had been building up among the new, predominantly realist-oriented and socially critical writers who emerged in the Ireland of the Thirties and Forties. This reaction came to the surface in the famous Irish number of Cyril Connolly's prestigious magazine *Horizon*, published in 1942 during the darkest period of the war. In this Seán O'Faolain, ambitious, articulate and consciously iconoclastic, seized the opportunity of attacking what he saw as an increasingly debilitating legacy: 'The young intellectual of the time had . . . an entry into an excitingly Eleusinian sub-world of hocus-pocus, half sincere, now soporific, now steaming, where thought could be levitated into the stratosphere . . . .' Here the joint target is plainly Yeats and AE, the first for his interest in occultism and the other for his religio-philosophical mysticism. Warming to his subject, O'Faolain goes on to say that Yeats 'had no interest in knowledge, fact, or objective truth for its own sake . . . He wished for the lightning flash . . .' He attacks 'his indifference to the common people, his Fascist tendency, his dandyism, his fastidiousness', derides Yeats's tendency in old age to become 'as bawdy as his friend Higgins' as well as his self-conscious role-playing, and declares : 'The new generation, while admiring his achievement as a lyric poet this side idolatry, felt that he was not assisting them.' As he saw it, that generation – his own – was faced with problems far more insistent, including political and religious questions; it had grown up in a period of socio-political revolution, it was tied closely to common life and could not evade its claims. As time went on, these problems became 'savagely acute'. The new Irish writers, O'Faolain pointed out, were nearly all Catholics, 'either by conviction or by atavism', and the Catholic Church in the new Ireland was making life impossible for them.

O'Faolain was being deliberately provocative, no doubt, but there is no reason to think that he was insincere, even if his argument was tantamount to saying that probably the greatest generation of Irish writers which had ever existed was becoming increasingly less relevant to modern readers and that the Twilight was precisely that – Twilight, a half-land of dreams, not the workaday, prosaic daylight in which people coped with immediate realities and even with basic survival. O'Faolain, like O'Connor, was an intensely ambitious and opinionated man who often consciously sought out controversy and debate, both to clear the air intellectually and because he enjoyed such cut-and-thrust. And it generally made good 'copy'. It was just these qualities that made him such a great editor of *The Bell* and, for a time, perhaps the chief standard-bearer of his country's intellectual conscience. Yet his virtual rejection of the spiritual legacy of the Literary Revival, while a common reaction of prose writers faced with the radically different psyche of poets, has a broad streak not only of dogmatism and insensitivity but of sheer philistinism. It is the polemicist and professional man of letters speaking, not the creative writer. However, O'Faolain was not speaking for himself alone; plainly he was articulating what others like him felt or were beginning to feel; and the reaction he expressed was a growing one. In a prosaic, self-limiting world, more concerned with vote-counting and population statistics and tax returns than with the heroics of Cuchulain or the fate of Deirdre of the Sorrows, the hieratic gestures of Yeats must have appeared to many readers rather as the latinised oratory of the nineteenth century did to the new race of professional politicians – splendid, but anachronistic. Besides, it was still wartime, and Ireland was concerned above all with the question of its own neutrality and with the outcome of the fighting, and ultimately with national survival.

In the post-war years, especially in the 1950s, the steady growth of Joyce's posthumous influence among the Irish intelligentsia made them look increasingly to him and *Ulysses* as pointers both to the present and the future; Yeats, while still obviously respected and admired, was now widely felt to mark the end of a whole cycle of modern Irish literature, while Joyce began another which was more relevant to the present and the immediate future. This view had already existed before the war and was particularly strong in the generation of Flann O'Brien/Brian O'Nolan/Myles na Gopaleen, one of the spokesmen for a new type of writer-intellectual growing to maturity in an Ireland where independence (relatively speaking) was taken for granted, and where a new academic and bureaucratic establishment had taken root. Disenchanted and rather bored with the Twilight, predominantly town-educated and caring little for the countryside, uninterested in mythology and intolerant of the occult, seeing around them not a country transfigured by AE's spiritual beings or forces but instead a petit-bourgeois society with little apparent cultural aspirations beyond the commercial cinema, this generation found in Joyce its spiritual ancestor and also a considerable innovator, both technically and linguistically. Though O'Nolan was a product of the National University and from a Catholic background, he and the Protestant Samuel Beckett from Trinity College are visibly of a common generation, and both look mainly to Joyce as their mentor and master. The fact that Joyce had become a voluntary exile on the Continent gave him an extra dimension in their eyes – a European dimension; and his choice of Paris as a domicile had a powerful allure for young men (and women) who reacted against narrowly folk and rural concerns and wanted to breathe the life of a great, cosmopolitan city and to savour its sophistication, its complex culture and perhaps even its sexual and other freedoms. (To have a French mistress was probably the daydream – and night-dream – of most young writers and artists.) They felt also, as Joyce had felt, that the mass of their fellow-countrymen had 'never got beyond religion and politics' and these forces overhung them like a low grey sky full of rain.

While Beckett became almost entirely Europeanised, O'Nolan never saw any more of Continental life than a brief, and apparently unsatisfactory, pre-war visit to Germany – then already launched into its Hitlerian era. Perversely, although this generation was cosmopolitan by aspiration, the political and economic realities of the time usually stood in the way of these aspirations becoming fact. The coming of the second World War, and often chronic shortage of money or lack of career prospects, permitted relatively few of them the kind of lifestyle and freedom to travel abroad which had been an accepted thing for the more patrician generation of Yeats, Moore, Synge, etc. – all of whom had been nourished intellectually by Paris. Denis Devlin was an obvious exception, but then he was a professional diplomat; most of the others underwent what might be called an unconsummated love affair with European culture. In general, they knew it better from books than from the living, first-hand reality. But Continental Europe was not the only magnet, since the discovery of modern American writing also had a considerable impact. The poetry of T. S. Eliot, the laureate of modern urban disenchantment, meant a great deal to this generation and so, to a rather lesser extent, did that of Ezra Pound (vide O'Brien's novel *At Swim-Two-Birds*, where a poet who is obviously the young Donagh MacDonagh is introduced as a follower of Pound). Among the prose writers, Hemingway, Steinbeck and even William Saroyan (who visited Ireland and was for a time friendly with O'Nolan) were widely discussed and censorship problems do not seem to have deterred people from reading them. Eliot made a famous visit to Dublin around this time, and to UCD to see and hear there a performance of his verse play *Murder in the Cathedral*.

It is stating the obvious to say that Yeats had become rather a remote figure to many of this generation – a monolith to be respected, or perhaps occasionally daubed with graffiti, but firmly of the past. Certainly it did not appear to feel overpowered by him as writers, or at least poets, of the older generation did. The intellectual Catholicism of the Thirties and Forties (a development, incidentally, which Yeats himself had anticipated) had many of its roots in contemporary French Neo-Thomism, so the Gnosticism, Neo-Platonism, and occultism which had obsessed Yeats must have sounded like remote, esoteric heresies. His Anglo-Irishness, too, probably seemed as archaic as the decaying Big Houses or the various academics of Trinity College who perpetuated a kind of colonial style and outlook. And his full-dress, ceremonious public persona, along with the oratorical ring of his later verse, often repelled younger poets who cultivated irony and indirectness and an artfully muffled monotone. The Suburban Muse now reigned, rather dowdy and charmless, but alert, sharp-tongued and recognisably 'contemporary', a cigarette in her mouth and a literary magazine tucked under her arm.

The Jeffares biography marked the beginning of a new but slow-moving surge of interest, and in the Sixties a succession of critical studies (several of them, interestingly, concerned with his plays) proved that Yeats's reputation had entered a new cycle. In 1965 the centenary celebrations set off a new round of debate and revaluation – a good deal of it critical or even hostile, but all of it showing that he was no mere museum piece (George Moore's centenary in 1952 had passed almost unnoticed.)[18] Slowly but inevitably, the wheel was turning again. Eliot's reputation, meanwhile, was sinking quietly and while there was a major Pound revival in the Fifties, it proved virtually impossible to refloat the 'Cantos' in their entirety. Suddenly, Yeats began to look and sound more intrinsically modern than most of the Modernists; it was his old critics the English poets of the Thirties (MacNeice apart) who now seemed dated and rather fatuous. Symbolism was also becoming respectable again, and poets such as Ted Hughes showed a new and intelligent awareness of the hermetic traditions which had nourished Yeats so deeply. Above all, the artistic and intellectual dominance of Joyce was finally beginning to lift and he was becoming increasingly the property of the universities rather than of the avant-garde.

Today Yeats is back grandiosely on his plinth, as the real founder-figure and father not only of modern Irish poetry, but of modern Irish literature in general. It is sometimes forgotten that the virtual creator of the Celtic Twilight was also largely responsible for bringing Swift, Berkeley and Burke back into intellectual currency, and that he demonstrated to his countrymen that these men were not simply periwigged figures in a colonial English regime, but as much an integral part of the Irish tradition as Aodhagán Ó Rathaille and Eoghan Rua Ó Súilleabháin, or Moore, Mangan and Ferguson. By stiffening late Romanticism with the hardness and dryness of the eighteenth-century intellect, he gave it a new fibre and resilience, and by evading the dominant current of popular realism he gave Irish writers an imaginative and philosophic base to work from. Somehow he also contrived to find a balance of folk and aristocratic elements, even if here he was outflanked by history and the future lay mainly with the petit-bourgeoisie – though again history is changing and 'folk' may well acquire a new, relevant meaning. It is true that the esoteric aspect of his thinking lay far apart from the interests of the mass of his countrymen (and from those of the ordinary English or American reader too) but in this field Yeats surely was thinking and writing as a practising poet, who knew historically that poets in almost all ages have cultivated their own lore and traditions, some of them quite occult and hermetic. Poetry after all, to state the obvious very lamely and tritely, is a very special calling, a vocation and not a trade, though also a craft which has to be laboriously learned; and after the journalistic verse fathered by the Thirties poets and their successors, it is quite possible that a more vatic and ritualistic view of the poet will emerge again (Robert Graves, though an enemy of Yeats, suggested something along these lines in *The White Goddess*, which became such a cult book in the Fifties). Like AE, Yeats gave Irish writers – that is, those of them who were prepared to listen and learn – an intellectual alternative to the dogmatic Catholicism or class-ridden Protestantism of their upbringing, and by doing so liberated both their thinking and their imaginations. In AE's case it was mainly Eastern philosophy and Blakean mysticism; in Yeats's case it was mostly Neo-Platonism, Gnosticism, Cabbalism and the hermetic traditions generally, with a smattering of Nietzsche – and, of course, of Berkeley. It could almost be described as a new bardic lore, and its effect on poets – not only on Irish ones either, by any means – has been incalculable.

The remote, arcane, almost inhuman element in his art and mentality continues to repel, or at least puzzle, many people who are otherwise drawn to him. It also repelled some who came into personal contact with him and encountered suddenly his cold, hawklike gaze, or who felt his intellectual detachment to be ultimately glacial and unfeeling. The grotesque, shamanistic, and birdlike quality in his work, as has been suggested here already, was present from quite early on and even in the masterpiece and culmination of his early period, 'The Shadowy Waters', there is a steadily increasing distance from ordinary human emotions and concerns as Feargal and Dectora sail or drift onwards to their lovers' rendezvous with the unknown.

> *Where the dead drifted, I could see a bird*
> *Like a grey gull upon the breast of each.*
> *While I was looking they rose hurriedly,*
> *And after circling with strange cries awhile*
> *Flew westward; and many a time since then*
> *I've heard a rustling overhead in the wind.* [19]

In that remarkable and even unique work – which seems to me to work best when read as a dramatic poem rather than a drama – it is clothed with the trappings of the eighteen-nineties Symbolism, while in the very late poems and plays it is *sui generis* as well as being gnomic, skeletal and strange. But in that curious, macabre poem 'Cuchulain Comforted', written only two weeks before his death, the timid 'Shrouds' which gather around Cuchulain as he strides among the dead, and tell him about themselves, in the very last line 'had changed their throats and had the throats of birds'. (This poem, and its poetic implications, are marvellously discussed by Seamus Heaney in his volume of critical essays, *Preoccupations*, written with all a major poet's special insight, and he also discusses Yeats's attitude to death with corresponding insight in 'The Redress of Poetry'.[20]) This is surely a perfect case of the snake with the tail in his mouth, the completed, annular O-shape of life and death. The poet feels himself already posthumous, or at least a transitory figure between this world and the next, as perhaps Ibsen did in his very last plays or Rilke in his final poems.

Chapter 5

JOYCE AND THE EXILE TRADITION

N
o other Irish writer in history has acquired such an international standing or mystique as has James Joyce. He has become both an academic industry and a virtual symbol of exile and alienation, a 'difficult' author who for decades was regarded as wilfully obscure and complex, yet has been translated into every world language and a number of lesser ones. In his lifetime he was a hugely controversial figure who nevertheless lived quietly, almost anonymously, and was a devoted husband and father, a refugee from both world wars in neutral Switzerland, speaking Italian at home to his wife and children, yet writing in English, a literary revolutionary who was almost petit-bourgeois in his personal habits, a man who refused to visit America in his lifetime, yet posthumously has become almost an American author by adoption or naturalisation. As a final contradiction, the writer who has become the symbol of deraciné modernism and universalism had almost no literary subject except his native Dublin, which he steadily refused to revisit.

Perhaps the best historical parallel is not with any other writer of the past century and a half, but with Wagner and the virtual dictatorship he established over the musical world, a dictatorship which continued for nearly a generation after his death. As men, of course, they were hugely different; Joyce was not power-hungry in the rather vulgar Wagnerian sense, was not an intriguer or art politician (though he showed considerable shrewdness and energy at times in pushing the fortunes of his books), and was never a lackey of kings, governments and politicians, as Wagner was with Ludwig of Bavaria. Yet there are many parallels, including their respective exiles in Switzerland and the kind of discipleship they aroused, as well as the single-minded fanaticism of their close followers, many of whom were devoted women.[1] The type of the perfect Wagnerian, now long extinct, closely resembles the dedicated Joycean – or, for that matter, the dedicated Proustian, a more precious and etiolated type which flourished until very recently. Both inspired cults – a futuristic and apocalyptic one in the case of Wagner (*Zukunftmusik*), and a Modernist one (with a capital M) in the case of Joyce. Both generated forms of almost cultural monotheism, from which no literate person was expected to stand apart or remain neutral. In that sense, the Joyce Cult can be compared with

Marxism in the political field, and Joyce himself has more than a touch of Lenin about him, an anonymous émigré sitting almost unnoticed in the cafés of continental Europe and quietly, obdurately working towards a revolution which would blow up the Old Order.

One strange result of this cult, or mythology, is that a great many readers and critics around the world, but particularly in America, view twentieth-century Ireland almost exclusively through Joycean perspectives, or rather what they believe are Joycean perspectives. His entire career and writings are widely taken to amount to, or at least to contain, a damning though impersonal judgement on his fatherland (or motherland), which is seen as too small, narrow and puritanical to accept and understand his cosmopolitan genius. Joyce has become the measuring rod not only for run-down Edwardian Dublin and its (admittedly rather provincial) society and outlook, but for the totality of Irish history and culture since then. It is rather as if modern London, and indeed the whole of modern British society, were to be viewed through the optics of Dickens's novels.

Now whatever about Dublin in 1904, Joyce neither knew nor wrote about the Dublin of 1924, or the Dublin of 1934 for that matter. He kept in touch to the very end with contemporary Irish life through his friends and what they told him, through newspapers and press cuttings, and through his own considerable curiosity, but he did not know or experience it at first hand. If he had returned, very possibly he would not have liked the reality of what he saw, and he might even have despised and detested it, but he never did return, as the world knows. For that decision he scarcely deserves either praise or blame, yet apparently in the eyes of a large section of his commentators it somehow enhances his stature as a martyr-saint of literature. By the same logic, his voluntary exile also registers as an implicit indictment of a country and society with which he had long lost contact at first hand, and which he no longer knew except through the eyes of others. But does every emigrant who, for one reason or another, settles abroad necessarily hate and reject the country he has left behind? Joyce may have done so, or at least for some of the time, but the evidence seems contradictory, and the man who wrote *Finnegans Wake* was plainly a very different Joyce from the one who spoke through the persona of Stephen Hero. There is a degree of acceptance, and even of celebration, in his later work which is very different from the narcissistic bitterness of his Dublin years. Shrewd critics such as Anthony Cronin have recently – and surely quite justifiably – tended to stress the celebratory and comic aspects of his writings, rather than the long-held view of the embittered exile cursing the memory of rabidly nationalist Ireland and the Church.[2]

Though Joyce personally was quiet and courteous, and as a rule deeply reserved with all except a handful of people, Malcolm Cowley has noted that 'from all his books three values disengaged themselves, three qualities of the man himself: his pride, his contempt for others, his ambition.'[3] Remarking on the famous (and, so it seems to me, rather youthfully fatuous) sentence in *Portrait of the Artist* about forging in the smithy of his soul the uncreated conscience of his race, Cowley suggests that in real life Joyce had chosen 'a still lonelier ambition. As he wandered through Italy, Austria, Switzerland and France, he continued to write about the Dublin of his youth and remembered the sound of Irish voices, but he half forgot that Irish race whose conscience was being forged in the smithy of revolution. He had chosen another destiny. Like Napoleon landing in Corsica, like Cortez or Pizarro marching into the highlands, he set himself a task of self-aggrandisement: he would be a genius! – he would carve out an empire, create a work of genius.'[4]

Joyce left Ireland as a very young man and his last visit to it was in 1912, when he was thirty. Nora Joyce with her two children visited Galway during the Civil War when they were fired on during a train journey, an experience which predictably soured her further towards her homeland and cannot have made her husband like it any better either. For the rest of his life he resisted all invitations or blandishments to go back, including a personal one from Yeats in the 1920s to visit him in Dublin, and later he refused membership of the Irish Academy of Letters. In that same year (1932) he declined to attend a St Patrick's Day party in Paris because the Irish Ambassador, Count O'Kelly, was to be present and, in the words of Richard Ellmann, 'Joyce did not wish to imply that he in any way endorsed the present Irish state.'[5] He never, it seems, changed his British passport for an Irish one, though that may have been mainly a matter of convenience since British citizenship was much more useful on the Continent. Nevertheless, it is not easy to judge just how he regarded his homeland, the Church, other Irish writers, Irish nationalism and Irish politics, or even if these things still interested him very much in his maturity. The evidence, and the various statements and random sayings attributed to him by friends, interviewers and fellow-writers, tend to suggest that Joyce said now one thing, then another, that his attitudes and opinions changed a great deal over his life, and that they even varied according to mood and circumstance and to whom he was talking at the time.

On occasions he seems gripped by the spirit of negativism and contradiction, at others he shows an almost benign detachment, at other times again – particularly as he aged – he appears to have been visited by an all-conquering nostalgia for the Dublin of his youth and what he had left behind. Certainly he disliked a great deal of what the Literary Revival had stood for, though he translated Synge's *Playboy* into Italian and early in the century had been friendly with Synge in Paris. (He also, at one stage, planned to translate some stories by George Moore.) He did, however, sometimes quote Yeats movingly in later life, though Irish mythology, which meant so much to Yeats and Lady Gregory – not to mention Austin Clarke, James Stephens and other younger writers – became for him chiefly material to burlesque, as Finn MacCool and other legendary figures are parodied in *Finnegans Wake*. Joyce at one stage had taken some lessons in Gaelic, but he never spoke it or studied it deeply and was rather opposed to attempts to revive it as the national tongue. Though he had a certain affection for popular patriotic ballads of his youth and liked occasionally to sing them, few writers – certainly very few Irish ones – concerned themselves less with rural life or rural traditions in the usual sense; Joyce has become almost a symbol of the modern big-city sensibility, although the Dublin he knew and was obsessed by was a city of fewer than 300,000 people. In his youth he had often been satirical and disrespectful – not to say resentful – towards Yeats and AE and others of his Irish elders, while the pulping of *Dubliners* by the publisher George Roberts, who had either lost faith in the book or was afraid of it giving offence, seems to have left a lifelong wound. He dreaded the malicious Dublin wits, such as Gogarty, and above all he must have found it hard to forgive Dublin for mocking his early pretensions and ambitions. These early smarts appear to have been rubbed sore on occasion by his brother Stanislaus, an awkward man, who was caustic, difficult and a frequent stirrer-up of strife and grudges.

As Joyce himself said, he did not live in Ireland for very long. The period in which he knew it was the 'dead period' against which Shaw before him had similarly reacted; Dublin then was a poor and probably a somewhat depressing city, a provincial or regional capital rather than a national one, while Joyce's own family background was shadowed and inhibiting, and he had broken with the Church which had educated him. The Literary Revival did not draw him to it or into it – rather the reverse – and virtually no figure in Irish history attracted him beyond Parnell, though he had a certain respect for Arthur Griffith. He liked the anonymity of foreign cities (he told Arthur Power that Paris was 'very convenient'),[6] he spoke several European languages though probably fewer than has been claimed, and he may have had in mind the example of Ibsen, whom he revered, and who had similarly escaped from his own small provincial country and its tensions and pressures by spending much of his life abroad. Plainly, Joyce felt that above all he needed air and space in which to spread his wings, and he also needed the artistic detachment towards his material which could only be achieved by distance and intellectual maturity. In short, he followed his own line of development, and that development did not lie in Dublin or along the lines indicated by Yeats. Even if he had been treated better or more sympathetically in his native city, it is likely that sooner or later he would have found himself at odds with the ruling literary elite there, and with Joyce, from first to last, it was a case of *aut Caesar aut nihil*.

So probably far too much has been made of Joyce the exile, and of the alleged native philistinism and narrowness which drove him abroad. For much of his life, he lived and moved among exiles from other countries and cultures who, like him, had moved from the European peripheries to its centre. The artists of the contemporary School of Paris, for instance, included Spaniards such as Picasso and Gris, Russians such as Chagall and Zadkine, Italians such as Modigliani and Severini, as well as numerous Germans and Scandinavians drawn naturally to the great international melting-pot which the city was then. His helpers, friends and admirers included numerous Americans, both male and female, while Pound and Hemingway were among his fellow-writers and supporters. Joyce, in fact, lived in a largely émigré culture and was at home and at ease in such a world. With most of the native French writers, on the other hand, he appears to have had rather distant relations – Proust, a famous snob, kept his distance, Gide was cool, while Claudel considered him an immoral writer and a bad influence. The Surrealists he avoided and was apparently irritated when their work was mentioned alongside his own; the Joycean 'stream of consciousness' was not to be confused with automatic writing or the random play of fantasy and free association.

Those French writers who did admire or actively support him were either of the second rank, or were primarily critics and theorists – Valery Larbaud, Louis Gillet, Philippe Soupault and Edouard Dujardin the alleged inventor of the interior monologue.[7] Joyce relied a good deal on their influence and support, social as well as literary, and he could be extremely possessive and manipulative towards his friends. He also cultivated a certain mystique of remoteness and inaccessibility which enhanced his personal legend and prestige, avoiding interviewers as a general rule and staying out of literary politics and feuds insofar as it was possible and feasible to do so. Joyce has gone down as a man who – his wife and children apart – lived entirely for his art as Flaubert had done, and there can be no serious doubt that this view of him is justified. The fact remains that he was exceedingly careful about the growth of his reputation, and from those featureless flats or dull hotel rooms in which he habitually lived and wrote, he actively presided over an international network of translators, admirers and well-wishers who could further his fame. His friends were expected to supply him with news and newspaper cuttings and miscellaneous items of information, and they also had to perform various errands and services – so much so, in fact, that Nora Joyce used sometimes to sigh: 'Jim is a tyrant!'

He kept in touch with Ireland from a distance, regularly reading Irish newspapers – especially *The Irish Times* – and corresponding or talking with old friends. As the early bitterness gradually drained away, and he found himself internationally famous if still a scandalous author in many eyes, he seemingly grew more mellow towards his homeland, though almost to the end of his life he nursed the belief that he might be subjected to physical violence if he ever went back there. Apart from the outside chance of his being menaced or even attacked by some crank or fanatic, this seems most unlikely, yet when told as much by friends and acquaintances Joyce refused to listen, and his wife apparently backed him in this attitude.[8] Padraic Colum, who was in touch with him throughout the Thirties in Paris, remarked in retrospect many years later that he had a persecution mania – perhaps the negative side of the Messianic self-importance which otherwise he either concealed, or had largely buried in maturity. In Colum's own opinion, as given to an anonymous *Irish Times* interviewer in December 1960: 'He would have come if he had been invited. I tried to organise a dinner party in Dublin for Joyce's fiftieth birthday. I talked to various people, but met with no success. When I went back to Paris, Joyce – in that way he had of asking about something, but trying to show that he had not been thinking about it – asked if that fiftieth birthday party plan had come off. He knew by my silence that it hadn't. He thought that political parties and the Church were down on him.' As has been mentioned already, he refused to join the Irish Academy of Letters, alleging privately that Yeats and Shaw merely wanted him there because of his name, not because his books were admired or even read in Ireland. This seems ungenerous and ungracious; after all, the battle against censorship concerned him as much as them, and surely he owed his literary peers at least some show of solidarity.

A talented young Dublin-born Jewish artist, Stella Steyn, got to know him in Paris during the late Twenties and early Thirties through a letter of introduction from one of her teachers, the painter Patrick Tuohy. She became friendly with the doomed Lucia, and at one stage Joyce asked her to do some illustrations for *Finnegans Wake*, a project which came to nothing. She thought that Joyce 'minded what Dubliners thought of him', though he showed no resentment when told that Arthur Griffith's widow had warned Stella and her mother against him as a 'thorough ruffian' who had written immoral books. She also recorded this revealing vignette of him in one of his moods of withdrawal and semi-depression: 'One late afternoon I had called for Lucia and was sitting waiting for her when he came into the room and, taking no notice of me, he went to the piano and with his head bowed over his hands, accompanying himself, he sang some melancholy Irish songs in a low, sad voice. I said, "You must miss Ireland." He replied, "I do." I said, "Would you not like to go back?" He replied, "No. They jeer too much."'9

Though he kept his United Kingdom citizenship, Joyce had no affection for modern England and admired very few contemporary English writers. The real England for him was essentially the country of Shakespeare and Donne and Duns Scotus, not the country of Tennyson or Hardy, and even less that of Wells and Galsworthy and Arnold Bennett. His three-month visit to London in the early Thirties was strictly to legalise his union with Nora Barnacle by marrying her in a registry office, and during that time he seems to have avoided meeting other writers. He refused several invitations to visit America, where he already had a strong following – though it is also true that *Ulysses* had been banned there for some years and there was a vocal anti-Joyce lobby, particularly among Irish-Americans. Latin Europe was his natural habitat, as it had been for Scotus Eriugena and those other Irishmen at the court of Charlemagne a millennium before; and Italy appears to have been his chosen land – if the first World War had not driven him to neutral Switzerland, he might well have settled there for good.

Joyce disliked Germany and the German language, though he knew German literature and even translated a poem by Gottfried Keller, while a visit to Denmark in 1936 proved disappointing. He liked wine cultures and wine was his natural drink; he was at home with café life and Continental cooking; he had the Italian's love of opera and singing, along with a relative indifference to orchestral and instrumental music; he loved the philosophy of Vico and the poetry of Dante, and his education by the Jesuits had soaked him in the influence of Aquinas. Joyce, in essence, was Celtic and Latin, a common enough cultural phenomenon, and in many or most respects he was profoundly un-English. England, in turn, has generally treated him as a foreign body and his works have never been widely popular there, nor has he left much imprint on English literature. The hysterical denunciation of *Ulysses* by D. H. Lawrence has often been quoted, and so has the icily snobbish reaction of Virginia Woolf, while he suffered from the English censors to the extent of having copies of his books burned by Customs. In short, he never has entered the bloodstream of Anglo-Saxon literature as Yeats has done, whereas his impact on modern Welsh literature in English has been considerable, including native-born Welshmen such as Dylan Thomas as well as Anglo-Welsh writers such as David Jones and John Cowper Powys. Jones's *In Parenthesis* could scarcely have been written without the example of Joyce, while Powys was an admirer virtually from the time *Ulysses* first appeared and he wrote enthusiastically about Joyce both in America and England. In Scotland Hugh MacDiarmid wrote his enormous poem 'In Memoriam James Joyce' in conscious homage. So while abstract-minded or obsessively cosmopolitan commentators probably will sniff at any notion of Celtic affinities, or even reject the adjective itself as meaningless, the evidence speaks for itself, since racially these are all Celtic authors writing in English.[10]

Joyce's blend of scholasticism and scatology, Rabelaisianism and cerebral introspection, and his continual use of Catholic imagery are quite alien to the English mind. On the other hand, he felt at home in France, where he has always been respected if not always fully understood, and there is an aspect of his work which has its ancestry in Flaubert and Baudelaire. In Paris, especially, he seems to melt into its Gothic past, while his hard, brilliant, scholastically trained intellect links him with the great medieval schoolmen and the age of Abelard. He told Arthur Power that he believed the modern epoch was moving away from classicism back to a quasi-medieval outlook, and he also remarked that Ireland was almost the last country in Europe which had retained a medieval character.[11]

Joyce never at any stage denied or disclaimed his essential Irishness; he accepted it as his birthright and hereditary curse-cum-blessing. His own familial and even tribal sense was acutely Irish, Irish accents sound through his writings like a key signature in music, and the ghostly voices of Irish legends, identities and essences crowd into the polyphonic texture of *Finnegans Wake*. When the young Arthur Power, newly arrived in Paris, expounded to him his idea of writing some great 'international' novel, Joyce told him quietly that one should 'write out of what is in the blood, not what is in the head'. He maintained his links with old friends such as Constantine Curran (who wrote his obituary in *The Irish Times*) and the Colums, and in general was at least civil, if not effusive, to the various Irish people he met abroad. According to Louis Gillet, he spoke well of Seán O'Casey,[12] he regarded James Stephens as the man who might carry on his work if he himself died without completing it, he encouraged (and used) the young Samuel Beckett and was impressed by Flann O'Brien's *At Swim-Two-Birds*. He was visited by various younger Irish writers, including Austin Clarke – who was disappointed to find that Mrs Joyce, once described to him as a beauty, was plain-featured and that their daughter Lucia had a squint.[13] According to Mary Colum, he was pleased by Irish praise or appreciation of his writings when they sounded spontaneous and sincere, and he was genuinely touched once in the 1930s when a Dublin admirer, newly arrived in Paris to watch an Ireland-France rugby match, recited to him some of his favourite Joyce passages by heart. He himself could quote passages from Yeats with equal feeling, including the familiar lines from *The Countess Cathleen* beginning 'The years like great black oxen tread the world . . .' And when Louis Gillet – who seems to have disliked Ireland and makes some risible blunders about it in his writings – proposed paying a visit to Joyce's homeland, he was told insistently not to miss seeing the rhododendrons in bloom at Howth.

Neither, after the anger of his early rebellion and recantation had quietened down, did Joyce deny the importance, for him and others, of the Catholic Church which had played such a role in shaping his psychology and dialectics. (Rather surprisingly, he admitted on several occasions to an admiration for Cardinal Newman, who had been the virtual founder of Joyce's old university and was revered there intellectually and doctrinally.) Though he refused to have his two children baptised, Joyce had Christian Latinity deep within him, and Jacques Mercanton has recorded a Good Friday encounter with him in Paris during which Joyce sang a verse from the old hymn 'Vexilla Regis' with deep feeling, and also quoted from the Gospel of St John. Examples like that could be multiplied, though, of course, so could examples of his anti-clericalism and Voltairean mockery. Mercanton also records that 'In his accounts of Ireland, he maintained his objective point of view. The English were very violent in their suppression of the uprisings, but the Irish were no less so in their rebellion, and no less so to one another in the Civil War . . . He took no sides. All the same, when Mrs Joyce spoke of the cantankerous character of the Irish, he said: "My wife detests her race and her nation. I am loyal."'[14] He was capable of dismissing the Irish as a priest-ridden race perpetually drunk on 'whiskey and Home Rule', or of saying that most Irishmen never got beyond politics and religion, yet almost in the same breath he could declare Ireland to be 'still the brain centre of the United Kingdom'.[15] Similarly he might in conversation paint Dublin as a place of almost mindless squalor, yet maintain that for him she was the second city in the world (after Paris, that is). Of the Jesuits who had educated him at Clongowes and Belvedere College, he said to Mercanton: 'They are tarts. They want you to flatter them, to fondle them. A heartless order that bears the name of Jesus by antiphrasis. But I spent sixteen years of my life with them, and I owe them a great deal.'[16] He also favoured the educational system he had gone through against the English public-school one with its tradition of fagging, a practice he particularly detested even though he had never experienced it.

His Italian friend from the early Trieste days, Alessandro Francini Bruni, called him 'the eternal contradictor'. Bruni, an academic, became militantly Catholic in his later years and was increasingly repelled by his former friend's irreligion, but he found Joyce 'as enigmatical towards politics as towards the Church. He told me one day: "My political faith can be expressed in a few words. Monarchies, constitutional or not, repel me. Republics, bourgeois or democratic, also repel me. Kings are clowns. Republics are worn-out slippers that fit every foot. The Pope's temporal power is gone and good riddance. What is left? Do we want monarchy by divine right? Do you believe in the sun of the future?"'[17] Certainly he did not show any obvious loyalty to the political systems of the various countries he lived in or passed through; he refused to take Mussolini seriously and thought that the Italians might be capable of silliness, but not of harm. Hitler was a very different phenomenon, and according to his Swiss friend, the art historian Carola Giedion-Welcker, 'Hitler interested Joyce as the personification of demonic powers and at the same time as an example of an individual's rise', the destructive side of the dualism whose positive aspect was art and creativity.

Joyce, then, was a man without a country, largely indifferent to his surroundings (thanks to his bad eyesight, he could not see much of them anyway), a kind of Wandering Jew of art. (It is highly significant, incidentally, how closely Jewish intellectuals have identified with his writings, and of course Leopold Bloom is himself a Jew. Ellmann, his definitive biographer, was Jewish and so are/were many Joyce followers and explicators.) In a wider sense, Joyce can be seen as that very mid-twentieth phenomenon, Man the Voyager, so it is no random choice which made him take Ulysses as his symbol. Probably he would have agreed with what Flaubert said to Maxime du Camp when his fellow-writers angered him by their constant talk about politics: 'They're nothing but bourgeois! We are neither French nor Algonquins, we are artists; Art is our country; a curse on those who have any other.'

It is curious, then, that in almost any discussion of Ireland in the period between the two world wars, he should automatically be brought in as the most august and obvious target of censorship and of Ireland's allegedly inward-looking mentality. In the first place, as has been said already, Joyce's books were not censored, with the exception of the early pulping of Dubliners (which Gillet and other partisans wrongly believed to have been burnt). It is true that for years Ulysses was not easily obtainable, though in certain Dublin bookshops such as Eason's it could be bought under the counter or from a high shelf where no prowling crank or amateur censor would easily see it. Nevertheless, virtually everybody who was anxious to read it managed to do so, and most of the Irish intelligentsia were familiar with it from a relatively early stage. The earlier books, Dubliners and Portrait of the Artist, quickly entered the bloodstream of Ireland's reading public and certain scenes from the latter book, such as the protracted family row about Parnell which spoils Christmas dinner, were in my youth quoted almost as regularly as Synge or

Yeats. On various occasions I heard them praised or cited by sincere Catholics who would not willingly have missed Sunday Mass, but who were not on that account burners of books or moral witch-hunters. *Finnegans Wake* was another matter altogether, not because it was a 'scandalous' work but because it was difficult, ultra-demanding and very long into the bargain; one Irish intellectual carried out a one-man poll of his friends and discovered that none of them had managed to finish it. The average reader merely found it boring or incomprehensible, or both. Nevertheless certain passages from it, particularly the ultra-musical closing pages, became virtually canonical and enthusiasts who could get hold of recordings of Joyce reading from the work treasured these as a bibliophile might treasure some rare edition of a classic.[18]

A friend of mine (now dead), who had been a high-ranking civil servant, once told me that during his final year at a Christian Brothers' school in a south-western Irish town, he and some like-minded friends repeatedly questioned their English teacher about Joyce and his writings. Finally, the teacher came in to class one day with a large green-covered volume, pushed it across the desk to them, and said: 'There you are – now judge for yourselves.' It was, of course, *Ulysses*. The painter Patrick Swift, a Joyce devotee like so many of his generation, similarly got his introduction to him via his English teacher at Synge Street Schools in Dublin – another Christian Brothers' institution – who could and did recite whole passages by heart and encouraged his pupils to read the originals.

Nothing could be less true, then, than to say that Joyce was neglected or ignored by his own countrymen, though it is certain that many Irish people – most of whom had not read him – considered him someone whose books no decent person would look at. (Denis Ireland, in his 1936 book *From the Irish Shore*, describes a frosty response from his otherwise genial Jesuit hosts when he mentioned Joyce during a visit to Clongowes College during the 1930s.) On the contrary, his work was enormously influential in his home country, both for good and for bad. Beckett and Flann O'Brian/Brian O'Nolan have already been quoted as examples of this, but Denis Johnston has also acknowledged the influence of Joyce on certain of his early plays. Austin Clarke plainly owes him a debt, though perhaps an intellectual more than a stylistic one, while Thomas Kinsella has recorded his early admiration for the *Portrait*. Joycean influences are visible in several of O'Casey's later plays and are also obvious – sometimes, indeed, far too obvious – in parts of his *Autobiographies*. Even the famous 'Exagmination' organised by Joyce and his close followers in order to restore confidence in 'Work in Progress', at a crucial stage when his original readership was falling away, included two Irish signatories, Beckett and Thomas McGreevy. A whole Irish school of Joyce commentators and admirers flourished in the immediate post-war years, including the architect and polymath Niall Montgomery and the high-ranking civil servant Tom Garvin, while in 1951 John Ryan's *Envoy* magazine brought out an entire Joyce number. In that same year, L. A. G. Strong published (in New York, incidentally) his study *The*

Sacred River: An Approach to James Joyce and in 1952 Arland Ussher brought out *Three Great Irishmen*, a quasi-philosophical study of Shaw, Yeats and Joyce, which is now out of print but contains many genuine insights alongside some rather dubious-sounding generalisations. A few years later, Ryan and another Joyce admirer, Anthony Cronin, organised a well-publicised literary pilgrimage to Sandycove which included both Myles na Gopaleen and Patrick Kavanagh as well as a surviving nephew of Joyce, and the tower itself, the scene of the opening chapter of *Ulysses*, soon became virtually a national shrine.

In fact, what had once been a minority enthusiasm was hardening into a cult and an academic industry, as well as a touristic one. Already by the late Fifties some people were beginning to voice their weariness of it, and in the Sixties this reaction was enhanced by the quickening flow of reminiscence and academic analysis, foreshadowing the development (predicted by the novelist John Broderick) by which Joyce would become increasingly the property of the university intelligentsia. The reaction was further strengthened by the orgy of bad writing by callow young imitators which began in the early Fifties, and which was marked by the overuse or abuse of compound words, an undisciplined flow of subjective impressions and associations in what was naïvely believed to be stream-of-consciousness style, and a lurid, tasteless jumble of sexual and religious imagery. In retrospect, Joyce can be considered fortunate that he did not live to see the worst efforts of his would-be followers and imitators.

Would he ever have gone back to Ireland physically? Joyce died before he had reached sixty, and if he had lived on into the post-war era he would certainly have been as revered an icon as Picasso or Stravinsky (neither of whom had interested him in his lifetime, incidentally; Joyce cared neither for contemporary music nor contemporary painting). Picasso never returned to Spain while Franco ruled there, but Stravinsky in old age did make a return visit to Russia, and my own guess – which remains purely an uneducated guess, nothing more – is that Joyce's admirers, and his own nostalgia or curiosity, would eventually have drawn him back briefly to Ireland, or at least to Dublin. In the Fifties Dublin was still largely the city he had known, but inside little more than a decade it had changed utterly as modern architects and tasteless developers had their way with it. A gap of forty years, combined with the self-assurance of world fame and perhaps some appropriate acts of homage, would surely have cancelled out his youthful miseries and frustrations and sense of rejection, and besides, the old mockers such as Gogarty had mostly departed. But would he have found the visit heartening or disillusioning? Would the dream city seem, once again, humdrum and provincial in the reality?

This, admittedly, is the merest speculation. The point which needs to be repeated here is that Joyce somehow has been turned into a measuring rod for Ireland's supposed mistreatment of its writers over several generations; he has become a symbol of the whole epoch this book deals with, though in fact he had little to do with it beyond exerting, from overseas, a considerable influence on its literature and thinking. He had nothing to do with de Valera, nothing to do with censorship or the trials of a new generation of writers, nothing to do with the Catholic Church of the inter-war years, nothing to do with the faltering steps of the new Irish state, and relatively little to do with the debates and polemics which were fought out in *The Bell* and other intellectual arenas. Those myopic, black-spectacled eyes were gazing retrospectively on a bygone era, as well as into the future. Whatever opinions he might give voice to in private life, in his writings Joyce was no social critic; he was essentially an imaginative artist, a great formal and linguistic innovator, who consciously distanced himself in space and time from the milieu he depicted, or rather transfigured. To read *Ulysses* as an indictment, direct or indirect, of a particular society is surely to distort and even shrink its real significance, since the book is a universal one, and incorporates as much fantasy and introspection as realism – the modern 'imaginative' novel, in essence, not the nineteenth-century novel of social chronicle and still less the Romantic novel of drama and violence and historical pageantry.

Yet various angry or disaffected Irish writers of a generation ago, looking for an iconic figure on whom to project their own inner tensions and frustrations, found him a convenient medium for the purpose. In particular, there was an influential school of opinion which saw him as essentially an inverted Catholic, the archetype of the believer turned blasphemer, and it was even fashionable for a time to view him as an intellectual type of 'spoiled priest' and as an upside-down Thomist. He was also interpreted in some quarters as innately rather sombre and Manichean, dominated dialectically and emotionally by his consciousness of sin and by his Jesuit-inculcated sense of man's guilt and fallen nature.[19] Today, these interpretations seem to tell us chiefly about the obsessions and prejudices of the writers concerned, not about Joyce's own inner demons. In yet another quarter, he was suspected of masking deep sexual inhibitions and complexes, an accusation which today seems to reflect mainly on the accusers and not on its object. The Hell sermon in the *Portrait*, and the moving scene in which the boy Stephen confesses his 'sins of the flesh' to an aging priest, are passages which spoke with special eloquence to many Irish Catholics brought up to regard extra-marital sex as sinful and Confession as a cleansing though sometimes harrowing ritual; but this is Joyce imaginatively re-creating his schoolboy past, not the objective outlook of the mature artist who had left that world far behind.

As some of his letters to Nora show, Joyce's sexual tastes had their outré side, and undoubtedly he had a streak of almost juvenile male bawdry, but then he had grown up in a Dublin where brothels were an accepted part of life, and he seems to have had his first sexual experience at fourteen. Male bawdry and male sexual banter were an integral part of the conversational modes of the circles he frequented during his early days and Gogarty, in particular, was a great propagator of bawdy limericks and verses. It is probably not a distortion to say that Joyce came to regard the relationship between the sexes, and the erotic field in general, as part of the universal tragicomedy or farce of existence, the rank forcing-ground of human life in general. As for his allegedly Manichean moral viewpoint, his general attitude reads or sounds at times very much like traditional Irish fatalism tempered by humour, and basically as much pagan and timeless as Christian. In this, as in so much else, his outlook was essentially medieval – or more accurately, both medieval and modern, as opposed to Victorian.

In spite of the much-quoted saying about 'silence, exile and cunning' he did not write about the ingrown world of an exile as Nabokov, for example, wrote about émigré Russian life in Berlin and Paris, or even in the celebratory way that Hemingway wrote about his early years in France when his fellow-Americans thronged the Latin Quarter. An entire mystique has been created where there need not be any. The Irish intellectual exile, after all, has a history of at least a thousand years, and medieval commentators in France speak of 'The Irish fashion of going away.' More recently, in the nineteenth century, Moore, Lady Morgan, the painters Maclise and Danby had all been voluntary exiles from their homeland without people seeing anything remotely tragic or unnatural in that fact; economics, the quest for fame and success, were the main factors which took them abroad. Joyce's contemporaries, Eliot and Pound, were voluntary exiles from America, just as Henry James and Edith Wharton had been a generation previously; similarly W. H. Auden, D. H. Lawrence, Christopher Isherwood, Max Beerbohm, Somerset Maugham, Robert Graves, Lawrence Durrell and P. G. Wodehouse are all examples of English writers who chose to live much or most of their lives abroad, as Shelley, Byron and Landor had done a century before. They were not in any way the less American or English for doing so, any more than Theodore Dreiser, Willa Cather and Thomas Hardy were hidebound provincials for choosing to remain at home. In fact, most countries – France is an obvious exception – have both an émigré cultural tradition and a home-based one, and the two are complementary to one another rather than hostile.

Those who naïvely, or idealistically, suppose that the ending of official literary censorship means the end of Irish intellectual emigration seem to me lacking in any strong historical sense; the probability is that it will go on more or less as it has always done, though the motivations for it obviously change. It has certainly continued in the years since censorship has vanished and today many Irish writers and artists pride themselves on their membership of a consciously cosmopolitan, jet-set elite. A small island nation, by its very nature, compels writers and artists to dream of other, greater lands and opportunities across the sea(s). The chief difference is that while for Joyce and the generation succeeding him Continental Europe was the magnet, in the last thirty years the Promised Land has been America.

Chapter 6

FOUNDING FATHERS

On the face of it, George Moore has little immediate relevance to the period covered by this book, since he lived only two years and a few weeks into the 1930s, dying in January 1933. Those two years were relatively uncreative and were plagued by ill health and growing world-weariness; Moore, seemingly unsubduable and indestructible, was at last breaking up physically and his formidable industry was finally running out. Nevertheless, as the closing scenes of a life which is woven so closely into the texture of twentieth-century Irish literature, they have their legitimate place here. What seems generally agreed to be his last important work, the novel *Aphrodite in Aulis*, first appeared (in a limited edition) in December 1930; but it had been written almost entirely in the previous year and while struggling with the book Moore, in letters to his *fidus Achates*, John Eglinton, had expressed anxiety about what he felt were his waning powers as a writer. Set in classical Greece, the novel was very much in keeping with the defiant paganism and aestheticism of his career as a whole.

The ambitious novel *Madeleine de Lisle*, which seems to have dealt with Moore's recurrent theme of convent life, somehow refused to be written and according to Moore's biographer Joseph Hone, Moore threw his first version into the wastepaper basket. A second version never quite coalesced or gathered impetus, while Moore also found it painfully hard to get on with his last book, *A Communication to My Friends*, a relatively minor work which remained unfinished – at least on Moore's own exacting terms – but was published posthumously. In the final months of his life, true to his lifelong custom of revising and correcting what he had written, he supervised the Uniform edition of his works, including *Hail and Farewell*. One of his very last letters, again addressed to his fellow-exile Eglinton (William Kirkpatrick Magee) who plays such a central role in *Hail and Farewell* and had been living in Bournemouth since 1923, was written on 14 January 1933. It said briefly: 'I am very ill today and feel inclined to abandon the project of writing anything more. I have written enough.' A week later, he was dead.

So ended the life and works of the most enigmatic and contradictory figure of the entire Literary Revival, a man remembered as much for his feuds as for his friendships, and a writer on whom any kind of final verdict apparently has yet to be given. By then Moore had largely outlived his reputation and his literary milieu, and an obituary in the *Dublin Magazine* – possibly written by Monk Gibbon – talked about the 'sleepy tapestry' of his late prose style and compared his power of character-drawing unfavourably with Thomas Hardy's. A few years earlier Katherine Mansfield in *Novels and Novelists* had rather bitchily written: 'While we are engaged in reading Mr George Moore's novels he is "there", but once they are put back on the shelves he has softly and silently vanished away until he is heard of again .. . Without emotion writing is dead; it becomes a record instead of a revelation.'[1] And Virginia Woolf, writing some years after his death, considered him 'a novelist who has no dramatic power, no fire of conviction within'. She thought, nevertheless, that 'the very qualities which weaken his novels are the making of his memoirs' and that Moore might still find immortality as an autobiographer, i.e. as the author of *Hail and Farewell*.[2] For such a sensitive critic, surely Virginia Woolf is being obtuse when she calls the trilogy an autobiography; it is as creative as any novel, the interweaving of reality and imagination, and as innovative as Proust in its handling of the time element.

Few reputations have declined as quietly, but inexorably, as Moore's did in the last decade of his life, and it went on declining after his death, although *Esther Waters* never quite went out of print and was always available in some library of classics such as Everyman or Nelson or Oxford. The early, immature *Confessions of a Young Man*, though in no way comparable to his later quasi-confessional writings, also continued to lead a kind of fringe life and many young Irish males read it over the years and dreamed of a similar, privileged bohemian life in Paris. Yet the *Ave-Salve-Vale* trilogy has only come back into the consciousness of the ordinary cultivated reader in the past decade or so, although older literary Dubliners had always cherished their familiar black-covered copies and the memory of Moore's own complex and prickly personality, his conversation, his foibles and his unending quarrels, lived on for many decades almost as a kind of psychic vibration (as a youth in the early 1950s I heard Seumas O'Sullivan talking about him and remarking, with rather donnish superciliousness, that Moore's conversational French had not been very good). Even Ely Place seemed still haunted by his un-benevolent ghost, just as the burnt-out shell of Moore Hall seemed a standing reproach to the Ireland he had left behind. In Dublin second-hand bookshops you might see, rather high up and looking dusty and ignored, a shelf of unsold (and at that time unsaleable) Moore novels, including *A Mummer's Wife*, *Vain Fortune*, *Evelyn Innes* and similar titles. They seemed, at that time, almost as extinct as the novels of Mrs Humphry Ward, or even those of Charles Reade.

Few men can have aroused such conflicting impressions and reactions; it might be true to say that he was loved by the few and disliked by the many. The aspect of his own nature which he called 'Amico Moorini', a kind of eternal juvenile always ready to shock and show off and play the intellectual buffoon, was sternly curbed by him as he grew older and wiser. Yet Moore all his life remained something of an *agent provocateur* and trouble-shooter, quick to take offence and rather slow to forget it. The rumour in Dublin that he was sexually impotent seems by now to have been disproven, yet though he was a lover of women he was not notably successful with them, and occasionally an edge of misogyny showed through the gynaeolatry. If Shaw cultivated paradox in his writing, then Moore might be said to have exemplified it in his life, and it is not hard to see in his strange tartan-plaid mentality a definite streak of self-dislike and even of self-hatred. Almost to the end he retained a capacity for putting himself in false positions and for making himself look slightly ridiculous, in spite of his social poise and his known shrewdness in business and professional matters. His vanity was considerable, so much so in fact that the Irish journalist Anna Kelly, who worked for a time as his secretary, remarked that he seemed mentally to be laying down a red carpet for himself wherever he went. This points in turn to the greatest weakness of his fiction-writing – his egocentricity; Moore manifestly found it hard to get inside the skins of other people, and generally he is more convincing in dealing with female characters than with men.

In spite of the renewed critical interest in Moore's work which began with Malcolm Brown's study of him in 1955,[3] and has been continued by other American scholars culminating in Helmut E. Gerber's magisterial edition of his correspondence,[4] his novels have been extremely slow in coming back into print, at least in the United Kingdom and Ireland. Those which have reappeared tend mostly to be relatively early works, such as *The Lake* of 1905, while several of the late novels are still virtually under a seal. *The Brook Kerith*, which dates from 1916, was for many years available as a Penguin paperback, but now appears to have dropped out of the average reader's canon. This seems inexcusable, since this novel of Jesus and his age is a remarkable work and stylistically comparable with Flaubert, whose *Temptation of St Anthony* may have supplied at least a hint for it. The medieval Irish tale *Ulick and Soracha* is no longer on any list of recommended reading. *Conversations in Ebury Street*, which admittedly is more of a literary curiosity than a masterpiece and, incidentally, infuriated Walter de la Mare by putting things into his mouth which he claimed he had never said,[5] leads at most a ghostly half-life. Even Moore the prodigiously versatile and professional man of letters is little known any longer; Moore the art critic, Moore the essayist and polemicist, Moore the aesthete and snob, Moore the sensitive friend and correspondent of women writers are all facets which have become unfamiliar. As for Moore the short-story writer, he is overshadowed in most Irish anthologies by people who are less than half his size, though Joyce – who plainly was influenced by Moore, but sometimes mocked him – had judged *The Untilled Field* to be one of the foundation-stones of the genre.

Conrad, whose reputation had similarly gone into a trough for a time, has been rehabilitated long ago, and so has Henry James – in fact, James has never stood so high as a novelist as he stands now. Gissing, who for some decades after his death had tended to be written off as a minor and overworked Edwardian, has also come back into serious contention, even if he is scarcely a novelist of quite the first rank. Even in his lifetime, however, Moore had relatively few followers (as distinct from admirers) or actual disciples, and though he made his career in London – in Ebury Street, to be specific, in the area of Chelsea and Pimlico – for the last twenty-two years of his life, he earned respect rather than enthusiasm or genuine understanding from the English literary world of the time. He never, for instance, seems to have sold very well and has always been something of a writer's writer. One of his few English followers, the novelist Charles Morgan, in 1935 gave probably the best definition of Moore's particular quality as a prose writer:

> In the continuous and deliberate calm of all his mature work, there is something spell-bound and trance-like. His detractors call it monotonous, frozen, dead. To me it is a calm enforced; I am aware in every line of the exercise of a rigid discipline; but it is a discipline which, though it touches me sometimes with unease, for I cannot escape knowledge of the struggle that produced it, fills me also with admiration and excitement. Here, plainly, at whatever cost to Moore himself, is something new in English literature that will have a lasting influence precisely because it is not new in the sense of being without roots. It will have a future because it has a past. Three great influences are perceptible in it: the majestic austerity of Landor, the translucence of Turgenev, whose stories are shaded by none of the mists that trouble other men; and Pater's doctrine that sensation is the touchstone of value, a doctrine which Moore, having less moral prejudice than the author of Marius, was able to accept more fully than Pater himself. Moore made no greater secret of these influences than he did of the earlier influence of Flaubert. His claim is that he had assimilated them, and the claim is just.[6]

Though his own style here is dated and mandarinesque, Morgan is writing out of genuine professional insight and admiration, so it is all the more curious that Virginia Woolf, whose fiction at its best achieves just the kind of rapt, trance-like quality defined in this passage, failed entirely to see that Moore's most characteristic works are built upon it. He is an exotic and outsider like Conrad, another un-English writer whose chosen medium was English, and it is significant that both men were fluent speakers of French (so also, of course, were Gissing and James). Moore's memories of Ireland were always at the back of his consciousness just as Conrad's memories of Poland and Eastern Europe were present in his, while the years of artistic awakening and discovery in Paris acted as a catalyst and also opened his eyes to modern painting. Like Joyce, Moore was a man without a country who could draw on the cultures of several nations simultaneously and, in fact, discovered and defined himself by doing so.

The intellectual battles Moore fought in his time are mostly old and irrelevant now, but it should be remembered that in his early days he was one of the most determined enemies of Victorian and post-Victorian prudery and fought a long campaign against the kind of genteel, middle-class, under-the-counter censorship exercised in Britain by the great circulating libraries such as Mudies. He himself was a considerable innovator in the treatment of erotic themes in fiction, so much so that for a long time he was considered a rather scandalous author and a potential corruptor who brought the influence of lubricious French novels into the wholesome, roast-beef and tweed culture of Britain. In Ireland, when he returned to Dublin early in the century for the period covered in *Hail and Farewell*, he fought hard also against the home-grown brand of Catholic middle-class prudery, though not always with tact or judgement – Yeats, for instance, was sometimes worried that Moore would bring down on them all the wrath of the Catholic Church, which was already suspicious of the Literary Revival. Apart from his known role in helping to introduce Impressionist painting to England and Ireland, and his advocacy of Wagner's music, Moore also played a major role – as Malcolm Brown has pointed out – in introducing French literature to English readers: 'He discovered Laforgue before Ezra Pound was born; and a generation before T. S. Eliot made Bloomsbury familiar with Gerard de Nerval's unhappy Prince of Aquitaine of the fallen tower, Moore was quoting with glittering eye the sestet of the same sonnet "J'ai revé dans la grotte ou nage la sirène".'[7]

After the burning of Moore Hall by republicans in 1923 Moore had vowed that he would never return to Ireland, and he kept his word. His younger brother Colonel Maurice Moore, who was for a time a Free State senator, also left Ireland, and late in life GM quarrelled with the colonel and his family and refused to be reconciled. Some at least of their differences seem to have been over religion, since the Colonel – as Moore always referred to him – was a strict and orthodox Catholic while Moore's hatred of his boyhood religion was obsessive and unbalanced. Yet the final gesture of this difficult, paradoxical man was to ask that his ashes be taken to Lake Carra, below Moore Hall, and buried in an urn on a small island there – a task which was duly performed by Gogarty. Richard Irvine Best read aloud a funeral tribute written by AE, although apart from himself and Gogarty the only other mourners present were Colonel Maurice Moore and his sister Nina. A cairn of stones was heaped up in Moore's memory, after which the small mourning party rowed back to the shore.

There was no reconciliation either with Yeats, although at some time during the 1920s, according to Monk Gibbon, Moore sat next to one of the Yeats sisters at a dinner and asked her to act, in effect, as an intermediary between himself and her elder brother so that their former relations might be resumed. She refused to do so, however, and for the rest of their lives they remained apart and unreconciled.[8] Just how deeply he had wounded Yeats, both in his vanity and his professional pride, Moore seems never to have realised; it was yet another facet of his curious character that he could not quite understand why people whom he had put into his books should resent it. For him they were always subject matter, 'copy', as we should say today, and so no more entitled to nurse a grievance against him on that score than artists' models were entitled to feel a grudge against those who painted them. He told correspondents such as the critic Ernest Boyd, who was planning to write a book on him, that others were free to treat him the same way, but Moore was a formidable antagonist if crossed, so very few took the liberty. His Dublin trilogy was never intended, in any case, to be read as strictly factual biography; Moore always claimed the artistic right to interpret his models/characters in his own fashion, just as a modern painter might use his models as a starting point only. This was a fashionable viewpoint at the time, when many writers had no artistic qualms about touching up reality, and even in the field of biography Emil Ludwig, André Maurois and others felt quite at liberty to add 'imaginative' touches to their lives of Bismarck, Beethoven, Shelley etc.

Moore's literary quarrels were not confined to Ireland and the Irish. His repeated attacks on Thomas Hardy infuriated the older writer so much that he referred to Moore as a 'blackguard' and never forgave him. Moore also quarrelled with Shaw, inquiring publicly: 'Why this affectation of the great man?' He was hypercritical of many or most of his contemporaries and he rarely kept his views to himself, so that over his long, active, abrasive life he acquired a steadily growing list of enemies or ill-wishers. Moore almost always got on better with women writers than with male ones, and in general better with painters – Tonks, Sickert, Mark Fisher etc – than with writers. Yet he received the young Austin Clarke in a friendly enough fashion at Ebury Street, though his hospitality there tended to be meagre, and he maintained a reasonably civil correspondence with Seumas O'Sullivan in his capacity as editor of the Dublin Magazine. Moore had not entirely cut off relations with Ireland, and when researching Ulick and Soracha in the Twenties he sought for details and descriptions of early Norman-Irish life and society from his old scholar-friend, Richard Irvine Best, and from Edmund Curtis the historian. This remarkable historical novel, incidentally, is full of the landscape and historical lore of Moore's native Connacht, as well as echoing the semi-feudal Ireland of his boyhood; and one of the great set-pieces in his entire output is the description of the Battle of Athenry in which the Norman-Irish under de Burgo defeated and almost annihilated the 'native' Connacht Irish under Felim O'Connor.

As the son of a patrician landowner, and as a man whose patrimony had suffered first under the Land League, then under social revolution and civil war, Moore can hardly have been expected to welcome the new levelling Ireland, nor did he. He belonged to a social caste which had largely been disinherited, and to a spacious, cosmopolitan milieu in which Irish writers and painters had three capitals: Dublin, London and Paris. Moore lived in London and kept in touch with Paris through frequent visits and through correspondence with old friends such as Dujardin; Dublin he had rejected, and after Hail and Farewell there were too many tensions in the air for him to live on comfortably in Ely Place. Probably he and Yeats, in any case, were too powerful and incompatible as personalities to cohabit in one small city. In the opinion of Louis MacNeice, 'he returned to his native country not to rediscover a lost continuity but to try to impose a Parisian-style salon upon Dublin. Ireland mattered for him as copy – nothing more.' This ignores the potent factor of the Boer War, to which Moore was as fiercely opposed as American writers were later to the Vietnam War, and which played a large role in his leaving England at that time. Yet MacNeice is surely right in his premise, just as he is in diagnosing Moore's ostentatious conversion to Protestantism as 'revulsion against the ignorant Catholicism of Mayo'. And he is surely right, too, in claiming that 'for all the realism of his early novels, (he) was essentially a child of the Aesthetic Movement'.[9] MacNeice might fittingly have added 'and a child of paganism'. His slightly farcical Protestant interlude apart, Moore by instinct and conviction was an aesthetic pagan, with a long ancestry in the nineteenth century, and in his late work he left Zola and naturalism far behind and went back to an idealised pagan antiquity and to his Symbolist-Parnassian youth.

Meanwhile, it is no exaggeration to call him the founding father of Irish prose literature, the equivalent of what Yeats is in poetry. The Irish short story could hardly have taken shape as it did without him, while *Hail and Farewell* obviously begot a sizeable, though very mixed progeny – works such as Gogarty's *As I was Walking down Sackville Street* obviously are based on Moore's mixture of present, past and reminiscence, although compared with Moore's practised, unobtrusive mastery Gogarty works with a heavy and rather dilettantish hand. More recently, Anthony Cronin has traced its lineage in Francis Stuart's *Blacklist Section H*.[10] Moore has also influenced many Irish novelists, though it is the early, realist Moore rather than the later; but above all his legacy can be seen in Joyce, who must have learned from his method of interior narration and his almost Proustian freedom in handling time sequences. This seems plain enough from *Ulysses*, but Moore's achievement in creating a sustained melodic prose – his 'melodic line', as he called it – probably also left its mark on *Finnegans Wake* in which Joyce writes consciously for the ear. His confessional side gave Irish writers some important hints on how to handle religious topics, though Moore's sophisticated insight into women passed on to relatively few of them. Few people ever knew the Irish countryside better or wrote about it with a more painterly eye, and though he came of landowning stock he knew at first hand the world of jockeys and jarveys and country fairs which also fascinated Jack Yeats.

Above all, in spite of his manias and quarrels and intellectual oddities, his notorious social snobbery, and his broad streak of spite and mendacity, Moore was a free spirit who gave an example of self-education and self-development to a generally backward country. Oscar Wilde's much-quoted jibe about him conducting his education in public may be justified, but much the same could be said of Yeats, since both men took many years to atone for their faulty, or inadequate, early education. He was also, of course, an example to his contemporaries and successors of the value of hard, dedicated work and unrelenting self-criticism – probably no writer, not even Flaubert, laboured more single-mindedly over his craft.

Since his relationship with Yeats – which only represented one phase of his long career – has bulked so large in literary histories, it might be pointed out here that Yeats has had much the more privileged treatment of the two from critics and analysts. No doubt the two men were incompatible ultimately, both as personalities and writers, but Moore did not underestimate Yeats as an artist and historical figure whereas the latter seriously and almost wilfully underestimated him. In spite of their estrangement, Moore in his later years fully recognised and admitted Yeats's role as a foundation-stone of Irish writing. Yeats, in contrast, never grasped Moore's full stature and failed entirely to follow his later development – if, indeed, he even read the late novels. In *Dramatis Personae* he quotes himself as warning him against the cult of 'style' with a capital S: 'Moore, if you ever get a style it will ruin you. It is coloured glass, and what you need is a plate-glass window.' By this massive piece of condescension, Moore is implicitly reduced to the stature of a commonplace realist who should leave genuine artistry to better men, and the imaginative, formal and stylistic advances of his writings after the Dublin trilogy are annulled as though they had never existed.

Moore has gone down in Irish literary tradition as the great quarreller, yet in this instance it is Yeats who did not forgive. Once again, it underlines Mary Colum's claim that he neither forgot nor forgave old injuries and slights. What is worse, however, is the fact that he endorsed the widespread view of Moore as a kind of intellectual grasshopper or stinging butterfly, a view which was held by Thomas Hardy among others – the view, so common among English writers, that the Irish are sometimes charming and absurd, sometimes malicious and amusing, but as a race untrustworthy, prone to exaggeration or distortion, and morally quite insubstantial. Moore's constitutional self-mockery has delivered him into the hands of his enemies, and his incurable sense of the absurd has been used inversely to illustrate his own absurdity. A sophisticate and natural cosmopolitan, a patrician with a plebeian (but never bourgeois) streak, he is a complex phenomenon and a pitfall for those who have less innate wit and intelligence than he expected from readers in his own lifetime.

Granted, then, that Yeats and Moore are the twin foundation-stones of modern Irish literature, where does that leave AE? At the time of his death in 1935, he still ranked high as a poet and even Yeats, who had become noticeably cold and hypercritical towards him in old age, felt compelled to allot him six pages in his *Oxford Book*. AE had an international standing as a poet-sage, Ireland's equivalent to Rabindranath Tagore; his quasi-philosophical writings were widely respected even if many people found them abstruse or over-mystical; he was one of the greatest and most influential Irish journalists of his age, both in his writing and editorial capacities; he was a hero of the co-operative movement; he was a painter of some quality; he was a noted discoverer and encourager of talent in younger people. His Sunday evening at-homes in No. 17 Rathgar Avenue were weekly cultural events where most of literary and intellectual Dublin met to talk, gossip, orate and listen, and the memory of these get-togethers, and the after-effects of the friendships and literary contacts they often set up, lived on for many years.

They have been described by many people ranging from Austin Clarke[11] to the sceptical Northerner E. R. Dodds, who had little time for AE's mystical monologues yet liked and respected him as a man. Here it was possible to meet James Stephens, Stephen McKenna, Austin Clarke, Padraic Fallon, F. R. Higgins, Seumas O'Sullivan, Frank O'Connor, Monk Gibbon, Lyle Donaghy, the painter Sarah Purser who was a formidable personality with a tart tongue, Ernest Boyd the critic, Joseph O'Neill and his wife Mary Davenport, George Eglinton, Constantine Curran, the scholar Osborne Bergin. A number of these people, particularly the poets, had been AE's protégés, his 'canaries' as Yeats contemptuously called them. Visiting writers and critics arrived there regularly too, as well as numerous American women who came, according to Austin Clarke, to ask AE about the Fairies on which he was an accepted authority.

At-homes were an accepted ritual in literary life, probably the closest Dublin got to a salon in the French style. Yeats's Monday evenings were select and prestigious affairs, as George Moore's Saturdays once had been (AE was said to have been left with a weekly void in his life after Moore returned to London in 1911). Sarah Purser's receptions were famous, and Gogarty too had his. Alcohol was rarely offered to guests at these informal, yet formalised social-cum-intellectual functions, apart from a little sherry; at some of them high tea was served, at others tea, sandwiches, and cakes, while AE and his wife Violet Russell simply offered plenty of strong tea and home-made scones. Unlike Yeats's carefully orchestrated and slightly ritualistic functions, AE virtually kept open house and relatively obscure, undiscovered young people were welcome there alongside the celebrities. Talk was what mattered, not ceremony, and it was largely against such relatively homespun, almost innocent backgrounds that the 'Dublin conversation' flourished which, deservedly or not, gained such a high reputation for decades and became part of the myth of Irish life in general. The literary pubs had not yet taken over as centres of debate, conversation, gossip and mutual bitchery, and in any case they were rarely patronised by women, who were not made welcome there until well after the second World War. At-homes, by contrast, welcomed wives and female companions and were therefore valuable as the cultural meeting-grounds of the sexes. Seumas O'Sullivan and his wife Estella Solomons, a gifted painter, were also noted hosts and it was during one of their at-homes that the young Samuel Beckett infringed etiquette by turning up obviously more than a little drunk. Probably the last of the Dublin at-homes was Arland Ussher's, which lasted into the Seventies, and gallantly upheld a native tradition of hospitality and intellectual stimulus.

The early Thirties, however, were for AE a time of shrinking prestige and personal misfortune, even tragedy. In 1930 the weekly journal which he had edited since 1923, the *Irish Statesman*, ran on the rocks. This incorporated the old *Irish Homestead*, which AE had edited from 1905 onwards and which was essentially the mouthpiece of co-operativism. The moving force behind it was Sir Horace Plunkett and the original choice of editor had been another Ulsterman, Robert Lynd, but he was unwilling to return from London where he had an established career. So AE was chosen, with J. W. Good and Susan Mitchell, the writer of light verse, as his editorial assistants. Broadly the editorial policy was pro-Treaty, and the board included Plunkett himself, James Douglas, Lionel Smith-Gordon, W. B. Yeats and George O'Brien. AE in his editorials took a characteristically broad outlook, standing out against the hysteria or complacency of so much Irish nationalism: 'We say we cannot merely out of Irish traditions find solutions to all our modern problems. It is no use reading Wolfe Tone or John Mitchel or Thomas Davis in the belief that they had a clairvoyance which pierced into our times with their complexities, or that by going back to Gaelic Ireland we shall find images upon which we can build anew. We shall find much inspiration and beauty in our own past but we have to ransack world literature, world history, world science and study our national contemporaries and graft what we learn into our own national traditions, if we are not to fade out of the list of civilised nations.'[12]

The matter on which the paper foundered seems to have been an unimportant libel case, which happened at the worst possible time. Seamus Clandillon – who at one stage of his career was director of Radio Éireann and gave his name to a popular type of céilidh band which for years was widely believed to represent genuine Irish folk music – had published a collection of folk songs edited by himself, which was reviewed rather contemptuously in the paper. Clandillon sued, and at a time when the journal's American backers found by Plunkett were involved in the Wall Street Crash. The action was therefore undefended because of lack of money, so the *Irish Statesman*, for years an outlet for liberal views and also a forum for creative writers, folded abruptly and was never revived. In its time it had carried contributions by Shaw, O'Casey, Hyde, Colum, Gogarty, Higgins, Padraic Fallon, Micheál Mac Liammóir, Walter Starkie, Lennox Robinson, Liam O'Flaherty, James Stephens, Edmund Curtis, Forrest Reid and Robin Flower. It remains unique in Irish journalism, since there has been no real successor to it in nearly seventy years. In its last issue the then Minister for Agriculture, Patrick Hogan, paid tribute to its 'outstanding moral influence on Irish journalism'. (Hogan himself supported co-operativism and had seen to it that the movement was grant-aided by his government.)

Two years later, AE's beloved wife died and the bottom fell out of his world; the Sunday evenings at Rathgar Avenue became increasingly sepulchral, and fewer and fewer people turned up at them. The co-operative movement, to which he had given so much time and energy, was under pressure from the new businessmen and from native gombeenery, while the Catholic triumphalism of the 1932 Eucharistic Congress nauseated him. The Civil War had horrified him by its intolerance and destructiveness and the 1923 burning by republicans of Kilteragh, Plunkett's home near Dublin, had been a personal blow; thirty of his own best paintings were destroyed in this, and it was in Kilteragh that he and Plunkett had often met to plan the future of co-operativism in Ireland. Its burning was part of a last-ditch campaign by republicans against the homes of Free State senators, which is why George Moore's ancestral home also became a casualty. Plunkett himself never recovered from the loss and emigrated to England.[13] So the coming to power of de Valera with his republican wild men brought no joy for AE, who began to foresee 'a nation run by louts'. He was increasingly estranged from his one-time friend Yeats, whose reputation continued to spiral upwards while his own was already fading, and fewer young writers sought his patronage. AE felt himself to be at the end of the road he had followed unselfishly for decades, and decided that he needed a radical change of scene if he was to renew himself in old age. One of his sons urged him to join him in America, a country which he had already visited and liked, but instead he opted for London where he had literary friends such as Helen Waddell. So he gave away his books and most of his furniture, the house in Rathgar Avenue was sold, and AE crossed over to England – first to London and then to Bournemouth, where he died.

Helen Waddell, the author of *The Wandering Scholars* and *Heloise and Abelard*, went to see him in the nursing-home in Bournemouth shortly before the end. This sweet-natured, high-minded yet lively woman shared his Ulster background and many of his intellectual interests, though she was more than twenty years younger. She wrote to a friend that AE looked 'very thin and waxen, and strangely young. The surgeon said that he told AE before he operated that it would be only temporary. AE never moved a muscle or flickered; he discussed the whole thing as if it were the tilling of a field . . . The surgeon was so shattered by the sheer saintliness of it all that he had to make some excuse and leave him, or he'd have broken down.'[14] The use of words such as 'saint' and 'saintliness' seem almost automatic with AE's friends, yet it is ironic that when Waddell had published her book *Beasts and Saints* in 1934 he had written to her urging her to get on with her projected sequel to *Heloise and Abelard* and 'don't think too much about saints. They don't bear looking into. The Irish bards said the saints told lies.'[15] Then, perhaps fearing he had offended the sensibilities of a woman who came from a family of missionaries, he explained: 'They are too much with us in Ireland, and I forget that elsewhere some might deserve the name.'[16]

Nevertheless these were prolific years for AE in terms of literary output; in 1930 *Enchantment and Other Poems* appeared, in 1932 came the prose work *The Candle of Vision*, and then *The House of the Titans and Other Poems* in 1934. He also kept up a continual flow of correspondence, much of which is still readable and relevant, and he continued to paint, returning to Donegal with his brushes not long before he died. As the letter from Helen Waddell shows, AE faced death with courage and spiritual calm. When the sands were already running out for him, he wrote to his former protégé James Stephens, also now living in England: 'They (the doctors) allow me a year or thereabouts. Don't think I feel anything melancholy. I hold to the spiritual verities I have believed in all my life and would be glad and more cheerful if my time were shorter.' To Austin Clarke, who had called on him in London, he said with a smile: 'Death will be an exciting adventure.' When it was all over and his body was brought back to Dublin for burial beside his wife in Mount Jerome, de Valera and several members of his Fianna Fáil government were present by the graveside, as well as most of literary and artistic Dublin. It may have been the apostle of co-operativism or the great journalist whom the politicians honoured, but the fact that they made the gesture is significant in itself. AE, however, had always refused public honours, including membership of the Senate in 1922.

AE and Yeats are inextricably intertwined, from their early years as art students and fellow-theosophists to the later years when they were, in effect, twin powers in literary Dublin and their respective followers were often in rivalry with one another.[17] Yeats, who liked to be the master in every situation, knew at heart that his rival was loved personally in a way he himself was not. According to Monk Gibbon – and he is not the only witness – he was envious of AE's influence over younger men. He even claimed that he himself was ill-spoken of at the famous Rathgar evenings – though Austin Clarke states expressly that this was not true; Yeats was attributing his own malice to a man who was singularly without any.[18] Above all, however, Yeats may have resented the presence or spiritual challenge of a genuine mystic, an illuminated man, who saw visions before his eyes while he himself had to have recourse to mediums and table-tapping and other machinery. As MacNeice puts it, AE had seen the Grail while Yeats, like Lancelot, could never do so because of his imperfect state, but it was 'because he did not see it that he was able to write poetry'. And Gibbon, after watching them together and noting Russell's tact and forbearance, felt that of the two AE 'is more likely to go to heaven, for Yeats, although he is the greater artist and perhaps the greater intellect, has none of AE's sympathy and benevolence and there is something of the crank and magician about him, whereas there is nothing about AE that is not wholesome and human . . . AE is the true mystic of the two.' He also discovered that AE professed no interest in spiritualism, which was Yeats's chief conduit to the other world, and cared very little about occultism.

AE was one of the few people to review *A Vision* seriously and sympathetically, though he disliked much of Yeats's late poetry and after reading through *Byzantium* for the first time, remarked to the young Padraic Fallon: 'Yeats is becoming all words.'[19] The Yeatsian cult of the mask was also repellent to him, and he felt that his old friend had recast himself into a public image or pose which damaged his sincerity as a writer. He could not see that his own high-mindedness got in the way of aesthetic objectivity; unlike Yeats, in his verse he was unable to reconcile his vision with everyday reality, so that while AE the journalist and activist was very well able to cope with the world of fact, as a poet he hides far too often in the clouds of idealism and quasi-religious aspiration. Though a few or even a small handful of AE's lyrics may live on, the bulk of his creative writing now seems dead beyond recall, the long poems as well as the songlike lyrics, and his plays have never entered the repertory even in a minor way. The quasi-philosophical writings for the most part seem curiously high-minded and unfocused – a mixture of editorialising and cloudy mysticism, rather like long-drawn sermons, though almost all of them contain passages of beauty and spiritual wisdom. A great deal of his talk seems to have been like that too, or at least the sustained monologues which he was always liable to launch into – and which thrilled some people while they bored others into silent rigidity. (One of the people who enjoyed his 'wonderful talk' was Beatrice Webb, though she also admitted that 'he bores Sydney'.)

When George Moore died and asked that his ashes be buried on an island in Lough Carra, AE was asked to write a funeral oration although he did not attend the ceremony. Moore being Moore, even AE had had his occasional brushes with him, but nevertheless he wrote: 'He loved the land even if he did not love the nation. Yet his enmities even made his nation to be as much admired or loved as the praise of its patriots . . . It is possible the artist's love of earth, rock, water and sky is an act of worship. It is possible that faithfulness to art is acceptable service. That worship, that service were his. If any would condemn him for creed of theirs he had assailed, let them first be certain that they laboured for their ideals as faithfully as he did.'

One of his strangest creations is the late novel *The Avatars* (1933) in which he attempts to set his usual shining mythic figures and spiritual beings against the landscape of modern Ireland, motor-cars, visiting Americans and all. As a novel it is obviously a failure almost from the first chapter; indeed it is scarcely a novel at all, yet the tone of rapt, passionate seriousness throughout commands a real respect even if the characters are little more than abstractions. At the end you may feel that while the man who wrote this had no gift for fiction, and indeed is hardly even a professional writer in the ordinary sense, he must still have been a man with a spiritual dimension far beyond the common level of humanity. Perhaps what AE had in mind was less a novel than a sustained Platonic dialogue with a quasi-realist background, against which he could set out his beliefs and ideas through the mouths of others. In the brief foreword, he remarks: 'I have, I fear, delayed too long the writing of this, for as I grow old the moon of fantasy begins to set confusedly with me. *The Avatars* has not the spiritual gaiety I desired for it. The friends with whom I once spoke of such things are dead and gone from me . . .' Certainly there is little gaiety, only eddying mists of metaphysical discourse set out in that tone of Sunday solemnity which is AE's greatest fault as a writer. Once again, the artist in him has surrendered to the lay preacher; yet in its odd way the book does act as a stimulus to thought; and he himself had written: 'The purpose of an avatar is to reveal the spiritual character of a race to itself.' AE can be counted among the select few who helped modern Ireland towards some degree of self-knowledge.

AE was of course by background a Northern Protestant, and combined with his early theosophical beliefs and his later debt both to the Bhagavad-Gita and to some form of Buddhism, this made him implacably hostile to Irish Catholicism. In his gentle way he was a fanatic, in some senses almost a bigot, while at the same time the most magnanimous and tolerant of men. Though in certain aspects a puritan, using the term in a rather specialised sense, he was also a prophet of sexual freedom as well as of sexual equality, and his influence can be seen and felt in the final, ecstatic chapters of James Stephens's *The Crock of Gold*, a book full of what Dublin called 'AEtheism' even if it is mixed up with a certain amount of Arthur Rackham-style whimsy. AE was also a mystic in the line of Blake and Samuel Palmer and Edward Calvert, though purely as a painter and draughtsman he never approached them in achievement. Like them, he saw reality transfigured by the holy light of the imagination, as Palmer saw the humble village of Shoreham transfigured or as Blake saw the most commonplace scenes illuminated spiritually and transformed into the New Jerusalem. But if he could never wholly capture this vision in paint or even in his verse, he could communicate it personally to others, and most of the visionary gleam which enters into the early work of Clarke, Higgins and other poets of that generation emanated through him to them. This not only gave their word-painting of the Irish countryside another, almost mythic dimension, it added to the philosophical and aesthetic range of an entire generation.

For young men raised in the tradition of post-Famine Irish Catholicism, with its harsh dogmas and narrow horizons, AE's mentality was an illumination and also a liberation – as it was too for various young Irish Protestants whose religion for the most part lacked ecstasy, or even real inner life. For them AE seemed to personify the timeless, mystic essence of Eastern thought, and somehow he combined this with a strong social conscience and a vigorous engagement in topical issues and controversies. His famous 'Open Letter to Rudyard Kipling' is one of the great, dignified apologias for Irish nationalism, just as his so-called 'Workers' Letter', addressed to the Dublin employers at the time of the 1913 lockout, anticipates the enlightened welfare-statism of the mid-century, before the socialist dream went sour.

Instead of the spiritualisation of life which he hoped for and predicted, he saw the advance of materialism almost everywhere, a world war and the shadows of another, mass philistinism and conformity, relentless mechanisation and the rise of huge overpopulated cities which he compared to Babylon. AE had an essential rural vision of things, which was one of the chief reasons why he threw himself into the co-operative movement, and like other Irish writers and thinkers of his generation, he had an almost religious horror of mass industrialism. This is one of the factors which alienate modern writers from the Celtic Twilight; it is seen as an escapist flight from the modern, predominantly industrialised urban world. Yet both AE and Yeats, growing up in the shadows of Ruskin and Morris, had inherited the reaction against the horrors of the Industrial Revolution which was widespread among sensitive, thinking men and women at the end of the nineteenth century. The terrible city slums, the forests of belching chimneys which darkened the skies, and the spoliation of so much of the countryside, seemed too high a price to pay for Europe's increased military-industrial power and prosperity. It is too easily forgotten that this reaction to the 'grim satanic mills' was a powerful factor in the rise of socialism – and it was based less on aesthetic grounds than on a recognition that millions of men and boys were being reduced to wage-slaves while their wives and families huddled together in urban squalor and deprivation in which disease, insanitary conditions, high child mortality, inadequate nourishment and almost compulsory prostitution were as much the rule as the exception.

At least, unlike so many Irish intellectuals sniping from the ditch, AE achieved some practical good in economic terms, though his dream of developing cottage industries never materialised. But his multitudinous activities were paid for at a high price: his own development as an artist. His verse has a reach-me-down quality, varying between Whitmanesque affirmation and ethereal Nineties half-lights; it lacks real verbal distinction, exactly what Yeats achieved in maturity, nor is his metrical ear as good as Yeats's. His visionary paintings are often weak and nebulous, and his more realistic landscapes, while sometimes good, cannot compare with the best of Paul Henry's or Nathaniel Hone's. He remained, to the end, a kind of superior Sunday painter with ambitions beyond his technical grasp or power to visualise in full. As an art critic, however, he was shrewd and sometimes inspired; he was one of the first people to recognise Jack Yeats's exceptional stature, and he was fully aware of Van Gogh, and even of Picasso and Matisse.

One of his most grateful disciples, Padraic Fallon, in reviewing Alan Denson's edition of AE's correspondence in 1961, wrote: 'An unfinished poet, an occasional painter, a clairvoyant born and a natural contemplative, a religious without an altar, a believer without a God, a seer, a visionary, yet a man of affairs, an organiser of country creameries, an inspired journalist, a ferocious controversialist, and the most gentle of men, here was a genius of a dozen vocations who mastered none of them, who was an amateur in everything, and yet emerges in my imagination as the one and only great man I have ever known . . . A man may be many things, but an artist is the singular of all the plurals and a dedicated person from the first. AE did not exist in his poetry. He was the occasional guest, arriving with a weekend bag, a pencil and a paintbrush – and all the arbitrary values of the other six days of the week. He never realised that his were not the values of poetry, but those of the religious visionary to whom verse was the inspired shorthand of the Infinite.'[20]

Yet Fallon also admitted that while he and others like him knew Yeats to be the greater poet of the two, it was to AE that they took their poems for criticism and positive response. Or as Roibeárd Ó Faracháin put it, if Yeats was the 'careless father' of so many Irish writers, 'then AE was the careful midwife who delivered them alive, and the wet nurse who suckled them.'[21] Much of his real greatness – and, in his way,

AE was genuinely great – lay in the magnetism of his personality, his deep humanity and patriotism, his basic sanity and above all his towering moral stature. Leaving aside those witnesses who have been already quoted, this spiritual dimension to him was recognised by people as diverse as George Moore the scoffer, and Frank O'Connor (it should be remembered that AE encouraged prose-writers as well as poets).[22] He retained, to the end, a remarkable capacity for responding to all sorts and conditions of people, and of drawing out the best in them.

Perhaps it is in his occasional prose writings and journalism that AE is at his best; they prove that the range of his intellect and the breadth of his interests were quite formidable. For that reason, the selection which Monk Gibbon published in 1937 under the title *The Living Torch* should be reprinted, since it contains many examples of excellent writing and clear thinking on various subjects. I quote some of these dicta here, to illustrate the span of AE's thinking:

'The arts are less the reflection of the age they were born in than a reaction from that age.'

'Nationalism in every country requires a strong admixture of internationalism to prevent it becoming a stupefying drug.'

'The patriotic idealist assumes a moral superiority because of his capacity for self-sacrifice. The humanist notes how many other things sacrificed may be regarded as of far more importance to humanity than the object for which the idealist strives.'

'It is only too true in the lives of nations, as well as individuals, that the dream which precedes action is nobler than the realisation.'

'There is always decay and apathy unless there are contraries . . . God is the great agitator.'

'We are quite sure any Devil would be well content to make a treaty with the Church, leaving it a free hand in the realm of the spiritual and the cultural, if he was allowed a free hand in the realm of the economic.'

'Continually I am excited by the theories of Jung, and almost as often I feel myself dubious.'

'Being an ignorant people, we distrust praise given to our own until it comes to us from other lands, and then we find to our shame that we have starved our prophets and our souls together.'

Of Yeats: 'He may be regarded as the pivot around which Irish literature turned from instinctive to conscious art.'

Of Shaw: 'The last veritable saint we produced in Ireland.'

Of censorship: 'It is a real peril in a country where there are vast numbers of semi-illiterates who can be roused to help in the denunciation of books which they never read, and so create the impression of a mass movement whose triumph would be to place genius in servitude to mediocrity, and to give the control of literature to those who have themselves produced nothing of worth or beauty or profundity.'

'Rhetoric has a dulling effect on the spirit.'

In epigrams and observations such as these, AE unconsciously proves that he is vastly more convincing when he deals with concrete problems and situations than when he is dimly trying to define intangibles or to walk in the ether. He needed the bracing shock or challenge of actuality to concentrate his intellectual powers. This is shown further by one of the very last pieces he wrote, a foreword to Joseph O'Neill's quasi-Orwellian fantasy *Land Under England*, which was published in 1935 (it has since been republished as a Penguin paperback, under a science-fiction label). O'Neill, who for many years was secretary to the Department of Education and was also a friend of Yeats, had previously written a historical novel about Viking Dublin and the battle of Clontarf, *Wind from the North*, which AE had admired. As an example of his political prescience even in old age and near death this foreword makes intriguing reading even. Again, I quote:

> *It is nothing new to humanity, the desire to surrender its soul to a leader, to be blinded and mindless and happy in the obliteration of its own free will and judgement. It is a remote simulacrum of the soul's self-abnegation before Deity. It is nothing new for a leader to demand such complete obedience to his will. It is the most subtle of spiritual luxuries, for it makes the soul feel in some way as if it were like Deity itself.*

> *Mr Arthur Waley tells us that, even in ancient China, there were political philosophers who held that a ruler should on no account encourage those who preach the perfecting of the individual life. But it is only in our time in Europe that we have had the spectacle of vast crowds hysterically cheering over the decaying corpse of liberty. It is only in our own time that we find a nation swearing blind allegiance to a leader who demands such devotion.*

> *The highest form satire can take is to assume the apotheosis of the policy satirised and make our shuddering humanity recoil from the spectacle of the complete realisation of its own ideals. And this is what Joseph O'Neill has done in imaging a State where the unity of obliterated individualism is complete, where the Master, or Hitler, of his Utopia has a selfless humanity completely malleable to his will; and we recoil from the vision of that perfection of mechanised humanity, as if we had peered into one of the lowest of human hells.*

This is recognisably the voice of a great European liberal, and the fact that AE was a dying man when he wrote it makes it all the more remarkable. At that time, Hitler had not yet shown his hand internationally, and many thinking people outside Germany regarded him as the regenerator of his nation, or at worst a bulwark against Communism. Perhaps AE was lucky to die when he did, since he was saved from living through the barbarism which ravaged Europe and only ended a decade after his own death. But it also shows that he too was appalled by the levelling mindlessness of twentieth-century populism gone mad, and that brings him within measuring distance of Yeats although their outlooks in many ways were so different. In spite of his democratic and quasi-socialist stance, there was a definite strain in him of the patrician and spiritual aristocrat, and even of an educator in the high Platonic sense. In many ways AE is Ireland's nearest equivalent to William Morris, and even if their respective spheres of activity were different, in essence they were labourers in the same vineyard.

G eorge Bernard Shaw is one of the very greatest Irishmen of the past two centuries, yet of all the leading Irish writers of his time, he now seems the most dated. It is possible, of course, that this is a passing phase from which his plays will re-emerge triumphantly for a new generation, or that at least a chosen handful of them will do so. Can three generations of theatre-goers, readers and critics have been so wrong, not to mention the many eminent writers who praised him highly? It seems more and more, sad though it is to admit it, as if they were. Even the most admired of his plays now seem whimsical, garrulous and emotionally evasive, lacking real body or heart – or even soul; it has become difficult to sit through a single one of them over an evening, unless they are superlatively acted and produced. So much for the writer-prophet who to many of his contemporaries seemed a giant and a demigod, Man and Superman combined.

There were, admittedly, shrewd judges who even in his lifetime prophesied that his works would not last, that his characters were unreal and little more than mouthpieces for a clever, brittle dialectic, that he lacked the ordinary human emotions and was quite inept when it came to depicting love and lovers. The one thing such people allowed him was utter professionalism and mastery of the stage. Even this quality, however, counts for less today because stage conventions have changed so enormously since his time, thanks to Brecht and certain other innovators. Within the lifetime of many living people, the Nobel Prize winner and proclaimed peer of Ibsen, Strindberg, Hauptmann, O'Neill and even Shakespeare has been dethroned in the most bloodless and noiseless of all palace revolutions. While biographical interest in Shaw has not waned (as Michael Holroyd's fine biography proves)[23] his literary works are scarcely even discussed outside academic circles. They are not even argued about any longer; they are simply ignored by the public.

While Shaw's literary reputation was probably sinking quietly in the last two decades of his life, no author in history can have been so much in the public eye down to the day of his death. His final weeks of life made front-page headlines in the world's newspapers, including the Irish ones – 'Mr Shaw sits up' ran a headline in *The Irish Times*, in a tone of optimism which quickly proved to be unjustified, since he died a few days later. For years he had been 'copy' and one of the first reactions of most British journalists to events in Ireland – whether it was the declaration of an

Irish Republic, or some speech of de Valera, or whatever – was to rush to Shaw in Ayot St Lawrence for some comment. Since his public image was primarily that of a wit and iconoclast, they automatically expected or demanded a witticism for their readers, and *The Irish Times* cartoonist, N. O'K., once drew a cartoon in which Shaw, surrounded by expectant newspapermen with notebooks and pencils poised, is saying desperately: 'Give me time, gentlemen – I'll think of a wisecrack yet.' Here we see an aged and probably world-weary man at the mercy of his own self-created legend, which would not allow him even elementary privacy, and one of the best intellects of his time is driven to playing the role of a public jester.

Shaw's standing as a writer had probably reached a peak with *St Joan* in 1923, and the worldwide praise for this tragedy had much to do with the award of the Nobel Prize two years later. *Back to Methuselah* had already established his role as a prophet and thinker, a seer to whom a whole generation could look for guidance. However, the various plays he wrote during the Thirties, such as *On the Rocks*, *Geneva* and *Buoyant Billions* did not add much to his reputation. *Geneva* mocked the contemporary Fascist leaders in an ultra-Shavian way, which made amends for his occasional gestures of sympathy with them earlier in the decade, while his famous visit in 1931 to the Soviet Union with Lord and Lady Astor and some others triggered off a great deal of controversy. Shaw, the socialist, libertarian and out-and-out individualist, seemed to have developed a queer leaning towards dictators, or perhaps it was towards the new mass ideologies which were dominant in many places. His old olympianism and detachment were prejudiced by this apparent political restlessness, which reflected the psychic unease and fluctuations of the decade rather than rising serenely above it. Or had he simply outlived himself? After all, no play of his had achieved a real success since *The Applecart* in 1928.

Graham Greene, writing in 1942, was probably expressing the consensus view of a new generation when he stated: 'Like Sterne, another Irishman, he plays the fool at enormous length, but without that little bitter core which lies hidden in *Tristram Shandy*. Ideas are often adopted for the sake of their paradoxes and discarded as soon as they cease to startle. He gives his audience a sense of intellectual activity – but they often imagine they have exercised their brains when they have really done no more than strain their eyes at the startling convolutions of a tumbler.'[24]

Ireland's attitude towards Shaw was usually an ambivalent one, since he represented something that most ordinary Irish people found particularly hard to come to terms with. His abstract outlook repelled the type of Irish mentality which is nourished by personalities, feuds, factions and foibles. Many suspected mockery and malice where there was none, snobbery and condescension where there was only good will, atheism and amorality where there was considerable moral seriousness, and cynicism where there was robust good sense. Shaw's attitude to the revival of Irish was typical: 'Nonsense! How can we be completely independent of our next-door neighbours? Are we not Europeans and citizens of the world?' And again: 'The English link, our most priceless acquisition, gave us three-quarters of the world for our audience, and to throw it away for a scholastic exercise, which was never common speech in any country on earth, would be like trying to revive fifth-century Latin.' When in 1946 an interviewer mentioned that a member of Dublin Corporation had declared him not to be a fit mentor for the young, Shaw replied simply: 'Who is?' Another Dublin councillor, the same interviewer remarked, had asked what Shaw had done for Ireland apart from 'an occasional long-distance wisecrack'. To which Shaw replied: 'English journalists often reproach me for ingratitude to their country, to which they attribute all my success and reputation. It is hardly polite to assure them that when I came to England I got nothing for nothing, and very little for a halfpenny; that I was abused, vilified, censored, and repressed to the limits of possibility, until my successes in Germany and America convinced my detractors that there was some sense in my evil doctrines. When my seventieth birthday was celebrated, the English Government prohibited the reporting of my speech . . . But the people in the market-place and at the street-corners stood by me, and I bear no malice. Now that I am ninety, British Cabinets are no longer so desperately afraid of me.'[25]

It was on a visit to South Africa in 1931-2, while his wife Charlotte was in hospital after a motor accident for which Shaw himself was largely responsible, that he wrote *The Adventures of a Black Girl in Search of God*. This enraged or upset many conventionally religious people, partly because of the way in which Christ is depicted merely as one of several great teachers of mankind, along with Mahomet and others, and partly because one of John Farleigh's illustrations showed the Black Girl naked even in the presence of Jesus. Several leading English libraries banned it and Ireland, of course, banned it altogether. (According to John O'Donovan in his brief life of Shaw, a motion came before the Co Wexford Bee Keepers' Association, of which Shaw was a life member through his ownership of a small ancestral property, that he should be expelled because of this irreligious book. Sanity prevailed, and the motion was dismissed).[26]

Shaw always rejected out of hand the idea of an Irish race as such, yet he insisted that he was Irish of the Irish, in spite of his long residence in England and his apparent assimilation to its culture. In 1948 he said: 'I have lived for twenty years in Ireland and for seventy-two in England, but the twenty came first, and in Britain I am still a foreigner and shall die one.' The depth of his patriotism was seldom recognised in his homeland, though AE had understood him and so had Yeats, after his early resentment of Shaw's anti-romanticism and contempt for the misty aura of the Celtic Twilight. Shaw had proved a considerable ally when Yeats was founding the Irish Academy of Letters, and he had a public serenity which allowed him to keep calm in the face of public vituperation, as well as the wit and presence of mind to make his attackers look ridiculous. Another warm admirer was Seán O'Casey, who made Shaw into a kind of intellectual father-figure – as Yeats had been before the rejection of *The Silver Tassie*. Shaw also frequently played a key role in an area in which he has had no real successor – that of an intercessor or mediator between Ireland and England, explaining his fellow-countrymen's case and viewpoint with unruffled clarity, and often meeting English prejudices head-on and refuting them. Though he strongly disapproved at first of de Valera's neutrality policy, he came to see its logic and expressed a measured respect for him as a public figure: 'He is a Paoli, a Garibaldi, not a Cavour.' And when Ireland finally became a republic, Shaw sent a personal message of congratulations to the new Irish Ambassador in London, John Dulanty. He also made the National Gallery a beneficiary of his will by leaving them the profits from *Pygmalion* – which became considerable with the success of *My Fair Lady*, the musical based on it.

Though Shaw the playwright may be in eclipse, his intellectual stature and the cogency and clear style of his prose writings are generally recognised and he is given a considerable role in the recent *Field Day Anthology of Irish Writing*. The prefaces to his plays contain some excellent prose and show the range and dynamism of his mind; the preface to *St Joan* reveals more genuine respect and awareness of the religious spirit at its best than the writings of most Irish Catholic intellectuals. Shaw, in fact, was no enemy to religion in the true sense (he declared late in life that his position was in certain respects close to that of St Thomas Aquinas) though he was always a foe to cant and woolly thinking – in England as well as in his homeland.[27] Unlike so many other exiles, he did not become negative towards the country of his youth and when offered the freedom of Dublin in his old age, he graciously accepted it instead of rebuffing the City Fathers of his native city, as Joyce might have done. No doubt, like Joyce, he needed to get away from that city early in life, but he never turned his back on it or made a virtue of necessity. Like Yeats, to the end he insisted on maintaining a positive outlook rather than what Yeats called a 'reactive' one.

Chapter 7

SECOND GENERATION

The death of Yeats marked, in effect, the end of the Literary Revival in its first, formative phase; Lady Gregory, Moore and AE were already dead, and Synge had died thirty years earlier. Only Hyde remained of the founding fathers, and he was scarcely an active literary force any more and was seen more as a Gaelic scholar and forerunner than as a poet, playwright and translator. Hyde served as a Professor of Irish in the National University until 1932 and was increasingly a public icon or figurehead; it was as such that de Valera pushed for his election (which was unopposed) as the first President of Ireland in 1938, a post he occupied until 1945. (Apart from Hyde's recognised eminence in the language movement, de Valera may have thought it a politic move to have a Protestant in the post.) Hyde published at least two more books during the Thirties, but without adding much to his reputation. He lived on until 1949, honoured as a figure of history, a pillar of the language and folklore revival, a decent and honourable man, and one of the first people to chart the history of Irish Gaelic literature with any authority.[1] Yeats included him as a poet-translator in his *Oxford Book*, and Hyde's book on the blind ballad-poet Antoine Raifteirí and *The Love Songs of Connacht*, though written many years earlier, were pioneer works which had a considerable influence on much younger writers such as F. R. Higgins and Padraic Fallon. Hyde played a central role in turning men such as these not only to Gaelic balladry and storytelling, but to the folk mind in general, and *The Love Songs of Connacht* is one of the genuine source books of the entire Revival. Allowing for the much smaller context, it could be said that it was a literary event comparable to the Arnim-Brentano collection *Des Knaben Wunderhorn* which helped to shape German Romantic poetry for at least two generations.

Similarly, Lady Gregory, though her stage plays were mostly rather slight affairs, bequeathed in *Cuchulain of Muirthemne* and *Gods and Fighting Men*, a legacy which fermented in the imagination of three generations of Irish readers and writers. When Yeats had praised these books on their original appearance, he was widely mocked in Dublin for putting friendship and policy before critical judgement. Yet as history has shown, they were popularisations and compilations of genius, which went through several editions, and for many Irish (and English and American) people they opened a door into the world of Irish myth and legend, especially the Ossianic and Red Branch cycles. It is only quite recently that they have ceased to be widely read. (The recent versions of the Gaelic myths and sagas by Marie Heaney appear to be fulfilling a similar role in our time.)

After this generation, the only living figure with a major reputation was Seán O'Casey, who had lived in England since 1926. After him in turn, T. C. Murray was probably the most respected dramatist, with the possible exception of Lennox Robinson, but both of these already had their most creative years behind them. Of the older poets, Padraic Colum was in America and James Stephens – at that time still very highly regarded for his verse, though this reputation did not survive the war years – was in England. The generally recognised heirs to Yeats were Higgins and Clarke, both born in the nineties of the previous century and often bracketed together, though in fact they were contrasting personalities. As Roibeárd Ó Faracháin put it, for years their respective careers had 'run in double harness'.[2]

However, it is possible after the canonical generation of Moore, Yeats etc. to trace another distinct generation born around 1880, and which includes Colum, Murray, Daniel Corkery, and George Fitzmaurice. Though they are sometimes classed as part of the second wave of the Literary Revival, or simply among its minor figures, they stand rather apart from it and can in no way be described as belonging to the Ascendancy class or the Twilight. They have much more limited horizons than the cosmopolitan generation of Moore and Yeats, their reputations have tended to be purely national or even local ones, and none of them pursued a literary career in England, though Colum emigrated to America where he lived as a professional all-round writer. With the exception of Fitzmaurice, the son of a Church of Ireland clergyman in Kerry who had married a Catholic servant-girl, they were all convinced Catholics and nationalists. These last two factors are important, since they show the gap which was opening up between Irish and English writing – a gap which did not exist for Yeats, for instance, who belongs equally to the literatures of both countries. They did not share the mythic and esoteric interests of Yeats and AE, and though they were predominantly realists it was emphatically not the cosmopolitan, French-influenced realism of Moore. Their moral and sexual codes, too, tended to be puritanical and their outlook was mainly rural and small-town, though Colum and Corkery, at least, were also widely read men of letters with good intellects. Their subjects were not the world of the Big House like Somerville and Ross, nor people in cultured upper-middle-class society like Moore's, nor colourful figures of history; instead they were mostly small farmers and townsmen and provincial petit-bourgeoisie. These writers were, in short, a new 'native' generation, even though they never banded together or claimed any communal identity.

Colum, who was the youngest of the four,[3] remains also the best known, and he was acclaimed at an early age – in fact, Colum as a writer was remarkably precocious. His early plays, such as *Thomas Muskerry* and *The Fiddler's House*, were

not only immediately successful on the stage but were widely praised as examples
of a new, unsentimental rural realism. Some of these plays, incidentally, predate
Synge's *Playboy* (Colum's father was among the protesters at its first performance in
the Abbey) and various Irish theatre historians give Colum the credit for
establishing, or at least helping to establish, the tradition of restrained, serious, even
sombre folk or peasant plays which lasted into the Fifties at least, and is in dignified
contrast to the tradition of Abbey rural farce. But in 1914, for reasons which appear
to have been purely economic, he emigrated to America with his wife, Mary (Molly)
Maguire, and after that Colum played little active part in the development of the
Irish theatre. The early book of lyrics *Wild Earth* established him as a poet, and
poems such as 'The Old Woman of the Roads', and 'She Moved through the Fair'
(still thought by many people to be a genuine folksong, though Colum actually
wrote it to a tune given to him by Herbert Hughes) quickly became not only
anthology pieces but recitation pieces as well, sung or recited by all sorts of people.
Reviewing this slim collection for his *Irish Homestead* in 1907, AE declared that
'Padraic Colum is the first Irish poet who has chosen to write of the common earth'
and predicted: 'If he fulfils the promise of those early verses, he may end by being
the most familiar and best-loved name in our literature.'[4]

Praise such as this would have turned most brains, and though Colum
remained to the end of his very long life a humane, modest man, in the long term
his early success probably did his reputation as much harm as good. His early rural
plays have not held the stage – admittedly I have never seen one acted, but when
read in book form the dialogue now appears stiff and literary, without Synge's verbal
flair or even any pronounced dramatic energy. As for 'The Old Woman of the Roads'
and similar once-loved lyrics, they were geared so exactly to the taste of an age
which has gone that today they read almost like parodies of the Georgian manner,
though with an Irish accent. 'The Drover', a poem admired by Ezra Pound, still
keeps its niche in anthologies but is disfigured by dead words such as 'kine' – which
no real-life Irish drover would use, or even understand – and Synge-influenced
literary flourishes such as 'And my mind on white ships/And the King of Spain's
daughter'. A real-life drover, slouching through cold and mud, would have been
more concerned about when and where he might next gulp a pint of porter. Far
from being a genuine folk poem, it is as much a genre piece of the period as any
Georgian lyric by Ralph Hodgson or John Drinkwater. This is not due to any lack
of first-hand contact with the land and the people since Colum, unlike the English
Georgians who were mostly city-bred, knew rural life from his childhood. It is
simply that he saw it mainly through the verbal and colouristic conventions of his
time, just as his readers did, and temperamentally he was a watercolourist rather
than a Jack-Yeatsian painter in oils.

Like so many Irish writers of peasant life, Colum's outlook was essentially
middle-class, and he was also an alert, socially sophisticated man behind his
outward simplicity. His folk vein was only one weapon in a large armoury, just as

his early plays are only a single aspect of his writing for the stage – the much later *Balloon*, for instance, has been compared to Strindberg and was influenced by German Expressionism. When he was in his eighties, he wrote a series of Noh-style playlets which were a partial reversal to the *Plays for Dancers* of Yeats – a strange and esoteric ending for the one-time folk dramatist! Colum, in fact, is one of the most versatile and eclectic of all Irish writers, one of the most difficult to pin down, and at present one of the least known; his achievement cannot be summed up merely on the strength of what he wrote before 1920. The popularity of his early lyrics has remained to dog his memory and give a one-sided impression of his large output, and the fact that much of his later verse is accomplished, sensitive and quite modern in spirit and technique is generally ignored. Some of it reveals the influence of Rilke – Colum knew something of contemporary German literature, and when Yeats near the end of his life asked if he could tell him something about the work of Stefan George, his wife Mary recited a George poem from memory.

The late novel *The Flying Swans* combines imaginative and symbolic elements with narrative realism, and the young sculptor Ulick O'Rehill may be partly a self-portrait. This flawed, but original work was praised by as shrewd a critic as Vivian Mercier when it appeared in 1957, while only two years after it was written Colum produced a very readable biography of Arthur Griffith, whom he had known. He was also a friend of both Yeats and Joyce, neither of whom suffered fools or hangers-on gladly, and he even wrote the preface for Joyce's *Anna Livia Plurabelle* (later part of *Finnegans Wake*) when it first appeared in 1929. The book in which he and his wife (who died shortly before it appeared in print) describe their relationship with that notoriously thin-skinned artist, *Our Friend James Joyce*, has become a source book for Joyceans and is still readable in its own right. Colum was such a consummate man of letters that he could turn out a good essay or introduction on a wide range of subjects – for instance, his preface to a translation of Rilke's study of Rodin, one of many such occasional prose pieces which should be reprinted. He was also an expert on world folklore, ranging from his native country to Hawaii, and a prolific author of books for children.

Apart from Joyce, the range of his friendships was astonishing; it included Griffith (who published his first poems in the *United Irishman*), the artist Marcel Duchamp, John Butler Yeats the portrait-painter and father of both the poet and the painter, the lawyer and art patron John Quinn, AE, Elinor Wyllie, Sarah Purser, Robert Frost. Americans had always loved him, and the Colums' New York apartment, in a brownstone house near First Avenue where John Cowper Powys had lived previously, received a steady stream of visitors. As Kevin Sullivan wrote for a centenary tribute in *The Irish Times* in 1981: 'The American public read Colum, and the American literary establishment honoured him: the Poetry Society of America, the Academy of Irish Poets, the American Academy of Arts and Letters, and that other academy, Columbia University, which conferred an honorary doctorate in 1958.' (His American pupils, incidentally, included J. D. Salinger.) But official Ireland had not forgotten him either, and in 1953 he was awarded the Gregory Medal by the Irish Academy of Letters.

The price paid for his versatility and productivity was high; Colum turned out a number of books which were little better than pot-boilers, and even his best work suffers from unevenness and a lack of hard, stringent self-criticism. He could have learned much from the disciplined artistry of George Moore or from Yeats's continual revisions, but he was not that sort of man or writer and in any case, as he remarked in old age to the young poet-critic Eavan Boland, 'I have to live.' He also told her on that occasion, 'Yeats hurt me. He expected too much of me,' a bitter admission to make in old age, and perhaps also a hint that his own poetic development had not been all that he and others had hoped for. In Eavan Boland's opinion, the prolific man of letters had damaged the poet, and, 'I find it hard to see his departure for America as anything but a loss in every sense.'[5]

As he was Joyce's near contemporary, this emphasises the gap of sensibility between the two men, since though they were friends from youth they seem to inhabit different cultural climates and even to belong to different generations. Morally and emotionally Colum was a late Victorian, or rather he was the product of an Irish society which prolonged Victorianism as a moral code well into the twentieth century. This was not a trait confined to Irish writers – Masefield's poetry, for instance, often shows the same simplistic morality and rather boy-scout outlook. Eavan Boland records a conversation with Colum which somehow or other came round to the subject of Alexander the Great. He praised the moral rectitude of Alexander in rejecting Oriental concubines who were brought to him, and when she showed or expressed scepticism he was huffed: 'Girls today know far too much.' An enormous gap of sensibility and code of behaviour is expressed in that reaction; yet Colum was a younger man than Yeats, who would have been suitably amused or sardonic.

The same simplistic mentality is the great barrier today in responding fully to T. C. Murray's plays, though the best of these are superior to Colum's in almost every way and from the start they worked effectively on the stage. Murray was not only a successful Abbey playwright, he was acclaimed in America in 1911 when the Abbey Players brought *Birthright* there on the tour which introduced Synge's *Playboy* to Americans, and sparked off riots which were a mirror-image of the Abbey riots during Synge's lifetime. The critics in New York and other cities voted it the best play of the season 1911/1912.[6] Murray, who came from Macroom, had been associated with Corkery and the so-called 'Cork Realists' and together they had founded the Cork Little Theatre which staged Murray's very first play, *Wheel of Fortune* – at the end of which, so Corkery recalled many years later in a radio talk, the local audience sat in 'appalled silence'. Since *Birthright* dealt with fratricide in a rural setting, and did so without setting off riots or protests, it raises again the question of just why Synge's masterpiece was considered so offensive, since its supposed patricide turns out to be a farce. Plainly, like Colum, Murray was more in tune with his audience than Synge and as a small-town Catholic, his sensibilities were closer to theirs. Possibly, indeed, they were just too much so, though he is a more honest playwright than Paul Vincent Carroll, who played a rather similar literary role some decades later.

Maurice Harte (1912) dealt with what was regarded for many years as a daring subject for Irish writers – the clerical student who discovers that he lacks a real 'vocation' but does not dare to confess this to his parents. It quickly got into the repertory and is still performed occasionally. A few years after this Murray, who was a schoolteacher by profession, moved to Dublin as headmaster of the Inchicore Model Schools, where he remained for nearly twenty years until he retired. During this period he wrote a succession of plays for the Abbey climaxed by *Autumn Fire* in 1925, which is generally regarded as his finest work and which, rather surprisingly, was also a success in London. After that, however, it was largely a downward curve, though Murray's work continued to be produced at the Abbey: *Michaelmas Eve* in 1932, *A Stag at Bay* in 1934, *A Spot in the Sun* in 1938, *Illumination* in 1939 and finally *The Green Branch* in 1943. A one-act play, *The Briery Gap*, was written in 1917 but was only given a production at the Abbey Experimental Theatre in 1948. None of these appears to have remained in the repertory, although Robert Hogan treats *Michaelmas Eve* respectfully in *After the Irish Renaissance*.

Though he was a retiring and rather sedentary man, Murray became vice-president of the Irish Academy of Letters and he has always attracted admirers and defenders – notably Andrew Malone during his lifetime and Micheál Ó hAodha since his death. Malone's influential *The Irish Drama* treats him with genuine respect as 'one of the most considerable of the Irish dramatists, and the outstanding Irish Catholic dramatist. Perhaps the greatest obstacle to the wider fame of Murray as a dramatist is his own incurable modesty. He is one of the shyest and most retiring of living writers, shunning publicity of all kinds . . .'[7] Malone noted that Murray tended to use the same devices and effects too frequently, 'suggesting a deficiency in the inventive faculty', but praised his dialogue in which he was 'surpassed by no dramatist of his time'. As late as 1950 the critic Thomas Hogan, writing in *Envoy* magazine, praised *Autumn Fire* as a masterpiece and 'greater and more profound' than O'Casey's *Juno and the Paycock*. Interestingly, *Autumn Fire* has several times been compared with Eugene O'Neill's *Desire Under the Elms*, dealing with a very similar theme, and both plays appeared quite close together in the mid-Twenties.

However, the best analyis of Murray's career as a whole is the essay on him in Micheál Ó hAodha's *Plays and Places* (1960). Here he is discussed in the context of what appears to be a kind of cyclical mood or reaction – we have seen a similar phase recently – by which the Irish intelligentsia, and possibly Irish audiences and readers as well, turn against rural or folk themes and demand urban, sophisticated, 'international' ones instead. As early as 1926 Lady Gregory recorded in her journal: 'Yeats has been saying that Dublin won't stand any more peasant work.' Or in the words of Brinsley MacNamara, himself an Abbey playwright as well as a novelist, 'the peasant play was to be considered a thing of the past and nothing further worthwhile could come from that source.' Murray tried to break with his rather monochrome rural and small-town settings by attempting a new range of subjects, but he was out of his depth and his milieu, as can be seen by the laboured suburban triviality of the one-act *A Spot in the Sun*, printed in the *Dublin Magazine* of April-June 1938. Unlike Lennox Robinson, he lacked urbanity and humour and the ability to depict a wide range of social types convincingly. His most interesting achievement during this period was probably the quasi-autobiographical novel *Spring Horizon* (1937) which gives glimpses of his childhood in Land League times and of his father's shop in Macroom.

Murray, it has been said, is the dramatist of small local tragedies involving land quarrels, ill-matched couples, thwarted hopes, religious aspirations and repressions, sometimes even outright violence and insanity. Perhaps more than anything else, however, he depicts inner and outer frustrations, the 'quiet desperation' which his friend Corkery expressed in his novel of Cork life, The *Threshold of Quiet*. Passive despair and resignation are more evident than genuine tragedy; it is a world of small lives and of a narrow society in which nothing much happens – very close, in fact, to what Brian Friel shows in *Philadelphia, Here I Come!*, though in that play young Gar has the twin outlets of a fantasy life and the emigrant boat. It is also the forerunner of much of what O'Connor and O'Faolain wrote about in their short stories, and Murray is very clearly one of the founders of a long tradition of Cork domestic realism. Morally, however, he is conventional and even timid, a regionalist writing for fellow-provincials and a prisoner of the petit-bourgeois values of his milieu rather than rising above them or challenging them. When *Autumn Fire* was revived by Jim Fitzgerald on RTÉ in the Sixties, the play's emotional sincerity and sure sense of rural background were obvious, but so also was the fact that the fire was burning low and that somehow the work, with all its good qualities, was of its period.

Corkery's plays have held the stage even less then Colum's – in fact they are known only to period specialists, although *The Labour Leader*, when performed at the Abbey in 1920, created a stir at the time through its trade-union militancy, which reflected Corkery's own background in Cork. It is difficult to define exactly what aspect of his literary output he lives by today; he wrote a good but not a major novel, verse which has not lasted, several short-story collections which are his most important achievement as a creative writer, polemics posing as literary criticism in *Synge and Anglo-Irish Literature*, a brilliant, thought-stimulating but apparently unscholarly re-creation of eighteenth-century Munster, its poets and its underground Gaelic culture in *The Hidden Ireland*, a mixture of polemics and shrewd analysis in his late book, *The Fortunes of the Irish Language*. He was also an amateur watercolourist of some talent, an influential Professor of English at University College Cork from 1931 to 1947, and an Irish senator from 1951 to 1954.

Corkery was an unregenerate cultural nationalist and his Catholicism was rigid and embattled, so much so indeed that at times he appears to be almost an intellectual bedfellow of his fellow-Corkonian, Dr Alfred O'Rahilly. The Literary Revival had left a legacy of European Symbolism and Continental Realism, neo-Platonism and Eastern philosophy, mythology and Muse-worship; Corkery rejected virtually all of these and insisted that a genuinely national literature should be based on the triple realities of religion, nationalism and the land. His own fiction echoes this, though not programmatically, and it would seem that – particularly in the collection *The Stormy Hills* of 1929, which is probably his best achievement in the short-story genre – what chiefly interested him was the need to invest peasant life with a certain heroic and monumental quality. This was also a preoccupation of many contemporary writers in Europe generally, from France to Scandinavia, as well as the theme of many painters going back to Van Gogh and, ultimately, to Millet.

In a passage of passionate polemic which has been quoted many times, he recalled how he had been present once at a Munster hurling final and had been struck by the idea of how this teeming, vigorous concourse of people, expressing an entire racial and cultural vitality, needed a literature which would speak to and for it, and would translate its reality into words.[8] One wonders how he would have reacted if taken to a rugby international in Lansdowne Road, or for that matter if he had been watching the Sunday afternoon queues forming in Dublin outside the picture palaces; yet both of these were, after all, as representative in their different ways of contemporary Ireland as the hurling followers he saw that Sunday in Thurles. As with Pearse and many other national idealists, Corkery's patriotism was as much subjectivity and emotional self-projection as a social and political reality; or to put it in other words, he was a romantic populist obsessed with his concept of 'the people'. Today this is anathema, confused with Fascism and racism and a dozen other outlawed -isms, although it is also in a sense a definition of democracy, and if Corkery had lived under Hitler he might very well have lost his life in opposing him and his policies. In spite of his professorship and his other public offices, he was never an Establishment figure and many of his intellectual stances were widely unpopular. *Synge and Anglo-Irish Literature*, for example, was savaged by P. S. O'Hegarty in a long review in the *Dublin Magazine*[9] as 'a bad book and a mischievous book'. O'Hegarty accused him of saying, in effect, 'that only an Irish Catholic Nationalist can write Irish literature' and went on to declare: 'Need I say more on this than that this theory of Mr Corkery's is wrong-headed and damnable. It is prejudiced and, in the real sense, ignorant . . . The Irish Nation includes all the people of this island, Catholic and non-Catholic, Gael and *Sean-ghall*, native and "ascendancy". An Irish national literature must include all of them, and an Irish "cosmos" – word beloved by Mr Corkery – must include all of them.'

Four years later Seán O'Faolain, who in his youth had been a follower and protégé of Corkery's, returned to the attack in the same publication, and he also repudiated Corkery's views on various occasions in *The Bell*. O'Faolain is a slightly suspect witness, since – as he frankly admits in his autobiography *Vive Moi!* – he himself had been a candidate for the UCC professorship which went to the older writer instead, and O'Faolain was an intensely ambitious and competitive man. However, Corkery was only reaping what he had sown, since essentially the book is based on a dubious thesis and argued polemically and dogmatically rather than objectively or logically. Yet many still-relevant points and statements are scattered through it, and underlying it all is a genuine, smouldering anger at the continuing willingness of Irish writers to compromise themselves and their talents in order to suit the preconceptions of English publishers, English readerships and English critics. On this point, at least, the book remains as valid today as it ever was and a valuable corrective to the mentality – by no means entirely, or even predominantly, confined to Anglo-Irish writers – which looks with provincial timidity (or career opportunism) towards London as the cultural arbiter of Ireland.

There seems no need to apologise for Corkery today merely because he flouts various dogmas of political correctness and belongs intellectually to what might be called the Radical Right. His interests were wide and he was one of the first Irish writers – though Moore had been there before him – to point to the Russians as literary examples and models for his fellow-countrymen. His views on certain subjects sound at times curiously like those of Gorky, while his quasi-nationalist and regionalist outlook was shared by many Continental (and American) writers of the time, when rural and regional themes had a considerable currency. If Corkery sometimes sounds ingrown and provincial, it is usually by conscious choice; and what in Murray are often moral and emotional inhibitions, or even intellectual limitations, somehow in him become positive qualities. Undoubtedly there was a streak of the male prude in him, as is shown by his obvious distaste (in *The Hidden Ireland*) for Merriman's *The Midnight Court* and by the fact that there is hardly a convincing female character anywhere in his fiction. He also displays little humour, another trait he shares with Murray whose spasmodic attempts in a comic vein are almost embarrassing.

Yet Corkery seems to have had genuine moral stature and even personal magnetism, so that the masterly first volume of O'Connor's biography, *An Only Child*, is virtually dominated by him, while even O'Faolain spent much of his later career arguing with or rejecting his views. His cultural importance to Cork can hardly be exaggerated, and in Seán Ó Riordáin's classic poem 'Cúl an Tí' the reference in the closing lines to 'an t-ollaimhín sin Aesop' is widely taken to mean Corkery: small, shy but combative. Many of his UCC pupils retained – some of them still do – lively memories of his lecturing and of his trenchant opinions, sometimes prejudiced or even one-sided, but almost always intellectually stimulating. In short, he was a seminal figure in several fields and the fact that contemporary writers such as Thomas Kinsella still find him relevant is proof in itself that Corkery is far from dead as a force.[10] Though he has been refuted or dismissed dozens of times over the years, he persists in coming back into currency, and most of his writings are still in print, which in itself indicates something in them that refuses to die. Certainly no literary or cultural historian of his period could ignore him without leaving a considerable Black Hole.

Where or how, then, can George Fitzmaurice be fitted into a cultural context beginning in 1930? Apart from Austin Clarke's staging of *The Dandy Dolls* and *The Magic Glasses* at the Lyric Theatre in Dublin in 1945, and a handful of fringe or semi-amateur productions, Fitzmaurice had virtually faded from the Irish theatregoer's consciousness since 1923 when the Abbey had performed *Twixt the Giltinans and the Carmodys*, one of his more conventional farces and not at all typical of the genuinely original aspect of his writings. After that, almost his only outlet was the always-staunch *Dublin Magazine*, where Seumas O'Sullivan published a number of his plays which had become increasingly fantastic and escapist, rather in the vein of Lord Dunsany. When he died aged eighty-five in 1963, in a tiny flat in Harcourt Street, his death was almost ignored by the newspapers and not only were his works not performed, but they were long out of print as well. The volume called *Five Plays* which he had published in 1914 was overtaken by the Great War, in which Fitzmaurice himself served; he was dead before Liam Miller of the Dolmen Press, who had known him personally, began to republish his works and bring them back into currency.

Yet, Miller apart, Fitzmaurice always had a coterie of influential supporters including Clarke, O'Sullivan, Colum, Micheál Ó hAodha, and Ernest Boyd. Robert Hogan praises him enthusiastically in *After the Irish Renaissance*, while one of the best short studies of his works was an article in the *London Magazine* in February 1965 by a respected English drama critic, Irving Wardle. In recent years there has been a small but growing literature on him, and even a television documentary, though whether or not he is now an integral part of the Irish dramatic repertory is another matter. His plays appear to be difficult to stage or bring off effectively, and in any case folklore and Kerry dialect – John B. Keane apart – are out of fashion. Perhaps Fitzmaurice has yet to find his producer? The works are close to puppet theatre, excluding his more traditional farces or the long early play *The Moonlighter* which deals with the land war, whereas the Abbey tradition was almost obstinately realist, in spite of Yeats's desire to get away from that mode or rise above it.

There was for decades an underground belief in Dublin, subscribed to by Austin Clarke among others, that Fitzmaurice was kept off the Abbey stage by the envy of Yeats and Lady Gregory; the latter was said to have resented some praise given by critics to his early plays at the expense of her own pleasant, innocuous farces. Certainly Fitzmaurice himself seems to have believed this too – at least according to accounts given to me by the late John Chichester, an old acquaintance and one of the very few people who were at all close to him in his last years. Chichester met the almost forgotten playwright in pubs along Merrion Row where Fitzmaurice, by then a gnome-like, grizzled, retired civil servant huddled into an old tweed overcoat, would sit occasionally over a glass of Guinness. Chichester remembered him as being 'very bitter' against Yeats and Lady Gregory for their treatment of him, which he believed had fatally damaged his public career as a writer. When he died alone, in his almost bare room where he had lived for years on his small pension, a note was found there saying: 'Author is prepared to sell outright all rights in 14 plays dealing intimately with life in the Irish countryside. Most have already been produced or published. Suitable on which to build musical, television, etc. Pass to anyone interested.' Yet when Micheál Ó hAodha spoke to him of radio adaptations of his plays, he was evasive or seemingly uninterested. He was, by virtually all surviving accounts, an odd and psychologically elusive man, one of twelve children none of whom married, and of whom he was the last survivor.

When the professional stage more or less abandoned him, Fitzmaurice published eight plays in the *Dublin Magazine* from 1924 onwards. Those that concern us here are *There are Tragedies and Tragedies* (1948), *One Evening Gleam* (1952), *The Coming of Ewn Andzale* (1954 – the name is an anagram of New Zealand), *The Terrible Baisht* (1954), and *The Enchanted Land* (1957). Several of these are one-act plays, a form which probably suited him best – in Micheál Ó hAodha's opinion, he was essentially a miniaturist who 'could carve a leprechaun on a cherry-stone, (but) could not hew a life-size figure out of a rock'. Ó hAodha also points out that his dialogue and idiom owe little to Synge or any other folk-dramatist and that his language is entirely his own.[11]

Leaving aside the allegedly negative attitude of Yeats, and the question of whether or not the Old Lady did say No, Fitzmaurice was plainly a writer out of step with his time. As Irving Wardle puts it, he was 'producing sombre works when audiences wanted comedy, bizarre fantasies when realism came into fashion, and anticipating O'Casey in tragi-comedy by nearly twenty years'. Perhaps the closest parallel is not with any Irish writer but with certain plays of Lorca, who understood thoroughly the world of puppet theatre to which Fitzmaurice's most characteristic works, consciously or unconsciously, seem to belong. Others have pointed out the example of Ibsen's troll figures, and of *Peer Gynt* in particular, though Fitzmaurice has none of Ibsen's intellectual power and range, even if he has his sense of the grotesque. His use of folk mythology is burlesque and surreal rather than serious, probably even with some debt to music-hall farce, and according to Robert Hogan he told Austin Clarke that *The Linnaun Shee*, which Clarke produced at the Lyric Theatre in 1949, was 'a satire on Yeats and his cult of the fairies'.

The Abbey style of acting lacked the pace or the brittle sense of fantasy his works required, and in any case Fitzmaurice's plays seem to work best on a small stage; a laboured, realistic production is entirely unsuited to them and clips their wings. And so possibly the most original Irish dramatist between O'Casey (who was actually some years younger than he) and the emergence of Behan and Beckett, lived almost half a century of obscurity. Yeats, who was trying to escape from a narrowly or dully realistic theatre, in this case ignored what was under his nose. Or, as Austin Clarke put it in the *Dublin Magazine*: 'George Fitzmaurice discovered what

Yeats, Lady Gregory and others were looking for and, as I have said, it is almost incredible that the interest of his experiments should not have been seen at the time. There are signs that our folklore may quicken an Irish ballet and, since we must assume that Irish drama will continue to develop, it is possible that dramatists will interpret our folklore before it is too late. If that is so, the precarious, difficult art-form in which Fitzmaurice experimented at the expense of immediate recognition will be its real turning point.'[12]

It seems now that Clarke was being uncharacteristically optimistic, because Fitzmaurice was almost forgotten by the time of his death and any revival of his plays since then has been slow and tentative. Apart from the almost inevitable American academics, there has been little interest shown in him outside Ireland – although Irving Wardle, in the article already mentioned, states that a version of *The Magic Glasses*, by the Japanese writer Kan Kikuchi, entitled *The Madman on the Roof*, was published in the early 1960s 'as a representative specimen of modern Japanese drama'. One wonders what Yeats, with his cult of the Japanese theatre, would have said to that.

Chapter 8

THE POETS AFTER YEATS

It is commonly said in literary histories that the generation of Irish poets coming directly after Yeats was dominated by his stature and his influence, negatively as well as positively. As a leading elder poet said to me once: 'There he was, out there in Rathfarnham, always towering above us all like the Wellington Monument.' Yeats was both an inspiration and an inhibition, a terminus and a beginning. When assessing any of the newer generation of poets, the more facile critics and literary journalists predictably took Yeats as their starting point or measuring rod. In this way Austin Clarke was hailed inevitably as 'a second Yeats', though as friends of his pointed out after his death, privately he found this galling because he did not want to be Yeats the Second, he wanted to be Clarke the First. Yet the habit persisted for decades – as late as the mid-Sixties, for instance, Thomas Kinsella was praised in many quarters as the finest Irish poet since Yeats, a comparison which backfired and harmed rather than aided his subsequent reputation. (Similarly, good or promising Irish novelists are still monotonously and meaninglessly compared with Joyce, even when their whole literary ancestry and outlook are notably non-Joycean.)

Yet while much of the contemporary evidence suggests that the better Irish poets from the 1920s onwards were only too well aware of Yeats's uniqueness, mostly they went their own various ways and achieved their own various individualities, major and minor. The Yeatsian legacy, in the broadest sense, meant that Irish poets could now write as Irish and not as honorary English ones – which did not infer a return to the journalistic balladry of the 'Nation' poets, or to the Thomas Moore drawing-room tradition, but simply meant that an Irish literature in English was now an independent reality, just as American literature was. Or as Roibeárd Ó Faracháin put it: 'Irish poets are now in the habit of assessing their work against the background of other Irish writing, instead, as was formerly the case, of measuring it against the work of English poets and writers.'[1] This represented an enormous liberation and the assertion of a newly found identity, but it was also open to abuse and misinterpretation by those with a blinkered, or at least limited vision. Yeats's intellectual complexity and depth were sometimes ignored, or else insufficiently understood, with the result that many younger writers took their cue or starting-point from the early, Twilight poems or the folkish Yeats of 'The Fiddler of Dooney', so becoming merely nostalgic or weakly Georgian, and putting themselves out of tune and out of touch with the changing modern world around them. Anthologies of the period are littered with such imitative verse, much of it no better than pastiche, though sometimes saved by a quality of genuine homespun innocence. Yet the overall impression left by these anthologies is of a quite surprising degree of eclecticism; the Yeatsian shadow is not as dominating as might be expected, and a large number of poets, good, bad and mediocre, seemingly went on writing as if they were unaware of it or had simply bypassed it.

Contemporary English poetry, of course, offered a variety of influences, and Masefield, Walter de la Mare, and Gordon Bottomley (who visited Ireland) all had Irish admirers. Even Chesterton, though his verse seems facile and journalistic nowadays, had a considerable influence on poets such as Higgins, particularly in his cult of the poet as a jovial, bucolic roisterer with a pint pot always in hand. Gerard Manley Hopkins interested some of the younger poets, and Monk Gibbon records Yeats warning him pontifically against his influence and recommending him instead to study Robert Bridges. Eliot and Pound were still minority enthusiasms and it is not until the 1930s (during which Eliot paid his famous visit to Dublin) that the impact of contemporary American verse is strongly felt. Robert Frost visited Dublin in the late 1920s, but it is hard to detect any obvious echoes of his style among Irish poets until after the second World War. And later, in the immediate post-war years, the poetry of George Barker strongly interested many Irish writers, including – so it has always seemed to me – Patrick Kavanagh. There were also influences from the Continent, notably Rilke in the 1940s and 1950s, and Lorca's poetry had been known in Dublin from the 1930s.[2]

Among the older figures, Seumas O'Sullivan is often quoted as a follower or even a mere epigone of Yeats, and of the early, Twilight Yeats in particular. Quite plainly, he is not a major poet and much of his verse is fragile and wistful, with a 'faery' element which suggests both Yeats and AE, yet predominantly his voice is his own and not theirs. O'Sullivan (or James Starkey, to give him his correct name) was above all a product of the eighteen-nineties, with one foot in French poetry (Albert Samain, Henri de Regnier, etc.) and another in the Celtic Twilight and in the English Aesthetic Movement. John Betjeman, who knew him personally, included him in an anthology of Nineties verse, into which he fits easily and naturally.[3] He had a fastidious ear and fine taste and if he lacks robustness or range, there is a sensitivity and a cultured, patrician note in his verse which are welcome among so many literary-minded men and women playing at being native-born folk-poets and balladeers.

O'Sullivan is a watercolourist and even a miniaturist, but he is an exact and sensitive one, particularly in his evocations of old, decayed Georgian Dublin – the lamplighter on his nightly round of the gas lamps, children playing in a run-down alleyway, old people shuffling down the streets, the ghosts of Buck Whaley and of the eighteenth century, a funeral going by. Nobody has been able to shut him out of Irish anthologies for long, even in an age when classical learning and classical allusions have become less and less current, and old-style, civilised bookishness such as his seems to most readers as divorced from real life as the dust in old libraries. Poet-critics as far apart as Clarke and MacNeice have treated him with respect and it might even be said that, in his minor-key way, he is something of a poet's poet. His verse apart, O'Sullivan did Irish literature a unique service through his long editorship of the *Dublin Magazine* and he was a respected bibliophile and book collector, with whom John Betjeman liked to talk during his stay in Dublin. He was also, by almost unanimous consent, one of the genuine wits of his age and milieu, as well as a man of patrician dignity and sense of style.

The case of F. R. Higgins is different, since he was an acknowledged follower and intimate of Yeats, whereas O'Sullivan occasionally crossed swords with the older poet and argued with or opposed him during meetings of the Irish Academy of Letters (this may have been why he did not appear in the *Oxford Book of Modern Verse*). Since he died in his mid-forties, a crucial or transitional time for most poets, there is no 'third-period' Higgins and speculation about how his later work might have developed merely underlines the unanswerable fact that his career leaves an overall impression of incompleteness. With many of the qualities of a major poet, he somehow did not become one; though an opinionated and argumentative man, he sometimes gives an impression of intellectual insincerity or evasion; and while he played energetically the role of a folk-poet and man of the people, he was bourgeois in his lifestyle and no mean hand at the complex game of Dublin literary politics. Great things were expected of Higgins both by his contemporaries and by his elders, Yeats and AE, and when he died in 1941 literary Ireland went into mourning, even though it was in the depths of the war.[4] Yet his poetry quickly went out of print and out of fashion, while intemperate attacks by Patrick Kavanagh, in particular, damaged his posthumous reputation badly – damage which still has not been made good.[5] Kavanagh in attacking Higgins's verse established a term of abuse, 'bucklepping', which became a catchword for certain younger writers – particularly among Kavanagh's own followers – and virtually marked the boundary line between two generations of Irish writers, as well as of two contrasting sensibilities.

Kavanagh, as a Borderer growing up in poverty on a small farm and poor soil, was sarcastically hostile to the tradition of verbal colour and exuberance that stemmed largely from Synge; these characteristics he viewed as 'phoney' (one of his favourite words) and as virtually a modern form of stage-Irishism. Yet it was also a legacy of the Gaelic tradition – which Kavanagh himself did not know at first hand, and liked to deride – while arguably the Stage Irishman himself, like most national stereotypes, has some basis in fact and represents one aspect at least of the native character. A conscious, half-humorous enjoyment of verbal opulence and overspill, a delight in piling on words as much for their phonic value as for their prose meaning, and a love of colour for its own sensuous sake are traits which are common and recurrent in Irish literature, from Eoghan Rua Ó Súilleabháin in the eighteenth century back to the Ossianic and Red Branch tales; one could even point to many passages in late Joyce and to the works of James Stephens, Flann O'Brien, George Fitzmaurice and Seán O'Casey. (They are, of course, also found in English literature – particularly the Elizabethans – and in French writers such as Rabelais, not to mention numerous figures of this century.) What Kavanagh was expressing was probably a temperamental dislike or incompatibility – that of a rather dour and hard-nosed Northerner for the more expansive, garrulous man of the West – which he elevated into a critical dogma and passed on to his followers. Underlying it is the old folk belief that the man with a flow of fine words is not quite to be trusted, as well as the endemic puritan prejudice in favour of the buff jerkin rather than the showy satin doublet.

Nevertheless, there is a valid core to Kavanagh's complaint, nor is there any doubt that Higgins frequently verged on self-parody and that his taste was always unsure. The favourite image of himself which he projects in his verse is that of a rollicking broadsheet balladeer who is also a wencher and drinker, rather in the style of Seán Ó Tuama back in the eighteenth century, though Higgins was quite respectable in private life and – according to Seán O'Faolain – an 'uxorious' husband.[6] His sources were partly Hyde's translations and probably the famous collection of folk songs, *Amhráin Mhuighe Sheola*, by the famous Mrs Costelloe of Tuam; but he also learned much from the English Georgian balladry of his time. Traces of Kipling, Masefield, Alfred Noyes and G. K. Chesterton can be found in his verse, and even echoes of the South African poet Roy Campell, though they become scarcer as he developed to maturity and in his last collection, *The Gap of Brightness* (1940), they have more or less vanished. By then Higgins was outgrowing his folk-bard phase, and was consciously striving for a more involuted, intellectual mode – which is also, of course, a part of the Gaelic tradition, as he was perfectly aware. The poem 'Heresy', while not one of his very finest, is a good example of this knotted, sinewy style. Near the end of his life, he told Padraic Fallon that he was tired of being merely a poet of 'atmosphere'. But death, in the form of a stroke, intervened, at what was evidently a transitional period in his growth as a poet. (As Austin Clarke puts it in one of his poems, 'Higgins was coffined in a clot.') His involvement in the affairs of the Abbey had also taken up much of his time and energies, particularly an exhausting tour of America in which he acted as manager – and capably and conscientiously too, it seems.

A rather insignificant episode in his career which has told against him posthumously, was the radio debate with Louis MacNeice, under the title 'Tendencies in Modern Poetry', broadcast from Northern Ireland in July 1939 (the text appeared duly in the *Listener* and has been reprinted since). MacNeice's oral put-down of his fellow-poet is often quoted; when challenged by Higgins who asked rhetorically 'Do the poets of your school ever sing?' he countered: 'Do the poets of yours ever think?' Of course MacNeice knew very well how to 'sing' when he wanted to while Higgins, though not a deeply-read man, did not lack thinking power. Yet the debate showed up his intellectual limitations and his exaggerated, neo-romantic belief in racial and ancestral traits, and it also marks a phase in which the entire rural and folksong tradition in Irish writing was coming under threat from the new urban-based, journalistic school of Modernism, whose headquarters were in London. However, too much should not be made of this impromptu radio exchange, about which Dylan Thomas, who listened to it, remarked sceptically in a letter to a friend: 'both of them, if you ask me, were pissed.'[7] MacNeice had a genuine respect and liking for Higgins, whose poetry he treats favourably though briefly in his study of Yeats and who also appears, posthumously, in the 1955 *Autumn Sequel* under the name of 'Reilly'. Since much of this long poem is taken up with a kind of poetic wake of Dylan Thomas ('Gwilym'), whose body had been brought back from New York for burial at Laugharne in Wales, MacNeice reverts in memory to his other dead friends and invokes Reilly, the poet from the West of Ireland: 'He too had a rolling eye and a fastidious ear/He too was proud of his landscape and his birth.'[8]

Higgins and MacNeice shared at least a Connacht ancestry and an Irish Protestant background, as well as an appetite for Guinness and the finer points of versification. About Higgins's qualities purely as a verse technician, there seems to be general agreement; Clarke, MacNeice, Roibeárd Ó Faracháin all agree in praising his craft and his ear. No Irish poet of his time had a finer feeling for landscape or local colour, whether he is invoking Mayo and the jutting peak of Nephin, or the rich grasslands of Meath traversed by the silvery Boyne. Where doubts do begin to enter is concerning his poetic range, his intellectual calibre and above all his ability – or inability – to remake himself at a period when his purely lyrical impulse was beginning to flag, and he had to face the laborious task of rebuilding and refurbishing his whole poetic psyche. Fallon, who knew him well, credits him with 'a rich, almost sensual pigmentation of sound and a marvellously pictorial line, the main portion of any poet's equipment'; yet he wondered also 'how Higgins would have developed in the fall and winter of his life. He had made no preparations for it mentally. His scholarship was nil. He regarded all learning with suspicion. Would the spontaneous poetry of his youth have failed him? The ego become too rigid? The vanity lose its humorous edge?'[9]

It is probable that Higgins never quite made up for the deficiencies of his early education as an RIC man's son in backward, impoverished Mayo; he knew no Continental language, and even the Church Latin which most middle-class Catholic boys learned was denied him. In his obsession with the poet as a Celtic singer (the phrase was one of the clichés of the time), he often forgot the emphasis the old bardic order had placed on acquiring a corpus of learning and knowledge. Yet from the various slim volumes of verse he published – mainly through the invaluable Cuala Press – there remains a handful of genuine anthology pieces which includes the 'Elegy for Pádraic Ó Conaire', 'Father and Son', 'The Boyne Walk' and – perhaps the finest of all – 'Auction', with its inexorable chorus of 'Going, going, gone'. This sustained, moving poem, which appeared in the last year of his life, was inspired by the public sale of the large country house once owned by Higgins's ancestors in Higginstown, County Meath, to 'beef-belted, pea-eyed men of Meath', the local farmers and cattle-jobbers and gombeen-men. It represents a complete *volte-face* from his early, man-of-the-people stance, when he had boasted: 'With these bawneen men I'm one/In the grey dusk-fall . . .' He had finally come full circle and, like Yeats, was mourning the decay and collapse of the Big Houses and the end of a culture. Instead of seeing himself as a kind of Raftery figure, he now speaks as an Irish Protestant who witnesses the steady shrinking of his own society and its gradual eclipse in favour of the new rural businessman sprung from the thatched cottages.

The wheel of history and conquest has come full circle. Here he may well have profited from Yeats's threnodies for Coole Park, but there is a personal note in 'Auction' which gives it emotional conviction and is very different from Yeats's lofty, distanced meditations upon history and tradition. Probably the direct influence of Yeats upon him has been exaggerated; the plain fact is that Higgins, at his most characteristic, does not sound like Yeats and that their respective voices were far apart in timbre. There may even have been a certain debt in the other direction – Fallon recalled that R. M. Smyllie, the famous editor of *The Irish Times*, once showed him a Yeats poem he was about to publish, with emendations in what appeared to be Higgins's handwriting. And the American critic Richard Fallis, in his book *The Celtic Renaissance*,[10] writes that from the period when they prepared together a series of broadside ballads for the Cuala Press, 'each began to influence the other. Yeats taught Higgins something about disciplining his art, while Higgins helped Yeats catch something of the authentic voice of folksong in his later poetry.'

Austin Clarke is credited with saying about him: 'Fred takes a little of the whitewash from every wall he leans against.' The two men were born in the same year (1896) and in the words of Roibeárd Ó Faracháin, 'ran in double harness for years'. This may sound surprising today, when Clarke's reputation probably stands higher than it ever did while that of Higgins is still partly in the shade. Also, Clarke's relatively late conversion to a form of Anglo-American Modernism – or more accurately, perhaps, his development along lines running roughly parallel to it – has largely buried or obscured his earlier identity. Before the second World War he was known and admired mainly as a poet of Irish mythology ('The Cattle Drive in Connaught', based on the Táin legend, was greatly praised when it appeared in 1925), for his imaginative re-creation of medieval Ireland (what he himself called Celtic-Romanesque) and for his 'nature' lyrics which have an inner, Samuel Palmer-like glow. The last quality probably derives in part from AE, always an inspirational figure, but even AE could only illumine or bring out what the young poet already possessed as his birthright. In short, the earlier Clarke seems to fit comfortably enough into a certain context, that of the second generation of the Literary Revival – less folksy and simple than Colum, less exuberant and more learned and introspective than Higgins, more imaginative and verbally inspired than Joseph Campbell, but basically belonging in the same camp as they.

Where he differed from them was that he went less to the Gaelic ballad tradition with its broad vowel sounds and more to the poetry of the Bards, whose (largely syllabic) metres he studied. This sharpened the cerebral, involuted quality which grew more marked from his middle years and which most Clarke commentators date to the appearance of the volume *Pilgrimage* in 1929. From then on, he became less a Celtic nature poet and more and more a nonconformist and individualist, at war with much of what was around him, and even with much that lay inside him. These tensions appear to have been chiefly sexual and religious, twin themes which have become a commonplace in Irish writing – prose as well as verse – in the past forty years, but Clarke was one of the very earliest to explicate them and his example has proved a seminal one.

To start with, Clarke had an obsessively religious mother, and he fell foul of the Church through his unconsummated first marriage to Geraldine Cummins, which took place in a registry office and probably cost him the renewal of his English lecturership in UCD. He left after this for London, where he worked as a literary journalist for fifteen years and met most of the leading English poets, critics and journalists, returning to Ireland in 1937 with his second wife and young children. His professional industry was remarkable; in 1932 he published a novel of medieval Ireland, *The Bright Temptation* (absurdly, it was banned until 1954); another quasi-historical novel, *The Singing Men of Cashel*, appeared in 1936 and in the same year he brought out his *Collected Poems* with an enthusiastic introduction by Padraic Colum. Shortly after his return to Dublin, where he settled with his family in Templeogue on the Dodder, he suffered a severe emotional and nervous crisis probably connected with the fact that Geraldine Cummins refused to grant him either a divorce or an annulment, so that his present marriage lacked full legal status. This impasse is reflected in the deeply introspective and sometimes obscure poems of the collection *Night and Morning* (1938); it is hard to recognise the earlier, lyrically expansive Clarke in a poem such as 'The Jewels' which appeared first in the *Dublin Magazine* of April-June that year:

> . . . *The sanctuary lamp is lowered*
> *In witness of our ignorance;*
> *Greed of religion makes us old*
> *Before our time. We are undone*
> *Within the winking of an eyelid,*
> *And there is nothing can be hidden:*
> *Love darts and thunders from the walls.*
>
> *The misery of common faith*
> *Was ours before the age of reason* . . .

Plainly the (rather crabbed and cryptic) imagery reflects conflict with the Church, sexual guilt or at least sexual rebellion, themes which had already been developed in his novels where pagan and Christian elements often collide. Clarke had probably ceased to be a religious believer, at least in any orthodox sense, but his paganism somehow appears incomplete and partial, seemingly unable to oust a Jansenist conscience and hereditary moral inhibitions, so that these co-exist like mutually hostile partners in an unhappy marriage. This deep-rooted conflict, however, is surely the key to his development as a poet and perhaps Clarke's anti-clericalism was given extra virulence by a definite clerical element in his own make-up – even his physical appearance suggested it, and there is a legend that once, while walking in Terenure, he was stopped by a small boy who asked him to bless his Rosary beads. The influence of Joyce – though it is mostly the early Joyce of the *Portrait of an Artist*, rather than the Joyce of *Ulysses* – seems strong, and Clarke had called on Joyce and his family in Paris and had been well received (though there is no mention of Clarke in the Ellmann biography). After all, he too had been educated by the Jesuits at Belvedere College, so on certain levels there must have been a strong degree of self-identification with the older writer. Both were tense, cerebral, introspective men with strong scholastic intellects and European cultures, both had made unorthodox marriages, both had rebelled against their early backgrounds and – a coincidence – each of them had married a woman named Nora.

Modern Irish Catholic writing can be seen, in retrospect, virtually to begin with Joyce who inaugurated a new cycle in his country's literature. Yeats had anticipated the emergence of a school of Irish Catholic writers and had even told Clarke, when the latter once visited him in Gort, that he wanted to see a neo-Catholic school of poets in the country, on similar lines to Francis Jammes, Péguy and Claudel in France. Yet he did not seem especially happy with the generation which emerged and he may even have felt threatened by the *novi homines* of the new Catholic middle class, socially as well as aesthetically and ideologically. (Or perhaps Yeats was simply hostile to any native literary development which he could not control or guide himself.) In any case, the tendency of his last period was towards triumphant affirmation – a kind of Nietzschean *amor fati* or 'tragic optimism' – while Clarke's was increasingly towards doubt, questioning, irony, social criticism and satire, and even a vein of narcissistic bitterness and negation. Certainly his lyric impulse was stilled for some years and he turned to the theatre, though his plays never enjoyed more than a coterie success. Between 1939 and 1946 Clarke, as Ó Faracháin points out, 'wrote, produced and published seven short plays in verse, one for broadcasting, and six for the theatre'.[11] The radio play was *As the Crow Flies* (1943) which contained the lyric beginning, 'Stop, stop and listen, for the bough top', familiar to two generations of secondary-school pupils. It showed that his lyric vein was not extinct, but he published no book of verse until the slim volume *Ancient Lights: Poems and Satires*, which appeared under his own imprint of Bridge

House, Templeogue in 1955. Finally, in 1961 appeared *Later Poems* which began the rise of his later reputation and was acclaimed by a new generation of poets, but also obscured his earlier achievements. The vein of social satire which became so prominent in his later verse was widely praised because it caught the essentially restless, transitional, even negative mood of the time, though in the opinion of Padraic Fallon, at least, Clarke's style was not well suited to the genre. Reviewing *Ancient Lights* for the *Dublin Magazine*, he wrote: 'He is not naturally a neat knifeman, having used the larger cutlery of the cavalry commander, and I do not think the smaller suit of the satirist keeps his elbows in. He refines too much for the fun to be effective, and he should learn of Swift not to be slow when it comes to hard clouting.'

Clarke's productive old age is outside the scope of this chapter, but with all due deference to his late verse and the deserved Indian summer of his reputation, it does seem a pity that so many critics have almost automatically praised the later Clarke at the expense of the earlier. For instance, Richard Loftus in his book *Nationalism in Modern Anglo-Irish Poetry*,[12] speaks of the 'flaccid romanticism of his youthful verse', a dismissive, even cocksure phrase which implicitly ignores the frequent mannerism and constriction of Clarke's late style, as well as the plain fact that some of the work of his old age would almost certainly have been rejected, or at least left unpublished, by his earlier, more critically fastidious self. He wrote good and bad poems at all stages of his long career, and time is already beginning to sort them out. But Clarke is also, in my opinion, underrated as a dramatist – even allowing for the fact that his plays are probably more alive on the printed page than in the theatre. He certainly deserves credit for trying so idealistically, often in the face of public indifference and half-hearted criticism, to keep poetic drama on the stage, and the Lyric Theatre (which he founded with Ó Faracháin) was a gallant venture that deserved better public support than, in general, it received. Beginning with its first public performance at the Peacock Theatre in 1941, it lasted until 1952 and performed plays by Yeats and Fitzmaurice as well as Clarke's own, and Donagh MacDonagh's still live-and-kicking *Happy as Larry*.

Clarke's novels are rather a specialised taste and occasionally look back to the archaising prose romances of William Morris and Maurice Hewlett, yet Benedict Kiely, a shrewd critic as well as a seasoned and respected novelist, has written: 'Even if "The Singing Men of Cashel" were to be regarded as nothing more than the notebook of a poet – and it is much more than a notebook – it would still be very important in the whole scheme of Irish prose literature. A poet who knows and loves a period in the past and who has used that period to great account, here writes down in prose, marred by a crawling story and amateurish dialogue but ornamented by knowledge and love, the richness that the past as he sees it can bequeath to the imagination.'[13] Incidentally, the portrait of Queen Gormlaí in this novel shows that though Clarke sometimes portrayed women in the old Irish misogynistic spirit, as tempters and troublemakers, he also had a sympathetic insight into female psychology. There is supporting evidence for this in the poem 'The Young Woman of Beare' (which, according to Richard Loftus, may have served as a prototype for Yeats's *Crazy Jane* poems) and, on a very different level, the portrayal of the religious spinster Martha Blake:

> *Early each morning, Martha Blake*
> *Walked, angling the road,*
> *To Mass in the Church of the Three Patrons.*
> *Sanctuary lamp glowed . . .*

Clarke had trials and frustrations to endure in his long life – private emotional stresses, painful brushes with censorship and with officialdom in general, periods of relative neglect, a constant struggle to make a living which involved a certain amount of journalistic hackwork. His application for the Chair of English in Trinity College failed and instead the post went to H. O. ('Ho') White, described to me once as 'a safe man with a few friends on the Board'. However, Clarke did not lack either official recognition or private support, in spite of what is sometimes stated. In 1932 he won the national award for poetry in the Tailteann Games, and apart from being chosen a foundation-member of the Irish Academy of Letters in that same year, he was elected its president twenty years later when T. C. Murray retired; he was also president of PEN (taken very seriously in those days) from 1939 to 1942, and again from 1946 to 1948. He always had well-wishers and supporters, including not only fellow-writers and critics but also influential figures such as R. M. Smyllie of *The Irish Times* and loyal friends inside the corridors of Radio Éireann. Clarke unfortunately was not a gifted broadcaster, and his weekly radio programme on poetry became tedious and repetitive in its later stages; similarly his weekly 'lead' review in *The Irish Times* every Saturday sometimes degenerated into dullness, pedagogic nit-picking and sitting on the fence. At his best, however, he was a distinguished, erudite critic and essayist and his two books of reminiscence, *Twice Around the Black Church* and *A Penny in the Clouds*, are minor classics of their kind. All in all, he was a considerable all-round man of letters and one of the very few Irish writers of the time who insisted proudly on earning a living by his pen alone.

The pity is that when, in the later Fifties and Sixties, he was rediscovered by shrewd poet-critics such as Donald Davie[14] and Valentin Iremonger, the tyranny of a fashionable new aesthetic demanded that his work from 1917 to the early Forties should be more or less denigrated as outmoded and derivative, the product of a provincial environment and a delayed maturity. On the contrary, Clarke was quite precocious in his development and to downgrade the bulk of what he created between the two world wars in favour of the (highly uneven) crop of later verse is to leave him a shrunken figure, not an enhanced one. It also underrates the judgement of an era which was at least as sophisticated and discriminating as our own, and finally, it creates a vacuum in the literary life of at least two decades.

The case of Joseph Campbell does not quite belong in this context, since the date of his birth (1879) puts him among the generation of Colum, with whom he has much in common. He even shares with him the distinction of collaborating with Herbert Hughes in a song-lyric which has become virtually a folksong, 'My Lagan Love'. Campbell's studied simplicity, his devout ruralism, his apparently unquestioning religious faith, and a kind of four-square, tweed-clad decency and wholesomeness and absence of complication in his character, belong to that generation and mentality rather than to those of Clarke or Patrick Kavanagh. Yet he is often placed in the Clarke-Higgins camp and Clarke was one of the writers who visited him regularly in the last six years of his life, when he lived alone in a small farmhouse in County Wicklow, increasingly estranged from the new Ireland to which he had returned and finding that life in the countryside was no idyll but contained its own sordid or petty realities. It is a strange irony that one of the most enthusiastic celebrants of rural Ireland should have found the latter-day reality to be disappointing and even disillusioning.

Campbell was a Northerner, born in Belfast, and was active in Ulster literary life well before the first World War. Later he emigrated to London where he published several volumes of verse including *The Mountainy Singer*, a title which became virtually his coat-of-arms. *Earth of Cualann*, which Austin Clarke considered his best book, was published in 1917 while he was living in Wicklow with his wife. He was involved in the 1916 Rising and fought on the republican side in the Civil War, for which he was interned in the Curragh for over a year; when released he went to America, like Colum before him, and like Colum he discovered the American university circuit long before most other Irish writers did. Campbell lectured for a decade at Fordham University and also founded a School for Irish Studies, as well as editing the *Irish Review* as a continuation of the Irish-based original which had foundered in controversial circumstances some years before. He returned to Ireland shortly before the second World War and the war cut him off from his overseas contacts, nor did he mix much in Dublin literary circles, though he broadcast several times on Radio Éireann. Campbell's last years in Wicklow were solitary ones apart from occasional visitors, such as Seumas O'Sullivan and his wife Estella, and when he died from a stroke in 1944 it was some days before his cottage was entered and his body discovered.

For decades his poetry bulked large in Irish anthologies; at least two generations of school-pupils learned his lyrics by heart, particularly the one beginning: 'The silence of unlaboured fields/Lies like a judgment on the air . . .' Yeats included him in his Oxford anthology but allowed him only a single lyric, 'The Dancer', a poem which once was hugely popular yet today seems merely another Georgian anthology piece. Campbell's moral decency and earnestness are inherent in everything he wrote, and on his own limited terms he was a committed craftsman, but his vocabulary, though pure, is conventional and rather colourless and he had no genuine gift for imagery, factors which give most of his verse a basic thinness of texture. Louis MacNeice classed him with Seumas O'Sullivan and Colum: 'Their poetry lacks brain work, but they succeeded better than Yeats himself in some of the objectives which he had proposed for Irish poetry.'[15] Clarke greatly respected him and credits him with being 'the first Irish poet to use free verse effectively'[16] – a factor which may have been influenced by the fact that Campbell in his London years was in contact with the Imagist group headed by Ezra Pound. Clarke edited the *Poems of Joseph Campbell* which appeared, with the blessing of the Arts Council, in 1963 but made little stir at the time; nor have they made much since. Somehow, he seems embedded in his age and its sensibility, and though there has been some biographical interest in him in recent years,[17] his verse has somehow not come back into currency. When he died, he left a long poem in manuscript called 'A Vision of Glendalough', which is in blank verse and was published, in two parts, in the *Dublin Magazine* of July-September 1952 and October-December 1953. A strange, apocalyptic, almost Blakean work, it is basically a sustained meditation on Glendalough's historico-religious past and whole passages read more like the work of an isolated religious mystic than of Campbell the familiar, homely lyricist. It would be an interesting experiment to print this poem in the company of Roibeárd Ó Faracháin's 'The First Exile', dealing with Colmcille, and the poems by Patrick Kavanagh and Denis Devlin about Lough Derg.

Considering that the conventionalised picture of Irish rural life which Colum had created became virtually an official image of the Free State, like the early paintings of Seán Keating, it seems ironic that Campbell never profited from this and that for the greater part of his active career he was either an exile or an outsider. He was one of those youthful revolutionaries who never forfeit their ideals in later life, do not chase after official posts and state pensions, and guard their independence at whatever cost. The circumstances of his death alone are proof of this. But poetry, as Mallarmé said, is made with words, and Campbell in his obsession with plain, pure, simple speech ignored the basic fact that life – peasant life, urban life or whatever – is a complex business, not a simple one, and certainly not a pure one. The Modernist revolution in poetry was based largely on this tough-minded recognition of life's complexity and impurity, though in turn it created its own conventions and evasions; and in the post-war years in Ireland, especially the Fifties, the rural pieties of Colum and Campbell were less and less the reality which people saw all around them. In this case, at least, life certainly did not come to imitate art.

Yet latter-day accusations and dismissals of 'rural escapism' are often very wide of the mark, apart from the fact that from the 1930s onwards such fashionable judgements have also echoed imported Anglo-American values which are/were quite applicable to industrial economies, but have little relevance to the largely agricultural Ireland in which Campbell, Colum and the other Irish Georgian poets (for that is what, in effect, they were) lived and wrote. Land hunger had been the dominant economic reality for at least three generations, rural emigration was a grim fact, and to a large extent both the so-called War of Independence and the Civil War had been fought over land and agrarian issues – the first between the peasantry and their Anglo-Irish overlords, the second between the landless men and the propertied middle classes and strong farmers. These are simplifications, no doubt, in which professional historians may quickly pick holes, but they are simplifications which moved thousands of men and women in their time and shaped modern Irish history. Though Campbell, in particular, was very much a representative figure of his age who did not see beyond it, he had a genuine social conscience and cared deeply about the small Irish farmer and his struggles. He may have idealised the Irish countryman, but he did not duck economic fact; and if it were possible for him to come back from the dead and see the modern Ireland which has succeeded his own, in all probability he would be saddened to find that much of what he had lamented or condemned still exists. Much the same, of course, could be said of AE, another man often dismissed as a Celtic dreamer, yet a man who attempted to live his visions and to realise them.

The generation immediately after that of Clarke in terms of age includes Louis MacNeice, Patrick Kavanagh, Padraic Fallon and Patrick MacDonogh. MacNeice is a special case, since his career and most of his life were in an English context; his attitude to Ireland resembles that of an aristocratic White Russian who sees the country of his ancestors delivered over to crude, half-emancipated peasants and revolutionary ideologues on the make. As for Kavanagh, he became so much a cult figure in the 1970s and 1980s, and has become so burdened recently with commentary and even rhetoric, that at this stage little new can be said about him. Perhaps a shift in critical perspective over decades has led in his case to a situation comparable to that of Clarke; the poetry of his later Dublin phase has tended to overshadow the earlier, more Georgian Kavanagh. Yet that earlier poetry has a special early-morning glow and radiance; poems such as 'A Christmas Childhood', mingling bitter-sweet self-awareness with earthy primitivism, quickly won their place in Irish anthologies and seem destined to keep it. They have a quality comparable to Chagall's early, folksy paintings. Personally I think that the 'natural magic' of these poems will endure longer than the rather soured and bleary verse of Kavanagh the world-weary pundit of McDaid's pub, or his generally heavy-footed attempts at satire which badly lack verbal wit. On the other hand, the long narrative poem 'The Great Hunger' remains unique in modern Irish literature, though I suspect that Masefield's narrative poems may have served as one of its models. Its dourness and earthiness, interspersed with moments of illumination, were a necessary corrective to the glib, idealised ruralism of which Irish anthologies of the period are so full.

Padraic Fallon, born the year after Kavanagh (1904 and 1905 respectively), was one of AE's protégés as early as the Twenties and a regular contributor to the *Dublin Magazine* – its editor, Seumas O'Sullivan, became a close friend. Failure to publish in book form handicapped the rise of his reputation, though his extraordinary series of verse plays for Radio Éireann in the 1950s reached a wide audience which surprised the poet himself. (They are discussed in a chapter of Micheál Ó hAodha's *Plays and Places*.) Fallon was a West of Ireland man, born in Athenry in County Galway where the old Norman castle and abbey entered the visual and imaginative world of his verse. He inherited from Yeats and AE an interest in Eastern and Gnostic philosophy, while both Higgins and Clarke offered him examples for writing imaginatively about the Irish landscape. 'Mary Hynes', for years a familiar anthology piece, shows him still embedded in the conventions of the time, but rising above them by a certain innate energy. His post-war poetry, however, moved far from either the first or second generation of the Celtic Twilight, and it sometimes shows an almost agonised awareness of Western civilisation threatened by war and the new barbarism – particularly in 'Yeats's Tower at Ballylee', written when the Korean War of the early 1950s seemed likely to escalate into World War III. Fallon was influenced by French Symbolism, by Rilke and by Rimbaud (a major influence on many poets in the Forties) and marginally, in his late work, by American Modernism. However, the Dolmen Press only published his *Collected Poems* in 1974, after they had hung fire for some years, and by then he was an unfashionable figure, and rather an isolated one (he died a few months after the book appeared in print). It is only in the past decade that there has been a gradual recovery in his reputation. Seamus Heaney, in an eloquent introduction to the 1990 *Collected Poems*, wrote that it could now 'be seen to stand in secure and complementary relation to the achievements of Austin Clarke and Patrick Kavanagh' and that 'Padraic Fallon comes to us now as much a contemporary as he was when he began.'[18] No poet has tried more resolutely to find an accommodation between the mythic and the everyday, and in that field his example may prove potent in the near future.

In the recent *Field Day Anthology of Irish Writing*, Seamus Deane has acutely remarked that Fallon – unlike Colum, Campbell, Higgins and certain others – 'found an enabling myth and was, therefore, freed from the provincialism of his predecessors'. Catholic imagery came easily and naturally to him, but so did the world of classical mythology, and there is no obvious conflict between the two as there is, for instance, in Austin Clarke, who had to contend with both a certain inborn asceticism and a romantic, highly-strung sexuality. Commentators such as the poet-critic Eavan Boland have noted Fallon's utterly un-Jansenistic outlook and have been tempted to explain it as a throwback to the spirit of eighteenth-century Ireland with its mixture of folk vitality and high-spirited aristocratic rakery. The poet himself said more than once that growing up in Connacht at the time he did, he 'got the last of the eighteenth century'. Perhaps the most potent expression of this aspect of his poetic psyche is the final version (there are two earlier ones) of his radio play *The Hags of Clough*, where the folk element is combined with, or offset by, a metaphysical dilemma of the kind which Calderón delighted in. The travelling student or scholar, with the gift or curse of healing the sick from which he himself must not profit, is tempted by the love offered to him in full sincerity by the beautiful, wilful young aristocrat whom he has saved from her father's unconsciously incestuous desires. Written mainly in blank verse with a basic iambic beat, this extraordinary play suggests not only the parallel with Calderón already mentioned, but the Romantic theatre of Kleist and Grillparzer whose heroes often similarly contend both with fate and with their own passionate, idealistic temperaments. The Christian element of free will is implicit throughout, but the black-and-white of traditional morality offers the tormented student no real solace or resolution.

In recent decades, Irish criticism and Irish literary polemics have tended to stress the gulf between cultural nationalism and cultural internationalism – an obviously simplistic categorisation, since probably many or even most good writers represent some sort of pragmatic amalgam of the two. It is doubtful, indeed, if they can ever be separated or demarcated, and most thinking men and women are aware of the simultaneous demands which local and international issues make on them. Fallon has suffered from some rather ignorant denigration in this particular area, based largely on his early work but sometimes applied to the whole corpus of his verse. He was never, in fact, particularly nationalist in outlook, at least in the conventional sense, but he accepted his own essential Irishness and once, in a radio talk, suggested that rather too many contemporary Irish poets made it their chief ambition to write like English ones. In this he was probably referring to the fashionable subjection to Auden, a poet for whom he himself had a good deal of respect. He was swimming against the tide, however, since Anglo-Americanism remained the dominant mode in Irish verse for several decades and it was according to its canons of style and vocabulary that his own work was criticised in the final decades of his life. This myopia endured until very recently, when the full range of his mind and sensibility was slowly and belatedly recognised, his intellectual range and very personal – and original – balance of the popular and the esoteric. Padraic Fallon, in short, can now be seen as a pure-blooded, intrinsic modern, evolutionary in his development rather than revolutionary, but scanning far horizons which many of his contemporaries never glimpsed. Verbally, the only modern Irish poet he can be compared to for the energy and resource of his language is MacNeice, who in most respects is his polar opposite.

His close friend Patrick MacDonogh died when not yet sixty, a sensitive, much-loved man who held for years a high position in Guinness's Brewery and was also one of the inner *Dublin Magazine* circle. MacDonogh had a small output, which his fastidious taste made even smaller, and apparently all the poems he wished to survive are contained in the slim volume *One Landscape Still*, which appeared in

1958. They show MacDonogh to be the possessor of a refined, musical ear (the poem 'Silent Worship' has in fact been set to music) and also to have been a genuine Modernist in his acute awareness of life's frequent, inextricable mingling of ecstasy and frustration, and in his sometimes hypersensitive sensibility. Some of the war imagery in these poems is particularly moving. For years MacDonogh was a firm presence in Irish poetry anthologies (he also published poems in American and British periodicals) though Thomas Kinsella ignored him in his *Oxford Book of Irish Verse*. More recently still, however, the *Field Day Anthology of Irish Writing* has restored him to his former position. At the time of writing, it seems likely that a new collection of this fine, and neglected, poet's work will be published shortly. It seems long overdue; MacDonogh may not have the vitality or the sheer output of a major writer, but his is work which demands a hearing, in its quiet-voiced way.

Chapter 9

THE FRENCH CONNECTION

Ireland for centuries has had close links with France, politically, ideologically and culturally. As any school-pupil in this country knows, or at least used to know, the Irish for centuries looked to France for succour against England and French armies fought on Irish soil – St Ruth in Williamite times, Humbert in the French Revolutionary age. French republicanism supplied much of the ideology of the Ninety-Eight Rebellion; the Tricolour which eventually became the national flag was modelled on the French flag, and later, leading Fenians such as James Stephens took refuge in France. (France is also alleged to have transmitted its Jansenism to Maynooth through clerics fleeing from the revolutionary Terror.) It was from this Fenian ambience that the young Yeats derived his early nationalism, particularly through John O'Leary, and this was intensified by the hold exercised over him by Maud Gonne, who not only had links in Paris with Fenianism and the Irish Republican Brotherhood, but through her lover, Millevoye, was involved in the right-wing political movement led by General Boulanger.[1]

The entire origins of the Literary Revival are closely connected with France and it was in the West of Ireland home of Count Florimond de Basterot that its initial foundations were laid. George Moore was virtually half French by culture and temperamental inclination, as was Oscar Wilde; Synge lived in Paris for some years and did versions after Villon; Yeats's debt to Villiers de l'Isle Adam, Verlaine and others has been mentioned already; Edith Somerville had studied art in Paris and spoke French well. So both French Symbolism and French realism entered the bloodstream of Irish literature, while Joyce was French-speaking and instinctively Latin by temperament. Even James Stephens studied and learned French, though when he visited Paris he was chary of speaking it; by contrast, his friend Thomas McGreevy was entirely at ease there and eventually France made him a Chevalier of the Legion of Honour. Padraic Colum, though America was his chosen land, lived in Paris for a time during the 1930s. This Francophilia was carried on into the generation of Beckett, who wrote his mature plays in the language of his adopted country.

A similar situation is seen in the history of twentieth-century Irish art. Since the generation of Nathaniel Hone in the third quarter of the nineteenth century, Irish painters had looked to France and many of them studied or even settled there. In the 1920s Mainie Jellett and Evie Hone had gone to Paris to study Cubism under André Lhote and Albert Gleizes, an event to which some contemporary art historians date the beginning of Modernism in Irish painting. The influence of the School of Paris was strong on the annual Irish Exhibition of Living Art, founded in 1943, though by then of course Paris was in the war zone and contact with it was cut off for another two years. Even so, artists such as Nano Reid and Norah McGuinness – to mention only two painters very active in the IELA – were to a large extent formed by French Modernism; and in the immediate post-war years, the Victor Waddington Galleries showed some prominent French painters including Henri Hayden (actually a Polish Jew by origin, but thoroughly naturalised in France, and a friend of Beckett). Irish art critics of this period, including James White and Edward Sheehy, show an informed awareness of French painting and Louis le Brocquy, the most prominent Irish Modernist then after Jack Yeats, was largely formed by Paris Modernism (though sometimes filtered through London). Incidentally, both Yeats and le Brocquy were awarded the Legion of Honour, an honour they shared with Yeats's old friend McGreevy – poet, art scholar, critic for a number of publications ranging from the *Studio* to *The Irish Times*, and finally director of the National Gallery of Ireland from 1950 to 1964.

It was not only admiration for French culture, French political structures and French thought which inclined the Irish intelligentsia towards Francophilia. France offered, in effect, an alternative to English domination or at least a corrective to it. France was republican while Great Britain was monarchist, and the fact that both had colonial empires was often conveniently overlooked in this Irish exaltation of France as the home of liberty, equality and fraternity. France was also seen as the land of artistic modernism and innovation, while English culture – as exemplified by a writer such as Galsworthy – was often considered stodgy, inward-looking and insular (this outlook was not confined to Irish writers and artists, it was strangely common among British intellectuals and artists as well, notably those of Bloomsbury who were almost all snobbishly Francophile). The French were also the 'civilised' nation, supposedly adept in the arts of cookery, haute couture and erotic life – again, an attitude prevalent also in Anglo-Saxon lands, where Colette's novels for at least a generation were widely regarded as the final word in sexual freedom and sophistication. But on a very different level, France was, or had been, a Catholic country with a lively, even aggressive Catholic intellectual wing, a long and illustrious succession of Catholic writers from the Middle Ages down to Claudel, a flourishing Neo-Thomist movement as exemplified by the philosopher Jacques Maritain, and at least the remnants of a deep-rooted peasant piety which drew thousands of ordinary, unintellectual Irish people to make pilgrimages to Lourdes.

This last consideration is hugely important and applies even to agnostics such as Joyce, who was anti-clerical yet soaked indelibly in the Catholic liturgy and had been trained from his schooldays in Thomistic dialectics. Joyce without his early Catholic background is unthinkable, but Joyce without France – or at least Paris – is equally so. A certain basis of Latin rational scepticism and inherited Latin faith is inherent in his writings, and both of these are elements which Anglo-Saxon readers sometimes find unintelligible or simply boring. Apart from the centuries-old battle between faith and reason, however, another conflict reflected in a large sector of French writing was the inner war between asceticism and sensuality, flesh and spirit, the soul and the senses – a dualism at least as old as Christianity itself. This dualism was not peculiar to men of active faith; it is fought out memorably and poignantly in the pages of Baudelaire, a banned poet and an agnostic – but a Catholic agnostic, who resorts frequently to theological and liturgical imagery at moments of emotional stress. In English literature of the nineteenth and early twentieth centuries this fission was less obvious, partly because middle-class prudery and respectability forbade its presentation in any obvious form, but also because increasing materialism, scientific rationalism and religious indifferentism had blurred the boundaries of such a conflict. No doubt many or most commentators today will view this sometimes agonising inner division as a product of religious taboos and moral or physical inhibitions which are no longer relevant. The entire erotic area of human life today apparently has been sanitised and rationalised to an extent where, in the eyes of the majority, any hint of sexual guilt is little more than a personal neurosis. But is there any special proof that this phase of our thinking will last much longer than the socio-moral strictures and the categorical thou-shalt-nots of forty years ago? A glance at European history would suggest that sexual attitudes and mores have more often than not oscillated wildly from one generation to the next.

This is not the place to discuss it, but the battle between physical passion and ascetic spirituality is many centuries old and goes far beyond Christianity. It is commoner in the literature of the antique world than is sometimes realised, it underlies the gynaeolatry of the Troubadours and the writings of mystics such as John of the Cross, it is found in various Asiatic and Oriental literatures, and it received a new force and direction with the coming of the Romantic movement. Yeats's early poetry is full of it, though he made up for his youthful scruples and idealism with the flaunted sexuality of his old age. The writings of Austin Clarke reflect it strongly too, and to depict Clarke's internal conflicts as merely the clash between modern libertarian instincts and a repressive upbringing and society is surely to miss their significance and minimise them. No doubt late Victorianism and petit-bourgeois respectability, which lingered on longer in Ireland than in most European countries, did enhance such conflicts among sensitive and imaginative individuals, who sometimes suffered torments of conscience or frustration as a result. A small society which made marriage virtually an imperative, and aimed semi-consciously to penalise bachelorhood or spinsterhood through sexual starvation, was an unpromising field of battle for advocates of Free Love. There was not even the outlet – traditional in Continental countries – of prostitution, since from the late 1920s the Free State Government had campaigned actively against this and Monto, the old brothel quarter of Dublin, was demolished. With it vanished Joyce's Nighttown and a place of nocturnal resort for numerous Dublin writers and intellectuals; Austin Clarke describes its last days in *A Penny in the Clouds*.

Plainly French Catholic writers had greater freedoms and less censorship than their Irish counterparts, not to mention a larger, more sophisticated and more emancipated readership. The sexual, marital and adolescent dilemmas depicted in the novels of Mauriac, Bernanos and other ostentatiously Catholic writers of the Forties and Fifties were keenly and sympathetically read and studied in Ireland, as were the novels of Graham Greene, their English equivalent. Seán O'Faolain is the most obvious case of an Irish writer influenced by this particular vein of Continental Catholicism, but he is only one of many; Francis MacManus is another, and so, rather later, is John Broderick who became a personal friend of the great Julien Green. Conor Cruise O'Brien took the title of a Mauriac novel for his study of contemporary French and English novelists, *Maria Cross* (1952), which is also notable for a detailed analysis of the novels of O'Faolain in this same context. O'Brien did not confine himself to novelists, since he considered the work of two poets, Péguy and Claudel, and of the latter he noted: 'The strength of a truly Catholic poet, as a poet, is that he takes poetry, in its highest function, seriously. He can believe in its giving access to a natural world, because he believes in a natural world; more than that, he can fuse the great common symbols of his faith and his own private system of symbols into a poetry that is at once personal and general, emotional and spiritual.' One wonders how many English or American critics could have written that.

Sexuality apart, however, Irish Catholic writers also gained courage by noting the frequent political radicalism of their Continental counterparts – for instance, the fact that Mauriac and Bernanos both were hostile to General Franco, a stance which in Ireland would have been considered by many people as a betrayal of their faith. They saw that while Ireland's narrower stage and generally narrower outlook very often made it hard for the mass of people to disentangle genuine religion from an almost tribal tangle of politics and inherited prejudice, the Continental writer could do so more easily and also was braced into greater awareness and dialectical self-sufficiency by the fact that he was surrounded by entrenched anti-clericalism and by vocal intellectuals of the Far Left. In short, they saw that an intellectual Catholic was not necessarily and unavoidably committed to the Right, or to dogmatic conservatism, or to puritanism and moral fundamentalism. This sometimes put them at loggerheads with the clergy, always suspicious of any religious initiative or opinion which they themselves could not control or had not sanctioned.

Many of O'Faolain's public editorial stances in *The Bell* could hardly have been formulated without the example of the engagé French intellectual – and by no means the Catholic variety alone. The public position and prestige claimed by writers such as Gide, Sartre, Camus was both an inspiration and a source of envy to the Dublin intelligentsia, who were only too well aware that their own opinions would never reach such a wide public or carry so much weight with the ordinary reader. The fact that these men could, and did, fearlessly criticise public men and institutions, even their own governments and heads of state, for policies and statements which they considered to be wrong or immoral, was a proof that the French took their intellectuals seriously and did not confine them to the role of mere literary specialists. In Ireland, by contrast, few people were given such a public hearing outside bishops and politicians. This was not a question of censorship, it was rather a matter of the intellectual's limited prestige and of the sluggish brains of a public unused to the discussion of ideas.

It became almost fashionable, also, to contrast the allegedly adult, intelligent, self-aware Frenchman with the stereotype of the often dull, or inhibited, or blinkered Englishman – even when many or most Irish writers relied on London publishers to bring out their works, and were largely unknown in France. This attitude, however, was not confined to Ireland; a degree of cultural Francophilia was fashionable in England, where Cyril Connolly[2] and other influential literary journalists tended to write off the great Victorians as naïve and sentimental, and urged their readers instead to turn to Stendhal or Flaubert, and to throw out their volumes of Tennyson and face up to real, complex, modern life in the poems of Baudelaire. O'Faolain himself subscribed largely to this view, though since he was a man of considerable independence of mind he was not merely trucking to fashion by doing so. In *Vive Moi!* he wrote that French novelists were far superior to English ones in 'the moral sense', a concept which he defined as 'the intelligence at work on man-in-the-world. The great French novelists are great moralists in this sense.' Even the greatest English novelists, he thought, were 'far less trenchant than the French. We only have to compare, say, the moral sense of Thackeray and of Stendhal, or even of George Eliot and of Balzac.'

Twentieth-century French poetry was less influential in Ireland, at least directly, though Denis Devlin's translations, or rather versions, of René Char, St-John Perse and others sometimes reach a high level and are generally more impressive than his original verse. Devlin's engagement with French literature in general began when he was a student at UCD and wrote his M.A. thesis on Montaigne, and in the early 1930s he visited Paris where he met Beckett and various French literary men. He also met St-John Perse during the war years in Washington, where Devlin had been posted as a diplomat and the French poet was in exile from occupied France. Devlin married a French wife and was an intellectual Francophile all his life – which was much too short for all he might have achieved, since he died at fifty-one of leukaemia. A gifted linguist, he also translated Italian and German poets and was versatile enough to produce Gaelic versions of poems by Baudelaire and Eluard. His close friend Brian Coffey, who had studied philosophy under Jacques Maritain at the Institut Catholique in Paris, translated Mallarmé, Eluard and Gerard de Nerval and as a poet had roots in French Symbolism. Both of these men were distinctly Catholic in sensibility and the influence of the neo-Thomism of the 1930s can be felt throughout their writings and their intellectual stances; both of them, too, spent much of their lives abroad. As 'difficult' poets in their own right, each often chose difficult poets to translate and Devlin's versions of Char's gnomic, oracular imagery are possibly the best in English.

Louis MacNeice's superb translations of some of Louis Aragon's wartime poems should be mentioned (they appear in the large *Collected Poems* edited by E. R. Dodds for Faber and Faber after his death). Aragon's poems had been smuggled out of France during the years of the Occupation and since he was an active member of the Resistance, as well as a committed Communist, these war lyrics of patriotic sadness, exhortation and nostalgia enjoyed a strong vogue in England for a number of years. Some of them, incidentally, were also translated by the 'myriad-minded' polymath and churchman, An tAthair Pádraig de Brún, who published at least one of his versions in *The Irish Times*.[3] Long after the war, de Brún met Jean-Paul Sartre as a fellow-guest in the West of Ireland home of John Huston, the American film director, who had hoped that Sartre would write a script for him. As it happened, neither the director nor the writer-philosopher took to one another, but after talking at length in French with de Brún (whose name, naturally, meant nothing to him and whom he assumed was a local priest) Sartre is said to have exclaimed: 'If your curé is like this, what men your bishops must be!'

However, perhaps the most devoted group of Irish Francophiles were those associated with the *Dublin Magazine*, including its long-term editor Seumas O'Sullivan. His links with French poetry of the eighteen-nineties have already been noted, but O'Sullivan also translated de Nerval's play *Nicholas Flamel* – not only translated but completed it, since de Nerval had left it unfinished. This version was published in an early number of the magazine, and years later Austin Clarke had it performed by the Lyric Theatre, though the audience must have been a small one. O'Sullivan also managed to get some leading French authors to contribute to his magazine, including Paul Valéry who published a poem in it. One of its regular contributors was the lady who wrote poetry under the name 'Michael Scot' (Kathleen Goodfellow in private life) and translated Villon and other French poets, and who is believed to have subscribed heavily from her private means in order to keep the magazine going. Another was the famous Professor T. B. Rudmose-Brown of Trinity College, teacher of Beckett among many others, freethinker, bon viveur and famous talker, who appears in Moore's *Hail and Farewell* trilogy though without actually being named. One of the Dublin personalities of his age, he was a genuine connoisseur of French literature and also a personal friend of many French writers including the Symbolist poets Stuart Merrill and Francis Vielé-Griffin (both of whom, strictly speaking, were American).

Rudmose-Brown's Trinity lectures were famous and he was as enthusiastic in inculcating his students with a knowledge of French wines, food and topography as he was in bringing alive the classical authors to them. Racine was one of his special loves and he maintained that the proper poet to translate him into English was Yeats, whose style was best suited to reproduce 'the Racinian music'. But 'Ruddy', as he was called, did not confine himself to Racine, Ronsard or even the French Romantic poets up to and including Verlaine. He also included in his lectures and writings contemporary authors such as Gide and Proust and Valery Larbaud, the friend of Joyce. His influence on the young Beckett was enormous and it has been acknowledged not only by the latter's various biographers, but by Beckett himself.[4] Incidentally, excerpts from Rudmose-Brown's unpublished memoirs were printed in the *Dublin Magazine* in 1952, long after his death, edited by his and Beckett's mutual friend, A. J. ('Con') Leventhal, a French lecturer in Trinity and yet another literary Francophile. After his retirement, Leventhal moved to Paris and died there – a suitable end, and probably the one he would have chosen himself.

Apart from neo-Thomism, the intellectual quarrels between Gide and Claudel were followed with (sometimes sardonic) interest in Dublin, though Proust seems to have been known to relatively few Irish people until after the second World War. Existentialism made a considerable impact in the post-war years and one of its earliest and best-informed commentators was Arland Ussher, another *Dublin Magazine* regular and a highly versatile man of letters. Existentialism, indeed, for a while became almost an obsession – or affectation? – with a certain type of Irish undergraduate who used its jargon as others might use the jargon of neo-Marxism a decade later, or even the Beat sub-language common in the late 1950s and early 1960s. The distinguished philosopher Gabriel Marcel came to Dublin in 1959, on a visit sponsored by the Arts Council, and lectured in English – but on contemporary French theatre, not philosophy (he was, of course, a playwright himself).

At this time, there was a strong vogue for contemporary French plays; Jean Anouilh's *The Lark* made a considerable impact when it was performed at the Gate Theatre in 1956, with Eithne Dunne outstanding as Joan of Arc, and another of Anouilh's dramas was translated, or adopted, into English by Donagh MacDonagh under the title *The Fading Mansion*. The same playwright's *Ring Around the Moon* (actually Christopher Fry's adaptation of *L'Invitation au Chateau*) had been staged at the Gate in 1953, with Micheál Mac Liammóir playing both of the twin brothers with typical aplomb. Anouilh had a prolonged vogue with Dublin audiences during the 1950s, since in the same year *The Waltz of the Toreadors* was performed at a long-vanished venue by the visiting Belfast Arts Theatre, and actually ran a week longer than was originally planned. Giraudoux's *The Madwoman of Chaillot* was staged at the Olympia Theatre in 1955, with the Madwoman herself played by the versatile

Eithne Dunne; various others of his plays were given performances by dedicated fringe groups. When in 1956 Cocteau's witty *Intimate Relations* was staged – apparently in a rather inept translation – at the Olympia, A. J. Leventhal wrote in his capacity of theatre critic for the *Dublin Magazine* that 'Cocteau has had something to say all his life and the years have not dimmed the brilliance of his manner of saying it,'[5] though the veteran writer was rumoured to be still under a cloud because of his alleged friendliness to the Germans during the Occupation years. In 1957 Pike Theatre Productions, a company which has its firm place in Irish theatrical history, put on Sartre's heavily political *Nekrassov* at the Gate, in a double bill with a long-forgotten work *The Hut* by André Roussin, adapted by Nancy Mitford.

Perhaps the first milestone in this run of French dramas had come in 1948, when Mauriac's *Les Mal Aimées* was mounted at the Gate, in a version by a nameless translator. Though it would probably seem musty and irrelevant today, the play's sexual frankness made one newspaper critic complain of its 'boudoir scenes'.

This list of performances is not in any sense complete, nor is it intended to be; it merely mentions certain highlights in order to demonstrate how strong a footing contemporary French theatre had in Ireland at this time. Apart from the productions mentioned, plays by Sartre, Montherlant, Cocteau and other topical names were performed at small theatres by various fringe groups and by university drama societies, including Montherlant's *The Master of Santiago* which was staged effectively by the UCD Dramsoc in 1959. Another favourite of Irish amateur groups for several years was Claudel's *Le Soulier de Satin*. The Pilgrim Players, virtually forgotten today, dedicated themselves to bringing French plays to Dublin and Leventhal, in his quarterly *Dramatic Commentary*, several times paid tribute to their initiative. And as early as 1951 another amateur group, the Dublin Arts Theatre, had staged Anouilh's *Antigone* in a production praised by John Montague in *The Bell* magazine.[6] This play had a strong political relevance, since the war was still a recent memory and Anouilh was widely believed to be referring, under the guise of classical characters, to the situation in France under the Occupation.

This vogue for plays from overseas was not, of course, exclusively French since Italian, Spanish and American works were also performed during this period, not to mention the usual classics by Chekhov and Ibsen and Strindberg. It was essentially a delayed reaction to the war years and their immediate aftermath, and in any case there was a growing feeling against the Abbey and its often stodgy, repetitive home fare, which had begun to seem like a diet of porridge. Ireland was reaching out to other cultures and countries for stimulation and renewal. Yet France in general, and Paris in particular, still exercised a unique hold or spell on the Irish intellectual until well into the 1960s, when it became clear at last that Paris had lost its primacy, and was no longer an art capital or even an important literary centre. New York had taken its place as the world capital of art, while the increasing Anglo-American – more American than Anglo – domination of Irish literary circles and taste meant that ambitious young writers generally thought more in terms of invading the American campus circuit than of joining the intellectual discussions in the Dôme or the Rotonde.

Throughout the 1950s, however, the old Franco-Irish pull had remained strong, especially to men and women who had been shut off from the Continent by the war or by what they felt was cultural isolation. Painters, including the gifted Belfast artist Dan O'Neill, were frequent visitors to Paris, but writers too maintained the tradition; Anthony Cronin's classic account of his bohemian pilgrimage with the young Brendan Behan, in his book *Dead as Doornails*, speaks for an entire generation as well as for himself for whom it was still a kind of Mecca, as Rome had been in the days of the Grand Tour. The poet John Montague is exceptional in that he actually lived in Paris for some years; others spent only a few months, or even weeks there, while others again merely passed through. In any case, fewer of the Irish intelligentsia spoke French well than in the old pre-war days, when it had been considered virtually indispensable.

Paris, in any case, had become simply too cosmopolitan and polyglot for its own good and in the bars and cafés of Montmartre, Montparnasse and other fashionable or once-fashionable bohemian quarters, the foreigners now tended to outnumber the natives. In particular, the city had become the stamping-ground for innumerable Americans, many of them with literary ambitions or with plans for starting small magazines or editing fringe publishing houses. There was also a new type of deraciné bohemian who might show up in the arty pubs of Soho one week, the following week in Paris, and the third week at McDaids' pub in Dublin. A month later, he or she might well be in Madrid, Rome or Munich, consorting not with the native inhabitants of these cities but with fellow-bohemians, beatniks and fringe artists of all kinds. Most of Brendan Behan's cronies in Paris seem to have belonged to this category. Such a type plainly was parasitic rather than creative, a kind of cultural transit passenger, absorbing little of real value and contributing even less. The Joycean tradition of prolonged, voluntary, self-aware exile in France had gone, apparently for good, and though few people at the time recognised it, Beckett was in fact the last of his line. In this sense, the famous first night of *En Attendant Godot* at the little Theatre de Babylone in Paris on 3 January 1953 was, in retrospect, as much a terminus as a starting point.

Perhaps the last surviving outpost of French cultural influence in Dublin was in the cinema, though apart from a dedicated minority, Irish intellectuals for decades had been relatively slow to accept cinema as a valid art form. Though the great French directors had been active since the Thirties and even the Twenties, there were limited opportunities for seeing their work in Ireland, since the picture-houses remained determinedly philistine and the basic cinema fare was dominated by vacuous Hollywood commercialism and 'family entertainment'. Enthusiasts such as Liam Ó Laoghaire were pioneers of good taste and knowledge in this area, though it was many years before they won sufficient converts to raise the taste of both the public and the cinema-owners sufficiently for them to show and sit through films of real quality. The long-vanished Astor Cinema, a diminutive place on the Dublin quays near O'Connell Bridge, in the 1950s courageously showed the works of Jean Renoir, Jacques Tati, Jacques Becker, René Clair and many others, while a little later the Irish Film Society made it possible for Dublin to see the works of their immediate successors, the so-called *Nouvelle Vague*, then much talked about. 'Art cinema' had arrived, but it, too, soon became increasingly less French and more international. The old magic which the term 'French film' exercised on people for a generation was no longer potent; *Hiroshima mon Amour* and *L'Année dernière à Marienbad* were fashionably acclaimed in Dublin, but a less vocal but more thinking minority damned them as pretentious and boring. The cultural spell of France was already a thing of the past.

Chapter 10

THE THEATRE

The Golden Age of the Irish theatre is, almost automatically in everyone's mind, synonymous with the early years of the Abbey Theatre under Yeats and Lady Gregory. The fact that Yeats was not essentially a man of the professional theatre, and that Lady Gregory had no professional grounding in theatre management or production either, does not seem especially relevant to their historic achievements in this field. Neither of them was primarily a playwright, and neither seems to have followed closely developments in contemporary theatre on the Continent or in America, though it is true that in 1918 Yeats had organised the Dublin Drama League, with Lennox Robinson as his right-hand man, to bring in foreign plays and to encourage translations for the Abbey. The Drama League achieved some distinguished results, and it can be seen as the predecessor of the Gate Theatre, which was founded in 1928.[1] Yeats, however, did not favour such a broad, eclectic role for the Abbey, which he believed should be an Irish theatre first and foremost; otherwise, he feared, it might lose its uniqueness and eventually become like any other theatre. Though Yeats was certainly no cultural chauvinist, he put Irish plays and playwrights first and, in effect, gave a vote of confidence to native talent, present and future.

The early years of the Abbey are history and need not be rehashed here. After Synge's early death, undoubtedly the next major figure to emerge was Seán O'Casey – even the very best plays of Colum, Robinson, Murray etc. can hardly be put on the same level as the best of his. His three great works, *The Shadow of a Gunman*, *Juno and the Paycock* and *The Plough and the Stars*, were all produced between 1923 and 1926, in that order. The demonstrations against the last-named play were largely the work of a vocal handful of women who included feminists as well as nationalists, and they seem to have been rather a genteel affair, though Yeats – as he had done before in the Playboy riots – was quick to see their value not only as publicity, but as part of the Abbey's entire mythology.[2] What he had not comprehended was that by rejecting O'Casey's next play, *The Silver Tassie*, he himself was adding another dimension to that very myth.

After O'Casey's departure to England – in fact, he had already gone there when he learned of the rejection – the Abbey board rejected the play by Denis Johnston which took its title from the rejection slip: *The Old Lady Says 'No!'* He took it instead to the newly-founded Gate Theatre Company which staged it in 1929 at the Peacock, also newly founded and intended originally as an acting and ballet school rather than the Abbey's experimental stage. In effect, however, the Abbey had lost the most interesting of the new playwrights to the Gate, which took full advantage of its acquisition. The title obviously refers to Lady Gregory, who did not in fact like the play, but the real nucleus of opposition in the Abbey to Johnston appears to have been Yeats himself – though Johnston himself suspected Lennox Robinson, almost certainly unjustly.[3]

Shortly afterwards, the old Abbey duumvirate began to break up; Lady Gregory died in 1932 and in 1935 Yeats decided to create a bigger board, bringing in Higgins, Ernest Blythe, and Brinsley MacNamara as directors in addition to himself, Robinson and Walter Starkie. This was a significant change, not only in numbers but in the fact that Blythe, a professional politician and language-revival activist, was now within the inner circle of power and would stay there for a long time. He had been a Minister for Finance under the Free State Government, but ruined his political career by introducing a Budget cut in the old-age pension – which was already minuscule. As a minister, Blythe had negotiated with Yeats the arrangement by which the Abbey became virtually a state theatre with subsidies, while the Government in turn could nominate a director to the board. Yeats appears to have been fully aware of the risks he ran in all this, and is said to have remarked that since the writers had not managed to cope with political and financial pressures, it was time to bring in the bureaucrats instead. Blythe, however, was a capable administrator, a shrewd boardroom manoeuvrer, and had training and experience in financial matters which made him valuable. While Yeats himself lived, artistic policy remained largely in his hands and there were no serious challengers to him – though when the Abbey finally staged *The Silver Tassie* Brinsley MacNamara resigned in protest, finding the play 'blasphemous'. He was succeeded by Frank O'Connor, who at this period had stage ambitions and whose play *In the Train* was produced in 1937.

When Yeats finally went, Higgins was made managing director in his place, but he died prematurely in 1941 – worn out, it is said, by the strains of a demanding American tour a few years earlier. Before that, however, O'Connor – who had been bidding for power – had been forced off the board, where he and Higgins had been clashing head-on for some time.[4] So the way was now clear for Blythe to take over, which he did and remained as managing director until 1967. By the virtually unanimous verdict of modern stage historians, he presided over the Abbey's decline and its Dark Age, from which it has only recently recovered. The age of Blythe is associated indelibly with kitchen farce, unspeakably bad Gaelic pantomimes, compulsory Irish, and insensitive bureaucracy.

The case against Blythe is a heavy and probably an unanswerable one, though he has been defended in recent years by men such as Micheál Ó hAodha and Tomás Mac Anna, whose views obviously must carry weight; certainly I myself lack anything like the detailed knowledge to argue or discuss the matter in detail. Blythe apart, however, it seems likely that the decay in standards had set in earlier. There has always been a school of thought – though rather an underground one – which holds that the great days of the Abbey have been much mythologised and that though it almost always had a core of outstandingly gifted actors, many of its productions were pedestrian in quality and its 'stars' played too much to the gallery. Visually, too, its levels of production do not seem to have been high, though admittedly it is more than difficult to sort out such things with any distinctness from the contradictory, and sometimes almost incoherent, impressions of sixty or more years ago. Certainly the advent of Hugh Hunt in the mid-Thirties – he had been recommended to Yeats by John Masefield, whose verse plays were then highly popular – appears to have produced a higher level of production and stage decor. Hunt, in turn, brought in the talented designer, Tanya Moiseiwitsch, apparently as a direct counterpoise to Mac Liammóir's costumes and sets. Yet when the company toured America in 1937 a leading Transatlantic critic, George Jean Nathan, wrote in the December issue of *Newsweek*: 'Lovely and musical speech aside, the present Abbey Theatre company has put the dub in Dublin. Not so long ago one of the finest acting organisations in the world, it is now a caricature of its former self.' He particularly complained of Maureen Delany – always above reproach with Dublin audiences – for 'outrageous overplaying, winking, snorting and mugging that wreck any serious play she is in'. Two years earlier, in March 1935, Seán O'Faolain had written an open letter to Yeats which was published in *The Irish Times*. This severely criticised the Abbey for its declining standards and contrasted it with the Gate, where an adventurous, modernist policy was paying dividends and attracting the more intelligent sector of the theatre-going public.

So it seems that the rot had set in before Blythe, and that the vanity of individual actors and a general tendency to rest on past laurels were already corroding the rigorous standards of the theatre's earlier days. Lacking the impact of a great modernising producer-manager – above all, a great writer-producer-manager – the company tended to give the audiences what they wanted, and the tastes of Dublin audiences were traditionally broad rather than subtle. One of the Abbey's keenest critics from the inside had been O'Casey, who so annoyed actors and stage staff by his constant cavilling, unsought advice and general opinionatedness that in the end he was virtually ordered out of the theatre – an incident which obviously and very understandably rankled, and was probably a factor in his voluntary exile. O'Casey was sometimes a crank and frequently a know-all, in certain respects almost the caricature of an autodidact intellectual, but he had the instincts of a born dramatist, he was not a self-seeker and he was certainly not alone in his strictures. Austin Clarke, for instance, complained of the tendency of actors and actresses, even after intense coaching, to revert to the stereotyped 'Kiltartan' accent which they had inherited and to fall back on their old mannerisms. And Seán O'Faolain – who, admittedly, had little innate feeling for the theatre – found that when his play *She Had to Do Something* went on the stage, the hard work of the producer was soon forgotten as the actors turned it into standard Abbey farce.[5]

The rejection of key plays by both O'Casey and Johnston, after all, took place when Yeats and Lady Gregory were the ruling powers and both rejections signalled, or should have signalled, that the pair had probably been there too long and that Lady Gregory in particular was simply too old to recognise new talent. On the other hand, the Abbey was virtually their own creation, they had no obvious successor to whom they could turn it over, and Yeats's enormous prestige and shrewdness, as well as the power of his personality, made him immovable if not absolutely indispensable. In any case, when both were dead, Higgins and O'Connor merely intrigued against each other, showing that writers rarely agree among themselves; Lennox Robinson had ceased to count, and it was left for Blythe, a combination of politician, technocrat and ideologue, to inherit the power vacuum. In the meantime, the poet Roibeárd Ó Faracháin and Gabriel Fallon, a theatre critic and civil servant, were brought on to the board.

The departure of O'Casey to England deprived Ireland of its only living dramatist with a world reputation, but he had made numerous enemies both inside and outside the Abbey, he was a notoriously touchy personality with many *idées fixes* and ideological obsessions, and for some time he and the Irish literary world had been on collision courses. Although many of his admirers and commentators – particularly American ones – have propagated the familiar idea that he was largely driven abroad by narrowness, philistinism and prudery, that seems to be no more than half the story, or possibly less than half. Though he always kept a staunch core of admirers in his homeland, he sometimes estranged and irritated even his well-wishers, and by the time of his departure he had few friends left among Irish writers. Higgins, Clarke, Denis Johnston were all in varying degrees antagonised – which was not a matter of mere professional jealousy. O'Casey, in spite of his professed Communism, was never genuinely a team player and once Yeats had gone there was nobody whom he respected greatly, or who could have controlled or managed him for long. For many years after his departure he fought a long-range battle with Irish society (with which he became less and less in touch), the Church, the politicians, most of the writers, and of course the Irish theatre. This war of words was given lavish publicity in the Irish newspapers and by literary journalists in several countries; it proved hugely diverting to some people, infuriating to others, and eventually, rather boring and irrelevant to the majority of thinking Irish people who increasingly saw the playwright-exile as a survival from another era. O'Casey's powerful American supporters – several of whom inclined fashionably towards the Left and so were sympathetic to a man whom they saw as a rejected prophet, reviled for his political and anti-clerical views – repeatedly praised his late plays as misunderstood masterpieces, while Irish audiences and most Irish critics regarded them as a sad falling-off.[6] Gabriel Fallon, originally a friend and admirer of O'Casey's, later turned against him and became one of his most nagging and persistent denigrators.

There are, of course, some notable exceptions to this negative reaction, including the critic John Jordan who argued eloquently for the merits of O'Casey's later phase. On the whole, however, the majority Irish view has probably been borne out with time; O'Casey's late plays have scarcely entered the repertory, some of them were and remain total failures,[7] and his attempts at social criticism and satire grew increasingly, and embarrassingly, divorced from any sort of socio-political reality. Yet his efforts to create a kind of quasi-poetic theatre enriched by a symbolic, imaginative element and by high-coloured speech, were genuinely courageous in themselves and were generally misunderstood by a milieu which seemingly wanted only stage realism, or rather the conventions which passed for realism. (*Cock-a-Doodle-Dandy*, for example, seems strangely poised between imaginatively poetic farce and total kitsch.) In England, O'Casey no more fitted into the theatre climate of Noel Coward and Terence Rattigan than he would have fitted into the world of J. J. McCann-style farce. Indeed an entire chapter of his 1957 book of essays, *The Green Crow*,[8] is taken up by an onslaught on Coward and the kind of artificial West End comedy which, in O'Casey's eyes, he represented.

Dublin between 1920 and 1950 was an acutely theatre-conscious city in which stage politics, stage personalities, theatre gossip and scandals were read or discussed avidly even by people who cared relatively little for literature *per se*. Abbey acting stars such as F. J. McCormick and his wife Eileen Crowe, Micheál Mac Liammóir of the Gate, emergent figures of the new acting generation such as Siobhán McKenna and Cyril Cusack, Lord and Lady Longford of Longford Productions, were all public figures known to most people by sight, and even prominent citizens were proud to be greeted or saluted by them in the street. Sometimes it seemed as if the actors and the personalities counted for more with the theatregoing public than the plays themselves did. Certain key roles were argued over almost to duelling point, in public houses and in private; who had been the best Joxer ever, the finest Playboy, the most moving and authentic Pegeen Mike? Who was best in Wilde and Shaw, and why couldn't modern Irish actors do that kind of comedy better? Abbey and Gate first nights were social rituals, and the verdicts of theatre critics next morning were eagerly read and often irritably dismissed. Inevitably, then, the question will be asked: why did such a milieu not produce more memorable plays?

The obvious answer is that dramatic geniuses do not appear to order and that contemporary London and Paris were not rife with them either. Yet it is probably too easy to blame the conservatism or limited tastes of Irish audiences, the vanity and intrigues of actors, and the commercial reliance on kitchen farce and on repertory plays which could be repeated without much expense or rehearsal time. It has been said, over and over, that the Abbey in particular virtually ceased to be a literary theatre and became both narrowly national and dully ruralist. Yet a look at the list of productions suggests that most talented writers got their chance there, including many of the better poets and fiction writers. Brinsley MacNamara, for instance, had a number of plays produced at the Abbey which were widely praised at the time, even if they have since dropped out of the repertory (with a background as a professional actor, he naturally had a knowledge of the stage which few other prose writers possessed). O'Faolain, O'Connor and even Higgins (with a one-act disaster entitled *A Deuce of Jacks*) all tried and failed, while Austin Clarke's dramas never won more than a coterie following. Murray and Robinson, as has been mentioned already, had their best work already behind them by 1930, though Robinson's *Drama at Inish* (1933) remains one of his best-loved plays and is still revived from time to time.

However, let us start in 1939 when Yeats died. In that year the Abbey produced *Tomorrow Never Comes* by Louis d'Alton, *Illuminations* by Murray and *Fohnam the Sculptor* by Corkery. In 1940 it produced d'Alton's *The Spanish Soldier* which was set partly in the Spanish Civil War, and *Strange Guest* by Francis Stuart, with an elaborate stage setting by Anne Yeats. The following year came Clarke's *Black Fast* and *La La Noo* by Jack Yeats; in 1943, *Faustus Kelly* by Myles na Gopaleen, with his friend Liam Redmond in the title role, which ran for only a fortnight before it was taken off. Other productions in the 1940s were of plays by Roibeárd Ó Faracháin, M. J. Molloy, Roger McHugh, Bryan MacMahon, and (in 1950) Seamus Byrne's *Design for a Headstone*, which anticipated Behan's *The Quare Fella* in its theme of prison life and in its semi-revolutionary outlook.[9] Byrne's play caused a genuine stir at the time, almost provoking riots, and its literary quality was high enough for Micheál Ó hAodha to devote an entire chapter to it in his book *Plays and Places*. Plays in Irish included Mac Liammóir's *Diarmuid agus Gráinne*, a version of Molière's *Le Bourgeois Gentilhomme* by Blythe himself, and a translation from the Spaniard Benavente, then a European reputation. The Abbey's 'experimental theatre' staged works by Strindberg, Lorca (*Blood Wedding* and *The House of Bernarda Alba*, both in 1949, in versions by Eric Bentley), and the version by Seumas O'Sullivan of Gerard de Nerval's *Nicolas Flamel*, already mentioned.

Allowing for the inevitable, in-between padding of rural farces and repertory pieces, this does not read as an unduly restrictive or unimaginative choice. It does, at the very least, suggest that the Abbey was searching intermittently for new, challenging authors and was prepared to give talented writers their chance, even if in most cases their gifts ultimately proved unsuited to the stage. Several of the productions mentioned were by Frank Dermody, who had originally been a Free State soldier and was discovered at the Taidhbhearc Irish-language theatre in Galway, from where, after much wire-pulling, he was sent to Dublin with strict orders to study the Gate Theatre production style closely. Along with Ria Mooney, he gave the Abbey long service in the days when the Gate was more fashionable because of its more obvious modernity and visual flair.

In the 1930s it had seemed as if Paul Vincent Carroll would dominate the Abbey stage for decades, especially after *Shadow and Substance* (1937) had proved that clerical themes could be introduced there if handled with a show of sympathy and tact. However, in 1939 *The White Steed* was rejected – ironically, for anti-clericalism according to some sources – and in disgust Carroll took the play to New York, where it was well received and won the New York Drama Critics' Circle Award for the best foreign play of the season. Alienated from the Irish stage, Carroll did much of his later playwriting in Scotland and England, though *The Strings are False* had a remarkable run at the Olympia in Dublin in 1942, playing for over a hundred performances. Yet Carroll ultimately outlived his reputation and the age of Beckett and Behan soon made him sound conventional and emotionally evasive, where once he had seemed frank and almost daring. Today his plays seem rather more shadow than substance, and there has been no Carroll revival in the sense that Teresa Deevy, for instance, has enjoyed a minor resurgence of interest, although in the early 1930s their careers ran virtually in tandem. (Deevy, incidentally, was treated badly by the Abbey from 1942 onwards.) Seamus Byrne, after the noise and excitement over *Design for a Headstone*, virtually petered out with his next play, *Innocent Bystander*, and today is almost forgotten. So too is Maurice Meldon, killed in 1958 at the age of thirty-two by falling off his bicycle, whose *House Under Green Shadows* and *Aisling* made many intelligent people at the time see him as the Green Hope of the Irish theatre.

Blythe, or Earnán de Blaghd as he liked to call himself, was not an uncultured or an unintellectual man, but he does seem to have lacked true literary flair or insight; and his concept of an 'Irish national theatre' was a narrow one. He even called it, officially, 'Amharclann na Mainistreach', though as various people pointed out at the time, this strictly meant 'The Theatre of the Monastery'. By tying the Abbey to the language revival and virtually enforcing a knowledge of Irish on members of the company, he gave it an ideological baggage which it had never carried in the past. Yeats had been a cultural nationalist, in the wider sense, but he always put culture first and nationalism second, whereas Blythe transposed the order. Almost inevitably, the result was a blurring of standards, especially in the ghastly Irish pantomimes which most critics found particularly objectionable, and in which seasoned, respected actors and actresses were expected to debase their talents in order to amuse children or simpletons. When the famous fire occurred in July 1951, forcing the company to move to the shabby but larger Queen's Theatre, the joke became widespread that it was the first fire to light up the Abbey in many years. Yet the move to this former music-hall of 800 seats meant that its spaces had to be filled in order to keep going, and to get the audiences into it there was a reliance on bread-and-margarine writers such as J. J. McCann and Donal Giltinan. Behan's *The Quare Fellow* was rejected, then produced by Alan Simpson at the minuscule Pike Theatre in 1954, and was not staged at the Abbey until after it had become a London success. This production, with its dragging tempo, lack of visual sense and general heavyhandedness, was sadly typical of the Abbey's general decline in style and intelligence.

No wonder, then, that the American dramaturge Eric Bentley, reviewing Peter Kavanagh's *The Story of the Abbey Theatre*,[10] wrote intemperately, but probably with a fair share of justice: 'An integral part of the Irish legend is the Abbey Legend: the Abbey as the Globe Theatre of our time. What a comedown for the visitor to Dublin to see performances that would scarcely pass muster in a German Stadttheater! He feels himself the victim of a hoax, a gigantic hoax that has been written into the history books and engraved on the general mind.' He went on to mention specifically the inadequate time allowed for rehearsals, as well as the lack of real authority given to stage directors: 'In Ireland, the director is often only the chap who tells the actors how to avoid colliding with each other and where to stand. Or, more often still, where to sit . . . Scenery is a matter of repainting the standard box-set representing a kitchen. Lighting is something added at dress rehearsal pretty much at the discretion of a lighting man who has not read the play.'

Blythe, however, remained unmoved by hostile or even constructive criticism, sticking dourly to his curious balance of ideological programming and commercial opportunism. One of the last works of any significance produced during this Queen's Theatre period of exile was James Plunkett's *The Risen People* in 1958, although certain critics – including Micheál Ó hAodha – felt that it worked better in its original form as the radio play *Big Jim*. In that same year the Abbey also produced Denis Johnston's strange play about the Easter Rising of 1916, *The Scythe and the Sunset*, which has been warmly praised by Robert Hogan and others, but somehow it never seems fully to have engaged an audience's deeper emotions. Undoubtedly, most of the laurels for the decade belong to the gallant little Pike: for its staging of Behan's masterpiece, for mounting Beckett's *Waiting for Godot* the following year, and for its 1957 performance of Tennessee Williams's *The Rose Tattoo* which led to the actors appearing in court under a police prosecution for indecency.[11] This hearing became a *cause célèbre* at the time, and the acquittal of the cast was a definite step nearer to the general relaxation of censorship which came in the Sixties. The law was made to look silly, always the most effective way to combat censorship – particularly in Ireland, where ridicule traditionally kills.

It seems almost redundant to write here about the achievements of the Gate Theatre under Micheál Mac Liammóir and Hilton Edwards; Mac Liammóir, in particular, won a national position comparable to that of Jean-Louis Barrault in France, and even that august parallel does not do full justice to him. Yet ultimately the Gate earned its unique place in Irish theatrical (rather than literary) history more by the quality and sheer style of its acting and production, and the breadth and catholicity of its repertoire, than by the discovery of any new playwright of genius. Its chief native-born talent was Denis Johnston, for whom major claims are no longer made – the advent of Beckett in the 1950s more or less unseated him from his chair as the leading Irish playwright of the avant-garde. So when the Abbey is so often castigated for not finding another Synge or O'Casey, it is only fair to point out that nobody else did either, and perhaps none was to be found anyway?

For many years it was devoutly believed that Mac Liammóir had Cork ancestry and he even perpetuated this belief himself (or at least tried to) in his autobiographical *All for Hecuba* (1946). It is now established that his original name was Alfred Willmore, not Michael Willmore, and that he had as purely an English background as Noel Coward – who began his career beside him in their child-actor days.[12] Hilton Edwards was the son of an English colonial official, and originally had ambitions as a singer as well as an actor. The two first met at Enniscorthy in 1927 while touring with the great Anew McMaster, Mac Liammóir's brother-in-law; the following year, along with Liam Ó Briain who was a language professor in University College, Galway, they played a leading role in setting up the Gaelic-speaking theatre, the Taidhbhearc, which opened with Mac Liammóir's own play in Irish, *Diarmuid agus Gráinne*. Remarkably, he had learned his Irish mainly through attending classes in London and had also studied for a time at the Slade School, which gave him his grounding in visual art. Together they formed the Gate Theatre Company, enlisting the gifted actress Coralie Carmichael, and their first production – at the Peacock, since they did not as yet have a theatre of their own – was in October 1928. The play was Ibsen's *Peer Gynt*, never yet produced on an Irish stage because of the heavy demands it makes in casting and staging; Edwards played the lead role and was also largely responsible for the production, while Mac Liammóir had no stage part but designed the costumes and sets, which were quasi-expressionist and novel to Dublin. By fairly general consent, the result was a triumph and the group's second production was Eugene O'Neill's *The Hairy Ape*, which had not been seen before in either Ireland or England. Plainly, a new epoch had begun.

The eighteenth-century Assembly Rooms next to the Rotunda Hospital were converted into a theatre by a talented young Dublin architect, Michael Scott, and the Gate Theatre proper opened with an equally ambitious performance of Goethe's *Faust* in February 1930. Once again, the occasion was a triumph, with Edwards playing the title role and Mac Liammóir as Mephistopheles. The new theatre was a small one with a correspondingly small stage, and there was little room either for backstage operations or for storing sets. What the Gate had from the start, however, was a recognisable stamp of style and intelligence and modernity, and the two men who directed it had complementary qualities. Both in their way were excellent actors, though Hilton was essentially a versatile character actor rather than a matinee idol – which Mac Liammóir emphatically was, a Leading Man in the tradition of Beerbohm Tree and a magnetic personality on the stage, or off it. Edwards – though he had no previous experience of directing before *Peer Gynt* – was a master of stagecraft: in the words of his partner, 'it was he who introduced to Dublin methods of production, decor, and lighting, handling of mass effects, experiments in choral speaking, in scenic continuity, in symphonic arrangements of incidental music, of mime and gesture, hitherto barely understood.'[13] These qualities seem to have proved particularly effective in the production of Denis Johnston's *The Old Lady Says 'No!'*, which was influenced by contemporary German Expressionism and is a play which largely lives or falls by its production.

By contrast, Mac Liammóir was temperamental, brilliant, exceptionally intelligent and intuitive, socially adroit, histrionic, multilingual and multi-gifted, with a genuine visual flair; he was also, of course – in his youth at least – exceptionally handsome, and as much a prima donna as a Leading Man. From the start, a personal mythology grew up around him, which he did nothing to discourage, and the press and public could never have enough of him and his doings. 'Meehawl' was a household name throughout Ireland, a personality whose autograph was eagerly collected and whose pronouncements on almost any subject were sure of a public airing. His professionalism, however, was just as committed and demanding as Edwards's and he had a genuine breadth of culture, speaking five languages fluently if not correctly (according to his own description).[14] Mac Liammóir was also a natural-born sophisticate and cosmopolitan, qualities which were particularly valuable at a time when so many Irish public figures had a homespun style totally lacking in panache or colour, and when the Abbey was widely regarded as being too folksy and too ploddingly nationalist. In fact, Ireland, or at least Dublin, was at this time in an 'internationalist' mood – the type of reaction which recurs at intervals and has already been described in the case of T. C. Murray, who was virtually swept aside by it. In the words of Edwards in his *The Mantle of Harlequin*: 'Theatrical revolution was in the air. Just as the Abbey had been swept along on the tide of naturalism, not in itself a native product of the soil, so the Gate bore a more obvious evidence of foreign influences. The Gate, although it has presented many plays by Irish authors and on Irish themes, is not a national theatre. It is simply a theatre. Its policy is the exploitation of all forms of theatrical expression regardless of nationality. It embraces, upon occasion, the naturalist play, but its concern has always been with the whole gamut of the stage.'[15]

It was precisely this cosmopolitanism, or eclecticism, which helped to give the Gate a very important aspect of its appeal – its snob value. It attracted people who disliked what they saw as the semi-official rural ethos, the sometimes dull, sometimes strident nationalism and the petit-bourgeois tone of de Valera's Ireland (not to mention its religiosity), and who felt themselves to be social and cultural sophisticates disinherited or sold short in such a backward society. This was not true of Mac Liammóir himself, a man who was a connoisseur of good living, with an almost unlimited sensitivity to all forms of social nuance, but who also possessed the common touch and whose devotion to the Irish language and the Celtic Revival was absolute. In fact, Mac Liammóir's personality was a highly eclectic or composite one, made up of various facets which at first glimpse might seem incompatible: it contained elements of Wilde and the Nineties, Yeats and the Literary Revival, the rhetorical, full-dress style of Beerbohm Tree and the brittle modernity of Jean Cocteau, Aubrey Beardsley alongside Michael Arlen – together, of course, with a certain leavening of homosexual high camp. To a large extent, he was his own greatest creation and of all the many roles Alfred Willmore played in his long, memorable career, perhaps the most brilliant and sustained was that of Micheál Mac Liammóir, Ireland's laureate of the theatre and cultural envoy-extraordinary abroad. To paraphrase Voltaire, if he had not existed, nobody could have invented him.[16]

To counterpart the great duo themselves, the Gate had excellent actresses in Betty Chancellor, Coralie Carmichael and Meriel Moore. Mac Liammóir's Hamlet appears to have been a memorable role, still remembered vividly by many people a generation later, though he was equally capable of playing knockabout farce in *The Drunkard* or the down-and-out Gyppo Nolan in *The Informer*. In the mid-Thirties there was the famous episode in which the teenage Orson Welles insinuated himself into the company and made a remarkable Dublin stage debut playing the lead role in *Jew Suss*, a chapter of his life which figures prominently in all Welles biographies. He did not stay in Ireland long, but he absorbed a great deal of the Gate methods and ethos, both in acting and production, as he himself admitted years later. The sheer professionalism of Mac Liammóir and Edwards was a revelation to him and he never lost touch with them over decades. Another eminent guest actor was James Mason, who eventually more or less gave up the stage for the cinema.

However, it is the quality and range of the plays produced which really weighs most in the balance, and particularly when we bear in mind that the Gate was a small theatre with small financial and other resources, they are remarkable in themselves. They included fourteen Shakespeare plays, eleven of Shaw's (including the complete *Back to Methuselah*), six by Wilde if Mac Liammóir's adaptation of *Dorian Gray* is counted, seven by Eugene O'Neill, three by Denis Johnston, two plays and a translation by Yeats. Besides recognised classics by Ibsen, Chekhov and Strindberg, their Continental dramatists included Pirandello, Cocteau, Anouilh and the Czech writer Karel Capek, whose *The Insect Play* was adapted by Myles na Gopaleen; and apart from O'Neill, there were American plays by Thornton Wilder, Lilian Hellman and Arthur Miller. The Irish contemporaries, besides Johnston and Mac Liammóir himself, included Mary Manning whose *Youth's the Season*, produced when she was in her mid-twenties, was one of the most striking first plays of the 1930s, Austin Clarke, Lennox Robinson, Padraic Colum (with his odd, exotic *Mogu of the Desert*), Donagh MacDonagh, T. C. Murray, St John Ervine. There was also a good proportion of frankly theatrical plays, by Coward, Kaufman and Hart, and various run-of-the-mill playwrights who are forgotten now. Literary merit was not always the criterion, since Mac Liammóir and his partner were above all men of the professional stage.

In the mid-Thirties, the Gate split into two virtually independent companies. This happened after Edwards and Mac Liammóir had taken other members of the company on a tour of Egypt which was disapproved of by Lord Longford, then chairman of the Gate board and the theatre's main financial support – for several years, in fact, he had picked up the bills. In their absence Longford went ahead on his own and ended by forming his own troupe, Longford Productions, which played at the Gate for six months of every year while the partners used it for the other six. The plays written by Longford himself and by his talented wife, Christine Countess of Longford, are 'of their time', a polite or euphemistic way of saying that they have become dated, though Christine Longford had a neat sense of social satire rather in the Lennox Robinson vein. Lord Longford was a knowledgeable enthusiast for the English Restoration dramatists and for Sheridan, Farquhar and Goldsmith, and he also produced a translation of the *Agamemnon* of Aeschylus which it might be interesting to compare with the better-known version by MacNeice. Shakespeare also was staged, so were Marlowe, Webster, Molière, and of course Wilde and Shaw, as well as Ibsen and Chekhov. The standard of these productions was generally below that of Mac Liammóir and Edwards – in fact, they sometimes had almost a village-hall flavour, but the idealism and commitment of Longford and his wife were generally respected and they bravely, and regularly, faced the gruelling round of provincial touring. Playing in local halls and similar settings, often mouldy or semi-decrepit, their company – together with that of McMaster – gave many people outside Dublin their first taste of real-life theatre in a time when the commercial cinema dominated everything. Finally, when Lord Longford died in 1961, his widow handed back the theatre to the old partners/rivals, who in turn made her chairman of the board. It was an admirable gesture, but by then the two elder statesmen scarcely had a theatre company any longer.

During the war years the Gate company took seasons in the much larger Gaiety Theatre, where several of its most successful productions were staged. It also toured regularly, going to the Balkans on the brink of war, and playing regularly in Belfast where it was respected and liked; after 1945, it took off abroad again. Here Mac Liammóir's multilingualism and social gifts were a major advantage, while both he and Edwards kept up an enormous range of contacts in many countries, both personal and professional. In 1949 this led to their one-time novice actor, Orson Welles, now a world figure in theatre and cinema, calling on their joint talents for the film of Shakespeare's *Othello*, in which Mac Liammóir played Iago, with Welles in the title role. Mac Liammóir's account of this spun-out episode in his *Put Money in thy Purse*[17] is a classic of its kind; much more than the twilight-and-tinsel texture of his plays, it shows the real Mac Liammóir – debonair, cosmopolitan, witty, intensely sensitive to other people's moods or feelings and to 'atmospheres', feline in his subtlety and his edge of malice. Yet vanity, narcissism, bitchery and clique-mongering were often the negative side to the Gate's undoubted stylishness, and there can be little doubt that its later years were as much an artistic decline as the Abbey's were. Perhaps Hilton and Michael (as they were usually called, both in public and in private) were victims of battle fatigue; perhaps they saw the public tiring of them a little as they aged; perhaps they discovered, like so many idealists in the arts, that high endeavour may win plaudits from critics, but does not bring the crowds – or the money. Certainly in the Fifties there were times when discontent seemed as common with the Gate as with the Abbey, giving birth to a number of half-forgotten movements or groups such as the Globe Theatre Company, built around the actors Godfrey Quigley, Norman Rodway and Denis Brennan and the producer Jim Fitzgerald. By fairly general consent, the standard of production in Dublin had by then become generally low, though shortage of money presumably had much to do with this.[18]

So the Gate did not, in retrospect, manage to find a new playwright of genius any more than the Abbey did, and it should not be used as a stick with which to beat the older theatre for lack of creative nerve. Denis Johnston was probably its major discovery, while the Abbey found dramatists of calibre – but not greatness – in M. J. Molloy, Carroll, O'Byrne, all of whom were hailed as major figures when their early works were staged. Perhaps, without paradox, it could be said that the great Irish playwright of the era was an American, Eugene O'Neill.[19] His plays had been produced in the 1920s by the Dublin Drama League and in 1927 *The Emperor Jones* was staged in the Abbey with Lennox Robinson as producer; in the following two years *The Hairy Ape* and *Anna Christie* were produced by Hilton Edwards in the Peacock, with settings by Mac Liammóir, and in 1931 Edwards both produced and acted in *Where the Cross is Made* in the Gate. In 1934 the Abbey staged *Days without End* in a production by Lennox Robinson and with a cast which included M. J. McCormack, Eileen Crowe, Maureen Delany, Shelagh Richards, Barry Fitzgerald and May Craig – an impressive roll-call of acting talent. In 1936 Longford Productions achieved a coup when it mounted the first European performance of *Ah, Wilderness!* with a cast which included Cyril Cusack, and two years later the Gate Company triumphantly produced *Mourning Becomes Electra* with a lengthy cast which, curiously enough, did not include Mac Liammóir, though he designed the sets. He did, however, act in the Gate's 1942 presentation of the same play at the Olympia Theatre, though not in subsequent productions there of *The Emperor Jones* and *Anna Christie*.

Other O'Neill plays followed; *Desire under the Elms* at the Gate in 1944, and in 1948 the first production in the British Isles of *The Iceman Cometh*, produced by the young P. J. O'Connor (the latter work, though staged at the Gate, was not performed by its own company). Finally, in 1959 came the famous production at the Abbey of *Long Day's Journey into Night*, by Frank Dermody with Tomás Mac Anna's sets. This was enormously successful and acclaimed, at a time when the Abbey's fortunes were sinking, and it was later revived.

Though the Gate never staged an O'Neill play later than 1953, over the years it had mounted no fewer than eleven productions of his works, including revivals – a number surpassed only by its productions of Shakespeare, Shaw and Wilde, and greater than those of Ibsen, Strindberg and Chekhov. O'Neill become virtually an Irish writer by adoption, since Irish versions of his plays were also performed at the

Taidhbhearc in Galway, and some of them were broadcast on Radio Éireann. It is one of the most remarkable facets of Irish theatre life in the whole period, yet it is rarely given the attention it deserves. What is also interesting is that though O'Neill was a daring and controversial writer in terms of his time, whose language shocked old Joseph Holloway and some newspaper critics, his work provoked no incidents or organised protests and both public and critical responses to it were usually positive as well as serious. Undoubtedly the elements of Catholicism and guilt were crucial to the special power he possessed over Irish audiences; undoubtedly, too, the almost claustrophobically Irish family sense in *Long Day's Journey* was a theme well suited to the emotional register of Dublin theatregoers. Yeats had been characteristically shrewd and calculating when, on the recommendation of a friend in America, he brought *Days Without End* to the Abbey, in the hope that its religious theme would buy some goodwill from that section of the Catholic hierarchy which disapproved of his theatre as irreligious. It did so, and turned out to be a considerable success in Dublin after failing in New York.

Yeats's admiration for O'Neill was genuine, however, and not mere opportunism. He invited him to become an associate member of the Irish Academy of Letters and when O'Neill won the Nobel Prize for Literature, Yeats expressed his delight 'because I have the greatest admiration for his work'. Somehow O'Neill never visited Ireland, but he had been an admirer of Synge and T. C. Murray since he had seen the Abbey perform their plays in America before the first World War.

In the face of such formidable activity, can it really be maintained that the Thirties and Forties were decades dominated by kitchen comedy and insularity? There was certainly a lot of the former – the figures are there to prove it, but in all likelihood the average Irish kitchen farce was no worse than the typical West End society play or any stock Broadway commercial production. The last two genres may habitually have been given slicker treatment and a more expensive staging, but in terms of literary and dramatic content probably all three were equally negligible. What at least cannot be denied about the Forties, in particular, is the sheer volume of theatre productions in Dublin, world war or no war. Writing in 1942, Gabriel Fallon surveyed 'Theatre for Forty-two' and pointed out: 'During the last twelve months plays were produced at four principal Dublin theatres – Amharclann na Mainistreach, the Gate, the Gaiety and Olympia. Our playgoers have had productions proffered to them at the approximate rate of one and a quarter plays per week, a rate which is considerably higher than the pre-war one.'[20] In other words, instead of war and isolation shutting the doors of Irish theatres and leaving their stages in darkness, they had brought a higher level of theatrical activity than ever before. It was not the only field in which outer darkness produced an almost defiant burst of creativity from within.

What should never be overlooked – though quite often it is – is the contribution which Radio Éireann made to drama over several decades. Brendan Behan wrote at least two plays for radio; Austin Clarke wrote several which are small classics of their kind; James Plunkett's play *The Risen People*, which made a stir at the Abbey in the 1950s and has since been successfully revived, was probably finer in its original radio version, *Big Jim*. These are only some of the highlights in an intensely creative age of broadcasting, and the history of Irish radio drama fully deserves a chapter to itself. Another was the remarkable series of poetic plays, some of them with a mythological setting, which Padraic Fallon wrote for RÉ, starting with *Diarmuid and Gráinne* in 1950 and including *Steeple Jerkin*, *The Hags of Clough*, *At the Bridge Inn* and several more.[21] Most of them were broadcast more than once, and a number were later produced on the BBC Third Programme, though they did not achieve the exceptionally high level of production they were given on the Dublin station.

The impact Fallon's work made on radio listeners can be gauged by reading the contemporary newspaper critics, though the number of listeners who heard them with genuine absorption must by now have dwindled to a minority of ageing people. They fully bear out the poet's own claim that radio offered a new and imaginatively challenging platform for poet-playwrights. The Radio Éireann Repertory Players were then widely held to be the best company of radio actors in Europe, and the RÉ Drama Department included people of calibre such as Micheál Ó hAodha, James Plunkett, P. J. O'Connor, and Dan Treston. Later, in 1962, Ó hAodha's adaptation of *The Weaver's Grave*, a short story by Seamus O'Kelly, won the internationally famous Prix d'Italia, while Treston later won it with his play *Piano in the Liffey*. But already by then, with the coming of Irish television, the golden age of radio drama had passed and there has been no obvious revival of it since.

Chapter 11

THE LITERARY PUBS

The days of the Dublin literary pub are already becoming a kind of legend, and they belong to yesterday or even the day before yesterday, though perhaps for a variety of reasons rather than for a single, dominant one. In retrospect they did not, in fact, have a very long life – scarcely more than forty years. Yet they are as interwoven into the cultural, intellectual and social life of the period as Vienna's coffee-houses are with its golden age, or the classic cafés and bars of Paris are with its great period from the years just before the first World War to the decade after the second.

Yeats did not go to pubs – there is a legend that he once asked Higgins, who was his semi-official guide to low life in Ireland, to take him to one in Dublin so that he might experience, or at least observe, the phenomenon at first hand. Higgins obeyed and led Yeats into a suitable tavern. Having stood or sat near the bar for a short while, looking about him attentively like a man in a zoo, Yeats said imperiously, 'Higgins, take me away!' whereupon the younger poet hurriedly finished his pint of Guinness or bottle of Bass No I Ale, and led Yeats out into the night. Had the older man altogether forgotten the convivial evenings of his youth at the Cheshire Cheese in London, or alternatively, had he remembered how his early friends Dowson and Lionel Johnson had drunk themselves virtually into the gutter and the grave?

If there is any solid foundation for this anecdote, the probable location was either the Bailey, the Palace Bar in Fleet Street, or Toner's in Merrion Row. Or, just possibly, it may have been some 'local' of Higgins's in the Rathfarnham-Templeogue area. He himself was a convivial, sometimes copious drinker, although tradition credits him with rather a poor capacity for holding his drink. Seumas O'Sullivan, by contrast, was a more staid, gentlemanly tippler who could quietly lower half-glasses of whiskey, produce an elegant bon mot at the proper interval, and without any obvious effort drink Higgins (and many others) into incoherence if he chose. His training as a chemist also enabled him to recover very quickly when it became necessary to do so.

The Bailey was frequented during the 1920s by a set of people which included the Gaelic writer Piaras Béaslaí, but its chief luminary was Gogarty who went there often after his day's surgery. It was a handy, central location and was used by many passing writers and intellectuals, as well as being for a time a favoured haunt of Liam O'Flaherty's. The Bodega in Dame Street, later renamed the Ouzel Galley and now vanished, stood just off the covered passage between that street and Merchant's Arch, giving access to the quays. Those entering it from Dame Street first went down a short flight of stone steps with a hand rail, and inside there were up-ended barrels to emphasise that this was a good, no-nonsense tavern. It was not at all squalid, however, and the fastidious Seumas O'Sullivan and various of his *Dublin Magazine* contributors often met there on Saturday mornings or at noon. Even George Fitzmaurice, odd, shy and gnome-like, sometimes joined them though he rarely attempted to take part in their quick-moving talk. When such sessions ended, O'Sullivan might cut through Merchant's Arch to browse through the bookshops and book-barrows which virtually lined the quay from O'Connell Bridge to the Metal Bridge.

The Palace Bar in Fleet Street emerged as a writers' pub rather later than the Bodega, which had been popular since the Twenties. It has been fortunate to have its vintage period recorded visually by a talented New Zealand-born cartoonist, Alan Reeve, whose depiction of one of the Christmas parties there has been reproduced many times and in many places (a large reproduction hangs still in the virtually unchanged back bar, though the original ink drawing is in the National Gallery of Ireland). This was done in 1940, before wartime shortages had bitten deep, though in any case Ireland never suffered from severe beer rationing, and whiskey could also be had. Wine rarely was drunk in pubs, but women – who were only welcome in certain lounge bars and hotels, though working-class women had their shut-off wooden snugs – might ask for port or sherry. There are no women present in Reeve's drawing, however. The Christmas drink was a general practice, but the proprietor of the Palace, Bill Aherne, made it into a special occasion in which for an entire evening, or at least for several hours of it, regular patrons could drink anything they liked and as much as they liked, on the house. The central figure in Reeve's cartoon is the massive, Chestertonian one of *The Irish Times* editor, R. M. Smyllie, but there is a remarkable assembly of writers present: Austin Clarke, Higgins, Brinsley McNamara, Padraic Fallon, Seumas O'Sullivan, Patrick Kavanagh, Brian O'Nolan *alias* Flann O'Brien *alias* Myles na Gopaleen, Francis MacManus, M. J. MacManus, Donagh MacDonagh, Roibeárd Ó Faracháin, Leslie Montgomery ('Lynn Doyle'), Ewart Milne. A sprinkling of visual artists includes the painters Harry Kernoff, William Conor and Seán O'Sullivan, and the sculptor Jerome Connor. Liam Redmond is the only actor present. Various *Irish Times* staff people sit or stand about, including Smyllie's successor as editor, Alec Newman, and a few 'characters' such as the gentle, eccentric and charming John Chichester. There are also various laymen – civil servants and others – whose names mean little today. All in all, it was a distinguished gathering which Reeve set down, and he has put himself on the far left of the picture.

Just across the intervening width of Westmoreland Street, in the continuation of Fleet Street, was the Pearl Bar, now long closed. Since it was advantageously placed almost directly opposite the (side) editorial entrance to his newspaper, Smyllie held court there when he had had a falling-out with the staff of the Palace, and vice versa. The clientele tended to be much the same in both places, though in the post-war years the Pearl attracted its quota of visiting Americans and British journalists, and there were rather more staff men from *The Irish Times* including W. J. (Jack) White and Bruce Williamson, both of whom were published authors in their own right as well as highly capable journalists. Women soon found their way there, though it was a long time before it was considered quite proper for a woman to enter a public house unchaperoned. Gus Weldon, the owner of the Pearl, was pious and ultra-respectable, but he knew better than to censor the behaviour of his customers unless they got completely out of hand – in which case they were banned, temporarily or for good.

Nearby on D'Olier Street was the Red Bank, which was also a restaurant and was on two floors. For a time in the post-war years its comfortable, almost luxurious upstairs lounge-bar became popular with writers, including the poets Patrick MacDonogh and (on occasions) Valentin Iremonger, until the dismissal of a favourite barman caused many of them to forsake it. From this desertion it never quite recovered its old status, although the rather bleak back bar downstairs was favoured by certain personalities such as the columnist Seamus Kelly ('Quidnunc' of *The Irish Times*) who once had an altercation with the staff of the Pearl Bar and never set foot in it again. The Red Bank marked a kind of intermediary or halfway house between *The Irish Times* and the rival *Irish Press*, whose ambience lay strongly over such quayside drinking spots as the Scotch House, with its great glowing, old-fashioned stove. Here in the 1950s you might meet the novelist Benedict Kiely – who was also literary editor of the *Irish Press* – the short-story writer Séamus de Faoite, and sometimes Brian O'Nolan/Myles, whose peregrinations might cover half-a-dozen or more bars in a single evening. Though he had his cronies in various places, he tended more often to sit alone in silence over his glass, black-overcoated and outwardly morose. If he felt that the bar service was slow or inadequate, he made a point of saying so.

McDaids of Harry Street became recognised as the bailiwick of Patrick Kavanagh, who tended to meet interlopers and newcomers there with his own special glowering, bespectacled stare. This milieu has been so well described by Anthony Cronin in *Dead as Doornails* that it is almost superfluous to discuss it here. Cronin himself, John Ryan the editor of *Envoy* magazine (when he was not attending to his own restaurant and bar in the Bailey), the critic John Jordan, the poet Pearse Hutchinson, were all regulars and sometimes painters such as Patrick Swift or Seán O'Sullivan might add to the numbers. Myles came there too, though he was scarcely a regular; so did Brendan Behan, although the rivalry or bad blood between him and Kavanagh tended to set up tensions which sometimes became explosive. It was a classic Dubliner-versus-culchie clash of personalities and while Kavanagh thought Behan a 'bowsey', Behan in turn called him 'the Monaghan wanker' and similar names. Admittedly Behan, at a certain stage in his drinking, might become unmanageable or vituperative, so that a number of Dublin pubs found it necessary to bar him altogether. Behan, however, also had his own working-class or semi-underground 'butties' with whom he drank in spit-and-sawdust houses in the Liberties or far down the quays, or sometimes in the market pubs around Smithfield which opened in the early morning. He was also to be seen sometimes in Neary's of Chatham Street, though the presiding genii of this house were the trio of Myles, Seán O'Sullivan and the great clown and comic, Jimmy O'Dea – joined sometimes by the half-crippled journalist Paddy Matthews, one of Dublin's very best conversationalists. Since the back entrance of Neary's opened on to a laneway which gave access to the Gaiety Theatre, there were often actors and actresses grouped around that end of the marble-topped bar.

'Davy Byrne's moral pub', on Duke Street, had long since passed into new hands, and from being a rough, old-style public house with bare wooden tables, much frequented by the rowdier type of student, it became in the post-war era one of Dublin's earliest cocktail bars, which also served edible food instead of the tasteless sandwiches and indigestible pork pies which were the staple fare of most other houses. Another notable innovation at Davy Byrne's was that in a period when lager was still widely regarded by Irish pint-drinkers as a dubious foreign substance, the management introduced genuine Spatenbrau beer from Munich, on draught. It also paid Cecil Salkeld, artist, writer and stage-designer, to paint the rather meretricious but suitably sybaritic murals which are still there and in which a Silenus-like figure was supposed to represent Shaw, and which helped to give the front bar its curious character. At one time, too, a number of Jack Yeats paintings hung on the walls. Davy Byrne's was never, strictly speaking, a literary pub but it did attract painters including George Campbell, Patrick Collins and various people from the nearby National College of Art in Kildare Street; it was also attractive to actors and actresses, who liked its arty, well-appointed, quasi-cosmopolitan style. A number of academics from Trinity College also found it convenient, as did their students.

Along Merrion Row, O'Neill's fulfilled the role of a drinking place for the Gaelic intellectuals, notably the scholar and academic David Greene, and George Fitzmaurice occasionally went there too, veiled in his usual quasi-anonymity. Farther south, over Baggot Street Bridge, were the pubs which Patrick Kavanagh frequented, including the Waterloo Lounge, and further south again was Reddins of Donnybrook where Myles/Brian O'Nolan often drank. These, however, were outer territory, since relatively few of the regular drinking intelligentsia were prepared to cross the Grand Canal from the city centre. Cultural Dublin was, in effect, bounded by the Nelson Pillar at one end and by Stephen's Green at the other.

North of the Liffey were the pubs frequented by the staff of Radio Éireann, then based in Henry Street at the back of the GPO, and by the actors and actresses of the Abbey and Gate Theatres. Since Radio Éireann employed bona-fide writers, actors, broadcasters, news staff, scriptwriters and musicians, either as staff members or as contributors and dependants, it was a small but intense world of its own, often ridden by internecine feuds and factions, but also with a genuine core of talented, witty people many of whom had a high degree of all-round culture. Gerry Dwyer's of Moore Street and Madigans nearby were liable to be crowded by RÉ people. They rubbed shoulders with the Moore Street traders and butchers who talked among themselves in their broad Dublin ('Dubbalin') argot. But probably the quintessential RÉ pub was the Tower Bar in Henry Street, close to O'Connell Street, where visiting BBC people usually drank with their Dublin colleagues and you might encounter Louis MacNeice or W. R. Rodgers, or even both of them together. Here Padraic Fallon, up from Wexford, drank with Roibeárd Ó Faracháin or Francis MacManus, both of them high in the Radio Éireann hierarchy, or with Seamus Kavanagh who was held by a number of people to be the wittiest and most amusing man in Dublin. Austin Clarke might occasionally be seen here too, after his weekly poetry programme, as well as various literati and journalists who came to hear and join in good conversation or simple gossip. Actors from the Abbey Theatre might also drop in, to mix with their colleagues of the Radio Éireann Repertory Company.

The Abbey people had various favoured drinking places in their own immediate area, including Dorans of Marlborough Street, and Tommy Lennon's long-vanished pub where the popular proprietor was famous for his judgement of new plays – it was said that after a first night he could almost always predict quietly whether one would succeed or fail. Farther north, opposite the Gate Theatre, was Groome's Hotel, which had a special status since it was possible to drink after normal hours there, and an entire clientele of politicians, journalists, writers, socialites and career drinkers went there nightly, as well as actors and producers. There were also, of course, the old hotels such as the Dolphin and Jury's, which offered good food as well as excellent bar service and were particularly popular with visiting BBC men and London journalists in the 1940s and 1950s, because they offered large steaks and other food items then unobtainable in Britain under wartime and post-war rationing. The classic Dublin restaurant, however, was Jammet's with its rich French-style cuisine, although its prices put it out of the range of most people except for special occasions. Special literary and artistic dinners were held there and it was one of the very few places where visiting international celebrities might be brought without loss of face. The tiled back bar – sometimes compared to a Victorian lavatory – attracted its own clientele, including Seán O'Sullivan.

Dublin pub conversation generated its own myths. Louis MacNeice has written of the 'cold gaiety' of the Irish intellectual, while V. S. Pritchett thought Dublin the most malicious city in the world. By contrast, James Plunkett always maintained that visitors failed to understand the native 'exuberant cynicism', which was not expected to be taken too literally or to denote any special malice – rather like Swift's definition of satire as 'a ball which is bandied to and fro, and every man carries with him a racquet, to strike it among the company'. Literary pub talk tended to be erudite, cynical, epigrammatic, personalised, occasionally bitter or malicious, often anecdotal or referential, sometimes bawdy in an all-male way, and sometimes genuinely witty or amusing. The sharp, cerebral quality which was a legacy from the days of Yeats, Moore, Eglinton, etc. and which is recorded in the pages of *Hail and Farewell*, lived on for at least another generation after them. Certain pages in Flann O'Brien's *At Swim-Two-Birds* reproduce its quality perfectly. Gossip, of course, was almost always welcome, and was sometimes retailed in a spirit of disinterested malice. Sometimes the wit was forced or flat, the anecdotes were too long or too prosily told, and outsiders were easily bored by the succession of inbred jokes or stories and by the long-winded raconteurs who buttonholed them for hours at a time. In fact Patrick Kavanagh, who himself was a confirmed literary pub-goer, defined most Dublin conversation as 'tiresome chatter between journalists and civil servants'.[1] Like Myles/Flann, Kavanagh had little taste for the give-and-take of repartee and preferred to deliver himself in monologues to his cronies.

Always touchy and rather lacking in *savoir-faire*, Kavanagh had gone through certain experiences which must have left their mark on him. On one occasion, during his early years in Dublin, he bought a broad-brimmed black hat of the kind worn by Smyllie, Higgins and others (the prototype for this was supposed to have been G. K. Chesterton) and with it jammed on his head entered the elite back bar of the Palace, where the literati were already in session. As he emerged through the door linking the front bar with the inner one, the assembled writers and journalists looked up, gave him first an astonished or unrecognising stare, and then broke out into one roaring, spontaneous laugh. Kavanagh, stung in his vulnerable ego, swung about and vanished, after which the Palace rarely saw him.[2] He was, however, present on another occasion when Louis MacNeice was drinking there with friends, and Kavanagh acted the role of agent provocateur by singing loudly and discordantly, to an Irish ballad tune: 'And go yez forth to labour/For Faber and Faber . . . .' According to the journalist Lionel Fleming, who was present, uproar and disorder ensued.[3] Pub rows and even fights were quite regular occurrences and one of the most notorious also occurred in the Palace – though in the front bar this time – when Higgins was rebuked by a fellow-poet who alleged that he was (verbally) bullying Austin Clarke. Higgins, who was sometimes bellicose in his cups, grew even more belligerent and was floored by the other poet with a right hook to his large stomach; then Brinsley MacNamara lumbered up from his bar stool to intervene, and was knocked down in turn.[4]

Kavanagh, in spite of his large, bony physique, was a poor fighting man and went in fear of Behan, who was a noted brawler until he grew overweight – he was believed to have fought man-to-man with and beaten (probably in the Bailey) Liam

O'Flaherty, who prided himself on his toughness. Their quarrel grew bitter after Kavanagh's long-drawn, much publicised libel action against the *Leader* magazine, during which he denounced Behan from the witness box and Behan, in turn, was blamed (wrongly, as it turned out) for an act of treachery which helped to swing the jury against the poet.[5] According to Austin Clarke, it came to a head one Saturday in the Pearl Bar when Behan attacked Kavanagh, but was thrown out by the combined bar staff. As it was approaching the Holy Hour which began at half-past two, Behan simply waited outside in a Fleet Street entrance or doorway until the pub emptied for the ritual break, then emerged and closed in again for his revenge. Kavanagh, with no stomach for a fight, turned and ran down towards Pearse Street with Behan pounding behind him; but Kavanagh's legs were longer and he gained a lead, swinging off to the right up Westland Row. Here he claimed the ancient right of sanctuary by running up the steps of Westland Row Church and, looking desperately around the interior, noticed that a confession box nearby was empty and had the curtains drawn back. He shot inside it, pulled the black curtains across for safety and remained there for a least half an hour until danger, and Behan, had receded.

It was in the Pearl Bar, too, that an incident is supposed to have occurred involving Dylan Thomas which was described to me by two eye-witnesses, one of them now dead, though I can find no record of it either in Thomas's own letters or in biographies of him. He and his Irish wife Caitlin, visiting Ireland in the immediate post-war years with their American friends Bill and Helen McAlpine, came at some stage to Dublin and climaxed a hard day's drinking with a session in the upstairs bar of the Pearl, among the usual literati and assorted hangers-on. By late in the evening both Thomas and Caitlin were very drunk and she got up to go to the women's lavatory, where she spent a long time. When she did not return, Thomas grew hysterically jealous and claimed that she had smuggled some man with her inside the cubicle. In spite of efforts to hold him back, he insisted on fetching a stepladder and climbing over the door to look down where she sat slumped in a semi-coma on the lavatory seat (a variant of this story has Thomas running out into the night and climbing the railings of the public lavatories in College Street, beside the Thomas Moore statue).

Pub arguments and even fights, however, were not merely the outcome of personal spites and grudges, or simply of too much alcohol. Feelings over literary matters ran high, free-verse poets might argue vehemently with traditionalists, admirers of Auden and Pound might attack more nationalist-minded writers, leftists might clash verbally with conservative Catholics, one clique might sneer at another, rival clique, and so on. Alliances and friendships were sometimes shifting ones, and there was always literary envy as a spur – even if it was aroused by something as trivial as another man getting work as a book-reviewer in some London weekly.

Cyril Connolly, in his capacity as editor of the literary magazine *Horizon*, travelled to Ireland in the depths of the war years and noted that Dublin literary society placed 'a sixteenth-century value' on conversation, but tended to keep apart from women. The Palace Bar seemed to him 'a male stronghold' and at first entry 'as warm and friendly as an alligator tank', but he went on to praise its habitués for being 'as witty, hospitable and kind a group as could be found anywhere. The Palace Bar is perhaps the last place of its kind in Europe, a *café litteraire* where one can walk in to have an intelligent discussion with a stranger, listen to Seumas O'Sullivan on the early days of Joyce or discuss the national problem with the giant, Hemingway-like editor of *The Irish Times*. Here one may also gather varieties of anti-British opinion, and see the war as a bored spectator, as a pro-Petain intellectual Catholic, as a pro-German, anti-Semitic Kerryman, as an Anglo-Irish Protestant disillusioned with England.'[6]

In her book about Ireland, *Mind you, I've Said Nothing* – a work which nowadays seems relatively lightweight and meretricious, but made a brief stir in the early Fifties – Honor Tracy recorded an evening visit to the Pearl Bar in its vintage days. Almost inevitably, the first personality she noticed was 'Bertie' Smyllie: 'Vast, genial, he would sit there hour after hour, his comfortable frame shaking with laughter at the sallies of his companions, and draw sagely at his pipe; but should one enter whom he really wished to avoid this seemingly inert, apparently rooted mass would suddenly vanish.'[7]

She and her English escort – who was there to 'meet Dublin intellectuals' – were immediately joined by 'one of Dublin's major poets, with a thirsty look on his face. He was glad to depend on our kindness that evening because the confidence he felt in certain racehorses had turned out to have been misplaced.'[8] This, presumably, is a reference to Patrick Kavanagh, who was a dedicated backer of horses and usually managed to lose – even when the money was not his own, as was often the case. He launched into 'a diatribe against Ireland and all her works, her passion for mediocrity, her crucifixion of genius: he lamented the passing of his best years among marshmen and Firbolgs: he threatened to shake the dust of her off his feet and to seek his living henceforward in strange places among foreign men.'[9]

Meanwhile, the Pearl regulars were arriving: 'In trotted a gnome with a face like a bottom and his hair *en brosse*, celebrated even in Dublin for the malignant venom of his attacks on all and sundry. Next came an Anglo-Irishman of letters with a mad light in his pale eyes, carrying with an air of decision and importance a briefcase that bulged with sandwiches and pyjamas. A literary editor with an air of gentle, refined melancholy about him. More poets. Some playwrights. Lawyers. One gaolbird. Civil servants. Some of this crowd showed signs of incipient persecution mania, due to their having in fact at some time or other been persecuted. A drunk reeled from one table to the next trying to find someone who would listen once more to a tale of ancient wrong. A little haze of cigarette smoke settled over the room. The bar boys ran hither and thither with their trays like men distracted.'[10]

Though the writing is journalistic and clever-clever, the overall picture seems accurate enough and several of the personalities described are at least half-recognisable. What is chiefly obvious, however, is that the Irish literary pub and its characters were very much 'copy' and no book of such a type could be written without taking them into account. In little more than a decade, however, most of the people described – including Smyllie himself, who died the year after Honor Tracy's book appeared – had vanished or dispersed, and the Americans and others who made literary pilgrimages to the Pearl found few genuine writers either to see or to accost there. The Dublin literary pubs mostly vanished with the coming of the Television Age, and are now as much a thing of the past as the epoch of the Café Nouvelle Athènes where, in the 1870s, young George Moore had gazed and listened pop-eyed to the conversation of Manet, Duranty, Villiers de l'Isle Adam, Degas and their peers.

Chapter 12

THE IRISH LANGUAGE

Next to the failure to curb emigration – the factor which, more than any other, disillusioned so many people with the road which national independence had taken – the greatest tragedy of modern Ireland is surely the failure to revive the Irish language. It vastly outweighs such period issues as censorship, the ultimate importance of which has been much overplayed. Its social and political importance scarcely matters here; its cultural role, however, can hardly be exaggerated. 'Gan tír, gan teanga' may have been as simplistic and one-sided a slogan as today's revisionists claim, but it has more than a core of truth. Formerly oppressed nations such as the Poles, the Czechs, the Finns, the Icelanders, the Hungarians have succeeded either in holding on to or reviving their ancestral languages, and minority races such as the Catalans, the Basques, the Flemings and even the Bretons have refused, in the face of heavy pressures, to let theirs die. Israel has successfully made Hebrew its national language in spite of the fact that a large percentage of its citizens had grown up speaking Yiddish.

It is scarcely necessary to underline how vital and central a role the language revival played in the Literary Renaissance. Yeats is almost alone of the major figures in his near-complete failure to learn it, so that he relied on Lady Gregory, Hyde, Frank O'Connor and certain others to inform him on it and convey as much of the Gaelic essence as they could. Yeats was, of course, a bad linguist but George Moore, who was a better one, similarly failed to learn Irish and had to have his short stories translated (according to Yeats's malicious account in *Dramatis Personae*, Moore had hired a native speaker to tutor him, but each time the man called at Ely Place he was told that Moore was out). Lady Gregory spoke and read Irish fairly fluently, and her versions of the old Gaelic myths were a potent influence on two generations; Hyde, it goes without saying, was the founder (or more accurately, one of the founders along with Eoin Mac Neill and certain others) of the Gaelic League. Synge learned Irish relatively late in his short life, but it was one of the elements which triggered off both *The Playboy* and *The Aran Islands*. O'Casey learned the language in his green-piper days, and never forgot it in exile; so did Austin Clarke and many other writers of his generation. Joyce, once again, stands outside this argument, but it seems to be increasingly recognised once more that the 'Celtic' element in his writing always remained strong – Joyce is not the out-and-out, deraciné cosmopolitan which today's wishful thinking tries to make him.

Anglo-Irish writers of the generation of Louis MacNeice and Elizabeth Bowen generally either ignored the Irish language or were vaguely hostile to it, though the entirely un-Irish John Betjeman, during his years in Dublin, made a point of learning it (I have seen a letter-card from him, addressed to an Irish literary man, written in fluent Gaelic and with excellent Gothic lettering in the old style).[1] Patrick Kavanagh knew little Irish and frequently derided those who did, though this seems to have been a typical Kavanagh tactic of making a positive virtue out of a personal shortcoming or blind spot. Brian O'Nolan/Flann O'Brien/Myles na Gopaleen is almost a classic case of ambivalence. Though he had studied Irish for his own degree in UCD, he regularly derided the Bicycle Clip Brigade of Gaelgeoirí, the (often Dublin-based) type known in the countryside as Law Braws and Taw Shays, and in *An Béal Bocht* he wrote the classic send-up of the Gaelic Establishment with its cult of often illiterate Irish-speaking peasants and its sanctification of the Blasket Islands school of writing.[2] He also expressed very rational doubts about the feasibility of reviving spoken Irish, the considerable gaps in its development since the seventeenth century, and its often-cited lack of an adequate vocabulary for expressing and coping with the modern industrial age. Yet he himself wrote it with considerable flair and brio (at the beginning, it should be remembered, 'Cruiskeen Lawn' was written exclusively in Irish), and he was capable of becoming quite surly towards any hint of West Brit condescension towards it. It is a familiar reaction among Irish intellectuals – a ready denunciation of national foibles, weaknesses and double-think, yet outrage towards any outsider who dares to criticise those without rights of cultural citizenship. The Irish, traditionally, are their own bitterest critics, yet almost inevitably they resent similar criticism when it is voiced by non-Irish journalists and intellectuals. Myles himself noted the national tendency towards paranoia, yet few have manifested it as strongly as he did.

The importance of Hyde's *Love Songs of Connacht* for two generations of Irish poets has been mentioned already. Without them, Colum, Campbell, Higgins, the early Padraic Fallon, and numerous others could scarcely have written as they did. But another, equally potent influence was Kuno Meyer's *Ancient Irish Poetry*, which dealt with poems in a style very different from exuberant folk balladry – the spare, allusive, epigrammatic style of the Bardic writers and of the early Irish nature poets. Meyer had a fastidious and scholarly mind, but he also had a good metrical ear, and his versions were probably influenced in turn by German translations of Oriental poetry – a tradition going as far back as the early German Romantics. In that, he was working along lines not dissimilar from those of Arthur Waley and Ezra Pound.

In recent years, leading Irish poets – notably Seamus Heaney and Thomas Kinsella – have concerned themselves deeply and committedly with the fortunes of the language, whether as translators, essayists and propagandists, or in their own original work. Another poet, Michael Hartnett, caused a stir when he announced that he had abandoned writing in English and intended to produce only Gaelic verse in future. In his play *Translations* Brian Friel has imaginatively recreated the crucial moment in Irish history when Anglicisation set in terminally and Gaelic became a minority tongue. These eminent examples do not stand alone; they appear to represent a strong contemporary mood or trend. So far from receding into the mists of forgotten promises and abandoned hopes, the Irish language stays obstinately in the foreground of intellectual, cultural and literary debate. Seemingly it cannot be revived on a nationwide scale, yet equally it refuses to die. (And is it some sort of pointer to the times that some of its most vigorous and vocal proponents today come from Northern Ireland?) It remains, along with all-Ireland unity, the nation's great piece of Unfinished Business.

That so many writers have concerned themselves with the issue is hardly surprising, nor can it be put down simply to literary nationalism, romanticism or chauvinism. There is, of course, a certain pathos or glamour about something which is inherently valuable and even beautiful, yet seemingly doomed, and this appeal is particularly strong to a writer who has a sense of the past and of historical and cultural continuity. When Wittgenstein, on a pre-war visit to Dublin, noticed the various signs in Irish and was told the language was dying in spite of attempts to revive it, he commented: 'It is always a tragic thing when a language dies. But it doesn't follow that one can do anything to stop it doing so. It is a tragic thing when the love between man and wife is dying, but there is nothing one can do. So it is with a dying language.'[3] As an intellectual outsider who spoke several European languages and was as fluent in English as in German, he could afford to be philosophically detached; but for the Irish writer, the matter was bound up with his very identity and self-expression (one wonders if Wittgenstein would have been quite so philosophical if attempts had been made to stamp out the German language).

Language, after all, is the writer's material and vehicle of expression, and since Gaelic was the written and spoken medium of communication in Ireland for well over a thousand years, the matter affects them deeply and directly. As Thomas Kinsella has said drily but unanswerably in print on a number of occasions, it is a serious matter when a nation loses its language. Kinsella, at least, can speak as someone who has studied Irish literature in depth and so for him it is not a *terra incognita* or a *terra perdita*; but for the average man and woman in this country, that literature is something he or she had to learn in school and was usually glad enough to discard afterwards. Probably even an under-educated English person is capable of quoting a line or two of Shakespeare from memory, but the average Irish person is unlikely to remember anything from Aodhagán Ó Rathaille. And of the many university-educated young Irish people today who can trot out an Eliot, Auden or Sylvia Plath quotation, relatively few will be heard quoting from Seán Ó Ríordáin. In short, the majority of educated people in this country today are cut off – whether by choice, circumstance or upbringing – from familiarity with most of the classics of their native literature. Probably many of them never think of it as such; Irish literature for them goes no farther back than Yeats. Even Kinsella's phrase (which he has used as a title for a book) 'The Dual Tradition', can mean little to such people since they are largely unconscious of this dualism.

The Irish State's first Constitution, in 1922, defined Irish as 'the national language', which of course did not infer that the speaking or teaching of English was to be downgraded. Compulsory learning of Irish at school – that bugbear to many people in future years – was not introduced until 1928, and not until 1934 was it necessary for a pupil to obtain a pass in the subject in order to pass the Certificate (Primary, Intermediate and Leaving) examinations generally. There was considerable pressure to conduct infant classes entirely in Irish, and even to teach all subjects at higher levels 'through the medium'. From the start, the main weight of the effort to revive the language was expected to come from the schools, since only in the Gaeltachtaí and in the households of a minority of enthusiasts was it possible to learn it in the home and from the cradle. That they failed, or at most achieved only a very limited degree of success, is now common knowledge. Even if the teachers had been good enough (and many of them seem to have been only a few lessons ahead of their pupils), even if the tendency to favour written examinations over oral ones had been less ingrained, and the obsession with grammar at the expense of conversational fluency had been less persistent, the odds were stacked against restoring Irish on a national scale. The native speakers were a small minority – at the turn of the century they had amounted to less than four per cent of the population of the whole island – and the adult world into which pupils were soon projected was not so much hostile to speaking Irish as largely indifferent to it. The 'taw shay mahogany gaspipe' jibe of the ordinary Dubliner was fairly typical of the country's attitude at large. The overall situation was officially acknowledged in a Department of Education report for the year 1928-9:

> While it may be taken for granted that the revival of Irish cannot be effected without the co-operation of the schools, the question whether the schools' unaided efforts can accomplish this purpose is another matter . . . In many districts in which Irish is being well-taught in the schools, the language has little existence outside the school walls, and as far as the general use of Irish is concerned, little progress seems to have been made in the last few years. It appears to be true that very few pupils speak Irish outside school hours, and a still smaller number can be classified as Irish speakers a few years after leaving school. The Irish they have learned is lost in the amount of English which they have to deal with on leaving school. English is the language of their sports and pastimes and one of the means of earning their livelihood, while Irish remains a school subject closely allied to lessons and examinations. Under such circumstances it is inevitable that a very considerable part of the work done by the schools must fail to bear fruit, and failing help from outside, it may well be that the revival of the language may prove to be beyond their powers.[4]

In short, the majority of Irish people did not care enough for Irish to bother speaking it in daily life, even if they had been able to do so. No amount of cavilling at West Brit snobberies and attitudes, no amount of historical alibis, no passing the blame back to the inadequacies of the education system and of Irish bureaucracy, can ignore the fact that the language was to a great extent abandoned by the people themselves. This was, and still is even today, a bitter pill for the Gaelgeoirí to swallow, yet the conclusion seems unavoidable. There was no major objection on a popular level to making it a Sacred Cow, a national ideal or aspiration, but there was considerable if mostly passive resistance to forcing it back into daily life and daily usage. Many ordinary citizens rationalised this in economic or utilitarian terms ('What use is it anyway? Sure it's only a dead language') while others suspected that it was something foisted on them by a minority of cranks and enthusiasts, or even by self-seeking careerists who were on to a good thing. Others probably felt that in a country where emigration was endemic, Irish would prove an obstacle rather than an asset in Britain or the New World.

Yet almost certainly, at the innermost core of this negative reaction there was the old, primitive, nineteenth-century rejection of something which they felt would drag them down to poor-peasant level, something which was associated forever with poverty and backwardness and social downgrading. To be English-speaking was, in the eyes of many ordinary people obsessed by the new spirit of ambitious gentility, to be socially respectable and upwardly mobile – even though the learning of Irish now carried new inducements for a successful career in the Civil Service or in teaching. It was a gut reaction rather than a reasoned one, but it erected a psychological barrier which was virtually unbridgeable. It was fairly common for men and women in the 1930s to have Gaelic-speaking grandparents as well as parents who knew Irish but did not or would not speak it, with the result that they themselves, the third generation, neither spoke nor knew it.

Richard P. Walsh, in an essay entitled 'The Death of the Irish Language', has pointed out: 'While the vision of a Gaelic-speaking Irish nation-state was being promoted, mainly by urban-educated people with a modern middle-class education and outlook, the last fragments of Gaelic Ireland, the foundation on which alone they could build, were crumbling away in bleak rural places, far removed from the middle-class scene, and indeed from the middle-class mind.' The late David Greene made a very similar point: 'The movement for the preservation and restoration of the language did not come from the people who spoke it, but from Dublin, and as one element of the great upsurge of national enthusiasm which was to produce an independent Irish state by 1922.'[5] For that, he gives much of the credit to the Gaelic League, even if it became fossilised in later decades. But there were inner weaknesses and divisions in the movement, including the dispute over which dialect of Irish should be used; for a time the West Munster one was officially favoured, but the native speakers there were decreasing rapidly, while many or most of the new Gaelic writers tended to come from Connacht or Donegal (the Blasket

Islanders were an obvious exception). The flood of translations produced by An Gúm (set up in 1923 by Ernest Blythe) seemed to include everything from Jane Austen to detective novels, though at least it did give certain native writers some financial outlets and support. Writing in Irish, however, proved a lean way to make a living, and those who mocked at the 'Irish language racket' were ignoring the high degree of idealism and unselfishness often shown by those involved.

D. P. Moran, the once-powerful editor of the *Leader*, had campaigned for the restoration of Irish as the only real badge of cultural identity and survival – apart, that is, from the Catholic Church. Moran does not deserve the denigration he has suffered in recent decades, but he was entirely a man of his time and his main interest to us today is as a representative of that time. He was not, however, a believer in simple rural pieties as the answer to Ireland's needs – in fact, he was an energetic proponent of industrialisation and though he was on the opposite side of the fence from de Valera and his followers, he greatly respected Seán Lemass. Daniel Corkery's *The Fortunes of the Irish Language* (1954) is typical Corkery – essentially polemical – but it puts over forcefully and coherently his viewpoint, the viewpoint of a strong cultural nationalist. As he himself admits in an introductory note, it is essentially popular and generalised in approach – a 'sketch'. Though at that stage of his career Corkery spoke for an older generation, the booklet is still worth reading, even if his conclusion that 'For the first time since 1169, the Irish language has a state behind it' has rather a hollow ring today.

Rather surprisingly, Yeats expressed his views on the teaching of Irish in an essay entitled 'Ireland after the Revolution' in which he cautioned people against trying to revive it overnight, or revising the educational curriculum too suddenly or too drastically. After advising the Irish Government, or rather the Department of Education, to 'teach nothing but Greek, Gaelic, mathematics, and perhaps one modern language,' he went on to say: 'If Irish is to become the national tongue, the change must come slowly, almost imperceptibly; a sudden or forced change of language may be the ruin of the soul. England has forced English upon the schools and colleges of India, and now after generations of teaching no Indian can write or speak animated English and his mother tongue is despised and corrupted. Catholic Ireland is but slowly recovering from its change of language in the nineteenth century. Irishmen learn English at their mother's knee. English is now their mother-tongue, and a sudden change would bring a long barren epoch.'[6]

As Yeats himself knew well, Gaelic literature had virtually died out with Raftery in the mid-nineteenth century, and even he was only a degenerate descendant of a great tradition, a balladeer rather than a bard. Hyde and a few others were born just in time to record a still flourishing Gaelic folk culture, so that his English versions of Connacht songs had a major influence on two generations – or even three – of Irish poets. James Stephens, Frank O'Connor and certain others brought Ó Rathaille and other Gaelic poets within the compass of ordinary readers through translations or renderings of varying merit. Higgins worked the folk and ballad vein energetically, until in the end it ran out for him and he found that the new Thirties poets were leaving him behind intellectually. Austin Clarke studied the techniques of Gaelic poetry, particularly its use of assonance and its syllabic metres, and tuned himself to its feeling for nature and its sometimes bitter dialogue between the sacred and the profane, or between the clerics and the laity. Padraic Fallon, growing up in Athenry where Raftery was still a local memory, made the tramp poet into a kind of lyrico-dramatic persona without, however, ever holding his verse in high regard. Fallon had only a limited grasp of the language and depended heavily on Hyde's translations – just as he only read the medieval tales and sagas in their English versions, before re-creating them imaginatively in his radio plays. However, the only major writer of the period with a direct access to Gaelic culture was Liam O'Flaherty, who was himself a native speaker from the Aran Islands, and who arguably wrote more idiomatically and personally in Irish than he did in English.

The school (if it can be called that) of writing from the Blasket Islands began with a volume of day-to-day impressions and records of island life by Tomás Ó Criomhthain, which was edited by Pádraig Ó Siochfhradha (*An Seabhac*) and published under the title *Allagar na hInse* in 1928. The islanders themselves were generally illiterate, but Ó Criomhthain had taught himself to read and write in Irish through schoolbooks he had picked up on the mainland in Dunquin. This was followed in 1929 by *An tOileánach*, which quickly became a classic and was read in translation the world over. Like Robert Flaherty's film *Man of Aran*, also an immediate and worldwide success, its island theme, its primitivism and a certain heroic quality – men versus the power of nature and the sea – caught the imagination of the time. Then in 1933 came Muiris Ó Súileabháin's *Fiche Bliain ag Fás*, more idyllic than its predecessor, more nostalgic, and with greater sensitivity to language. Ó Súileabháin, after the early death of his mother, had been left in an orphanage in Dingle, and when his father came to reclaim him as a small child, he could speak no Gaelic. Back on the Blaskets, however, he picked it up rapidly and he seems to have read some Gaelic literature too, since in one chapter of his book he quotes the opening lines of Bryan Merriman's 'Cúirt an Mheán-Oídche':

> Ba ghnáth me ag siúl le ciumhais na habhann
> Ar bháinseach úr, is an drúcht go trom
> In aice na gcoillte, i gcoim an tsléibhe,
> Gan mhairg gan mhoill ar shoilseadh an lae . . . .

to which his companion, a typical dour islander, responds by telling him that he has 'a power of nonsense inside his head'. In his late teens he became friendly with the Englishman George Thomson, scholar, Communist and nonconformist, who persuaded him to join the newly-formed Garda Síochána rather than emigrate like others of his family. *Fiche Bliain* was written while he was serving in Connemara and it appeared in English translation – by Thomson himself and Moya Llewellyn Davies, the supposed mistress of Michael Collins – before the Irish original came into print. This seems to have been because An Gúm, the official Irish publishing house, objected to some episodes in it – though a book less likely to harm youthful morals could hardly be imagined, and it was soon being read in schools. The original text was published instead by the Talbot Press, and in the opinion of most critics who can read Irish well, it has a raciness and muscularity in the writing which the English version somehow lacks. Ó Súileabháin, unfortunately, petered out as a writer; the sequel, called *Fiche Bliain fé Bláth*, was rejected by publishers and the manuscript has either been lost or destroyed. He tried briefly and unsuccessfully to run a hotel, was forced to rejoin the Garda, and was drowned while swimming off the Galway coast, aged only forty-six. The garrulous and rather lachrymose Peig Sayers, whose autobiography *Peig* had been published in 1936, outlived him by several years, dying in 1958 at the age of eighty-five. Though her books of personal reminiscences have genuine folkloric and social value, they often verge on self-parody, and it was partly Peig's style which Myles na Gopaleen burlesqued in *An Béal Bocht* of 1941. Entire generations of Irish schoolchildren have suffered under them, and some have not forgiven her for the fact.

Gaelic novelists were isolated figures, such as Seosamh Mac Gríanna, who spent most of his energies on translating for An Gúm anything from *Ben Hur* to *Ivanhoe*. Nevertheless, in the opinion of David Greene, 'by the end of the Thirties Irish prose was a medium in which any theme of modern life could be handled.'[7] He instances the writings of Mgr Pádraig de Brún and León Ó Broin, who used it as a medium for scholarly and biographical works – a direct disproof of those who claimed that Irish lacked the vocabulary to cope with the complexities of the modern world and with contemporary abstractions. However, the true imaginative leap into literary Modernism occurred with Máirtín Ó Cadhain's novel *Cré na Cille* which was first published by Sairséal agus Dill in 1949 and had been preceded by a volume of short stories – between which Ó Cadhain's career had been interrupted by his internment during the war years as an IRA member. Its importance was recognised almost at once, and though the book's episodic structure and stylistic unevenness were admitted, it was plain that Irish prose had leaped into the Joycean or post-Joycean era. Here was a gifted modernist writer who was also a native speaker, and to whom the Irish language was a living medium which he did not feel enforced to handle like a museum piece.

Ó Cadhain came from Connemara, and his poet-contemporary Máirtín Ó Díreáin was also a Connachtman – a native of Inishmore in the Aran Islands, who had been involved in Irish-language theatre in Galway in the 1930s before moving to Dublin as a civil servant. He published his first verse collection, *Coinnle Geala*, in 1942 and the second, *Dánta Aniar*, in 1943; *Rogha Dánta* followed in 1949. Explaining his working methods and the dilemma facing his fellow-poets, he explained: 'We had two choices when we began, to go on using the traditional style which had been squeezed dry long before we were born, or to use the natural power of the language as we knew it. We took the second choice.'[8] His simple, sincere, rather rugged use of language – Hardy offers a rough parallel in English – was a landmark of its kind, especially since Ó Díreáin, although a 'man of the people' in his origins, did not employ folk pastiche or pseudo-balladry. Ó Díreáin was not a sentimentalist; he knew that the way of life he had seen in Aran was doomed by a dozen factors, and the lines (translated into English) in which he gives poignant expression to this awareness are often quoted:

> *My people's way is failing fast,*
> *The sea no longer a guarding wall.*[9]

Then in 1952 came Seán Ó Ríordáin's epochal *Eireaball Spideóige*, which made its author virtually a national figure inside a few months; among the most discerning of its reviewers was Valentin Iremonger who spoke with judicious enthusiasm on Radio Éireann. Here at last was what the more intelligent Gaelgeoirí, and many others, had been hoping for against the odds – a poet writing in Irish with a balance of native, idiomatic force and a recognisably mid-twentieth century sensibility and outlook. Ó Ríordáin had been born into a Gaelic-speaking area, Ballyvourney in County Cork, but he spent most of his life in Inis Carra, just outside Cork City. Cork at that time had a vigorous coterie of intellectuals, writers and artists of whom Corkery was the elder figure, but which included the poet-academic Seán Ó Tuama, the sculptor Seamus Murphy (also author of a prose classic, *Stone Mad*) and the language enthusiast An tAthair Tadhg Ó Murchú.

Ó Ríordáin suffered from TB from his early twenties, and for much of his life he was a semi-invalid nursed by his widowed mother, whose death in 1945 was probably the central event of his life. His moving elegy for her is one of his best-known poems, in fact probably the best-known after the much-loved *Cúl an Tí* known to thousands of schoolchildren as well as adults. The latter poem has a directness and 'natural magic' (Keats's phrase) which Ó Ríordáin rarely achieved; like 'Alice in Wonderland' it sets the ordinary, everyday world upside down, yet without flying off to Dreamland as Lewis Carroll did:

> *Tá Tír na nÓg ar chúl an tí*
> *Tír álainn trína chéile . . .*

Ó Ríordáin is more essentially a Modernist than Ó Díreáin, and also a more complex, divided, cerebral poet in general. His technique is often rough-cast and his versification is occasionally hard on the ear, a factor which is compounded by his sometimes crabbed, ingrown, eliptical style of thinking. He inherits much of the old Bardic mentality with its cerebral scholasticism and knottiness, to which he adds some of the erotic conflicts of a modern man and the inner divisions of a Catholic sensibility in a secular, materialistic culture (*Cnoc Mellerí*). A parallel with Austin Clarke suggests itself at once and there are many similarities between them.

Four years after *Eireaball Spideóige* had appeared, Máire Mhac an tSaoí, then a civil servant in the Department of External Affairs, published *Margadh na Saoire* which made many people hail her as the third major figure of a trinity of contemporary Irish poets. There had scarcely been a woman poet of stature writing in Irish since the days of Eibhlín Dubh Ní Chonaill, but hers was unmistakably a feminine voice though not in the domestic sense which that word conveyed to the average Gaelgeoir. It was passionate, self-aware, and uninhibited, recognisably the tone and sensibility of an emancipated European woman of the mid-century. She opened the way for a whole crop of younger women poets, of whom the best known is Nuala Ní Dhómhnaill.

No Irish dramatist of real stature appeared, however, unless Brendan Behan can be regarded as that on the strength of *An Gíall*, produced at the Damer Hall in Dublin in 1958, but better known in its English form *The Hostage*. Behan had been writing poetry in Irish for some time before that, and at least two of his poems have gained anthology status – the familiar elegy for Oscar Wilde, and the haunting 'An Irish Jackeen's Lament for the Blaskets' – or to give it its proper Gaelic title, 'Jackeen ag Caoineadh na mBlascaod'. Its two final lines virtually write an epitaph for the Gaelic past of the Great Blasket, now uninhabited (its surviving population had been moved to the mainland, at their own request) and with the wind sighing through half-doors that no longer opened or shut to neighbours, or even to home-dwellers:

> Séidead na gaoithe, ag luascadh go bog leathdhoras
> San teallach fuar fliuch, gan tine, gan teas, gan cosaint.[10]

Some of Behan's poems appeared in the epochal anthology *Nuabhéarsaíocht*[11], which was edited by Seán Ó Tuama and laid special stress on Seán Ó Ríordáin's work before his poetry had been collected in book form. With this fine anthology, modern poetry in Irish may be said to have come of age, and the introduction in itself was an important critical essay. Besides the poets already mentioned, it included lyrics by Roibeárd Ó Faracháin and the always versatile Micheál Mac Liammóir. Behan's two poems appear under the Gaelic version of his name, Breandán Ó Béacháin. Ó Tuama was yet another Corkery pupil, a notable scholar, critic and academic as well as a poet in his own right, and his 1960 study *An Grá in Amhráin na nDaoine* was an important scholarly work which analysed the links between Irish love-songs and the Continental *amour courtois* tradition.

The world of the Irish exile in Britain – not that of a middle-class intellectual, but that of an ordinary working man trying to keep afloat in a bleak industrial society very different from anything back home – was depicted in Dónal Mac Amhlaidh's *Dialann Deoraí*, which appeared first in 1960 and was translated into English by Valentin Iremonger a few years later under the title *An Irish Navvy*. It is of documentary value rather than great literature, but it did remind people in Ireland of a social reality they often liked to shut out, and it also set down the odd patois and lifestyle of the Irish-speaking worker in Britain, often living precariously or fecklessly in a series of 'digs' in industrial towns, and as shut inside his own racial identity as the West Indian emigrants alongside whom he worked. Once again, modern Irish had shown itself well able to cope with the realities of contemporary life.

Journalism, from the 1940s onwards, also showed a good deal of vitality. In 1942 An Comhchaidreamh, an association of Irish-speaking university graduates, founded the monthly magazine *Comhar* which from the start had energetic, forward-looking editors and proved a major outlet for the new literature in Irish. Virtually every writer of merit in Irish published there, both in prose and verse – including, incidentally, Brendan Behan. In 1945 Seán Ó hÉigeartaigh and his wife founded the publishing house of Sairséal agus Dill, which was not the usual semi-amateur, state-subsidised affair but an enterprise run with professional efficiency and sound literary judgement. Three years later An Club Leabhair was set up, which could guarantee a certain circulation to books of its choice and so make the lot of publishers easier. Meanwhile, the Gaelic League, perhaps aware that its prestige and relevance were waning, launched its own literary monthly, *Feasta*, whose editorial policy was far from being hidebound; it too published many of the best Gaelic writers.[12] An tOireachtas, the national language festival which had fallen into disuse, was revived with a fair measure of success in 1939 and included an annual art exhibition.

The newspaper *Inniu*, launched in 1943, was originally planned as a daily publication as its name implied, but had to confine itself to appearing weekly. Its long-time editor was Ciarán Ó Nualláin, a brother of Myles na Gopaleen and an excellent journalist in his own right, inheriting the family scholarship, irascibility and integrity. In the post-war decades, Dublin swarmed with talented writers and/or broadcasters in the Irish language: Dominic Ó Ríordáin, Seán Mac Réamoinn, Breandán Ó hEithir, Proinnsias Mac Aonghusa, Micheál Ó hAodha, to mention only a few. Dublin, it was said, was now the leading Gaeltacht in the country, a joke which had a good deal of truth since the actual Gaeltachta continued to decline, and of the estimated ten per cent of the population, North and South, which could read Irish with reasonable fluency, a high percentage lived in the capital. Near the end of the Fifties, a new energy showed with certain cultural activities of the organisation Gael Linn, which was responsible for the films *Mise Éire* and *Saoirse* and the early recordings by Seán Ó Riada and his Ceoltóirí Chualann. Both were landmarks of their kind, which heralded in a kind of Celtic mini-Renaissance during the 1960s, when the new mass following for folk and traditional music on occasion tended – literally – to run riot, as anyone who attended the typical Fleadh Ceoil of the period can testify.

Meanwhile, Tomás de Bhaldraithe's monumental *English-Irish Dictionary* had been published in 1959 – a landmark in many senses. It not only supplemented Dinneen's much less systematic one which had held the field for decades, but it standardised Irish spelling and put an end to much or most of the scholarly wrangles about dialect differences and other matters on which so much ink and emotional energies had been expended. Readers of Irish were now slowly becoming accustomed to the romanised alphabet in place of the old Gothic script, which arguably had always been better suited to the scribe with his quill pen than to the modern printing press. A whole generation was growing up which learned this romanised print at school and knew no other. For older readers, however, the break was traumatic, especially since the 'h' aspirate now seemed so ugly and obtrusive. Some never got used to it and hoarded their old copies of the Gaelic poets, or kept from their school-going days the familiar *Filíocht na nGael* which introduced many people to poetry in Irish. (This splendid anthology, first published in 1940 and edited by Pádraig Ó Canainn, has rarely been given its due. Though no doubt modern scholarship would be more demanding in terms of textual editing, its choice of poems is consistently good and at times inspired, though almost entirely pre-Modernist.)

In spite of a certain institutional stuffiness, the energy of the 'language movement', as it was almost unavoidably called, is quite remarkable in retrospect. The language itself, of course, was not revived on a national scale and perhaps no human agency could have done so by then, though that is not to slur over the blunders and narrow horizons often shown by the revivalists themselves. A typical mixture of schoolmasterishness and puritanism seemed to cling obstinately to it, in spite of the racy and rabelaisian streak which various Gaelic writers often showed in private – but much more rarely in public. To some people, such as Corkery, it was closely linked to Catholicism and a neo-Victorian code of moral behaviour; and the pagan, orgiastic, or anti-clerical elements in Irish literature were carefully skirted around or simply planed away. Even Irish dancing was desexualised to an almost grotesque degree. There was also – as in the Literary Revival itself – too great a mystique created concerning the folk mind and the folk imagination, a bias which goes back to the early days of Romanticism: This led to too great an emphasis on preserving the Gaeltachtaí, even when they were obviously backward areas gradually caving in under the pressures of economics and modern communications. In more recent decades, writers such as Desmond Fennell have earned themselves some unpopularity by pointing out that the Irish spoken in these areas is no longer the 'pure' speech which was once praised and jealously guarded, but is increasingly adulterated and hybrid. Perhaps the future of the language largely rested in the hands of the writers, intellectuals, folklorists and simple enthusiasts who loved it for its own sake and made it a living force, and not in the hands of a dwindling number of fishermen, small farmers and labourers who had spoken it from childhood.

There were also numerous splits, rivalries, and internecine wars in which various factions of the language enthusiasts seemed more intent on their private feuds and quarrels than on getting on with the job in hand. In that, of course, they were far from unique, and though Yeats's now over-quoted line 'great hatred, little room' sometimes applies, to them, they had more excuse than most other dissidents for their mutual paranoia. If the language enthusiasts often acted and spoke as if every man's hand was against them, they had to cope with something possibly worse than that, or at least more demoralising – mass public apathy and indifference, as well as a good deal of private mockery and begrudgery. The anti-language lobby was often vocal and sometimes even influential, particularly among parents who liked to think that the shortcomings of the Irish educational system, or their children's lack of success at school, were really the Dead Sea Fruits of compulsory Irish.

There was also widespread, though generally irrational, resentment against the importance given to Irish in Civil Service entrance requirements, or in the marking of school examinations, and against the new type of careerist who used fluency in the language to pave his or her climb to success and influence. Other people, more sensibly, resented the implication (much bandied about by a certain kind of obscurantist) that only the Fíor-Ghaels were genuine citizens and patriots in the new State. Yet to have created virtually a modern literature in a language which many or most people believed to be dead or moribund is a major achievement by any standard. As so often in its history, Irish Ireland had come back from the grave's edge.

Chapter 13

GAELS AND ANGLO-IRISH

In an epoch which apparently never tires of proclaiming its liberalism and pluralism, it is difficult for most people to understand the extent of the gap between Catholic and Protestant Ireland which was, in some ways, so unavoidable two generations ago, if not even more recently than that. They tend to view it now as they view the divisions in the North of Ireland – as a sort of largely irrational, inherited sectarian and racial divide which time, reason and commonsense, increased prosperity and enlightened education gradually make irrelevant. How easily it is forgotten that it was virtually an inbuilt element in the class, economic and socio-political realities of the time and that doctrinal and confessional differences often had relatively little to do with any of these hard basic facts. Protestant Ireland was ineluctably 'there', in some ways an integral part of the Irish State, in certain other ways a statelet within that state, and politicians, writers and social commentators could not afford to ignore this basic truth.

Protestant Ireland is an abstraction, no doubt, since Irish Protestants (leaving aside the separate issue of the Ulster Presbyterians) were never a homogeneous body. However, Yeats, AE, Hyde, Lady Gregory, Synge, Somerville and Ross, were all Protestants or at least of Protestant stock – the great exception again is George Moore – who had the social self-confidence, or even the sense of cultural superiority, which their caste(s) gave them, and without which they might not have triumphed as they did. One even has the impression, at times, that many of their Catholic fellow-citizens secretly rather liked them for their uppish tone, while at the same time they actively envied or resented it as rank snobbery. At heart, they probably felt that the stereotype Anglo-Irishman, Brendan Behan's 'Protestant with a horse', was preferable in some ways at least to their own jumped-up Beggars on Horseback. Even among the Dublin working-class, the imperial pageantry – which had never been very much or very spectacular in actuality – of the old Vice-regal Lodge and Dublin Castle days was missed and mourned. And the legends of royal visits, including that of Queen Victoria, were part of Dublin folklore, even among working-class republicans.

Nevertheless, many Irish Protestants must have felt virtually under siege in a new State which was not religiously or politically intolerant, but was certainly overwhelmingly Catholic in ethos and outlook. Just as the Penal Laws had disinherited the Catholic majority, politically the former Ascendancy was now disinherited in turn,[1] even if Protestants kept a grip on many of the professions, or at least a firm footing in them (accountancy was virtually their last monopoly and was not challenged much before the Sixties; Catholics gradually took over the law and medicine). They were the class who had created institutions such as the Royal Dublin Society, whose gardens somehow almost always managed to look better than those of their Catholic neighbours (generally they still do), who had created and maintained the more gracious aspects of Irish urban and suburban living. Born into a privileged social position, like the Brahmins in India, they now had to face the real possibility of dwindling into near-extinction – particularly as the Catholic clergy were zealous in enforcing the Vatican's *Ne Temere* decree on their flocks, thereby making mixed marriages increasingly difficult if not impossible. At the time of the Treaty they had numbered a quarter of a million at most; and between 1926 and 1936 they fell from seven per cent of the population to six. So for many of them it was often a severe conflict of loyalties, as in the case of Brian Inglis who piloted a bomber for the RAF during the war, but had agreed with some of his Irish friends to desert if Irish neutrality was violated. Others detested the neutrality policy as a betrayal of all they stood for (it was such people whom Gray, the American Ambassador, had listened to) while others again, almost to their own surprise, came to respect de Valera and to defend him. As Cyril Connolly (himself the son of an Anglo-Irish mother) put it: 'The Ascendancy made the best of de Valera, partly out of expediency, partly out of patriotism.'[2]

Inglis noted that from the start of independence many of the Anglo-Irish simply pretended that it had not happened and that nothing basically had changed, so accordingly they went on behaving more or less as they had always done.[3] But while such a head-in-the-sand attitude might suit the type of persons whose activities and interests outside their offices or estates or farms were limited to bridge games and golf and watching rugby at Lansdowne Road, or to the racecourse and the hunting field, it could not possibly satisfy the more thinking Irish Protestants– of whom there were plenty, since they were an educated class with good schools and a tradition of scholarship and professional exactitude. They felt themselves to be genuinely Irish, if not Gaels, and justifiably resented the familiar 'West Brit' taunt or label; they knew themselves to be 'no petty people' (Yeats's phrase in the Senate), fully capable of taking an objective and informed view of politics both at home and abroad; and they were often impatient with those among their fellow-Protestants to whom Churchill was not only a great statesman but a demigod who could do no wrong, while the native politicians were jumped-up peasants who had utterly no business measuring their parochial opinions against his.[4] For the latter type, the second World War was not primarily a war to save democracy, or the struggle of the

Atlantic Alliance against Hitler and Fascism, but simply the British Empire against Germany plus a few dubious Continental nations such as Italy (the 'Eye-ties' as I often heard them called contemptuously in my youth). And to be fair to them, they did not flinch from fighting in it, almost always with bravery and often with some distinction. The Anglo-Irish military and naval traditions still lived on, and even today they are not extinct.

However one-eyed or bigoted a certain school of nationalist opinion might seem today (and seemed then also to any thinking person) the unavoidable fact remains that it had deep socio-historical roots. Arland Ussher in *The Face and Mind of Ireland* records the mentality of the Anglo-Irish 'Quality' into which he had been born: 'The males seemed to be every one of them a captain, a major or a colonel: Ireland was the land of colonels as Hungary was a land of counts. From the conversation of these people, whenever it strayed from sport or the iniquity of the Asquith Government, there emerged a far-from-flattering picture of the "natives". No Irishman, it appeared, could be trusted so much as half a yard; their language, the Erse, contained no word for "gratitude"; they were taught by "their priests" that it was not wrong to lie or steal, and such of them as were members of the Ancient Order of Hibernians (a harmless friendly-society) took an oath that they would murder Protestants whenever they got a chance; more than this, there were those among them who were not above shooting a fox; and at the same time every word and action of an Irishman was somehow inimitably, incredibly funny. Young as I was, it struck me that the Irish were a patient people, to put up with the things that were said about them.'[5]

When such a mentality is taken into account, it becomes easier to understand why a certain type of prickly nationalist with a small-cottage origin or background, and who personally was morally earnest, socially insecure and with little real humour outside folk farce, could take offence at the stories of Somerville and Ross. In spite of the enormous popularity of their books, both in England and at home, the collaborating cousins occasionally touched on sore points and vulnerable nerves. This was partly through their Big House slant on Irish life – which was inevitable, given their upbringing and backgrounds, and is also one of the elements which gives their work its value – and partly because of their comic/ironic view of human nature. Even relatively well-read people sometimes claimed to see in a character such as Slipper, Flurry Knox's disreputable but faithful hanger-on, only the continuation of Lover's and Lever's stage-Irish caricatures and ignored the fact that Somerville and Ross treated their own Ascendancy class very similarly – that they were, in fact, chroniclers of a society in decay. Such hostile critics also ignored the mastery of dialogue, the accurate version of country speech which was generally less mannered or artificial than Synge's, and the marvellously evocative word-painting of the Irish landscape. Yet the R.M. stories continued to be read and enjoyed – even when, for a time, they could only be obtained easily from second-hand bookshops[6] – and Edith Somerville was honoured by the Irish Academy of

Letters in her old age. They never went into virtual eclipse as most of George Moore's books did. However, it was many years before *The Real Charlotte*, written in 1892, was fully recognised as the great novel it is; one of the first post-war critics to do so was V. S. Pritchett.[7]

Contrary to what is sometimes said, Big House literature never died out and in fact has flourished into our time with such books as Molly Keane's *Good Behaviour* of 1981. Probably the best-known example is Elizabeth Bowen's novel *The Last September*, written in 1929 and set in a county house in Tipperary at the time of the Troubles, in which erotic tensions and intrigue take place against a background of violence culminating in the burning down of the house by the IRA. Elizabeth Bowen later wrote the now-classic account of her family home and history in *Bowen's Court*[8] – which did not prevent that rather bleak County Cork mansion, after she had sold it, from sharing the same fate as Coole House had suffered in 1941.[9] She herself, both in her personality and her career, exemplifies the divided loyalties and demands of her social caste; her life was lived mainly in London, and during the war years she acted as a kind of freelance intelligence agent for the British Ministry of Information, travelling between the two countries and reporting on the climate of opinion in Ireland without actually being an agent or spy. She went courageously through the Blitz and apart from *A World of Love* (1955) her later novels have English themes and settings, while the prose style tends to get increasingly ceremonial and mandarinesque. Her childless marriage to Alan Cameron, a blimpish Englishman who drank rather too much, her unlikely yet seemingly intense affair with Seán O'Faolain, her masterful character and energetic professionalism in all she did or wrote, are familiar by now from the fine biography by Victoria Glendinning and from her other commentators.

What is notable about Molly Keane's career, however, is how thoroughly London-oriented it was (in spite of her election to the Irish Academy of Letters in 1937), and how divorced it seems from the Dublin literary world of Clarke, Kavanagh, etc. When she was interviewed in 1942 for *The Bell* by the 'Bellman' (H. L. 'Larry' Morrow, an excellent and versatile journalist) she was treated like a visiting celebrity more than an Irish author, and seems to have behaved rather like one. Whatever political and racial ecumenists may claim today, usually with the best intentions, it is a fact that the Anglo-Irish and the Gaelic or 'native' Irish temperaments and traditions do appear, at times, to be remarkably dissimilar and even poles apart, though much of this may be simple class differences. In Elizabeth Bowen's case, one feels that she was probably closer spiritually to Virginia Woolf and Bloomsbury than even to other Big House writers such as Somerville and Ross.

Yet in spite of all this Elizabeth Bowen always considered herself to be quite unanswerably Irish, and in *The Bell* interview she stressed her sense of nationality, which she called 'a highly dangerous emotion' but not mere sentimentality. She disapproved of Irish neutrality, though she understood its rationale, and disliked the increasing tendency of Ireland to dissociate itself from Britain; she was also faintly hostile to the language revival, which gained ground during the war years, and as a true-blooded, undemonstrative Irish Protestant of her class, she was sometimes repelled by Catholic populist religiosity. Yet her high degree of anglicisation did not make her think of herself as an Englishwoman, even if she was accepted by the London literary world of Cyril Connolly, Christina Wedgwood, William Plomer, Raymond Mortimer and even Virginia Woolf as one of themselves. She always retained a certain detachment about England and things English, the sure mark of the émigré writer, though her allegiance to them was firm. And in the end she was buried in Cork, in the graveyard at Farahy near the site of the now-demolished Bowen's Court – of which hardly a stone by then remained.

The early novels of Molly Keane, written under her pen-name of M. J. Farrell, have mostly been republished over the past decade and a half. They are not heavyweight or searching works, in fact they now seem very much of their time and place, a world of hunt balls, keeping up appearances, worldlywise girls on the lookout for eligible boyfriends, occasional family bickering and, of course, horses, the totem animal of Anglo-Ireland. Nevertheless they are knowledgeable, professional, polished and shrewd, and quite essential for an understanding of the milieu they depict. Two are set in the inevitable Big House against the (almost equally inevitable) background of the 'Troubles'; *Mad Puppetstown* (1931) and *Two Days in Aragon* (1941) – Aragon, incidentally, is the name of a house and does not allude to the Spanish Civil War. Virago, the English publishing house which has brought back many good women writers from neglect or semi-neglect, has recently issued a series of these books with good, knowledgeable prefaces. Less known, but with rather more emotional substance, are the two novels of Barbara Fitzgerald, who like Elizabeth Bowen was born in Cork and was the daugher of Dr Gregg, the Church of Ireland cleric who became Primate of All Ireland. *We are Besieged* (1946) deals with the burning out of an Anglo-Irish family in 1922, while *Footprint upon Water* (not published until 1983, the year after her death) depicts the displaced children of a similar family now grown up and facing the reality of a changed society.

Yet probably too much has been made of Big House literature, and indeed of Big Houses in general – even if Yeats wrote about Coole so magisterially, while O'Faolain showed a country mansion from the radically different viewpoint of a republican rebel or 'gunman' in *Midsummer Night's Madness*. It was not the whole of Protestant Ireland, or even its most representative institution, and it is easily forgotten that Britain also contained many such decaying mansions and run-down historic families until the National Trust came to save them.[10] Allowing for the considerable contributions to national life made by patriotic peers such as the late Lord Moyne (Bryan Guinness) and the Longfords,[11] the real vitality of Protestant Ireland was in its middle class, even after Yeats and his generation had vanished. It continued to produce – naming them more or less at random – people as various as Beckett, Lennox Robinson, Edmund Curtis the historian, Maurice Craig, Bruce Williamson, Patrick MacDonogh, Denis Johnston, Mary Manning, Hubert Butler,

William Trevor, Robert Lloyd Praeger, Francis Stuart, Frank Mitchell, W. J. White, Douglas Gageby, and perhaps the greatest and most ecumenical-minded Irish churchman of the past half-century, George Otto Simms. In the visual arts, the early years of the Irish Exhibition of Living Art were dominated by men and women – chiefly women – with a Protestant middle-class background – Norah McGuinness, Anne Yeats, Hilary Heron, Oisín Kelly, etc. Protestant Ireland may have been squeezed out politically – its small numbers, in any case, prohibited it from playing a major public role in the new State – but there was never any question of it being squeezed out intellectually and culturally. Yet the sense of estrangement from the majority, and even a certain sense of social redundancy and uselessness, can be felt in some of their writings – for instance, in this extract from a poem by Bruce Williamson, entitled 'Afternoon in Anglo-Ireland':

> We must go, yet cannot leave Hell or Heaven.
> We get no choice whether we rise or fall.
> Fold up the deck-chairs, dear. There will be some
> Not needed next year, no matter how warm the sun.[12]

Though there were many Protestants who, for reasons of policy or out of sheer indifference, made a point of keeping their heads down, there was always a minority who made it a point of honour to stick their necks out. Some of them pursued the role of public gadfly in the Senate and elsewhere, occasionally getting up the noses of party politicians or antagonising the more right-wing type of Catholic – though curiously enough, the Trinity College senator most active and vocal in this role was Professor Owen Sheehy Skeffington, whose parents were Catholic though he himself was an agnostic with leftist tendencies. Similarly, Hubert Butler stirred up a hornet's nest by his public exposés of Catholic atrocities in Yugoslavia, at a time when Cardinal Mindszenty of Hungary and Archbishop Stepinac of Yugoslavia were portrayed in the Catholic press as victims and virtual martyrs of Communism. In his native Kilkenny he was attacked and expelled from various learned bodies to which he belonged – an example of misplaced zeal which showed that there were areas of native bigotry still alive behind the facade of official religious tolerance. Sheehy Skeffington too was sometimes attacked as a crypto-Communist, though he was no more than mildly Socialist and Fabian – or in effect, a romantic radical of the old school. Butler was essentially a liberal with leftist leanings, like so many other intellectuals at the time, and occasionally manifested a certain paranoia towards Rome and its works and pomps. That, however, was equally true of many Irish writers with a Catholic background, most of whom were assiduous readers of the London-produced *New Statesman* whose views set the tone for a surprisingly large proportion of the intelligentsia. (In any case, several of them had personal scores to settle with the clergy.)

No greater example of the gulf which yawned occasionally between the two societies could have been cited than that of the contrast between the National

University of Ireland and Trinity College Dublin. Trinity, once the intellectual nursery of Tone, Emmet, Tom Moore, Davis etc. had acquired a reactionary and West Brit reputation early in the century, which on the whole was deserved. The historian F. S. L. Lyons, writing as late as 1962, remarked: 'In the generation before the Treaty, Trinity made practically every political mistake it could make and the crude and ignorant gibes of Mahaffy and others at the renaissance of Irish culture aroused a deep resentment for which the university is still paying.'[13]

Since Lyons himself was a prominent Trinity academic who later became Provost, he can be absolved of any intellectual bias against his own college. Yeats, who never attended it, remarked (apropos the case of Synge, who had), that it seldom produced creative or original minds, Synge for him being an exception. Intellectually its finest products were usually either historians (like Lyons himself) or classical scholars, ranging from the famous Professor Tyrrell in George Moore's time down to comparatively recent figures such as W. B. Stanford, H. A. Parke and J. V. Luce. Otherwise it mainly turned out competent doctors, lawyers and engineers, a high percentage of whom emigrated to the British Colonies – a tradition which continued until well after the second World War. Samuel Beckett cannot be counted as a typical Trinity project, nor can the gifted poet Patrick MacDonogh, who was several years older (born 1901). Both men, however, were excellent sportsmen, Beckett in cricket and MacDonogh in hockey (he played for Ireland over thirty times).

Neither can Beckett's friend and patron, Professor Rudmose-Brown, be counted in any way as a typical Trinity academic. His fellow-dons seem mostly to have regarded him as eccentric or dangerously bohemian, and barely accepted him socially – which to a lesser degree also applied to that other professor and voluminous writer, Professor Walter Starkie, brother of the more famous Enid. The typical 'Fellows of Trinity' tended to be hidebound, stuffy, intellectually incurious, voluntary half-prisoners inside the confines of a kind of exclusive club or social enclave – Trinity itself, where they ruled the roost as they had done in Mahaffy's time. In Lyons's words: 'The world had changed overnight and too many Fellows were too set in their ways to change with it. The result was that though individual scholars of repute were still in evidence, the Twenties and Thirties rank among the darkest periods of the College's history – it was poor, the buildings became steadily more dilapidated and a great tradition of learning seemed destined for extinction.'[14]

With the death of Provost Alton in 1950, the old regime was shaken and so was the power of the Fellows. However, the Provost who probably did most to effect the steady recovery of the postwar period was Dr A. J. McConnell, a career mathematician and a Northerner with the traditional shrewdness of his race. He struck up a good relationship with de Valera, whom he appears to have flattered occasionally as a fellow-mathematician (Dev apparently was vain about his qualifications in this field) and managed to obtain the state grants which Trinity had never before received, even under the old Dublin Castle regime. This allowed the college to come back from near-penury into playing the institutional role which its historic past and traditions deserved. McConnell also introduced internal changes and, in general, did much to bring it into line with postwar thinking. Trinity, however, continued to be largely a Protestant institution, though no longer a Unionist one, with a School of Divinity and relatively few Catholics on its teaching staff – a factor not helped by the ban imposed by Archbishop McQuaid on Catholic attendance there, which remained in force until 1970 though by then few paid any attention to it. Well into the Fifties, students at the evening meal ('Commons') still prayed for the Queen of England and many of the old Anglo-colonial trappings and ceremonies remained. It was still, in many or most people's eyes, the Protestant university, just as the National University of Ireland was the Catholic one in spite of its non-denominational constitution.

This, however, did not imply public hostility in any sense, ban or no ban, since the old university with its fine buildings and incomparable situation was at the very heart of Dublin and commanded a special respect. The English poet-critic Donald Davie, who came there to lecture in English in 1950 and remained for several years, found that 'there was nothing more touching than the common Dubliner's pride in Trinity and affection for it, however he was opposed to what it had stood for'.[15] The special and even unique visual aspect of Trinity, with its squares, campanile, eighteenth-century library and playing fields, had and still has something strangely self-contained and self-sufficient about it, and this was noticed by the philosopher Wittgenstein when he first visited it shortly before the second World War with his Irish friend and disciple, M. O'Connell Drury. Looking about him in Front Square, he remarked: 'Now I understand what was meant by the phrase "the Protestant Ascendancy". These buildings have the appearance of a fortress. But now the gypsies inhabit the castle.'[16]

University College Dublin for many years was dominated by the powerful figure of its President, Dr Michael Tierney, originally a classical scholar but a man whose real vocation was academic power politics. The intellectual legacy of Cardinal Newman and his Catholic University ideal were naturally very strong there, but Tierney was also at one time identified, or linked, with the corporate and syndicalist ideals which were much debated in the Thirties and were associated with Mussolini's regime in Italy (not yet disgraced by its links with Nazism). This school of thought – which was far from being Fascist in the accepted sense of today – achieved its most coherent expression in *Church and State in Fascist Italy*, written by the great Gaelic scholar D. N. Binchy and published in 1941. Binchy himself had been Professor of Jurisprudence and Roman Law in UCD, before turning to a highly distinguished career in diplomacy.[17]

Nuns and budding priests attended lectures in the UCD building in Earlsfort Terrace,[18] and it was widely believed that Archbishop McQuaid had more influence than was healthy in some of its staff appointments. (Certainly he was very influential in obtaining a kind of lectureship there for Patrick Kavanagh in 1955, when the poet had just recovered from a major illness.) Compared with the venerable architecture – and history – of Trinity, UCD had a functional bareness which looked forward to the modern degree factory, and it was fashionable to sneer at it as 'a glorified technical school'. Certain aspects of student life there had an inbuilt grottiness, brilliantly recorded in Flann O'Brien's comic novel At Swim-Two-Birds, whereas Trinity students consciously preserved – or tried to preserve – a certain social style and what outsiders rather sourly called snob appeal. Its much smaller student body – during the mid-Fifties Trinity had only a little over two thousand students, while UCD had about three-and-a-half thousand out of the NUI total of eight thousand – helped to give it a certain elitism and exclusiveness.

Certainly the typical upper-class Protestant undergraduate, son of a successful businessman, surgeon or solicitor, often cut a smarter figure socially than his UCD counterpart, usually the son of a civil servant or farmer or national schoolteacher who had scraped and saved to give him the third-level education which probably he had never enjoyed himself. Yet in the Thirties it was UCD which produced the bulk of the writers and intellectuals, while Trinity could only point to Beckett and a few other isolated figures such as the sculptor Oisín Kelly. The remarkable generation of O'Nolan, Devlin, Mervyn Wall, Donagh MacDonagh, Brian Coffey, Charles Donnelly, Liam Redmond, Cyril Cusack, had no real equivalent in Trinity at the time. UCD also broke new ground with its School of Architecture, and it too produced some excellent historians, as well as supplying a forum for the great art scholar Françoise Henry. On the other hand, Trinity did educate some of Ireland's most brilliant journalists, including two future editors of The Irish Times, Alec Newman and Douglas Gageby (who had studied classics and law respectively). W. J. (Jack) White and Bruce Williamson were also TCD graduates who became brilliant journalists and respected writers; both studied in Trinity during the second World War, when it had become rather a strange, inward-looking institution, facing backwards to its historic past of Berkeley, Goldsmith and Burke rather than forward to its eventual postwar resurgence in a socially levelling society. For a time, it even seemed as if it might shut its doors for good and its site and buildings be sold to some other institution.

Even by then, however, Trinity was shedding much of its exclusive social tone, so that the wealthier or haughtier landowning Protestants often preferred to send their sons and daughters to Oxford or Cambridge, as a matter of class prestige. It represented a society at the crossroads, since even the old Protestant professional class was losing its energy and identity; William Trevor, whose father was a bank manager, was one of the last Trinity-educated writers to emerge from this background. By the Sixties much of its old image – some would even say, its essential character – had changed radically, and in any case waves of religious (and political) ecumenism had altered the cultural climate in Ireland out of all recognition. A new generation of writers now emerged: Derek Mahon, Eavan Boland, Michael Longley, Brendan Kennelly. Its new Business School, too, turned out a succession of men and women who carved out successful careers. Today the staffs, and the personalities, of TCD and UCD are in many respects interchangeable, and UCD has realised the dream of its former President, Michael Tierney, by becoming a large-scale campus university in south Dublin – rivalled only by the splendid new Limerick University.

Women had been admitted into Irish universities at an early stage, but until postwar times they remained very much a minority. Personalities such as Beckett's Trinity contemporary Ethna MacCarthy were untypical of their times – emancipated women who smoked, drank, talked to men as frankly as they would to their women friends, and expressed their views and opinions without inhibition. Ethna MacCarthy was also remarkable in that as well as being a poet whose work was included in Irish anthologies, she was a practising medical doctor and lectured in Trinity in Spanish and French.[19] Beckett seems to have been in love with her, and so too probably was Denis Johnston, but eventually she married A. J. (Con) Leventhal. Another factor often forgotten by those who threw the 'West Brit' taunt at Trinity was that, in spite of Mahaffy and his legacy, it produced or harboured a number of excellent Gaelic scholars. One postwar example is David Greene, an outstanding scholar and author of *The Irish Language* and other books, who was Professor of Irish for many years. In 1955, Trinity courageously brought in as a lecturer in Irish the novelist Máirtín Ó Cadhain – then still a controversial figure, and a man with no obvious scholastic qualifications to his name. Stranger still, Ó Cadhain stayed on to become Professor of Irish in 1969.[20]

Chapter 14

THE CHURCH

A long with sex and literary censorship, the power of the Catholic Church is one of the dominant obsessions of modern commentators on the Ireland of a generation ago. Undoubtedly it was one of the dominant realities of the period, and continued to be so until little more than a decade ago. Nothing impressed, repelled or simply puzzled intelligent visitors to the country quite so much as the atmosphere of religion which seemed all-pervading – and it is interesting that they found this in the Protestant North as well as in the Catholic South. If, like Chesterton coming to the 1932 Eucharistic Congress in Dublin, they were fervent and even militant Catholics, the sight of worshipping thousands with their priests and banners was heart-warming and inspiring – *Vexilla Regis prodeunt*, the Europe of the Crusades come back to life.

To others with radically differing viewpoints, Ireland viewed from this aspect seemed a theocracy rather like Islam, and as such repellent and retrogressive in the modern secular, rationalist, democratic world. To others again it was interestingly primitive and picturesque from a quasi-aesthetic angle, rather like a Spanish religious procession in Seville or Malaga with its pageantry and large painted effigies – Croagh Patrick pilgrims crawling up their sacred mountain, an old man or woman bending reverentially over a holy-water font, a High Cross standing apparitionally in a stretch of almost empty countryside, children in white lining up for their First Communion. All these sights were singled out regularly by visiting photographers, in particular, as though they were recording the nation's heartbeat. To a largely secular world – England, America, Continental Europe – they carried the fascination which the irrational, the archaic, and the ritualistic often have for urbanised, industrialised people who have long since discarded or lost touch with such things and have no particular wish to see them revived in their own environment, or as part of their own daily lives.

Conversely, to the average Irish Catholic the atheism of most of contemporary Europe in some ways appeared as strange or even perverse as his own country's religiosity seemed to the average Frenchman or Swede. In this sense, at least, Ireland was/is out of step with most of the contemporary world, so that the believers in 'isolation' do have a strong argument here to support their wider claims. There were plenty of fervent or even bigoted Catholics in Spain and Italy, but they had atheists, socialists, communists, and simple agnostics in plenty to offset or counterbalance them. In Ireland, Catholicism was overwhelmingly the majority creed, and it seemed to be everywhere and to infiltrate among all circles and types. The cold, ambitious, precisionist civil servant who nevertheless devoted his spare evenings to confraternities and prayer circles; the jovial publican who had no scruples about selling one more pint of porter to a drunken man with a family to support, but who on no account would ever miss Sunday Mass; the good-humoured, chatty housewife who listened regularly to 'Mrs Dale's Diary' on the BBC and enjoyed gangster films and love stories, yet would enforce the strictest Lenten fasting on herself, her husband and children; the bookish schoolteacher who was prepared to discuss with impartiality, over a bottle of stout, anything from nuclear fission to the coming US presidential election, but who might feel personally insulted if anybody made fun in his presence of Lourdes or Fatima – all these were typical of various aspects of Irish life. To outsiders they were contradictory and even mystifying; to a native Irish person, they were merely part of the normal, everyday texture of life.

In the same vein, Myles na Gopaleen records a conversation with a Christian Brother in which he himself jocosely brought up the subject of the various supposed relics of the True Cross, and pointed out that these fragments, if pieced together, would weigh far more than any single wooden cross. To which the Brother replied 'stiffly' that he could see no obstacle to believing in miraculous multiplication of the material (in the style, presumably, of the Loaves and Fishes in the New Testament). Yet no doubt when he went back to his desk the next day, he would have punished his pupils for every misspelling, every small inaccuracy, and every minor mistake in adding and subtraction. Nor would he have seen or felt the slightest discrepancy between these two attitudes or have regarded them as belonging to mutually incompatible worlds. Neither, for that matter, did the groups of ordinary people who made the ritual pilgrimage to Lough Derg, where they fasted and performed the penitential rites, then relaxed and gave the flesh its play with a week of hard drinking, dancing and generally orgiastic behaviour at the nearby resort of Bundoran.

Contrary to what is said over and over, Irish religiosity was not primarily the result of being cut off from the rest of Europe. This factor might explain some of the oddities and extremes of Irish Catholicism, but it does not adequately explain the obstinate fact of the nation's piety, any more than it explains the passionate Catholicism of the Poles, or the dour, decent Calvinism of Scotland and Wales. In any case, it was not a purely national, insular religion like Anglicanism in England; Catholicism is a world religion, and Irish newspapers followed almost obsessively the sayings and doings of the Pope, the reported massacres of priests and nuns in the Spanish Civil War, and the various religious persecutions behind the Iron

Curtain. For some of them, it was their strongest link with the world overseas, apart from the letters home of relatives working in Britain or the occasional cheque or money order from the States. At a time when travel abroad was relatively rare (chiefly because of national poverty) organised pilgrimages to Lourdes or Assisi, or even to Rome, were regular events.

A French visitor, Camille Bourniquel, remarked: 'There is no people in the world for whom religion holds a more important place, or influences customs and behaviour more conspicuously. One feels enveloped from the start in an atmosphere of militant clericalism.'[1] That is an obvious exaggeration, since Ireland was not a Christian version of Islam, and the atmosphere of an Irish Sunday with the pubs noisy and cheerful, crowds making their way to hurling and football matches, off-duty farm labourers lounging and chatting at crossroads, and queues forming outside cinemas, was a very different thing from Scottish, Welsh or even English Sabbatarianism. (One of the typical would-be jokes of the period was: 'How would you fancy a rainy Sunday in Belfast?') On the other hand, the power of sometimes despotic and overbearing parish priests, and the arrogance of some of the bishops, had few parallels in Europe except, possibly, in Spain. The Church was sternly paternalistic, taking the attitude that it alone knew what was best for the Irish people in terms of faith and morals and matters of conscience. To say – as has often been said – that it was resolutely anti-intellectual is not true, since it contained plenty of able academics and scholars and the education it gave, through the diocesan colleges and other institutions, was basically a good one. Certainly an entire generation of Irish men and women owed most of their schooling to priests and nuns, who voluntarily subsidised their education since they themselves were paid little. Mainly for reasons and interests of its own, the Church maintained the teaching of Latin and classical Greek, while a surprising number of teaching priests and brothers were keen mathematicians and amateur scientists – an Irish tradition going far back into the nineteenth century.

Perhaps the degree of paternalism is exaggerated today in one particular area – the teaching of women. That was usually carried out by nuns, who were very numerous – at certain stages of the nineteenth century, in fact, they had heavily outnumbered the priests. So nowadays, when so many Irishwomen are reacting against what they see as a male-dominated Church, this important factor should be borne in mind. It was nuns who taught them to read and write, to cook and sew (though most Irishwomen tended to be poor cooks) and learn a little French or Spanish or Italian, to strum the piano and sing, or perhaps to dance in the traditional Irish style; it was also the nuns who gave most Irish girls their moral schooling and impressed on them their responsibilities as future wives and mothers. They, too, were a power in the land, just as priests were, and Irish convents contained some powerful, autocratic personalities. (The writer Dervla Murphy has recorded her positive memories of 'the nuns', and she is only one of many.) Personally, I have no doubt whatever that the real backbone of Irish Catholicism were the ordinary Irishwomen, Mná na hÉireann, just as women are also to a great extent the backbone both of Judaism and Islam. It was on women that the clergy chiefly relied to maintain religious morale and to carry out most of the small, regular rituals (e.g. the family Rosary) which kept Catholicism an active force in the home, and it was to the consciences of women that they appealed most frequently in their sermons and in the hushed, private, sealed-off world of the confessional. The short stories of O'Connor and O'Faolain often convey the power of this world-behind-curtains. In 'The Great Hunger' Patrick Kavanagh depicts the typical rural matriarch, for whom religion is not so much a moral force as a numinous aspect of life, which it is necessary to placate like pagan deities:

> Now go to Mass and pray and confess your sins
> And you'll have all the luck, his mother said.[2]

Priest-worship, too, was predominantly a female phenomenon, and clerical celibacy was an important, even essential ingredient in it; a man who could dispense with normal sexual satisfaction, so women reasoned to themselves, must indeed be apart from most other men and probably superior to them. This was particularly true of working-class mothers, who spent much of their adult lives dreading yet one more pregnancy and who must often have wished that their husbands would 'leave them alone'. Yet here, too, it was the priests who sternly forbade virtually any form of birth control outside abstinence. They had learned to do what Communism, for instance, never quite achieved in Eastern Europe, though it tried hard to do so – that is, to create an ideological power-base in the private home, and they achieved it in a country where the family unit counted above and before anything else.

Against this, however, Irish Catholicism very rarely took political forms, at least not party-political ones. The obvious comment on this is that since it had an overwhelming majority there was no need for it to do so; in Austria, for instance, during the 1930s Dolfuss's Catholic and nationalistic policies were often carried out against strong Leftist and other opposition, while the old Centre Party in Germany, which represented most of the organised Catholic vote there, was only one facet of a bewildering political kaleidoscope soon to be shattered by Hitler. Catholic groupings in France, too, were only a segment of the entire body-politic. In Ireland there were no such groupings, nor – contrary to what is often said – did the Church as a rule intervene in political life. De Valera resented political interference by bishops and on two occasions he even appealed to the Vatican, where the Irish Ambassador was usually listened to with respect. The famous/infamous case of the Mother and Child Scheme in 1951 was a notable exception to this non-intervention policy, for which the Church paid heavily in terms of popular support and is still paying to this day. But badly and dogmatically – not to say stupidly – as the hierarchy behaved on that occasion, their intervention was genuinely seen to be on the grounds of 'faith and morals' and not of political ideology – even if the line in this case happened to be a rather fine one.[3]

What was really more reprehensible, not to say downright contemptible, was the behaviour of some of the Inter-Party politicians involved, who virtually kow-towed to the bishops' whims, and by doing so did themselves no good at all with the overwhelmingly Catholic electorate. They paid for this by losing office, but even then few of them appear to have felt any degree of self-reproach. Long afterwards, J. A. Costello – who had been Taoiseach at the time – was interviewed on RTÉ by David Thornley, historian, television journalist and politician, who asked him if he still held the same views as he did then. Costello told him quite vehemently, in effect, that he regretted nothing and that for him the bishops' views were tantamount to law for any believing Catholic. Television viewers hostile to the Church can only have been confirmed in their view that State and Church in Ireland at that time were one, and that the true seat of power was not the Oireachtas, but Maynooth.

The architect for this state of affairs is frequently claimed to be de Valera, largely through his 1937 Constitution with its now-abolished 'special position' clause concerning the Catholic religion. The Cosgrave Government of the Twenties, though more overtly clerical than de Valera's party ever was, had given the Catholic Church no special legal or official status and was generally careful not to offend Protestant sensibilities in any way which might rebound on Ireland's image abroad. De Valera, however, came to power in 1932 against a good deal of clerical hostility – clerics even spoke against him from election platforms – and he still carried the stigma of his and his followers' excommunication during the Civil War. An accommodation with the Church was therefore essential, and from that angle his Constitution might be seen as a kind of Concordat, equivalent to what Mussolini had signed with the Vatican in 1929. He and his party needed the facade of religious respectability, while the Church for its part must recognise and accept him as the country's legally elected and legitimate leader.

The Constitution he produced was heavily influenced by Catholic social teaching, in particular by the 1891 *Rerum Novarum* Papal Encyclical and by Pope Pius XI's *Quadragesimo Anno* of 1931, which was closely allied to it. These were not reactionary documents; they showed a considerable degree of social conscience and were logical and coherent in their thinking, though the later of the two also showed traces of the corporate and vocational thinking of its time.[4] It was widely believed that de Valera had allowed Dr John Charles McQuaid – who shortly afterwards became Archbishop of Dublin with de Valera's support – a considerable input when he was shaping the terms of the Constitution, but it appears that he only consulted him along with a number of others. In the end, a national referendum approved of it by 685,105 votes to 526,945, which does not seem an overwhelming margin.

It is sometimes said that this vote made Catholicism the official Church of the State, but the wording of the controversial clause was deliberately ambiguous, or at least capable of varying interpretations. Many of the clergy themselves seem to have felt that they had been let down, and some spokesmen for the Catholic Right even denounced it – notably Dr Alfred O'Rahilly, in a pamphlet called *Thoughts on the*

Constitution.[5] De Valera had once again shown his sense of verbal and diplomatic shadings; he was keeping his options open, as usual. He cannot, however, have been unaware that the Constitution helped to copper-fasten Partition, since the Northern Unionists would inevitably view it as the official creation of a Catholic State. (On the other hand, when the religious clause was repealed during the 1970s, Orange opinion which previously had condemned it paid virtually no attention to its abolition.) Perhaps, in retrospect, the verdict should be that while de Valera had not established a State Church, he had established an official Catholic State, or at least a State permeated by a Catholic ethos. (It is interesting to note that his Constitution was studied closely by certain other countries and that Burma, for instance, modelled its own on his, giving Buddhism a corresponding 'special position'.)[6]

That in itself is anathema to contemporary thinking, which is essentially secular and often anti-clerical. Yet de Valera was neither looking back to the Middle Ages nor forward to the kind of regime which Spain got a few years later. As his record then and later showed, he was hostile to Fascism and his policies on land distribution and other matters were actually closer to those of the Spanish Left than to Franco's. What, then, was his real motive? He was always a believing Catholic, though not a clericalist one – in fact, this deep and almost mystical religious belief was one of his strongest traits. However, his Constitution was not a personal declaration of faith; it was a carefully pondered political document for an entire nation. I believe that he viewed it primarily as yet another stage of national self-definition, by which Ireland took its place among the historic old Catholic states of Europe – Poland, Austria etc. And as a pragmatic politician, he may have calculated that in a decade when extreme political ideologies – both Left and Right – were winning converts in Europe at a terrifying rate, Catholicism at least gave Ireland a broad, popular, stabilising faith. He must also have been fully aware of the clergy's value in maintaining some moral balance and order in a country with a long though intermittent history of violence, and in a largely rural society which in many respects was still unruly and crude and under-educated. Even Yeats, viewing the legacy of Civil War violence and anarchy and the moral vacuum which threatened to grow out of it, did not shrink from saying that the Church was now badly needed, to restore order and values among young people.[7]

Irish Catholicism is often described as repressive, and so it was in many or even most senses, but how effective would it have been as a grassroots moral force if it had been anything else? The question has to be faced realistically and today's ready-made answer, that of the liberal middle-class agenda, does not seem adequate in the context of two generations ago. Like Scottish and Welsh Calvinism, the post-Famine Church in Ireland had developed as an antidote to the poverty and degradation of the mass of the population in the mid-nineteenth century, when evangelical religion proved to be virtually the only force which could lift demoralised human beings to some level of self-discipline and self-respect. To have undermined this foundation, whether deliberately or arbitrarily, would have been socially irresponsible.

Here, perhaps, we have the key to much of the hold which the Church exercised on the mass of the people until very recently. It gave them the only morality they knew, it enriched their often hard, underprivileged lives with its rituals and Sacraments, baptised their children, married their young people and buried their dead. With institutions such as the Sunday Mass ('half-eleven Mass' was the standard one to attend in rural areas) it provided both a sense of ancestral Sabbath rites and a communal meeting-place, and while it sometimes looked sourly on dancing and other amusements, it encouraged sport as an outlet for surplus energies – something which Communist regimes also discovered. Through its parades and other activities it gave some public pageantry to a country which – thanks largely to the socio-political revolution – was woefully short of that dimension of public life, and even confirmed atheists, agnostics and anti-clericals often remembered their First Communion all their lives as a day of radiant innocence. In short, it was woven deeply into the texture of daily life and while it may have terrified people intermittently with the threat of Hell Fire, it promised redemption for the sinner and eternal life for all.

The clergy themselves were drawn heavily from the small-farmer class and from the small-town bourgeoisie, and as such had the asset of being close to and representative of their parishioners, usually sharing the same outlook and values. In spite of the pomp and circumstance adopted by some of the higher clergy, the privileged appearance of the bishops' palaces with their spacious gardens, and the decree-from-on-high tone customary with the hierarchy in its public pronouncements, the Catholic Church in Ireland was essentially a people's Church, except when it moved into theological areas where the ordinary man could not follow it and probably did not care to. It was the willing obedience of the people towards their priests which incensed and bewildered many liberals and others who could only put it down to educational brainwashing from childhood upwards, or to folk superstition and ignorance, or to the Wiles of Rome about which most Anglo-Saxon or Anglo-American liberals were traditionally paranoid.[8] And, no doubt, there was a very strong culture of obedience in Ireland in those days, though that was true of many other countries at the time, when belief in authority was still strong at nearly all levels. (A New York Jewish author once told me that he grew up during the 1930s in an atmosphere of unquestioning obedience, both to his parents and the rabbis, and that on the whole he considered this a positive and stabilising force.) Yet the – possibly unpalatable, yet unavoidable – fact seems to be, more or less, that the mass of people liked the Church as it was, and either did not want a different one or lacked the vision to imagine any alternative. Or if they did not actually like it, they accepted it as part of the scheme of things, just as they accepted the reality of being ruled by party politicians few of whom they admired personally.

All this is to state the positive side. The negative one was a moral narrowness and sometimes a crippling lack of tolerance and charity – common defects in any simplistic, black-and-white code of morality. The priests were, for the most part, very ordinary men (very often younger sons of farmers) without original ideas or judgement, and untrained in any method of constructive criticism – something which would certainly not have been encouraged officially, in any case. Relatively few of them had ever been abroad and so had no standards of comparison with other European countries, including Catholic ones; a visit to Rome once in a lifetime, with a possible view of the Pope addressing crowds in St Peter's Square, was an ambition which many of them nursed but only a handful realised. This gave their outlook a certain fundamentalist harshness and crudity, unsoftened by Continental humanism or by the spirit of compromise and moderation which priests had (often very unwillingly) acquired in countries where anti-clerical traditions or religious indifferentism were strong. This was exemplified at its worst by the so-called 'Missions' in which the Redemptorists were prominent, and which were, in effect, communal emotional orgies looking back to the worst and most mindless excesses of nineteenth-century religious revivalism.

Culturally the clergy were mostly philistines, as was immediately obvious from the ugliness of many or most of the parish churches, the vulgar plaster saints (usually imported from Italy), the crudely painted Stations of the Cross, the mass-produced benches with their varnished glaze like cheap shop furniture. Intellectually they were often naïve – an admiration for G. K. Chesterton, for instance, was equated with mental sophistication, and the bulk of them regarded modern thought, literature and art as predominantly 'pagan' (a favourite word of the period), dangerous, and subversive, part of the corrosive modernism which was eating away at the foundations of the whole Christian world. Politically they mostly inclined towards the Right,[9] seeing the Left as an agent of secularisation and materialism, or even as an active enemy of religion in any forms – which was not unreasonable, given the persecution of the Church in Mexico under a left-wing government, in Spain under the Republic, in all Communist countries, and even in republican France earlier in the century.[10] This gave their general outlook a distinctly paranoiac tinge, and also reinforced the 'missionary complex' which had been an Irish characteristic through the ages. Concerning the latter aspect, an anecdote (probably apocryphal) circulated about Gogarty walking down Grafton Street in Dublin one day and being stopped by two nuns with collection boxes. For what or whom were they collecting? he asked civilly. For the Maynooth Mission to China, they replied in unison. Gogarty brusquely refused to contribute, though as the two offended sisters walked off, he had a sudden inspiration and ran after them. 'But listen,' he called out, 'if you ever hear of a Chinese mission to Maynooth – I'm your man!'

It is obvious that there could be few areas in common between these people and the typical Irish intellectual. The clergy wanted the people to believe, to 'keep the faith' first and last; in contrast, the intellectuals wanted them to think and to question things rather than to swallow them unconditionally. Liam O'Flaherty fell foul of priests on a number of occasions, though he often gave back as good as he got, while Frank O'Connor was regarded by many clergy with a dislike and suspicion which was enhanced by his divorce – an unpardonable sin in their eyes. O'Faolain seems to have been perceived by at least a section of opinion in Maynooth as a special threat, because much of his writings encouraged a kind of Catholic liberalism and a broader, more humanistic standpoint which allowed some degree of doctrinal and even moral flexibility.[11] The fact that O'Faolain sometimes evoked the hallowed name of Cardinal Newman made things worse in their eyes, since Newman's greatest propaganda value to the clergy was as a converted Englishman who had laboured to give Irish Catholics their own university, and as an intellectual who had submitted with due humility to Rome. Writing in *The Bell* after the Mother and Child controversy of 1951, O'Faolain coined the phrase 'The Dáil proposes; Maynooth disposes' and apart from quoting Newman to bolster some of his arguments, in the words of Maurice Harmon he 'pointed to the figure and the example of Daniel O'Connell, the liberal layman, ready to work with the Church but ready also to resist the Church when he thought it necessary'.[12]

Criticism such as this must have flashed a red light to the hierarchy. The last thing most of the bishops wanted, it seems, was a new generation of independent-minded, highly educated and literate Catholic laymen quoting Pascal or Mauriac, who might ask awkward questions and undermine the people's unquestioning belief in their priests. This, in retrospect, was one of their most tragic mistakes, and one which goes far to explain why today the educated classes in Ireland have steadily fallen away from religion. The flock must dutifully follow the God-appointed shepherd and not stray after its own whims. This, after all, was an attitude formulated many years before in Canon Sheehan's novel *My New Curate*, in which the parish priest Father Dan – a decent, kindly clerical bigot of the old school – is portrayed as a wise and gentle pastor controlling his flock like errant children, for their own spiritual and moral good. Such a mentality could only be fatal to itself in the long run, as Ireland moved farther away from being a society of under-educated peasants to a modern middle-class one. Obviously a time must come when even the uneducated and the simple-minded would realise that they lived in a world where Communism would not be abolished by mass Rosary rallies, or the danger of world war by pilgrimages to Lourdes.

Still, O'Faolain was in no danger of excommunication, and while he was more than once in trouble with the Censorship Board, his opinions were read and respected. Once again, we should beware of seeing the epoch as homogeneous and monolithic; there were many shades of opinion, and among the intellectuals and writers there was a wide range of religious – and irreligious – viewpoints. Certainly it does not follow that most sincere Catholic writers were right-wing bigots, or at least reactionaries; there were liberal Catholics who were sincere believers, yet who also reserved the right to think and analyse with a certain independence of judgement. Francis MacManus was Catholic through and through, and in most respects a very typical Irish writer-intellectual of his time, but his novels and other writings bear witness to a great deal of inner questioning and conflict as well as a firm basis of faith. In this sense, he probably represented a wider section of Catholic opinion than is realised today. He was certainly not the man to be bullied by priests, as he showed in his long years of service in Radio Éireann which were marked by intellectual courage and independence. His immediate superior in RÉ, the poet Roibeárd Ó Faracháin, was a strong neo-Thomist and an admirer of Chesterton, yet he was also a supporter of the Labour Party and he protected the writer James Plunkett in 1955, when a section of the Irish press had attacked Plunkett for being one of a number of people who travelled to the Soviet Union as more or less official guests.[13] The outlook of the English artist/thinker Eric Gill, who was both a zealous Catholic and a Leftist, had some influence on Irish Catholic thinking – particularly his Chestertonian admiration of the medieval guild system; and Ó Faracháin belonged to this trend.[14]

Kate O'Brien, though she too suffered under the censorship and for periods of her life chose to live abroad, seems in some scarcely orthodox sense to have kept her religious faith, which had been mellowed by the experience of Continental Catholicism. Her novels remain especially valuable because they depict the impact of the Church on thinking, educated, middle-class women, through the medium of nuns as well as of male clergy. She spoke to and for people who, while they might be critical of many of the Church's sayings and doings, still counted themselves believing Catholics in spiritual communion with millions around the world. Criticism of Rome did not necessarily imply rejection of it; there was an intellectual appreciation of the greatness of its traditions and its enduring relevance. Even the negative bitterness of numerous writer-intellectuals was a kind of inverted tribute to it and its potent spell; while the conversion to Rome of Evie Hone, the best-known stained-glass artist of her generation, created ripples in the Irish art world which still have not entirely ceased.

A tradition which was strong well into the postwar years, but has since steadily weakened and is now virtually extinct, was that of the old European Right which Chesterton and Belloc, in particular, had given a new interpretation and a new, almost romantic currency. Chesterton's much-anthologised poem 'Lepanto', which glorified Don John of Austria's victory over the Turkish fleet in 1571, expressed a kind of triumphalist Catholicism which still saw itself as defending Christian Europe from its traditional enemies, both within and without. Historically this attitude made a special appeal in Ireland, which was aware of its identification with Catholic Europe in past centuries and previous wars. Chesterton particularly admired the Poles, who for him represented a heroic, knightly, idealistic people guarding the frontiers of Catholic Europe – an attitude, of course, endorsed by the present Pope. His attitude towards Ireland was rather similar, which added to his already high standing there, and both he and Belloc lectured at various times in

Dublin.[15] Certain Irish intellectuals, however, including Austin Clarke, detested Chesterton and his influence.

Doctrine apart, there remains the black-letter issue of Catholicism and sex, which has tended to dominate discussion of religious issues now that sex, from being a taboo subject, has become almost an obsession – precisely, in fact, what it supposedly was with the Irish clergy a generation ago. In the case of a writer such as Austin Clarke, who was the son of a religion-obsessed mother but who also inherited the romantic paganism of the eighteen-nineties and its cult of physical beauty, the conflict between sexual desire and austerity or self-denial – nowadays called 'repression' – is particularly acute and at times agonising. This, however, is neither exclusively Irish nor even exclusively Catholic; it is part of a European dialogue between flesh and spirit which is carried out in the writings of Baudelaire and many others, and is at least as old as the Middle Ages or even neo-Platonism. It underlies the poetry of the Troubadours and runs like a *Leit-motiv* through that of Keats, Tennyson, Hopkins, not to mention Yeats. In Clarke's own words:

> *Burn Ovid with the rest. Lovers will find*
> *A hedge-school for themselves and learn by heart*
> *All that the clergy banish from the mind*
> *When hands are joined and head bows in the dark.*
> — 'Penal Law'[16]

In Patrick Kavanagh's work, by contrast, sex is not so much a moral issue as a need whose satisfaction is obstructed by personal inhibition and awkwardness, by social and moral convention, above all by the sheer shortage of available women – what Brendan Behan called 'the great scarcity of crumpet'.[17] Tarry Flynn, who is obviously the young Kavanagh in person, personifies a certain type of rural Irish male who is uneasy with the other sex and finds it almost impossible to cross the gulf between them. Such a man goes to a dance but lacks the courage to dance; he talks and boasts to his friends about sexual exploits, but these are imaginary and they know it. Tarry is also one of the earliest of what soon became a literary stereotype that, strangely enough, is still acceptable not only to English publishers but to Irish readers, who presumably know that it is a cliché decades out of date. There are only two recognised options for Tarry, marriage or bachelorhood; and the lot of the rural bachelor – another Irish literary obsession – is portrayed sombrely in the character of Maguire in *The Great Hunger*. (There is of course a third option, that of a successful lecher, but Kavanagh/Tarry was temperamentally unsuited to the role.) In such a society, women hoard their virginity for the marriage market, or because they are afraid of being gossiped about in the pubs, and the supply of sex – as far as human nature allows it – is cut off from young unmarried males. As a result, these are either forced to the altar, or have no opportunity to seduce other men's wives and daughters, and so wither into lonely bachelors.[18]

Today this, too, is blamed routinely on the clergy and their inflexible taboos, but though often dressed up in moral and religious platitudes, it was essentially a social, financial and familial pattern, determined above all by poverty or mere subsistence living and by a scarcity of jobs. In post-Famine Ireland many males, remembering the evils of population sprawl in the past and barely able to support themselves, seem to have preferred loneliness and infertility – though that scarcely justifies the claim by Arland Ussher that the Irishman 'notoriously shies away from marriage and sex'. Meanwhile many of the young women, unwilling either to slave on farms or become dependent relatives, chose to emigrate. Nevertheless, many people did marry. Irish marriages might often be relatively late and seemingly reluctant, but they tended to produce large families of children. Here again, the moral issues seem to have obscured the economic base.

Other writers preferred simply to damn the Church and religion generally, a reflex which has had plenty of support in recent years. So powerful was the psychological imprint of an Irish Catholic upbringing that most sensitive people were/are marked by it for life, some hating its whole ethos and feeling that it had left them emotionally stunted, others rejecting it doctrinally and morally, yet remembering its rituals and sonorous Latin and the atmosphere of Good Friday leading on to the joyous, half-pagan festival of Easter Sunday and the Resurrection. For instance, certain poems of Padraic Fallon, such as 'Coat of Arms' and 'Christmas Vigil', celebrate Sunday mass-going and religious festivals through the eye of a complex agnostic recalling his childhood:

> The fields unyoked and
> Turned loose, all occupation gone
> But the business of man
> In the holy city
> That had no spires
> Visible or choirs, a faint angelic land.

For its visual aspect, one has only to look at some of the brooding Good Friday paintings of the artist Tony O'Malley to realise that 'Irish spirituality' is no myth, even if so many Irish men and women looked for it in confraternities and Rosary rallies, where it was not to be found. Under all the sentimental popular religiosity, and the dogmatism and myopia of unimaginative clerics, there was a pure underground stream of something which can only be called 'soul'. When John Betjeman was in Ireland during the early Forties (see Chapter One), this quality impressed itself on the consciousness of the ultra-clever, deeply cultured Anglican poet and scholar who had a genuine religious strain himself, as many of his poems show. And a greater poet than Betjeman, Louis MacNeice, in one of his late poems written in Donegal, surmises what his life would have been like if he had been born locally (as a Catholic presumably) and had put down roots there:

As though the window opened
And the ancient cross on the hillside meant myself.[19]

It was a fantasy, of course, but MacNeice in later life appears to have viewed Catholic and nationalist Ireland with more tolerance and understanding than before. Perhaps he now saw or sensed that in spite of all its crudities, ugliness and blind spots, Irish Catholicism enshrined something which went back in time and penetrated deep into the national and racial psyche, linking men and women to previous centuries and reconciling them to the trials and threats of the present.

W hen the Eucharistic Congress was staged (probably the appropriate word) in Dublin in 1932, the Catholic Church in Ireland arguably reached its zenith of triumphalism. Many of the people involved must have felt that the Penal Laws and the Famine were now cancelled out, that the ghosts of Cardinal Cullen, Archbishop Mac Hale, Archbishop Walsh and other clerical potentates of the nineteenth century were smiling down from Heaven, and that Ireland had finally come of age as a Catholic country. Chesterton, who was treated almost like visiting royalty, was deeply moved by it all, by the huge crowds, by the general atmosphere of popular devotion mixed with good humour, by the magnificent hospitality, and by the climax of the mass in the Pro-Cathedral when St Patrick's Bell was solemnly rung.[20] The once-golden voice of the great tenor John McCormack, now grown a little reedy and thin, was heard by thousands singing 'Panis Angelicus'. One of the few 'begrudgers' was AE, who had fled for refuge to the Wicklow Hills (some even say, to Donegal) from where he allegedly called on the heavens to rain and thunder on what, to him, seemed no more than a mass mummery organised by Rome. However, the entire event appears to have been splendidly organised and ran smoothly, one of those flashes of Celtic flair which the Irish occasionally produce, as happened on the visit to Ireland of Pope John Paul II half a century later. It was a multinational affair, with groups attending from all over Europe and even farther afield – possibly the most remarkable feat of organisation since the 1908 Durbar called by Lord Curzon in India.

Many of the participants and spectators felt that they were seeing the apotheosis of the true, timeless, Christian Ireland, stretching back to St Patrick and forward into another millennium. A colder, more historically conscious verdict might be that they were witnessing the climax of the post-Famine Church, making amends for the times when the landlords and the Protestant establishment had confined their worshipping to bare chapels on bog and waste land and had not allowed them to build their own cathedrals. In reality, the triumphalist period of the Irish Church lasted little more than another thirty years, since, in my opinion, 1951 sowed the seeds of its gradual decline. But were not the seeds of that decline already present, in any case?

This may seem rather paradoxical, but it is not when the issue is viewed historically. In the nineteenth century Catholic prelates such as Mac Hale, 'J. K. L.', Cullen, Walsh and a few others had been among the greatest Irishmen of their age; indeed their fellow-countrymen sometimes looked to them for the guidance and reassurance they did not get from their politicians. Yet search the history of Irish Catholicism from 1925 to 1955, and what do you find? It is hard to see even one genuinely major figure – McQuaid, Lucey, Browne, etc. may have seemed so to their contemporaries, but they are not to us. They were conscientious, single-track men with (on their own definition of it at least) a genuine social conscience, and not quite the rampant zealots of contemporary propaganda; but most of what they stood for has been swept away. Ceremonial figureheads such as Cardinal McRory are simply forgotten. There are remarkable individual churchmen of the period such as Monsignor Boylan the great Biblical scholar, or Mgr Pádraig de Brún the 'myriad-minded' scholar, academic and poet, or Canon Hayes the founder of Muintir na Tíre which did so much for Irish rural life, or various distinguished theologians, educators and scholars who left their mark on Irish life. Yet the fact remains that there is no unarguably great public figure among them who has created history. Similarly, the typical Irish priest of the period now appears limited and dogmatic, a provincial dealing with other provincials, unable to pull off the blinkers of his upbringing and education and to see into the heart of his age. Until quite recently, his training was often narrow and 'religious life' at its worst and most claustrophobic amounted to little more than ideological brainwashing – a fact borne out in a recent short book by a Redemptorist priest who began his training during the 1950s.[21]

There is no Irish Catholic philosopher of European stature in the modern epoch, no thinker/theologian of the calibre of Barth or Tillich or the Austrian Karl Rahner. The native vitality of Irish religion seems to have been swallowed up in almost slavish obedience to Rome, and the creation of a closely-knit, disciplined but largely unquestioning clerical bureaucracy took precedence over the discovery or encouragement of men with original minds and forward-looking vision. There was, to be blunt, an overriding conformity and mediocrity, a decision to go almost always for the 'safe' man and the orthodox mentality, for which the Church is paying in Peter's Pence today. Outspoken and intelligent men were distrusted, as they so often are in other walks of Irish life. When there was a departure from this narrowness, as in the importation from America of Father Peyton and his Rosary Crusade in the postwar years, the result was mere populist vulgarity – the Catholic equivalent to Billy Graham. The cult of Lourdes and Fatima might be understandable on a populist level, but to many thinking people, the quasi-official cant propagated about these highly dubious phenomena can only have seemed nauseous (though Yeats, curiously enough, was interested in 'miracles' of this kind, while Francis Stuart at one stage of his life acted as a stretcher-bearer at Lourdes Basilica. In the poem from 'Vacillations' addressed to the Catholic thinker Friedrich von Huegel, Yeats wrote:

The body of Saint Teresa lies undecayed in tomb,
Bathed in miraculous oil, sweet odours from it come . . .)

In its intolerance of any opposition, its inability to accept even constructive criticism from others or to criticise itself, lay the seeds of the Church's dilemma today. Thanks to an overwhelming Catholic majority, it had no organised anti-clerical groupings to contend with, no equivalent of the old Radical Party in France, nothing which would have kept it alert, self-aware and sensitive to changing circumstances and modernist currents. Instead, it had an unfocused, paranoid obsession with 'paganism' and materialism in modern life and with Communism in the East; of these, the first two had little relevance in as poor a country as Ireland, while the third had none at all. Its vocal critics were largely confined to a handful of rather old-fashioned and prosy liberals writing in the letters column of *The Irish Times* and to the scattered intelligentsia who had negligible public support. The old Fenian and republican tradition of anti-clericalism was virtually moribund, and de Valera was not the man to encourage or revive it.

Schoolchildren learned that Ireland was still the Land of Saints and Scholars, while the version of Church history which I was taught at secondary level intemperately demonised Luther, Voltaire, the Eastern Schism and virtually every important thinker of the nineteenth century from Hegel to Nietzsche. Ecumenism was an unknown word, though to be fair, none of the priests who taught me ever declared that Protestants, Jews or Moslems were damned – they were merely misguided and led astray. Some of these clerical teachers were even capable of discussing the theory of evolution in the classroom, though without quite admitting its plausibility. But almost always, at a certain stage, the massive, opaque curtain of orthodoxy descended, and with it the tacit implication that what Rome had spoken on was beyond discussion or argument. For the most part Ireland, lay as well as clerical, was proud to think that the Pope had a special affection for it and regarded it as the brightest jewel in his crown, or rather in the papal tiara. There was even a serious proposal, in the years just after the war, that Ireland might offer Pius XII official sanctuary in the event of a Communist victory in the Italian elections – a kind of historical repeat, in effect, of the Babylonian Captivity of the Papacy at Avignon in the late Middle Ages. It had, apparently, the backing of some leading Irish diplomats but was never put to the test.

The Catholic Church in Ireland seemed an immovable, massive, broad-based monolith, probably comforting and reassuring to the majority, though overbearing and even hateful in the eyes of a minority. It had a certain fundamentalist quality rather like the religiosity of the American Mid-West – a Rosary Belt, it might be called, instead of a Bible Belt. However, its hold on the mass of people, though powerful, was not absolute and certainly not the timeless, changeless edifice the clergy and lay zealots thought it was. Patrick Kavanagh was one of the few people to realise and even say, with blunt and earthy sense,[22] that many people believed in it more out of convenience than out of any deep conviction – that it was, in fact, something which suited them for the moment, but from which they might withdraw allegiance if and when it failed to do so in the future. So it has proved, since all forms of belief are subjects to swings and reactions; as John Cowper Powys remarks in *The Pleasures of Literature*, both religion and rationalism (the orthodoxy of our own time) are as much matters of fashion as most other human activities are. After all, what society could have been more vocally Christian than Victorian England, and where are its values now? English Protestantism has faded into English rationalism and agnosticism.

However, with all of its numerous blind spots, its narrowness and frequent lack of charity, the philistinism of which it was so frequently accused, and its bouts of sheer stupidity, the record of the Irish Church in some fields is better than is often realised. In spite of its continuing feuds with the intelligentsia, it almost always respected scholarship and even the most bumptious parish priest might turn out to be, in private, an ardent reader (though not of banned books) and an enthusiastic amateur historian, archaeologist and local chronicler. Priests were often – like Father Dan's New Curate – initiators of local enterprise and parish activities, such as amateur drama and musical societies. As teachers and educators, they did not spare themselves and they were capable of taking extra pains to encourage pupils whom they considered bright or gifted beyond the ordinary. (This is true of nuns as well as priests.) In the visual arts, it should not be forgotten that they patronised the work of Harry Clarke and other stained-glass artists, while churches all over the country are enriched by the craftsmanship and vision of Oisín Kelly (a Protestant, incidentally), Imogen Stuart, Patrick Pye and other artists of note. In the 1940s and 1950s, Father Jack Hanlon was one of the central figures in the annual Living Art Exhibition in Dublin. When in 1946 Rouault's picture 'Christ and the Soldier' was attacked and rejected publicly by Dublin Corporation, it was given refuge in Maynooth, where there were visually educated priests who fully recognised what the dim-witted public representatives did not or could not see – that Rouault was a great religious artist. The clergy also built some handsome churches and colleges, though they found no architect equal to Pugin in the nineteenth century or even his leading Irish disciple, McCarthy (perhaps there was none to be found?). The generally high level of the Jesuit-edited magazine *Studies* deserves notice and so does the remarkable florescence of the *Capuchin Annual* under Father Senan.

These are not isolated instances; in all areas of Irish life it is possible to find the influence of cultured, intelligent priests and nuns. But it is necessary to peer behind the dour, dogmatic, public face of the Church in order to see and identify them. Nor should the conservative or even reactionary character of so much clerical thinking be blamed purely on native Irish crankiness and introversion – though quite undeniably there was a good deal of that. Roman Catholicism in general had been on the defensive since the days of Pius IX ('Pio Nono') and the virulent anti-Christianity of many twentieth-century regimes made many sincere and unaggressive believers feel that their Church was going through its worst period of persecution since the Catacombs. To a considerable extent, the Irish bishops were merely echoing the Vatican which felt itself lapped about with enemies – and often was, in practice. As late as 1950, Pius XII in the document *Humani Generis* came down decisively against the progressive Catholic theologians in France, which was followed by a wave of intellectual repression in seminaries and religious orders; some years later came the clamp-down on the French worker-priests. It was not until 1961, with the saintly and benevolent John XXIII's *Mater et Magistra*, that the great Thaw genuinely began.

Chapter 15

THE LITERARY CENSORSHIP

Literary censorship is for many people the chief stumbling-block to any intellectual reconsideration of what is still regarded as the Thirty Years' Darkness. Along with the Church and intemperate nationalism, it has done more to create the *legenda negra* that clings to an entire epoch than any other factor, even economic ones. The basic facts cannot be refuted – the list of the works banned under the Censorship of Publications Act speaks for itself, and so does the anger and humiliation of the Irish writers who found themselves classed with mercenary pornographers, or deprived of a large share of their legitimate income. It is almost irrelevant that in its last ten or dozen years of life the literary censorship was an anachronism, increasingly ridiculed and condemned, yet retained because politicians would not risk losing the votes of ageing prudes and zealots, or provoking the anger of the clergy, by abolishing the institution which had made Ireland look absurd in the eyes of all Europe. By that stage it had relatively few public defenders, while Irish writers had been steadily denouncing it for decades, and it had even become counter-productive by throwing the publicity spotlight on to the very books it banned.

Virtually every leading Irish fiction-writer between 1929 and the mid-1960s suffered under censorship, the exception being, once again, James Joyce, the eternal outsider. Frank O'Connor, Seán O'Faolain, Kate O'Brien, Liam O'Flaherty, Samuel Beckett, Benedict Kiely, Norah Hoult all had at least one book banned, while some of the poets too suffered for their occasional ventures into prose writing; Austin Clarke's novels were put on the censored list, and Patrick Kavanagh's *Tarry Flynn* was briefly threatened with the same fate (heaven knows why) but escaped it. One of the most controversial acts of the censorship was the banning of Francis Hackett's almost forgotten *The Green Lion* in 1936, which provoked a furious bout of polemics and led to Hackett's emigration from Ireland along with his Danish wife, the writer Signe Toksvig.[1] Hackett had been at Clongowes with Joyce, and his novel is a kind of *Bildungsroman* portraying a young Parnellite who undergoes a perfectly normal and unremarkable sexual awakening of the kind which any adult could see around him anytime. Possibly it was the criticism of the Jesuits and of clerical celibacy which angered people more than its harmless, rather sentimentalised sexuality. Hackett, however, was a formidable controversialist and polemicist who had learned in the hard school of American literary journalism, and he knew exactly how to put his case over to the public and to raise hell. The dust raised over his essentially unremarkable novel hovered in the air for decades afterwards. By contrast, the banning of O'Faolain's *Bird Alone* at about the same time seems virtually to have removed it from public consciousness for years, although a handful of followers (e.g. the short-story writer and critic Maurice Kennedy) maintained over decades that it was 'the' great Irish novel. When, eventually, it was republished in the early 1980s, it made disappointingly little impact – in fact, the relatively lurid quality of most modern fiction made it seem almost old-maidish. *Bird Alone* had missed the tide, and its public.

Kate O'Brien's *Land of Spices* brings in, very briefly, a homosexual incident, described in highly conventional language, but that was enough to secure its condemnation. Since she was a believing though unconventional Catholic, this piece of official stupidity at least showed that the censors struck with impartial hostility. In fact, there was much embarrassment among the more intellectual members of the Irish clergy when the Censorship Board banned Graham Greene's *The Heart of the Matter* just when Greene had become one of the Church's showpiece Catholic writers. The treatment of O'Faolain, who had run into trouble with the censors from early in his career with the banning of *Midsummer Night's Madness*, was another proof that the Catholic intellectual was not immune from condemnation – though Francis MacManus went unscathed throughout his busy years of writing. Frank O'Connor suffered both as a fiction writer and as a poet-translator: his second novel, *Dutch Interior*, was banned in 1940 and five years later his translation of Merriman's *The Midnight Court* was also proscribed, although it was not banned in the Irish original nor was the alternative translation by Arland Ussher. In general, however, poets and verse-writers went immune, presumably on the philistine but factually sound supposition that only a small minority of readers bothered to take poetry seriously.

The banning of Behan's *Borstal Boy* in 1958 was a major blunder in every sense, since it was one of those obvious classics which caught on with the public almost straightaway, and Behan's own personal popularity was high. The ban did not stop it from being widely read, but it was undoubtedly one more nail in the coffin of censorship. Behan himself, who characteristically appears to have enjoyed much of the resultant publicity, went around Dublin singing, to the tune of 'MacNamara's Band':

> My name is Brendan Behan, I'm the latest of the Banned;
> And though we're few in number we're the best Banned in the land . . .

However, the Board had not learned its lesson, and well into the Sixties it was still active, banning novels by Edna O'Brien and John McGahern's *The Dark*. In the case of these writers, it merely helped to project them into media notoriety and consequent literary fame, since the debate over these decisions showed that public attitudes were changing greatly. By now, the censors were not only odious but ridiculous – and in Ireland, ridicule kills more painfully than moral denunciation.

The belief is widespread that Irish censorship was primarily a clerical initiative, growing in strength and arrogance after the period of triumphalism initiated by the Eucharistic Congress of 1932. The facts, however, do not appear to bear this out, since a large number of the worst censors were laymen and the Censorship Board sometimes included Protestant members. The passage of the original Censorship of Publications Act through both Houses of the Oireachtas in 1929 was largely a secular initiative, with the notorious Senator McGuinness a key figure – though there is no doubt at all that he had considerable clerical backing. Neither was the mentality it represented a new phenomenon, since the turn-of-the-century Irish society which George Moore presents in *Hail and Farewell* teems with self-appointed censors. As Patrick Maume says in his excellent short study of D. P. Moran, the influential editor of the *Leader*: 'The xenophobia, censorship mentality and Gaelic chauvinism which disfigured the post-independence state were present before 1914.'[2] They merely became more codified and institutionalised from the 1920s onwards, so both Shaw and Yeats were adequately forewarned and forearmed before the 1929 Act became law. Much of the impetus towards creating the Irish Academy of Letters came from this knowledge of the wrath and repression to come, since it only legalised what already existed.

Joyce apart – and copies of *Ulysses*, though in theory obtainable, were often in practice hard to track down – a high percentage of the leading twentieth-century writers were banned in the Free State/Irish Republic. They included Thomas and Heinrich Mann, Shaw himself, Stefan Zweig, Wyndham Lewis, Scott Fitzgerald, Ernest Hemingway, Henri Barbusse, Maxim Gorki (very strange indeed, since he was a major influence on the Irish short story and was greatly admired by Corkery, rather a sexual prude), André Malraux, Mikhail Sholokhov, Aldous Huxley, Theodore Dreiser, Henry de Montherlant, Erich Maria Remarque, Compton Mackenzie (a regular visitor to Ireland and greatly esteemed there), Charles Morgan, D. H. Lawrence, John Cowper Powys and his brothers Theodore and Llewellyn, Robert Graves, Evelyn Waugh, Scholem Asch, Romain Rolland, Somerset Maugham (though his books were enormously popular in Ireland, this did not prevent *Cakes and Ale* from falling foul of the censors). Somehow the censors even detected something 'indecent and obscene' (the stock epithets) in certain novels of A. J. Cronin, a Scottish Catholic (though a socialist) and a great favourite with pietistic Irish readers who also trooped to see the sentimental films based on his books.

The Papal Index (*Index librorum prohibitorum*) also operated in Ireland, though it was not legally binding and the bookshops – at least in theory – could ignore it if they saw fit, or rather if they thought it safe. This meant that for many years the novels of Dumas were extremely hard to find, even in second-hand bookshops.

Sometimes, too, the booksellers went beyond the decrees of official censorship and refused to stock certain works which they considered less than respectable, or liable to excite the interest of those scourges of Irish culture, the self-appointed lay censors. It was often such people who, in their senseless zeal, sent marked passages of books they had read and considered offensive to the Board. The Legion of Mary (caricatured in Mervyn Wall's novel *Leaves for the Burning* as the Daughters of Glory) were also an intermittent source of nuisance.

Book censorship, however, was not supported only by puritans, zealots and cranks. There was the married, well-off woman ('I'm no prude, but there are limits') who might be horrified to find one of her children reading a copy of the mildly scandalous bestseller *Forever Amber*. There was the suburban father, usually a normal and even jovial fellow, who would go purple at the thought of 'filth' falling into the hands of his teenage daughters. There were also the sophisticates who felt that *non-legenda* passages, old or new, were best kept out of the hands of the constitutionally smutty-minded Common Man. Early in the history of the State the Film Censor, James Montgomery, had more or less maintained that the mass of people lacked the wit or self-control to be shown explicitly sexual scenes, whereas a sophisticated man or woman of the world could cope. As a result, for decades some excellent (and many bad) films were hacked to a point at which some of them were almost unintelligible. Curiously, however, there was relatively little censorship of plays; in fact, it frequently happened that Irish plays crossing to London were verbally softened there because their language was considered 'crude'.

It should be emphasised, however, that there was no official censorship on ideas, and that even some strongly anti-clerical literature was allowed to circulate relatively freely, including H. G. Wells's *Crux Ansata* which was a sustained diatribe against the Catholic Church. The Censorship Board was not empowered to dictate to people what opinions they might or might not hold, although the clergy were frequently zealous in condemning virtually every prominent non-Christian thinker of the last century and a half. (The Church history which formed part of my secondary school course denounced Hegel, Nietzsche and Schopenhauer collectively as 'pantheists'. At that time, admittedly, Nietzsche was *persona non grata* with many political and intellectual camps and was frequently denounced as a forerunner of Nazism. His works were hard to obtain and I read many of them for the first time while sitting in the National Library. He was, however, frequently discussed in the *Dublin Magazine* by Arland Ussher.) The opinion which one hears stated again and again, and which is sometimes treated as historical fact, that censorship was fundamentally an expression of anti-intellectualism, is in itself very dubious. In the first place, 'quality' literature represented only a fraction of the total amount banned, so writer-intellectuals were not especially targeted. Secondly, the polemical and socio-political writings of these people was scarcely interfered with, and they were generally free to denounce in print whatever institutions – including censorship – they thought fit. The claim that Ireland lacked intellectual freedom is a travesty of the facts. Literary, political and intellectual controversy was constant, though it was also often outspokenly personal, and too much energy was spent on internecine quarrels rather than in combining in a triumphal march against the philistines.

Whatever about the general Irish readership for modern literature, which suffered a definite degree of deprivation, the average writer or intellectual usually had relatively little difficulty in obtaining the books he or she wanted. My own, strictly subjective impression is that censorship was inefficient in practice and operated like a large-holed net through which all sorts of things could seep in. From the middle Fifties, in particular, it became particularly porous, and it was not uncommon to find banned books openly on sale, while newspapers and magazines often reviewed them regardless of officialdom. The younger generation was increasingly impatient with the old interdicts and inhibitions, while the system itself had become mechanical and semi-obsolete, running on out of habit, mental laziness and ingrained double-think more than from conviction. Probably no more than a certain minority still supported it – though that minority could periodically prove itself to be not only vocal, but active and influential, and it was also well organised. An Appeal Board had already been set up in 1946 to mitigate the Board's worst decisions, and though the reactionaries struck back at intervals during the Fifties and even later, their power was ebbing. With successive post-war Governments proclaiming Ireland's growing modernity and forward strides, the Censorship finally had become an intolerable embarrassment and a blot on the country's international image, a blot which needed to be excised.

‚ÄîÔøΩ‚ñ∫

Though Irish literary censorship was certainly no myth, it has been much mythologised and I believe myself that its long-term influence on the development of Irish writing has been a good deal exaggerated. After all, censorship in some form or another existed virtually everywhere, and the average professional writer or publisher usually learned how to cope with it or circumvent it. This is not intended to be, in any sense, an alibi or apologia for it, since a considered one simply is not possible. Whether or not the censors and their supporters actually managed to change or subvert the course of Irish culture, they certainly succeeded in alienating a number of the country's finest talents and intellects, in causing them shame, embarrassment and financial loss, and in making Ireland look ridiculous to the world. Ireland's writers were its major asset internationally, yet they were subjected to the kind of treatment which should have been reserved for professional pornographers and peddlers of dirty pictures. Support for censorship was not necessarily blind or reactionary, as has been pointed out already; it was often merely wrongheaded, or based on insufficient data and knowledge. The growing literacy (or semi-literacy) of the masses was something relatively new in society, and there was a widespread fear of commercial exploitation of ordinary people through the medium of print – and, of course, through the cinema.

However, though Irish censorship was extreme and some of its decisions now seem, in retrospect, almost lunatic, it certainly was not unique for the time. It was, of course, accentuated in a poor and insular country, where educational standards were still low (the majority of people finished school at fourteen) and where – thanks largely to history – there was undue reliance on the Church for guidance even in fields where it lacked the proper qualifications to give it. There was also the phenomenon of the new, raw, uncultured petit-bourgeoisie – the 'nation of urbanised peasants' defined by Seán O'Faolain. To such people, morality was black and white, and all intellectual or aesthetic values were high-falutin' and irrelevant. All of this had created a quasi-fundamentalist mentality, though the fact remains that much of the initiative for imposing a censorship came from people who were themselves relatively well educated.

If they were educated, however, they were rarely cultured and the idea that a literary masterpiece should have privileges which pulp fiction did not deserve would not have made any sense to them. 'Dirty books', whether written by a genius or a hack, were equally dangerous – in fact, of the two the genius was likely to prove the more subversive and dangerous to society. Discussing the ban on *Land of Spices*, Arland Ussher wrote in 1949: 'What conclusion are we to draw from this? Simply (or so it would seem) that the Censorship is maintained, primarily, for the purpose of baiting the intellectuals. It is a pity, for I should like to have seen my country show the world a really fine example of Censorship and How to Do it. It is a problem which will have to be tackled some day by every free democracy, and Ireland has the incomparable advantage that she still recognises a spiritual authority and the necessity for specialists in the field of morals. But unfortunately, Irishmen have sung for so long the line of Thomas Davis "for righteous men must make our land a nation once again" that they have forgotten that *cultured* men should also have a say. And righteousness without culture has a tendency to turn rancid.'[3]

On a wider level, however, censorship was part of a general trend or reaction which showed itself throughout Europe and the United States. The Twenties had been, broadly speaking, a permissive age, as is usually the case with any decade which directly follows years of war and social upheaval. The Thirties, by contrast, was a decade in which respectability, security, and a general spirit of retrenchment were emphasised – often at the expense of personal freedom and originality. In particular, middle-class family values were paramount, a factor which was recognised above all by the film industry in Hollywood when it began to turn out mass 'family entertainment' and set up its own censorship machine. The Twenties flapper became a model housewife in an apron, the Latin Lover so popular in the Twenties was replaced by the kind of Regular Guy or Decent Chap whom any woman could trust, domesticity was sacred and a coating of safe, reassuring conventionality was laid on over almost all emotional situations like a glaze of varnish. Child stars such as Shirley Temple became the focus for a worldwide cult of populist sentimentality. Much the same is true of popular literature; in Britain, it was largely a time of anodyne mass fiction, ranging from J. B. Priestley at the upper level down to James Hilton on the lower. The anxieties and self-questionings of the intellectual Left were still strictly a minority affair.

Anyone who thinks the Irish censors unique in their stupidity is advised to read *Censored* by Tom Dewe Mathews,[4] a study of British film censorship between the two world wars which reveals a world of old colonels, prudish spinsters and sheer fatuity which would seem wildly implausible even in a novel by Evelyn Waugh. The story of the banning of *Lady Chatterley's Lover* has been rehearsed many times over, but equally influential had been the banning in 1928 of that sentimental story of lesbianism, *The Well of Loneliness*, which caused many British publishers to reconsider their lists and drop various 'daring' or potentially controversial authors without delay. One of them was the gifted Gamel Woolsey, the not-quite-legal wife of the Hispanophile writer Gerald Brenan, whose fine novel *One Way of Love* was rejected because the heroine – who, like Gamel Woolsey herself, was tubercular – undergoes an abortion for health reasons. It was not published until long after her death.[5] She was, it seems, only one of many to suffer under the climate of the times. Writing in the mid-Thirties, the popular woman author E. M. Delafield remarked dryly that the average middle-class Englishman at heart believed all nice girls to be sexually frigid. Morality apart, sexual 'coarseness' was not acceptable to contemporary social mores; it ranked with the use of bad language before ladies, the telling of lavatory jokes, and picking one's nose at the dinner table.

The BBC was equally strict in ensuring that the sensibilities of its listeners would not be shocked, and popular comedians with a 'blue' tendency were either closely monitored, or simply dropped, or (as happened in the case of the comedian Max Wall) cut off in the middle of their act. The Corporation even forced Noel Coward – who, one would have thought, was by then safe and sacrosanct, a public idol – to rewrite some of the lyrics of his musical play *Ace of Clubs*; in one the lines 'New Jersey dames / Go up in flames / If someone mentions bed' were amended to 'in Tennessee/ The BBC/ Would blush to hear what's said.'

That relatively trivial incident happened as late as 1950, when thinking people believed or hoped that the war had shaken a generation out of its former smugness; but there were far weightier cases of English censorship in the same decade. In 1954, magistrates presiding over a court in Swindon ordered the destruction of a two-volume illustrated edition of Boccaccio's *Decameron*, which had been one of over 300 volumes seized by police in a raid on a local bookshop. When the owner of the shop appealed against this, the Wiltshire County Appeals Board reversed the decision and declared that Boccaccio's work was not obscene, but only after lengthy argument from the lawyers involved. During the hearing, the counsel for the

Director of Public Prosecutions made a statement which provoked the ridicule of the self-consciously liberal-leftist *New Statesman*: 'To suggest that women may be susceptible to these overwhelming urges which only need touching off is obscene according to our ideas.' It could almost have come out of the mouth of an Irish censor! And in 1958 the Lord Chamberlain refused a licence for public performance of Beckett's *End Game* at the Royal Court Theatre. According to a *Daily Telegraph* report of 10 February 1954, 'the principal objection by the censor is to a scene of about 30 lines in which three of the characters are seen in prayer. The official view is that this is blasphemous.' In view of Beckett's much-publicised withdrawal from a Dublin Theatre Festival because of clerical disapproval, it might have been expected that he would withdraw his play also on this occasion. However, though he refused to cut or alter the prayer scene, he did agree to make four of the five alterations demanded, and the licence was duly granted. (Incidentally, he appears also to have made various minor changes in the language of *Waiting for Godot* some years previously, also at the Lord Chamberlain's request.)

Many parallel examples of prudery and repressiveness could be quoted from America in the immediate post-war years, including the fact (only recently revealed) that the famous Dr Kinsey, whose researches into American sexuality caused such a stir, was for a time under close surveillance from the FBI, which suspected that his activities were un-American and deliberately subversive of public morality. Kinsey was even publicly denounced in Congress as a probable agent of Soviet Communism, whose writings were intended to undermine family solidarity and the American way of life. The film actress Ingrid Bergman's adulterous affair with the producer Rossellini, by whom she had a child, led to public denunciations by American women's organisations and the virtual collapse of her career in the US for several years.

When *Life* magazine published large colour reproductions of Modigliani nudes in 1959, to illustrate a feature article on the artist, many readers cancelled their subscriptions because the women were depicted with recognisable pubic hair – which at that time was, I understand, one of the factors by which nude photographs were judged illegal and pornographic. And a few years previously, the *Saturday Evening Post* had caused almost a national scandal by running a serial story in which a girl secretary and her boss, after driving to his holiday home in the woods, were shown in the next episode sitting down to breakfast together. Today this would be as acceptable as a valentine (though a modern readership might feel cheated because the intervening *nuit d'amour* was not described in some detail), but in the moral climate of the Fifties, it was shocking and decadent. After a shower of angry letters and phone calls, the fiction editor was forced to compose a facetious reply saying that the magazine was not responsible for what its fictional characters did in private and between instalments.

When all this is remembered and placed into context, the follies and excesses of the Irish Censorship Board no longer seem as extreme or as isolated as they did.

In fact, they are much more typical of a general climate of opinion than is recognised today. For instance, a recent biography of the Australian novelist and Nobel Prize winner Patrick White describes his long-drawn martyrdom at the hands of the Australian book censors and shows, once again, that the experience of various Irish writers was very far from unique.[6] In Canada, a rather similar situation seems to have existed some decades ago – which raises the question of whether Ireland's case should possibly be viewed as much in a British post-colonial context as a European one. Though it would probably infuriate old-style Irish nationalists to be told so, certain aspects of their mentality typified a mindcast still to be encountered in the more backward areas of North America, and presumably also in Australia. In an essay written originally in 1962, but recently reprinted,[7] the distinguished American film critic Pauline Kael records that a congressional sub-committee had recently been set up under the chairmanship of Kathryn Granahan, 'a Democrat from Pennsylvania who is known as America's leading lady smut-hunter', to explore the possibility that French films such as *Les Liaisons Dangereuses* might be part of a Communist plot to undermine American morality and weaken national morale, through encouraging Americans into a preoccupation with sex. Ms Kael commented: 'In other words, she takes the position that a strong state, a state capable of defending itself, must be a Puritan state, and that individual freedom and the loosening of sexual standards threaten the state. This is, of course, the present Communist position.'

The mentality represented by Congresswoman Granahan was, until recently, a familiar and very vocal one, and it seems to have resurfaced in recent years, though with nothing commensurate with its former hold on public opinion. In the 1950s it took an almost comic turn when British pressures persuaded the French Government to ban for a time Nabokov's bestselling novel *Lolita* because, so it was alleged, too many people were buying the French edition and smuggling it into Britain. The belief that sexual licence (or sexual permissiveness, to use the fashionable term) is linked closely with moral, social and political decline is at least as old as the Roman Empire; in more recent times, it was prominent in the trial of Oscar Wilde and in certain murder trials of this century which involved women. Usually in such waves of semi-hysteria, it is represented as an insidious import from abroad which threatens the social fabric at home. Even after the second World War, Lady Nancy Astor was making speeches warning British society that its unhealthy interest in sexual matters would 'make us all go down the drain like the Roman Empire', and in this outlook she was only one voice among many.

The English popular press of the 1950s occasionally ran campaigns against public libraries for allegedly stocking the kind of 'dirty' fiction which was liable to corrupt the young. We tend to forget that the permissiveness we now take for granted is a fairly recent growth, and that the battles fought for it were often hard-won. In his biography *A Life at the Centre*,[8] the eminent British Labour Party politician turned Social Democrat, Roy Jenkins, describes his long, arduous campaign for censorship reform in the years 1957 to 1959, before the relevant Private Members' Bill was narrowly passed by the House of Lords. This in turn opened the way for the now-canonical *Lady Chatterley's Lover* trial and the general victory of permissiveness during the Sixties.

Even in Sixties France, censorship was intermittently active; under General de Gaulle's regime, for instance, there was a renewal of film censorship, and rather earlier a novel by the writer, jazz musician and Montmartre night-roamer Boris Vian was banned, and he himself was briefly imprisoned as a pornographer. During the early 1950s the novels of Françoise Sagan provoked the kind of fashionable, semi-scandalous notoriety which Colette had achieved in the previous generation. So if one considers that Brian Lenihan's legislation of 1967 signalled the end of an epoch, Ireland was not so far behind the times as is usually claimed, just as Sagan's novels preceded those of Edna O'Brien by only a few years. The Censorship Board was not, of course, swept away or abolished, and on paper it retained a good deal of power, but in practice it no longer mattered very much. The bitterness and wounds it had left, however, have not been forgotten and, in some cases, possibly never will be. It was, from every point of view, a bad business.

Yet curiously enough, for at least a decade after it had ceased to be a power in the land, various ambitious writers looked back almost with nostalgia to the days of 'a good old censorship row' and several of them even tried to foment situations in which they and their books could once again figure as victims of official repression. Given the traditional gullibility of many people in the Dublin and London media, they were sometimes successful in doing so, probably with favourable effect on their sales. None of this, by the way, is based on hearsay, since I knew of most of these cases personally and professionally, and in at least two of them the writers even tried to enlist my aid to publicise them. However, the Sixties brought the more fashionable publicity outlet of the protest industry, which flourished for some time and offered a field day to press and TV photographers, and the old-style controversies over 'banned books' had had their day.

Chapter 16

NEUTRALITY AND DE VALERA

As the true facts of Irish neutrality in 1939-45 become better known, the old sneers and misunderstandings become less and less relevant. An increasing number of contemporary historians now appear to accept that this policy was favourable towards the Allies in the long term, rather than a two-faced ploy for covering up a basic hostility to England, or even a degree of pro-Fascism.[1] Yet to a whole spectrum of opinion, ranging from liberal to imperialist, Ireland (or 'Southern Ireland') in general, and de Valera in particular, stood indicted of deserting Western democracy in its hours of greatest need. Dev was accused of an emotional obsession with Ireland's past wrongs, and with myopic nationalism. H. G. Wells typified a certain kind of English outlook on Ireland when he wrote in a London paper, the *Evening Standard*: 'God, of course, is Minister without Portfolio in whatever Cabinet happens to be in power . . . Awkward problems can always be referred back to Christ or Cromwell . . . Yesterday is continuously being shoved in front of the public eye to bamboozle them about the problems of today.'[2]

There seems to be no doubt that de Valera was the chief architect of this policy, even if it had the support of the country at large and of virtually every Irish politician of note, with the exception of James Dillon. It has been almost axiomatic to describe many or most of 'The Chief's' mental processes as tortuous, devious, hair-splitting etc. and his ability as a political casuist has generally been admitted even by his admirers. Yet neutrality was based on a broad, simple principle, even if de Valera had to employ all his cunning and resource as a politician, negotiator, diplomat and (not least) manipulator of public opinion in order to make it work. He was a product of a school of thought which insisted that small nations had the right to stay out of wars in which they were not directly involved and could achieve nothing positive against *force majeure*. The first World War had (allegedly) been fought to protect the rights of such nations (i.e. Belgium and Serbia) and this doctrine was an important component in the policies of the League of Nations. De Valera was therefore acting true to type when he insisted that Ireland had the right to keep its national territory inviolable from both sides of the conflict, and that

Britain should not regard it merely as a kind of offshore island integral to its own defence system, to be treated accordingly.

Though an anti-British mood certainly helped to swing national support behind de Valera, it is difficult to see how his stance was, in itself, particularly anti-British. As has been noted already, de Valera was not an isolationist. He played a role of some importance in re-defining the British Commonwealth for a new political and economic era, and as his speeches and actions in the League of Nations had shown, he was no friend of Fascism.[3] His relations with Chamberlain appear to have been quite amiable, although with Churchill he was forced to lock horns with a committed, bullish imperialist who had little time for the idea of an independent Ireland and whose sometimes intemperate rhetoric against it stirred up rancour on both sides and achieved nothing positive. To some extent this was probably a personality clash – the aristocratic, rakish, bellicose Whig-turned-Tory, personally flamboyant and with a taste for verbal bullying, had nothing in common with the ascetic, ultra-Catholic, slightly pedantic former schoolmaster whose politics he had always detested. Another personality clash was evident in de Valera's wartime dealings with Roosevelt; from the start, the anglophile New England patrician had no time for the populist Irish politician from the wrong side of the tracks.[4] Roosevelt, in his way, was also a committed imperialist – which is not to disparage his belief in democracy, or what he saw as democracy, nor the real greatness of his New Deal policy – and encouraged by his courtier, Gray, he saw Ireland's neutral stance as virtually a stab in the back for the great Anglo-American crusade against Fascism. De Valera's treatment at his hands was not unique, however, since he was almost equally intransigent in his handling of a greater European and politician than Dev – Charles de Gaulle.

Looking back, what is perhaps most striking about this chapter of Irish foreign relations is the naïve trust in American goodwill. Encouraged by certain of their politicians, by emigrant relatives living in 'The States', and by the Irish popular press, many Irish men and women persisted in seeing the US as the benevolent, republican Big Brother which would always stand by them – even, if necessary, against the overweening dictates of the British Empire. Their chronic overestimation of the power and status of Irish-Americans, the belief that even anglophile politicians such as Roosevelt would favour a fellow-republic against a monarchical empire, the belief (fostered particularly by the propaganda of the popular cinema, which was overwhelmingly American) that the US was not only the arsenal of democracy, but a friend to all small nations and an active defender of them – all these were articles of faith which survived among the mass of Irish people until long after the war. (It was strengthened by the post-war spectacle of American opposition to global Communism, which most ordinary Irish people hated and feared while knowing relatively little about it. Communist persecution of religion had much to do with this, and the plight of the Croatian Archbishop Stepinac in particular – a highly dubious figure politically, as Hubert Butler and others had shown – received enormous coverage in Irish newspapers). At the back of this idealisation of America was perhaps a kind of popular emotion going back to the Famine, and to the years when the Statue of Liberty rose like an angel of mercy over the horizon to welcome shipfuls of Irish emigrants to a new life in the New World. And looking at things from a more prosaic angle, many poor rural families relied heavily on the packages of money, regular or occasional, which were sent home to them from across the Atlantic. This kind of mentality is burlesqued in Brian O'Nolan's *An Béal Bocht*, where America is called 'Thar Lear', 'Across the Sea' – a reference to the Gaelic proverb that cows over the sea have long horns.

The wartime issue of the Irish ports became such an explosive and emotional one that even today it is often difficult to discuss it objectively. I once had to assure an English journalist (who, I suspect, remained largely unconvinced) that in the war years German submarines did not, in fact, put in regularly to Cork and elsewhere on the Southern coast to refuel and refit and take on food and fresh water. To this day, quite responsible writers often refer to Ireland as being a 'nest of German spies' between 1940 and 1945, though the dropping of twelve German agents by parachute was a farcical affair which resulted in all of them, except the ill-fated Goertz, being captured within a day or so (see Enno Stephan's book *Spies in Ireland* for an account of this). That there were numerous German sympathisers in Ireland is undoubted – there were in virtually every country, until the facts of the Nazi tyranny became known – and certainly the attitude of various people in public life was highly ambivalent towards the second World War, though I have seen no real proof to back the allegation that Frank Aiken, the Foreign Minister, was privately pro-German. Above all, there was a great deal of anti-Englishness, some of it fully understandable or even justifiable while much or most of it was atavistic and unthinking – mere tribalism, like the behaviour of a football crowd or the maudlin emotionalism of such popular songs as 'Galway Bay'. But distrust of imperial Britain was not confined to Ireland, by any means. In France, for instance, it was so strong in whole sections of the French Army and navy, not to mention the politicians, that it contributed to France's downfall by making effective co-operation with Britain virtually impossible.

Neither was isolationism a peculiarly Irish characteristic. Roosevelt had great difficulty in manoeuvring his country into a warlike frame of mind, and as the Spanish statesman, philosopher and author Salvador de Madariaga pointed out in his *Victors, Beware!* written in the immediate aftermath of the war, probably most European countries would have opted for staying out of the fighting if they had been given the opportunity to do so. He also categorically declared: 'If we maintain the separate and independent existence of national entities, there is no reason why a neutral should cease to be a neutral unless *in its own eyes it is in its own interest to fight*.'[5] In this context, he expressly absolved Ireland or 'Éire' of blame. In the case of Poland, Czechoslovakia, Belgium, Holland, Denmark, Norway, Greece, Yugoslavia, no such option was offered; they were attacked and overrun, some of them with little resistance. Even the two superpowers, America and the Soviet Union, only entered the fighting at a relatively late stage when they, too, were attacked – America at Pearl Harbor, and the Soviet Union in Operation Barbarossa. As for Britain and France, they had jointly declared war on Germany with the nominal intention of saving Poland – for whom, in the end, they failed to fire a shot. The strange interlude known as the Phoney War intervened before fighting began in grim earnest.

As for the familiar allegation that Ireland remained insularly indifferent to the war, and uninformed or incurious about its course, even a glance at the Irish newspapers of the time will disprove it (though it is true that late in 1941, the *Irish Press* carried as its lead headline 'Pope sends Christmas message to Ireland'). The much-ridiculed phrase 'the Emergency' was largely an official, Civil Service euphemism designed to stress the nation's neutrality, a piece of official jargon which was never part of popular currency. I was a junior schoolboy during the second World War, but my memories of the time are vivid, and apart from the food, fuel and petrol rationing and other inevitable discomforts or deprivations, the atmosphere of fear, menace and foreboding was constant and almost tangible. Quite simply, one just could not shut it out, at least for long. I remember following, with my elder brother, the whole North African campaign on BBC radio, the battle of Stalingrad, the loss of the battleship *Hood*, and other key events.

On the Wexford coast, near where my family lived, naval mines constantly drifted ashore and either blew up or were dismantled by experts; so did empty dinghies and rafts from sunken ships, and even the bodies of soldiers and airmen of various nations. German bombs fell a few miles from where we lived, probably jettisoned after unsuccessful raids on English ports, while from time to time both Allied and German planes crash-landed around the coast. And one frequently met, or saw, or knew of Irish people who served in the British army or navy, or worked in English wartime industries. I remember relatively little overt pro-German sentiment except among the ignorant, and while there was still a good deal of vestigial anti-English feeling, America's entry into the fighting helped enormously to swing popular feeling behind the Allies.

Yet there lingered, and still lingers, a core of genuine moral shame that Ireland did not openly take sides in what was obviously a struggle against an evil tyranny. Just how evil it was, of course, could not be known at that time, and when in the final months of the fighting the facts about Belsen, Buchenwald *et al* began to spread, many Irish people at first refused to credit them because they remembered the lies perpetrated by British atrocity propaganda of the first World War. Yet even if they had known about them, the ineluctable facts of Ireland's situation remained the same. Neutrality split the Irish intelligentsia deeply, and half a century later the argument is still fought out periodically in print. Even many of those who reluctantly recognised its realism felt that in return for passive immunity from bombs or invasion they had bartered their moral conscience, ignored a historical imperative and would pay for it in the eyes of posterity. And while certain rabid nationalists exalted sheer necessity into a moral struggle in which the Celtic David was defying the Anglo-American Goliath, there was (and is) an uneasy recognition that Ireland's role was an unheroic one. If she had, at least, acted as a haven to refugees fleeing from Hitler, especially the Jews . . . But instead, she made bureaucratic difficulties about admitting them, only let in a handful, and again wrong-footed herself historically. Today, in fact, the Holocaust threatens to overshadow all other aspects of what was a world catastrophe.

Certain eminent writers had been against neutrality from the start – George Bernard Shaw, for instance, who declared that it would 'make invasion a certainty'. He elaborated on this: 'When I was a child, Galway was defended by an exciseman with a wooden leg. If it has any more formidable defences now, I am not aware of them.'[6] (Yet Shaw, with his moral greatness, eventually came to admit more or less that he had been wrong and that de Valera had been right.) O'Casey, in his subjective, digressive, rather cranky way, seems to have felt that ultimately neutrality was justified: 'The Ireland of today has been largely moulded by an English lord of misrule for the past thousand years; and this boyo is more responsible for her present day neutrality than Ireland can ever be . . . We must take Ireland as she is, forgetting that she is technically neutral; remembering, rather, that as far as fighting goes, she has done as much, and in many ways more, than the next to stand in with the United Nations.' (Presumably, O'Casey was referring to the thousands of Irish who fought for Britain.)[7] George Birmingham (Canon Hannay), for years an exile in England, was strongly against Irish neutrality and stronger still against Chamberlain's policy of appeasement.

Today, as the cold rationale of de Valera's stance becomes clearer and the true factors of it are made public, this sense of shame seems less justifiable, if still fully understandable. The hard truth is that neutrality was scarcely a moral issue or a moral choice at all, since Dev had no realistic option except a policy of non-belligerence, and at heart he knew it very well. Ireland's army was tiny, her navy was non-existent, her air force only a token one, and she would have found it virtually impossible to defend her extensive coastline from invasion, just as her cities would have been defenceless against air attack. She was denied adequate arms for her troops – Britain needed all she had – and had no munitions industry of her own, no industrial base for a long war, no petrol or oil supplies.[8]

Realistically, then, it was not so much a question of fighting actively against Germany as of allowing, or denying, England the right to man the ports – in effect, of bringing garrisons or forces of occupation back into the country they had left only seventeen years before. As de Valera himself claimed many times, this would almost certainly have played directly into the hands of the IRA and put Ireland back to Black-and-Tan times – precisely what, on the face of it, Britain should have feared most. It would also have made things difficult if not impossible for the national Government, since the military commanders would have had considerable powers and would *de facto* have been answerable only to Churchill or Eisenhower or Montgomery. Dublin's civilian authority – in fact, Ireland's limited degree of independence – might thereby have been gravely discredited and undermined. Considering that some leading generals including Montgomery – the intransigent son of a Northern Ireland rector – favoured invading 'Éire' from across the border, it is not hard to imagine how a military governor with virtual plenary wartime powers might well have walked booted and spurred over the native administration. The predictable reaction would have been a burst of anti-English emotion of the most recidivist kind.

The presence of German and Italian embassies in Dublin infuriated many people in the Allied camp, even if we know now that this presence was only a token one, that Minister Hempel's moves and messages were closely monitored, and that Irish Army intelligence was in close touch with London.[9] Though recruiting for the British forces was officially discouraged, in practice de Valera turned a blind eye and as has been mentioned already, many thousands of Irishmen served in the British forces and thousands of others worked in British industry.[10] Ireland also allowed English and American planes to infringe on its air space repeatedly, it discreetly repatriated Allied air crews by sending them across the border to the North, and even supplied weather forecasts for the D-day invasion. And when Belfast was bombed, Dublin sent fire-engines there to help in fighting the flames – a gesture unlikely to be reciprocated. Northerners were generally, and understandably, more bitter about Southern neutrality than the English were, particularly since they themselves endured the usual wartime blackout but could see the lights of Irish towns and villages glowing directly across the border.

Yet outward defiance of Anglo-American pressures was never quite forgiven by either of the Atlantic Alliance partners, even though by 1942 the American High Command had decided that Ireland, in spite of the fuss about the ports, had now little strategic importance in the Battle of the Atlantic. For this defiance Ireland paid a heavy price in terms of international reputation, as pointed out by Bernard Share (see Chapter 1). Until recently, it was customary to compare Ireland's selfish, insular neutrality with the courageous independence of those two liberal democracies, Switzerland and Sweden. However, the recent furore over the quantities of German-Jewish money and gold still lodged in Swiss banks has cast a certain shadow over that country's previously unquestioned integrity, while it is now admitted that Sweden allowed thousands of German troops to cross its territory into Russia.[11]

Irish neutrality was far from being a passive or purely isolationist policy. It involved constant diplomatic manoeuvres and a war of words on an international level, which the nation followed with close interest; and when, at the end of the war, de Valera made his famous radio reply to Churchill, almost all segments and shades of opinion from the border to the Cork coast felt that he had spoken for them. It was probably his finest hour, and if he had retired inside the next five years and allowed Seán Lemass to succeed him correspondingly earlier, his reputation today would probably be higher than it is. Like Churchill, Roosevelt and Admiral Horthy of Hungary, and unlike de Gaulle, Adenauer and de Gasperi, he did not emotionally belong to or fully understand the postwar world. It was largely out of mutual prostration, collapse and economic distress that modern European unity, both political and economic, was born. Perhaps, in the words of Thomas de Quincey, 'less than these fierce ploughshares could not have stirred the stubborn soil'. It was a fearful price to pay, and in retrospect we may wonder if all the disaffected Irish intellectuals, then and since, would have been prepared to pay it. Arland Ussher, writing only a few years after the war had ended, declared: 'Ireland, that has missed every great historical experience, has missed this one also, and perhaps we may be thankful – the dreadful twentieth-century experience of the Abyss.'[12]

Leaving aside the exceptional case of Samuel Beckett who worked for the French Resistance, or the antithetical case of Francis Stuart marooned in wartime Germany and – on his own admission – at one stage writing virtual propaganda for German radio, the reactions of certain Irish writers on both sides of the Irish Sea must have been representative of the thinking of many ordinary people. Louis MacNeice in his much-quoted poem 'Neutrality' spoke not only for many English people but also, probably, for many Irish people too – particularly the Anglo-Irish to which he himself largely belonged:

> But then, look eastward from your heart, there bulks
> A continent, close, dark, as archtypal sin,
> While to the west off your own shores the mackerel
> Are fat – on the flesh of your kin.[13]

MacNeice, crossing the Atlantic on his return from America to England in 1940, had travelled on the ship which picked up the survivors of the *Jervis Bay* voluntarily sacrificed by her captain in an attempt to divert German submarines away from the convoy she was guarding. He also lost several close friends in the war – including Graham Sheppard, a college contemporary, who was lost on a destroyer – and had gone through the London Blitz, experiences inevitably mirrored in his poetry. To ask him to display a dispassionate, peacetime attitude towards the small neutral country just across the water would have been almost an insult; war and the death of friends and unarmed civilians were too cruel and immediate a reality.

Elizabeth Bowen, as has been already noted, was opposed to neutrality, though when she blamed it largely on traditional anti-English feeling she was mistaken – de Valera, in contrast to his actions in 1922, refused to let emotion sway him. She was, however, level-headed in her approach and could see the arguments on both sides. As she herself said, she wished that the English could remember more of history and the Irish less. Kate O'Brien, who mainly because of passport difficulties had been forced to spend the war years in London,[14] like Elizabeth Bowen worked for the Ministry of Information there and as part of her duties turned out a good deal of quasi-propaganda. She was strongly against Irish neutrality and appears to have kept this attitude in later life; in any case, those who saw Britain's wartime ordeal at first hand were generally angry or contemptuous of other nations who appeared to be only saving their skins – and justifying it with a line of moral humbug.

For a rather intemperate yet closely argued defence of what was probably the majority Irish view, M. J. MacManus's article in the special Irish issue of *Horizon* magazine (January 1942) is still worth reading, under the title 'Éire and the World Crisis'. It is spoiled in part by conventional Celtic-harping on the 'centuries of oppression' and the legacy of distrust which it left, yet MacManus was strictly factual in pointing out that when de Valera in his League of Nations speeches had called for sanctions against Mussolini after his Abyssinian aggression, Sir Samuel Hoare for Britain had joined with Laval of France in helping to sabotage these. Similarly, when Dev had warned the League that Japan's action in Manchukuo was a 'testing time' for the League and that it must now assert its powers, Sir John Simon had favoured appeasement.[15] In retrospect, de Valera's disillusionment with the Big Powers on these occasions was a turning-point in his life and career; he must have recognised by then that official rhetoric about the rights of small nations was little more than a catch-cry and that Powers, as A. J. P. Taylor has said, will be Powers.

MacManus, probably smarting both from Churchill's attacks and from the distortion of Ireland's motives in the British press, went over to the counter-attack: 'They look for Fascism and they fail to find it. They look for hostility to Britain and they find little of it. The one thing they do find is that people are almost aggressively neutral . . . No small nation has entered the present war of its own volition, and those who have been swept into it have not escaped any of its horrors through being afforded the protection of powerful belligerents. Irishmen feel the same about it. Their country has had more than enough "history"; it badly needs rest.'[16] He might have added that considering the fate of Poland and the treatment of Czechoslovakia, not to mention the collapse of France, Ireland had no compelling reason to believe in the power of Britain's wartime protection.

One thing at least which cannot be refuted, either on a factual or an emotive level, is that de Valera had most of the country behind him and in that sense he can be said to have acted 'democratically'. The fashionable travesty of the man and his motives which has gained such currency in recent years greatly underrates both his shrewdness of judgement and his humanity, as well as the inbuilt European dimension to his thinking. During the early stages of the Spanish Civil War, for example, he had refused to recognise the Burgos Government of General Franco, who already had the covert backing of Britain and of other major powers. De Valera was no hayseed Republican or religious fundamentalist, as he is sometimes portrayed today. He was a statesman of real calibre, who earned the respect of men as diverse as Gandhi and Salvador de Madariaga. The historian Nicholas Mansergh, who knew him well, describes his personality as resembling that of a university don; and Lord Keynes, the economist and intellectual patron of Bloomsbury, was favourably impressed when he called on him in Dublin. Even Harold Nicolson, who had Ulster Unionist connections and was no friend to 'Southern Ireland', found himself liking and respecting de Valera during their meeting in the very depth of the war years, when Nicolson came to Dublin and lectured there. They talked about the progress of the war, of Churchill's difficulties and of American attitudes, and afterwards Nicholson recorded: 'He is a very simple man, like all great men . . . Deep spiritual certainty underneath it all, giving to his features a mask of repose.'[17]

T he Spanish Civil War had previously split Irish opinion as radically as it split opinion in France, England and America. A poll carried out among English and Irish writers at the time showed that Seán O'Faolain, interestingly, was neutral towards the conflict while O'Casey predictably saw it as a clear case of light versus dark – the workers and Humanity against clericalism and Fascism and a bigoted upper crust. Samuel Beckett, when asked for his views, simply wrote back UPTHEREPUBLIC! Elizabeth Bowen favoured the Leftist cause and so did Louis MacNeice, whose visit to wartime Spain – in the Republican zone, that is – is described in his autobiography *The Strings are False*. He met on that occasion Spain's greatest living poet, Antonio Machado, but since he knew little Spanish and Machado did not speak English, the encounter did not yield all it should have done. (MacNeice had also visited the country shortly before the Nationalist rising, when he heard people prophesy war in the near future – a theme which forms part of the long poem 'Autumn Journal'.)

Kate O'Brien knew Spain at first hand and spoke the language well. As a young woman, she had lived and worked as a governess in Bilbao – experiences which she drew on later for her novel *Mary Lavelle*. Her *Farewell Spain* (1937) is mainly a book of subjective impressions and personal jottings rather than an attempt to analyse Spain, its history and politics in any great depth, nor was Kate O'Brien essentially a political animal. She did not romanticise what she saw, though her approach on the whole was sympathetic, and she did regard the Republican government as the legitimate one; but the book was written too early for her to offer any definite perspectives about the war itself. Its chief value is that she wrote from the vantage-point of someone who genuinely knew and loved Spain and the Spaniards, which set her apart from the legions of intellectuals – British, American, French, Irish – who dogmatised about the war on the basis, for the most part, of almost total ignorance. Robert Graves, who had to leave Mallorca in a hurry with his family early in the fighting, soon grew extremely caustic about the young, callow writers (mostly Left-wing) whom he met back in England, and whose views on Spain he found intolerably simplistic and uninformed.[18]

By contrast, Peadar O'Donnell was very much a political animal, from a militant republican-leftist slant, and his book *Salud! An Irishman in Spain* (which appeared in the same year as Kate O'Brien's) is a committed work written by a whole-hearted admirer and supporter of the Spanish Left. It is not, however, mere propaganda, because O'Donnell was too good a journalist and too sharp an observer to see everything through Red spectacles. He was predictably caustic about many of the Spanish clergy, whom he found snobbish, money-minded and arrogant, though he also discovered that a number of them were highly critical of Cardinal Segura, head of the Spanish hierarchy and a strong Franco supporter. He noted how bitterly people talked about illiteracy and the poor quality of education in Spain, and naturally he was enthusiastic about the spirit of the working-class while seemingly oblivious to most of their excesses. O'Donnell, however, was essentially too liberal-minded not to be repelled by the bigotry of the extreme anti-clericals he met. Back in Dublin, he found himself a centre of controversy when Catholic Action accused him of visiting Russia some years earlier and of being involved in a church-burning in Moscow (O'Donnell had never been to Russia at this stage). He records that at a public meeting in support of Republican Spain, some of the speakers were pelted with a 'mild drizzle' of bricks, bottles and other missiles. O'Donnell also complains of the journalist Aodh de Blacam 'hosing the country' with atrocity stories about the desecration of convents, the raping of nuns and the digging up of dead ones. However, Hugh Thomas and other historians have proved since that such stories were frequently true and not mere propaganda fantasies of the Catholic Right.[19]

Such divisions were reflected in the Irish national press, with the *Irish Independent* predictably incensed against 'the Reds' while *The Irish Times* sent Lionel Fleming to report on the war from behind the Republican lines. Frank Geary, the long-term editor of the *Irish Independent*, was prominent in the Irish Christian Front and middle-class, Catholic Ireland was predominantly pro-Franco, though not necessarily pro-Fascist. However, General O'Duffy's attempt to lead an Irish contingent in Spain ended in near-farce[20] and the general was the target of ridicule, particularly from Dublin intellectuals most of whom seem to have been anti-Franco. One piece of topical doggerel, parodying a familiar music-hall song, ran:

> *My name is Owen O'Duffy*
> *And I'm rather vain and huffy,*
> *The side of every Bolshie I'm a thorn in.*
> *But before the break of day*
> *We'll be marching right away,*
> *For I'm off to Salamanca in the morning.*[21]

By contrast, a number of Irish men did fight, including some (I met a few of them as a very young journalist) who found it politic, or even necessary, to play down their involvement later in life, for the sake of their careers or their families. The case of Frank Ryan, the republican socialist who was amnestied from a Francoist prison and died in hospital in Germany, is probably the best known. A more relevant case here, and perhaps the saddest of all, is that of the young poet Charles Donnelly, killed fighting with the International Brigade at Jarama in February 1937. Donnelly, originally a Northerner from Tyrone, was one of the brilliant UCD generation which included Brian O'Nolan, Mervyn Wall and many more, though he left college without a degree and went to London, where with the genial Irish-Jewish poet Leslie Daiken (Yodaiken in private life), he briefly edited a publication called *Irish Fronts*. He was barely twenty-three when he died, so the big claims sometimes made for his poetry are scarcely realistic, and my own guess is that he would eventually have abandoned verse for prose (he had in fact published essays and short stories in student magazines).

Donnelly is one of the might-have-beens of Irish writing, and any attempt to speculate on how he would have developed is complicated by the fact that a good deal of his later work appears to have been lost. What survives is mostly typical Thirties verse, much closer to the politically minded English poets such as Stephen Spender or Charles Madge than it is to Higgins or other practitioners of the Irish quasi-folk mode. Like Julian Bell and John Cornford, he was the victim of his own boyish idealism and of the political obsessions of his age. Donnelly is claimed to have said just before his death, while fighting at the Jarama from behind an olive tree: 'Even the olives are bleeding' – which is possibly his most memorable line. His UCD contemporary, Donagh MacDonagh, wrote a moving poem on his lost friend, which has recently been reprinted; and Ewart Milne, Blanaid Salkeld and her son Cecil Ffrench Salkeld also wrote poems in his memory.[22] (Incidentally, another Irishman killed at Jarama was Eamon McGrotty, a former Christian Brother who had later become a member of the IRA and of the Gaelic League. He was a friend of Brendan Behan, who had served under him as a Fianna scout.)

In 1940, a year after the War in Spain had ended and a world war had begun, Louis d'Alton's play *The Spanish Soldier* was presented at the Abbey Theatre. Forgotten today, it made a minor stir at the time by its depiction of an Irishman who returns to his homeland after supporting the Nationalist cause in Spain. Another writer who employed a rather similar theme was the novelist Ethel Mannin who, though English-born, was a popular figure in Ireland and is rumoured to have been, briefly, the mistress of Yeats and possibly also of Liam O'Flaherty (her *Connemara Journal* of 1947 is still worth reading). *The Blossoming Bough* (1943) brings a young Irishman to Paris, where he has a love affair, and then to Spain and the Civil War. In the end he returns home to Ireland and finds happiness with his actress-cousin, in the undemanding, slightly saccarine style of most middlebrow fiction of the period. And for those with a taste in literary curiosities, a poem appeared in the August 1938 issue of the *Workers' Republic*, which was more or less the organ of the Communist Party of Ireland, under the title 'Red Envoy'. The final verse read:

> *I see this old bad order die*
> *In a great swift blaze of fire,*

> *A structure, clear and mighty high,*
> *Born in its funeral pyre,*
> *Worker, know the world's for thee,*
> *Wert thou to raise the servile knee*
> *From off the ground.*

The author was a sixteen-year-old Dubliner, Brendan Behan, soon to be arrested in England and to serve a term in Borstal.

T he most recent controversy about the War period in this country has tended to fasten on the non-admission of Jewish refugees fleeing from Hitler. No reliable figures are available, but it seems that fewer than a hundred were admitted, a miserably inadequate number (there had been persistent, though unofficial reports of numbers of them passing through on their way to America and elsewhere, but no factual evidence for this was ever produced). There is, of course, no credible excuse for the Irish Government's action or lack of it, even though the reality of the Holocaust was not then widely known or understood, and if the mass of people had realised that they could have saved significant numbers of Jews from gas-ovens, the response might have been very different.

What is largely forgotten, however, is that the numbers and influence of Irish Jews were much greater then than today – there were at least 5,000 families living here, while today the number is less than half that. Dr Izaac Herzog, later Chief Rabbi of Israel, had moved in 1919 from Belfast to Dublin (his two sons, Chaim[23] and Jacob, attended a Protestant school there), and later became Chief Rabbi of Ireland. When he left Dublin in 1937, his departure was a major event with many tributes paid to him at an official reception in the Mansion House in Dublin, as well as an eloquent editorial in *The Irish Times*. Herzog was a personal friend of de Valera's and negotiated with him over the plight of Jewish refugees, though the obstacles proved almost impossible to overcome; Irish bureaucracy, Irish officialdom, failed lamentably and even tragically to rise to a unique historical challenge.[24]

Irish Jews were influential in the arts, however; Victor Waddington with his famous Dublin gallery virtually pioneered modern art in Ireland, Louis Elliman was for years Dublin's leading theatre impresario, Harry Kernoff was a well-known and much-loved painter and Dublin character, David Marcus was one of the editors of *Irish Writing* and later literary editor of the *Irish Press*, Maurice Fridberg's good work as an independent book publisher – it was he who published Frank O'Connor's translation of *The Midnight Court* which was subsequently banned – is noted in another chapter, and Leslie Daiken ('Yod' to his friends, who were legion) was well known as a poet, even if he was not a particularly good one.

There was the whole Solomons dynasty, including Dr Bethel Solomons who was Master of the Rotunda Hospital in Dublin at the astonishing age of twenty-five, while his remarkable sister Estella was both a fine painter and the wife of Seumas O'Sullivan of the *Dublin Magazine*. A. J. (Con) Leventhal, the lifelong friend of Sam Beckett, was both a respected lecturer in French at TCD and the equally respected drama critic for the *Dublin Magazine*. Certain Jewish families were also active in music. Serge Phillipson, a hat-manufacturer of Polish ancestry who fled to Dublin from Paris in the Thirties, became an esteemed and very active member of the Board of the National Gallery. (For many years Ernest Schrödinger, the nuclear physicist brought to Ireland at de Valera's initiative, was believed to be Jewish, but his background was Austrian Catholic.)

There were also Jewish businessmen – at one time the whole dry-cleaning industry seemed to belong to them – and even Jewish politicians, notably Robert Briscoe, a personal friend of de Valera, and twice Lord Mayor of Dublin. In Cork, David Goldberg was both the city's Lord Mayor and one of its key cultural figures. And, of course, the great Wittgenstein came to Ireland for long stays, finding warmth on cold days in the great heated glass-house of the Botanic Gardens in Dublin. In fact, this Jewish element was in its way an essential part of Dublin cultural life until well into the Fifties, when it declined steeply, for no obvious reason – though the lure of the new state of Israel was potent for some younger people. It was never, of course, even remotely comparable to the Jewish presence in pre-1914 Vienna or in Berlin between the wars; but if Irish Jews never achieved such visibility, neither did they suffer active persecution, either racial or intellectual.[25] Meanwhile, ironically, on each 16 June Ireland in general, and Dublin in particular, celebrates Bloomsday and Joyce's fictional Jew – admittedly a poor substitute for an Irish Mahler or Schoenberg, a Wittgenstein or Einstein, a Celan or a Rothko.

Chapter 17

PRESS AND PERIODICALS

Although native Irish publishing fought a courageous battle against costings, a limited buying public, and above all the weighty competition of London publishing houses, it ultimately lacked either the financing or the distribution to make it a major force. The long and honourable record of the now-vanished Talbot Press is exceptional, as is the Cuala Press which ran from 1908 to 1978 when it published its last title, Arland Ussher's *From a Dark Lantern*. The Cuala's best years, however, were between the first World War and 1940, when Lolly (Elizabeth) Yeats died; its small, beautifully bound and printed volumes were collectors' items (and, of course, still are). Patrick Kavanagh, F. R. Higgins, Elizabeth Bowen and Jack B. Yeats were among its authors. Until the coming of Liam Miller's Dolmen Press (which itself owed much to its predecessor) it was unique among Irish bookmaking in its emphasis on visual quality, its fine typography, its quality paper and printing, which could compare with the 'art' publishers on the Continent such as Count Harry Kessler's Cranach Press in Germany. The Talbot Press, by comparison, was plain bread-and-butter in the sense that it dealt mainly with fiction and non-fictional prose works, and its list of titles and authors was a long one. Its books had a stolid, four-square, old-fashioned look, curiously typical of a whole sector of taste at the time, but it was a genuine institution in Irish life and Talbot Press publications could often be seen displayed in the old glass-fronted bookshelves which stood in the front parlours of doctors and priests and prosperous farmers. In their slightly homespun way, they proclaimed the values of literacy.

The Three Candles Press of Colm Ó Lochlainn was a small affair, but highly influential and respected, the creation of an enthusiast who loved what he did and lived for it. An almost forgotten episode in Dublin postwar publishing was the series of slim books brought out by Maurice Fridberg, who had made money as a bookseller in London during the war and began his Irish list in 1945 with O'Connor's translation of *The Midnight Court*. His venture lasted a few years only, but it deserves at least a footnote to cultural history. Gills, Fallons and other family publishers have survived to this day, but many lesser ones have vanished over decades and this is not the place to write their obituary.

Most of the national newspapers of the period, however, have survived, with the notable exception of the *Irish Press* group whose collapse in the past decade has been one of the tragedies of Irish journalism. The Right-wing Catholic paper, *The Standard*, has also vanished, the victim of changing tastes and the triumph of liberalism, or at least what now passes as that. The *Evening Mail* has gone too, so that the once-familiar Dublin street cry, 'Herilomail! Herilomail!' ('Herald and Mail') is heard no longer except in memory. The *Mail*, though loved by many Dubliners of the old school, was never a good newspaper, but in its odd, prosy, inconsequential style it was a way of life. (It was, incidentally, almost the only prominent Irish paper in the Thirties to oppose the cause of Franco in the Spanish Civil War.)

The Irish, like the French, the English and the Austrians, were great newspaper readers. They had no special respect for them, disagreed with most of what they said, and variously attributed their opinions and editorial slant to the machinations of Fianna Fáil, the Freemasons, the Knights of Columbanus, the clergy (a minority view), mysterious and unnamed business interests, the British Empire, and even the Jews. But newspapers offered such attractions as crosswords (very popular in the days before television), horse-racing results to a nation of gamblers, reporting of court cases (popular with the lower orders in particular, as a kind of cheap form of theatre), sports columns, radio programmes, letters to the editors. The letters column of the *Evening Mail*, especially, sometimes reached such bizarre heights of crankery and oddity that it was widely believed that the staff of the paper often wrote them – which was quite untrue; the native capacity for opinionated eccentricity and garrulity has been unfailing over the ages and is splendidly anatomised in the writings of Myles na Gopaleen/Flann O'Brien. For the snobbish, there was even the Court Circular which used to be printed in *The Irish Times*.

The launch of de Valera's *Irish Press* in the early 1930s was born out of the republican party's long-standing exasperation with what it perceived as the Protestant snobbery and West Brit stance of *The Irish Times* and the Cosgraveite, conservative, clerical mentality of the *Irish Independent*. Its first editor was Frank Gallagher, a close follower and personal friend of de Valera's, yet a man of moral courage and no mere party hack or apparatchik.[1] It was predictably populist and nationalist, frequently biased and propagandist in its reporting and interpreting of national politics and issues, while careful at the same time not to annoy Maynooth and the Catholic hierarchy. It was, in short, a party newspaper, produced by and for a populist party, much of whose support came from people who were barely literate. This did not preclude the presence of many excellent journalists on its staff over the years, ranging from able newsmen to a great literary editor in M. J. MacManus, who was himself an author as well as a noted bibliophile,[2] and Anna Kelly, who had been at one time secretary to George Moore in London and was one of the best Irish journalists of her time. The 'Roddy the Rover' column was written for many years by Aodh de Blacam, a prolific and very well-known journalist who inclined to the nationalist Right in politics. There was always a strong tradition in Irish newspapers that – good staff reporters and writers apart – their columns should also carry the views of eminent writers, public figures, specialists in various fields, academics and economists – a tradition dating back a long way. On certain occasions, these people even wrote the leading article(s).

As a distinguished former journalist remarked to me recently, the Dublin morning papers of those days had a considerable brain pool to draw on. So while the front page of the *Irish Press* might shriek in heavy black headlines against the misdoings of Fianna Fáil's political enemies, the inner pages might contain articles which were not only literate but also highly informed, balanced and thought-provoking. Like all the other national papers, it also had capable critics on the theatre, cinema, music, radio, and (sometimes) the visual arts. This applied equally to *The Standard*, whose campaign against the Irish writers who went on an officially sponsored trip to Russia in 1955 (they included Anthony Cronin and James Plunkett) was little more than demagoguery posing as moral crusade, aimed less at maintaining standards of political morality than at raising circulation. Yet *The Standard's* panel of critics included, at one time or another, Patrick Kavanagh who wrote spasmodically on films, James White (later Director of the National Gallery) on art, and Benedict Kiely. Peadar O'Curry, who was editor for many years, was an excellent professional journalist with a nose for the right talents and the right contributors.

The *Irish Independent* was more balanced in its reporting of political events, and less demagogic if in ways rather more philistine, but unfortunately its mania was clericalism. It is to be doubted if any national newspaper, in any European country, has ever given so much space or emphasis to the doings and sayings of its country's priests and bishops. Just how, and why, its readers could stomach so many column inches about them on a daily basis is one of the genuine mysteries of the period. Yet clericalism apart, the *Independent* was a hard-headed business paper, as well as laying stress on accurate local news coverage and farming events – a factor which paid off well in terms of its rural circulation. It was also one of the first Irish national publications to realise the value of cartoon strips in attracting readership, and 'Curly Wee and Gussie Goose' – English in origin – ran for at least a generation. Its long-serving humorous columnist, John D. Sheridan, was a national institution, whose articles were regularly collected into book form and sold well even in Britain. Though the *Independent* was never a 'class' newspaper, and its conservative outlook was sometimes stifling, it always had an excellent, hard-bitten, old-style news staff of unfailing accuracy.

The *Irish Times* under R. M. (Bertie) Smyllie, who had succeeded the Unionist John Healy as editor, has become a legend and Smyllie was a legend even in his lifetime. His great bulky figure – 'Falstaffian' was the stock adjective applied to him – topped by a black sombrero or sometimes by a beret, and with a pipe almost always stuck in his mouth, made him one of the sights of Dublin. He was among the last, if not the very last, of the patriarchal, larger-than-life, Victorian-style editors, a man whose Jupiter-like approach made his staff turn suddenly studious and silent, or caused heads to turn as he entered the Pearl or Palace Bar. Few editors have been more written about than he – by Patrick Campbell, Lionel Fleming, Tony Gray among those who served under him, and he also turns up in various books written by visiting English and American writers (Cyril Connolly and Honor Tracy have already been quoted).[3] Smyllie liked to have writers around him and he liked to listen to them and join in their talk, yet he himself was not an intellectual, and his idea of great poetry was Burns's line 'My love's like a red, red rose'. Though he was glad to have Austin Clarke at the top of the Saturday book page, he privately considered Clarke's poetry 'esoteric stuff' and responded more to writers as individuals than he did to their work – probably he had little real taste in literature, particularly modern literature. Smyllie either liked a man or he didn't, regardless of literary abilities. His personal kindness, though not always on display, was great and was shown even to people who had let him down badly, including Brendan Behan on a famous occasion when Behan had drawn advance expenses for a journalistic trip to France. Predictably Behan squandered the money (a small sum by today's standards) in advance, and ended by being arrested in England, but Smyllie magnanimously forgave him.[4]

Smyllie's outstanding achievement as a journalist was to bring the traditionally Unionist, stuffy, ultra-conservative *Irish Times* into a new 'liberal' stance. Though a tolerant man, he was not a liberal in that sense – in fact he was a rather old-fashioned Presbyterian from Sligo, with the simplistic public-school ethos of his era, which stressed 'decency' and uprightness rather than cleverness. Nor was his newspaper owned or run by liberals – the Arnott family, who then owned it, was a Dublin business dynasty whose chief interest outside commerce was horse-racing, while the board of The *Irish Times* was full of Protestant Freemasons of the old, limited, hard-nosed type. Smyllie, however, judged the mood of the time shrewdly and saw that between the ultra-nationalism of the *Irish Press* and the post-Redmondite clericalism of the *Independent*, a new course could be steered – and one which could also give the Dublin Protestant a new role or relevance. In this sense Smyllie may be said to have largely invented the liberal Protestant, a myth which scarcely existed in Ireland before his time. Divorced from his old identification with Dublin Castle, landlordism and West Britishness, such a type could now see himself as the humane, rational, objective man in the centre, or above the party and sectarian battles. It was an image, and a stance, which made the paper's correspondence columns a favourite outlet not only for disillusioned Protestants, but for angry liberals and intellectual dissidents of all kinds. Nevertheless Smyllie was careful to avoid an overtly anti-clerical image for his newspaper, even if Right-wing Catholics often regarded him and it with detestation.

The coming of the second World War gave Smyllie probably his finest hour, when he clashed repeatedly in public with de Valera's Minister for External Affairs, Frank Aiken, on the issue of press censorship. The public, and the paper's readership especially, were unaware that Aiken's virtual gelding of war reports and commentary was done largely under pressure from England – a point which has been made several times since.[5] Most thinking people at the time saw in it only Civil Service interference or myopic provincialism, so that once again Smyllie emerged as an apostle of free speech, while his newspaper gained in status accordingly. Though staunchly pro-Allies, Smyllie had a streak of emotional sympathy for the Germans as a people, which he had learned as a civilian internee in Germany toward the end of the first World War. The Anglo-Irish landowning class, in particular, sometimes regarded him as a traitor to their hereditary cause, which was that of the British Empire, and many years later one of them snarled at me about 'that fellah Smyllie' who had been 'so bloody pro-Jerry in the War'.

Smyllie had some distinguished journalists working under him, notably W. J. (Jack) White and Bruce Williamson, as well as an outstanding sports writer in Paul MacWeeney; he also had a genius for discovering original talent. He showed this above all in hiring the almost untried Brian O'Nolan to write his 'Cruiskeen Lawn' column, which at first appeared in Irish but gradually became bilingual, then almost wholly in English. This unique column was probably at the peak of its style and inventiveness during the Forties; personally I have always believed that its anarchic, sometimes surreal, ultra-personal brand of humour rather declined during the Fifties, and was too often replaced by a moralistic sourness. It became a national institution, read and quoted by people ranging from disaffected intellectuals to the type of pub-going Dubliners whom Myles had so often made fun of, and who were not put off by the Gaelic scholarship, the scraps of Latin, and the numerous esoteric references in which the column habitually indulged. Myles showed himself to be one of these very rare writers who are able simultaneously to appeal to the intellectual and the man in the street – who can combine extreme mental sophistication with broad entertainment value.

Another of Smyllie's discoveries was his choice of Patrick Campbell as the first 'Quidnunc' of the daily 'Irishman's Diary', which was so stylishly written and so consistently entertaining that much of it was later reprinted in book form. In G. A. Olden *The Irish Times* possessed probably the finest critic of broadcasting Irish journalism has known, while Bruce Williamson was (among other things) a perceptive writer about the cinema and Seamus Kelly, in spite of a later falling-off, was a fine theatre critic (he also was Campbell's successor as 'Quidnunc' for many years).

Smyllie, however, by the early 1950s had virtually burned himself out by years of overwork and was losing his grip. He had never been a good organiser or administrator, so that the overall quality of the paper declined while the *Irish Press*, under the editorship of Jim McGuinness, was making new efforts to win intelligent readers. McGuinness, too, had a flair for choosing contributors, as he showed by picking Brendan Behan whose regular column (later collected in book form under the title *Hold Your Hour and Have Another*) became hugely and deservedly popular. McGuinness also employed Lennox Robinson and Padraic Fallon as weekly columnists during this period, but as an editor he fell foul of the eccentric and unpredictable Major Vivion de Valera, whose almost autocratic power on Burgh Quay was not matched by any obvious corresponding qualities of judgment or ability. He was, by almost unanimous testimony, a difficult and almost impossible man to work under.

It is often written – and sometimes by people who, to judge by what they say, have scarcely bothered to look at the relevant files – that Irish journalism of these three decades was predominantly introverted, provincial and uninformed. There was, of course, a great deal of flatness, provincialism and dullness, but apart from the fact that Irish newspapers of the period gave a good proportion of their features space to specialists of all kinds and even to intellectuals, a glance at old yellowed copies will often reveal a quite surprising awareness of the outside world. The various crises of the Thirties which culminated in the World War were covered very thoroughly, for instance, and during the Spanish Civil War *The Irish Times* maintained a correspondent, Lionel Fleming, behind the republican lines. League of Nations proceedings were covered fully and so, in the postwar years, were United Nations debates, as I can testify personally since I worked as a youthful news sub-editor for *The Irish Times* during the Fifties when the majority of front-page stories were often foreign rather than home news. Certain Irish journalists earned their spurs as foreign correspondents – Douglas Gageby by his reports on Germany, Erskine Childers Junior by his coverage of affairs in the Middle and Near East. Benedict Kiely in the late 1940s wrote a series of outstanding articles for the *Irish Press* giving his impressions of Yugoslavia under the early years of Tito's rule. Few books got more publicity in the immediate post-war period than Denis Johnston's *Nine Rivers to Jordan*, which was based on his experience as a war correspondent. Radio Éireann, too, gave much radio space to 'foreign affairs', as they were rather loosely called, which frequently triggered off edgy debates. In general, both in newspapers and on radio, the right of free speech was generally respected and, wartime restrictions apart, the censors did not as a rule intrude. That there were political and other pressures from behind the scenes is undoubted, but except for the *Irish Press* these were not overt; and Maurice Gorham, in his history of Irish broadcasting, recalls that in his own spell as director of broadcasting in Radio Éireann, clerical interference at least was non-existent.[6]

The Irish literary magazine has a respectable ancestry, but in this particular context it might be said to begin with Seumas O'Sullivan's *Dublin Magazine*, which apart from its innate qualities had a remarkable life-span. It was launched in 1923 as a monthly, ran a few years and then was started again as a quarterly, which it remained until it virtually folded with O'Sullivan's death in 1958, aged seventy-nine. Later attempts to revive it were short-lived, and by then the age of the literary magazine was over in any case. Its early issues had been elaborately produced, with art reproductions and a decorative format, but as a quarterly it was elegantly austere, with a distinctive grey cover and without art reproductions or graphic illustrations.

The *DM* had several features which were virtually exclusive to itself. One was that it was prepared to print plays, usually one-acters. The works by George Fitzmaurice which appeared in its pages have already been mentioned, but it also printed plays by Austin Clarke, T. C. Murray, Lord Dunsany, the text of *Diarmuid and Grania* written by Yeats and George Moore in an ill-fated collaboration many years before, and the last act of Padraic Fallon's elaborate radio play *Diarmuid and Gráinne* – the whole being too long to include in a single issue. Another feature was its emphasis on poetry, and not only on original poems but critical articles (often by practising poets) and on poetry reviewing. Yet another was the size and scope of its reviewing section, not only of books but of theatre and visual art. A. J. (Con) Leventhal was for years its drama critic, and a much respected one, while Edward Sheehy's regular Art Notes were probably the most extensive of their kind in Ireland at that time.

As for the list of the *DM*'s contributors, it constitutes almost a who's who of cultural Ireland over decades: AE, Samuel Beckett, Thomas Bodkin, Joseph Campbell, Austin Clarke, Daniel Corkery, Padraic Colum, Maurice James Craig, Edmund Curtis, Lord Dunsany, John Eglinton, Padraic Fallon, Oliver Gogarty, Bryan Guinness, F. R. Higgins, Francis Hackett, Norah Hoult, J. M. Hone, Patrick Kavanagh, Mary Lavin, Donagh MacDonagh, Patrick McDonogh, Francis MacManus, M. J. MacManus, Brinsley MacNamara, Rutherford Mayne, Constantia Maxwell, T. C. Murray, Frank O'Connor, Liam O'Flaherty, Seán O'Faolain, P. S. O'Hegarty, Seumas O'Kelly, Joseph O'Neill, Lloyd Praeger, Lennox Robinson, Blanaid Salkeld, Niall Sheridan, James Stephens, Francis Stuart, Helen Waddell, Maurice Walsh, Terence de Vere White, and the Yeats brothers, W. B. and Jack. Those names, in themselves, would guarantee it a special niche in Irish literary history; but it also printed contributions by Gordon Craig, Gabriele d'Annunzio, Selma Lagerlof, Hugh MacDiarmid, John Masefield, Llewellyn and T. F. Powys,

Henry Treece, Francis Vielé-Griffin, and Paul Valéry. No other Irish publication has come within measuring distance of such a roll-call.[7]

The *DM* represented, in effect, a direct continuity with the whole Literary Revival, since O'Sullivan had known most of its leading figures personally and also knew Joyce. Personal contact, by letter or phone when man-to-man meetings were not possible, was O'Sullivan's modus operandi, and his patrician manner and sarcastic wit did not hide a considerable gift for friendship. The house in Morehampton Road which he shared with his painter-wife Estella Solomons was a place of call for many writers and artists, not all of them Irish by any means. About O'Sullivan himself there hung an aura of literary Edwardianism, a breath from the spacious milieu of Moore, Gogarty and John Eglinton, even of Beerbohm, and he retained to the end of his life the fastidiousness of the old-style bookman and man of letters. It was precisely these qualities, however, which brought his magazine into slow decline in the postwar years, since the new generation of writers tended now to gravitate towards O'Faolain's *Bell* or John Ryan's comparatively short-lived *Envoy* magazine. The *DM* was too gentlemanly, too old-fashioned; it was not controversial, it was non-political, it did not indulge in regular denunciations of censorship or the shortcomings of Church and State, and while O'Sullivan was no prude, there was little in his magazine about sex, directly or indirectly. He and his entire outlook belonged to an older generation. Yet up to its last issues, the magazine maintained standards of literacy and good manners – perhaps too much of the latter, in fact – in a society which was speeding towards the raucousness and self-advertisement of the Sixties.

The Bell has been so often discussed, and appears in so many studies, biographies and other contexts, that to write about it here at length is probably redundant and even boring. It was as different from O'Sullivan's magazine as whiskey is from old claret, since O'Sullivan was primarily a poet, a scholar and a bibliophile while O'Faolain was primarily a writer of realist fiction, as well as being an engagé man of letters who sought controversy with the enthusiasm of a fairground bully looking for a fight, a man for whom politics and the contemporary world were the writer-intellectual's natural material, a challenging critic both of society and of letters, a committed professional where O'Sullivan was a gentleman amateur. As an editor he merely served for half a dozen years, but then *The Bell* was a monthly publication from first to last, whereas the *Dublin Magazine* after its first few years of life was merely quarterly. That O'Faolain was, in every sense, a great and influential editor is fully recognised, and he took his duties and responsibilities very seriously. Since prose and polemics were his chosen field, he relied for the choice of verse on a series of poetry editors who included Geoffrey Taylor and even, for a time, Louis MacNeice. O'Sullivan had been his own sub-editor and factotum, while *The Bell* had various assistant editors and helpers including Anthony Cronin, Hubert Butler and Val Mulkerns.[8]

In the very first issue, O'Faolain in his editorial promised that the magazine would stand for 'Life before any abstraction, in whatever magnificent words it may clothe itself'. This was not entirely true, since he was as fond of abstractions and generalisations as most engagé intellectuals are, but it did imply a commitment to engaging head-on with the here and now, not just roaming comfortably in the world of books and belles lettres. O'Faolain was, among others things, a great journalist, and he also had a strong sense of history which prevented him from sinking too deeply into the bog-pools of topical controversy, however strongly he cultivated it. He spoke out boldly on issues such as the need for a successor to the League of Nations, before the United Nations Organisation had been founded;[9] he (inevitably) denounced petty acts of censorship and obscurantism; he challenged fashionable chauvinism and did not spare the Catholic Church; he attempted to see local issues in a wider, European context when the war had produced a defensive, introverted mentality among many people. O'Faolain, it might even be said, was an eloquent spokesman for the nation's conscience, though it was not the conscience of the orthodox or the entrenched.

Along with all this, he and his successor as editor, Peadar O'Donnell, managed to discover or encourage young talent, and Brendan Behan (who published in *The Bell* a piece which was the germ of *Borstal Boy*), James Plunkett and Brian Friel were among the prose writers who first came to attention through the magazine. Other contributors included Austin Clarke, Padraic Fallon (who, as well as contributing poetry, wrote a remarkable *Journal* which should be reprinted), Patrick Kavanagh, Kate O'Brien, Frank O'Connor (who contributed critical and polemical pieces as well as stories), Mary Lavin, Val Mulkerns, Liam O'Flaherty, Micheál Mac Liammóir, Patrick Campbell. There was an editorial policy of encouraging Northern Irish writers, so John Hewitt, W. R. Rodgers and Michael MacLaverty all contributed. Anthony Cronin (who served under O'Donnell rather than O'Faolain) was a strong presence in the magazine's later stages, both as poet and as critic/polemicist. One entire issue was given over to the views of young writers, their aims, ideals and complaints, to which Francis MacManus was chosen to reply as a representative of the middle-to-older generation. MacManus, unfortunately, rather lost his balance and sense of humour and as a result his article became schoolmasterish and hectoring, so that an excellent chance was wasted.

The Bell had a good, though not outstanding, section of book reviews and its theatre columns were genuinely crisp and informed; it also carried music criticism, which was an innovation. As Vivian Mercier wrote, it was 'to Ireland a sort of *Horizon*, *New Statesman* and *Nation*, *John O'London's Weekly* and *World Review* all rolled into one'. It had its weaknesses and blind spots too, including the columns of pretentious arty chat by 'Gulliver' (later to become posthumously famous as the novelist Michael Farrell) and some of its topical articles were worthy, well considered, but prosily dull. Visually, too, it was as penny-plain and functional as a trade magazine, allowing for wartime paper shortages and other problems. Even

O'Faolain's topical commentaries themselves could be predictable and self-righteous; as Vivian Mercier wrote in the issue of May 1945: 'The Editor's heart is in the right place. He is against the Government, as every intellectual should be in a capitalist country. And his basic approach to the historical situation is sound. Ireland has, as he is never tired of saying, merely achieved her bourgeois revolution, and has reached a stage of development very similar to that of England or France in the early nineteenth century. The Philistine is rampant in Ireland, and Seán is ever ready to play David to him. But his ammunition is always the same old set of well-worn pebbles – half a dozen generalities, one or other of which has done duty for every editorial in the past four and a half years.'

Though *The Bell* had a much shorter life than the *Dublin Magazine* it still ran for fourteen years, whereas John Ryan's *Envoy* ran for less than three, or twenty issues in all. It spoke for the generation which Seumas O'Sullivan had notably failed to attract, the postwar one of Brendan Behan, Anthony Cronin, Aidan Higgins, John Montague (though most of them had also written for *The Bell*) as well as older, more established figures such as Flann O'Brien and Francis Stuart, who had recently returned from Germany. Ryan himself was a painter, and he was knowledgeable about visual art, which *The Bell* had largely ignored. So *Envoy* carried articles on contemporary Irish painters such as Nano Reid, several of them written by the talented young painter Patrick Swift who moved to London in 1952, a year after *Envoy* had ceased publication. Here, together with the gifted South African poet David Wright, he edited the remarkable magazine *X*, a quarterly which ran for only a few years (1959-1961) but had an outstanding list of contributors while it lasted.

John Ryan ran the Bailey bar and restaurant, where his contributors were usually sure of getting drink on credit, or even of getting a loan (which was rarely paid back, incidentally). His milieu embraced the famous Catacombs, the curious set of people described in J. P. Donleavy's novel *The Ginger Man*, and of course McDaid's pub, which was close to the offices of *Envoy*. This was Patrick Kavanagh territory and inevitably Kavanagh bulked large in the magazine, contributing a 'Diary' regularly while it lasted, besides poems. And since Ryan and many of his contemporaries were Joyceans – it was the era in which Joyce's intellectual and artistic ascendancy over the Dublin intelligentsia was at its peak – Joyce's shadow lay sometimes heavily and even opaquely over *Envoy* which devoted a special number to him, as well as another to Yeats. Somehow or other, it also managed to obtain contributions from Heidegger and from the French novelist Nathalie Sarraute, as well as from Beckett who seems to have been favourably disposed to it. *Envoy* did not display the politico-social conscience of O'Faolain nor did it range so wide, but its purely literary quality was probably higher on average than *The Bell* achieved, and Ryan never used it as a vehicle for his own ambitions, being quite content to provide a forum for his generally distinguished contributors while staying in the background. It was also financed largely from his own money. Ryan has told the story of those years in his *Remembering how we Stood* (Dublin, 1975).

Irish Writing, the fourth of the distinguished quartet, was published from Cork on a quarterly basis and was edited from 1946 to 1954 by David Marcus (later literary editor of the *Irish Press*) and Terence Smith; they were succeeded by Seán J. White, who edited it until it folded in 1957. Inevitably, Cork writers bulked large and O'Faolain and O'Connor of course contributed, but so did Liam O'Flaherty, Beckett, Kavanagh, and the playwright Teresa Deevy. *Irish Writing* had a notably plain, even nondescript format, but its content and editorial policy were never shoddy.

One of the stranger products of the 1940s was the emergence of the *Capuchin Annual*, a religious periodical, as a cultural force under an eccentric monk called Father Senan. For a time, though his superiors can scarcely have approved, he extracted contributions from many well-known writers, critics and journalists including Benedict Kiely, Aodh de Blacam etc. and attracted a readership who normally would not have given a glance at what was, after all, supposed to be a religious journal. At one stage, Roibeárd Ó Faracháin worked for it in an editorial capacity and may have been at least partly responsible for the attempt to enlist 'progressive' Catholic writers to its columns. Somehow or other, Senan even succeeded in paying his contributors reasonably well, until he fell from power and the *Capuchin Annual* relapsed into clerical primness.

Another Catholic journal which has never received its due was the *Irish Monthly*, which was edited by the Jesuits and during the Thirties, Forties and at least the early part of the Sixties printed articles by prominent Catholic writers and journalists including Ó Faracháin, de Blacam, Gabriel Fallon, Denis Gwynn and Alfred O'Rahilly among others. Nor did it confine itself to Catholic apologetics; its brief was wide, and as early as 1950, for example, it carried an article by Colum Gavan called 'Can Europe Unite?' which considered the issue of European unity in an exceptionally well informed way. Other contributors wrote about the possibility of an Irish television service long before such a thing became a reality, the Catholic novel in France, and many other topical issues and controversies. When the hackneyed charge comes up once again that the Irish clergy of the time were fundamentally anti-intellectual, a look at the files of the *Irish Monthly* might qualify the accusation. Or, for that matter, the files of *Studies*, a serious and scholarly publication which is still in existence and was/is also produced and edited by Jesuits. Contrary to what is often assumed, all the best brains in Ireland were not ranged in the anti-clerical camp.

And finally, it would be ungracious not to mention the long-running humorous journal *Dublin Opinion*, the brainchild of a senior civil servant, C.E. (Charley) Kelly. He contributed his own topical cartoons, which had plenty of bite. In later years *Dublin Opinion* became over-amiable and rather woolly, but in its early stages it was influential enough to be quoted in Dáil debates.

Chapter 18

THE VISUAL ARTS

It is only comparatively recently that Ireland's contribution to the visual arts has been recognised, or indeed even seriously discussed. Nobody of sense and discernment would claim for a moment that it can compare with that of twentieth-century France or Germany, or even with those of England, Italy and Spain. Here again, Ireland remains on the outer rim of Europe, outside most of the great movements – Cubism, Expressionism, Abstraction, Futurism, Surrealism etc. As usual, it follows its own rules, or rather lack of them, though looking constantly to France where the prestige of the School of Paris lasted until after the second World War. The result is a good deal of provincial mediocrity, a number of fine individual talents most of which are virtually unknown outside Ireland, and one genuinely European genius in Jack Yeats.

The better Irish artists of the nineteenth century had either looked to England (Maclise, Danby, Mulready) or to France (Nathaniel Hone, Roderic O'Conor, Frank O'Meara and many more). There was little market at home for pictures and sculpture, particularly in the years after the Famine, and the Royal Hibernian Academy was not only a conservative body but a narrow-minded and provincial one. Early in the twentieth century, the few Irish painters who won European fame were active outside Ireland – William Orpen chiefly in London, Sir John Lavery in France and later in England, Nathaniel Hone for years in France before he returned home to farm his estates near Dublin. The outsider was John Butler Yeats, father of the dynasty, whose genius as a portraitist failed to gain him a living either in Ireland or England, so that he died a virtually penniless exile in New York in 1922.

The 'official' art of the Free State, which continued to be the official art of the period leading up to the second World War, was from the same school of thinking which produced the early Irish postage stamps, the Tailteann Games, some rather grim and four-square pieces of architecture, the typical Abbey rural play etc. Seán Keating, Charles Lamb and the other practitioners of Free State style were, in their day, hailed with some excitement as the first genuinely Irish school of painting, a new art reflecting both the realities and the aspirations of the new state and its citizens. In fact, there was very little in their work which was recognisably Irish except the subject matter, and even that was stylised – not to say stereotyped – rather than realistic, laying a weighty stress on strong men and fair colleens in rural or Western seaboard settings and wearing picturesque peasant clothes. Instead of resembling real people, these seemed to have just walked off the stage from a play by Synge or T. C. Murray. A major exception was Paul Henry (1871-1958), who had studied in Paris and absorbed the style of Van Gogh and the final wave of European realism, with a certain admixture of early French Modernism. His paintings of the West of Ireland landscape are still alive and potent – artfully simple and stark, tonally subtle inside a rather small range of colour, monumental without being rhetorical. To a great extent, they have created our visual image of Ireland west of the Shannon. Unfortunately Henry did not remain on this level for very long and during the Thirties, which was probably his period of highest popularity, his pictures grew increasingly stereotyped and ended by being barely distinguishable from those of a number of less gifted contemporaries such as James Humbert Craig.

The trio of major sculptors composed of Andrew O'Connor, John Hughes and Jerome Connor were past their peak of creativity and influence. O'Connor, who was Irish-American, was not given the public role which he deserved in the Free State, when his flair for vigorous, democratic (in the best sense) public statuary should have been recognised officially and have led to numerous State commissions. As it was, his bronze 'Christ the King' was allowed to lie half-concealed in a corner of Merrion Square for many years, because of ecclesiastical disapproval – often blamed on Dr John Charles McQuaid, but in reality the doing of the great Biblical scholar Mgr Henry Boylan. Hughes had lived abroad for many years before dying in Nice in 1941. Jerome Conor worked for more than a decade on his *Lusitania* memorial in Cobh, but his later years were blighted by a lawsuit which effectively bankrupted him, and when he died in hospital in Dublin in 1943, he was not only virtually penniless but because of wartime shortages was denied the basic fuels he needed to cast his work in bronze. The other great Irish-American sculptor, John B. Flannagan, never exhibited in Ireland and his work – mostly in stone – remains virtually unknown there.[1] Yet Flannagan visited Ireland twice for lengthy stays, in 1930 and 1933, which were largely spent in Connemara. A star-crossed man, alcoholic, depressive, and the victim of several bad accidents which partly crippled him, he died by suicide in 1942.

The foundation of Irish Modernism – if such a thing really existed – is often credited to two remarkable Anglo-Irish women, Mainie Jellett and Evie Hone. Like so many others before them, they studied in France; but while earlier Irish artists who worked there had brought back a rather dour, literal, late-Realist style, they broke the mould by absorbing the teaching of two Paris-based Cubists, André Lhote and Albert Gleizes. Neither Lhote nor Gleizes was an outstanding painter, and their version of Cubism was the kind of watered-down, formalised one which for a time was adopted by mildly 'progressive' young artists almost everywhere. (Certainly Braque and Picasso, the original Cubists, appear to have despised them.) In provincial Ireland, however, this style was not only novel but virtually heretical, so Jellett and Hone became spearheads of a New Age. Though not revolutionaries, they were both energetic, inspirational women with a talent for teaching and organising, and their personalities and examples set up ripples which spread through the small Irish art world and even into official circles. Both, too, had aspirations to create a new religious art, which flowered particularly in Hone's stained glass for churches, teaching institutions and other public places in Britain as well as Ireland. Evie Hone eventually became a Catholic. She was an invalid for most of her rather short life, and her courage and genuine spirituality had a considerable impact on more than her own immediate circle – indeed some people close to her seem to have regarded her as virtually a lay saint.

It cannot really be claimed, however, that either of them founded a school, though both had talented followers. Jellett and Hone were good painters, but scarcely major ones – the stained glass is another matter – yet their historical importance in an Irish context is considerable. In the first place, they made Paris-oriented Modernism relatively acceptable and respectable, even to the Church (or Churches); in the second, they established a kind of artistic and ideological platform from which a new generation of Irish artists could jump into the future. This was due as much to the force of their personalities, and to their pioneering energy, as it was to their creative work. They had made what nowadays we call a 'breakthrough', broken the sight-barrier for Irish art-lovers at an ultra-conservative time; and though the moguls of the RHA did not realise the fact, their star was already beginning to sink. For years the Academy had been under the die-hard presidency of Dermod O'Brien,[2] a competent painter himself, though better known as a social figure and a leading light in the Dublin Arts Club. O'Brien was a man of another age, and although the Academy had able, solid talents in Leo Whelan and James Sleator (both pupils of William Orpen, incidentally) its annual exhibitions relied heavily on dull, semi-official portraiture, laboured genre pieces, and tritely 'picturesque' landscape. The great Jack Yeats, of course, exhibited in its shows, but he was a solitary figure who was generally respected even when his later style baffled many of his admirers.

In 1943, in the darkest period of the World War, the Irish Exhibition of Living Art was founded, and it remained the outlet for the country's best visual talents for roughly a quarter-century. It was an unpromising time to launch an annual avant-garde event, but war has often proved a stimulus to creativity and in this case there were several important factors at work. One was growing dissatisfaction with the RHA, which had come under increasingly heavy fire from the critics and from various artists who resented its conservatism and its virtual stranglehold on public taste, or at least official taste. Another was the Academy's rejection of works by certain talented younger artists including Louis le Brocquy, who with his strong-minded mother, Sybil, was one of the most active figures in setting up the new grouping, if it can be called that. And yet another factor was the presence in Ireland (mostly in Dublin) of a number of English artists who were mildly avant-garde in outlook, including Basil Rakoczi who was actually Hungarian by blood, Kenneth Hall, and Nevill Johnston. The coming of war had either attracted or stranded various people in Ireland for its duration, including some who may have been genuine conscientious objectors to fighting, or simply draft-dodgers. Rakoczi was not a very talented artist – it was said of him, more than once, that he could paint competently in any style except his own – but he was energetic and persuasive, a mixture of enthusiast and artistic adventurer. The White Stag group with which he was associated may seem small beer today, yet it had a genuine role at the time, and around it germinated a new type of Dublin bohemian life which echoed that of Soho or Chelsea.

Mainie Jellett's name was prominent among the initial organisers of the IELA, but she was already a dying woman and was more useful for her prestige and connections than as an active participant. Another generation was taking over and during the first dozen years of the IELA's life numerous fine talents emerged, making this a vigorous and characterful period of Irish art. Artists from Northern Ireland were prominent, including Colin Middleton, Norah McGuinness, Daniel O'Neill, Gerard Dillon and George Campbell, but there were also Nano Reid, a Drogheda painter whose style was powerful and expressionistic, and Patrick Collins from Sligo, one of the most poetic and original talents to emerge since Jack Yeats. Sculptors were rarer, but the sensitive, versatile, rather eclectic talent of Oisín Kelly quickly found admirers, and Hilary Heron showed an ability to work convincingly in various media including metal. These were not international figures (a term much used and abused today) nor was the Living Art an event of European significance, but in a sense it marked the coming of age of Irish art, since all these gifted men and women had their own individual idioms which were at once recognisably Irish and recognisably modern.[3] Nano Reid and Collins, in particular, showed that a national sensibility was no hindrance to modernity, though in any case Jack Yeats had already blazed such a trail, and while he had no direct followers, his example and his strong, though reticent personality were potent forces for at least two generations. Unfortunately, few of the Living Art painters equalled his capacity to grow and develop over a lifetime; Yeats's 'third period' remained unique in its technical boldness and visionary power, while many of his juniors tended to repeat themselves after early middle age. (Admittedly, this was true of many of their literary contemporaries as well.)

Yeats's late works puzzled many people who had followed him faithfully from his early days, but who could not make the quantum leap of comprehension when his style grew increasingly broken, irridescent and full of shapes and figures which half-emerged through a thick veil of paint. His idiosyncratic picture-titles were often taken as riddles or jokes, while those well-wishers who earnestly searched for recognisable subject matter were thwarted or repulsed by his seeming obscurity. The man who earlier in his career had been regarded as the national laureate of painting had seemingly retreated into a world of private mythology or fantasy, to which any public access was closed and sealed. Yet his pictures sold steadily, there were always the understanding or enlightened few (such as Beckett, Sir Kenneth Clark, Oskar Kokoschka[4] and Thomas McGreevy, who became Director of the National Gallery in 1950) who could and did follow him in his artistic pilgrimage, and he did not lack recognition either at home or abroad. In 1942 he had a retrospective exhibition at the National Gallery in London, another major exhibition was mounted at the Tate Gallery in 1948, and in 1951 yet another toured a number of cities in America. France awarded him the Legion of Honour. In old age Yeats stood on a pinnacle, unapproached in stature and prestige by any other living Irish artist, though the death of his wife Cottie saddened him and left him terminally alone. In the last two years of his life he was an invalid, until his death in a Dublin nursing home in March 1957.[5]

The Living Art Exhibitions always relied heavily on a certain type of masterful, organising woman-artist which had been a phenomenon of Dublin art life since the days of Sarah Purser at least. Norah McGuinness was in this sense the heir to Purser, and to Hone and Jellett as well, but other women artists were prominent in the groundwork and organising chores, notably Anne Yeats (daughter of the poet, and a talented painter in her own right) and the strong-minded Hilary Heron. Another prop was the young James White, a former pupil of Jellett who had turned to art criticism and became a very effective lecturer and propagandist for the new art; in due course, he was to revitalise first the Dublin Municipal Gallery of Modern Art, and then the National Gallery. Herbert Read, then England's leading Modernist pundit, came to lecture during the 1947 exhibition on 'The Present Situation on Art in Europe'. There were also some sympathetic and relatively well-informed critics such as Edward Sheehy of the *Dublin Magazine*.

But perhaps the most decisive ally this generation possessed was Victor Waddington, the remarkable Dublin Jew who had once been a fairground boxer, then through the lower ranges of picture-dealing eventually became the most successful gallery-owner and art entrepreneur that Dublin – and Ireland – ever knew. The Living Art exhibitions might exhibit modern Irish art publicly, James White might publicise it verbally, a coterie of Dublin snobs might patronise it socially, but Waddington performed the essential service of selling it. His gallery in South Anne Street – which opened in 1942 and was officially called the Victor Waddington Galleries – was not the first or the only one in Dublin to show such art, but Waddington was a salesman and showman of genius, as he later showed when he emigrated to London in 1957 and in a few years had become a power in the art world there.[6] The buying public for his artists was never large, but it was adequate for a city of Dublin's size and Waddington knew how to turn exhibition openings into social events which attracted both a monied clientele and a fair share of press coverage. He himself had an excellent social sense and the former booth boxer rapidly developed the manners and appearance of a grand seigneur. The artists he exhibited included O'Neill, Dillon, Paul Henry and many more, but of course his crown jewel was Yeats. Waddington was not a disinterested idealist; he was a hard-headed businessman. But his flair and vision were undoubted and they were not restricted to Irish art and artists. He also showed works by many leading English and Continental artists, including Picasso, Bonnard, Matisse, Braque, Rouault, Kokoschka, Ben Nicholson, Ivon Hitchens, Stanley Spencer, Henry Moore, Barbara Hepworth, André Masson – a remarkable list for a city widely regarded as a European backwater. When he finally moved to London, some of his leading Irish artists were taken over by Leo Smith for his Dawson Gallery, while others went to the recently opened Ritchie Hendriks Gallery (later the David Hendriks Gallery) on St Stephen's Green.

It goes without saying that there were also distinguished Irish émigré artists, a tradition which went back to the eighteenth century. Probably the best known was William J. Leech, who had left Ireland as early as 1910 and spent his later life in England, dying in Surrey in 1968 in his eighties. Leech was essentially a late Realist painter, trained in France, whose style became conservative in later life but never quite fell back into academicism. He continued to exhibit in Dublin in his years of exile, chiefly at the RHA, but in 1945 the Dawson Gallery managed to organise a one-man show of his work and showed him regularly from then on to his death. Leech was a typical product of the cultured Dublin Protestant middle class and so was Mary Swanzy, if she can be said to be typical of any class or background. She represented the new 'independent woman' and travelled in Eastern Europe and the South Seas before settling in London in 1926, when she was in her forties; during the second World War, the London Blitz forced her to return to Dublin for a time. She was one of the exhibitors in the IELA's very first show in 1943. Swanzy lived on until 1978, lucid to the last, tart in speech, and something of an old dragon, able to recall with perfect clarity her studies under Walter Osborne early in the century. She, too, continued to exhibit in Ireland during her exile, and was given a retrospective exhibition at the Municipal Gallery of Modern Art in Dublin in 1968, which brought her back before the Irish public. Swanzy was everything Leech was not: unorthodox, original, surreal rather than realist, a visionary with a notably black, sardonic side to her psyche. In spite of the higher critical standing of Jellett and Hone, I still regard her as probably the finest Irish woman painter, with the possible exception of Nano Reid.

The careers of the sculptor F. E. McWilliam and the painter William Scott belong more in the area of British than of Irish art, which is fully understandable since they were both Northern Irishmen who spent most of their active lives in England. Both also served in the second World War, McWilliam as an RAF pilot and Scott as a map maker with the Royal Engineers. McWilliam ('Mac' to his friends) came into prominence as early as the 1930s with the English surrealists, and won an international reputation and many public commissions – although, most regrettably, the Irish Republic never commissioned a work from him. Stylistically he was an eclectic, and a remarkably versatile technician who created impressive stone carvings, portrait heads in bronze, woodcarvings, even pieces in cement. There is a strong erotic element in his work, probably stimulated by his contacts with Indian classical sculpture during his years as an airman, and in an epoch when the abstract-versus-figurative debate sometimes grew fierce and wordy, he moved between both camps with apparent ease. In spite of his outward Anglicisation, McWilliam was very conscious of his Irishness (or Anglo-Irishness, some would have called it) and exhibited regularly in Dublin. He was a personal friend of Scott, and his bronze bust of him is in the Ulster Museum; yet two more contrasting personalities it would have been hard to name. Scott, who was born in Scotland of working-class parents but always counted himself an Ulsterman, had been living and working in Brittany in 1939 when the war forced him and his wife to decamp almost overnight, leaving many of his paintings behind. He then lived in Dublin for a time before returning to England and war service.

Scott too won an international reputation, developing from his early, French-influenced style into virtual abstraction; he was included in the Sao Paulo Biennale in 1953 and the Venice Biennale in 1954, as well as the Kassel Documenta in 1955 and 1959. Scott first showed his work at the Living Art in 1945 and from the start he had supporters and admirers in Dublin. His Calvinist upbringing comes out in his mature style, which is often bare and austere ('minimal' in the fashionable sense) yet always beautifully crafted and never lacking a degree of sensuous appeal. He was one of the first British artists to appreciate the importance of the post-war New York School, and he was also close to the abstract painters and sculptors grouped in or around St Ives in Cornwall. St Ives was also a landmark in the career of another eminent Irish painter, Tony O'Malley, who was born in the same year as Scott (1913) but thanks partly to a late start as a painter, and partly because he found himself at odds with many facets of Irish life, found it very much harder to find any recognition until he was on the verge of old age. He was still almost unknown in his homeland when he moved to Cornwall in 1960, so the most important stages of his career lie outside this book. For most of the Fifties he painted in obscurity in various Irish towns, producing in private works of a high originality most of which were exhibited only many years later. All in all, his is one of the strangest stories in the history of Irish art.

The fact that as strong and original a talent as his was cold-shouldered by the Living Art selection committee was in itself a proof that the arteries of that institution were already hardening. Some new talents appeared, including the portrait painter Edward McGuire, the elegant abstractionist Patrick Scott, and Patrick Pye who in some ways was the successor to Hone and Jellett as a religious artist; but these were isolated individuals rather than a coherent new generation. The fact was, the axis of the international art world had shifted from Paris to New York, but relatively few people in Dublin fully realised this as yet – and when American styles did flood in, at the end of the Fifties and in the early Sixties, too often the immediate effect on Irish artists was to make them produce works which were banal, imitative and provincial rather than electrifying. At least a decade had to pass before New York art was properly absorbed and understood, and by that time the Living Art was past history. Later attempts to revive it were ill-judged and short-lived. It had served its purpose and was no longer needed, since the stranglehold of the RHA was thoroughly broken and the public was no longer baffled or frightened by Modernism. In fact, the shoe was now on the other foot and it was the academics who found it hard to discover outlets or selling opportunities for their work. However, the conservatives held on to power in the National College of Art and Design until the late 1960s, when they were driven out at last and a more rational, up-to-date generation of teachers and administrators took over.

In retrospect, the NCAD under the Old Guard was probably the greatest obstacle to progress in the visual arts, since in general it gave young painters, sculptors, graphic artists and designers a training which was not only old-fashioned but sometimes technically inadequate as well (an exception should be made of Maurice MacGonigal, who was respected as a teacher even by pupils who disliked his work). This was particularly true of the 1950s, when a combination of petty bureaucracy and academic dogmatism bore down heavily on students who showed any obvious nonconformity. In minuscule, this was typical of an entire generation clash in Irish life, in which parental control and ancestor-worship were challenged head-on by young people whose own thinking was sometimes confused and contradictory. In England, this took the form of the Angry Young Man generation, most of whom had little of any real originality to offer when they managed to win some degree of success and prestige.

Sadly, the flowering of Irish crafts which had begun at the turn of the century, and survived the first World War, largely died out in the 1920s and was never revived with its old energy. The great tradition of Irish stained glass lasted longer, but with the death in 1955 of both Evie Hone and Wilhelmina Geddes (who had lived in London for thirty years) it came to an end, and no real successor has emerged if we except a few outstanding windows by Patrick Pye. Harry Clarke, the real genius of the school and also a remarkable book illustrator, died of TB early in 1931 while returning home from the sanatorium at Davos in Switzerland – Thomas Mann's Magic Mountain. His life had probably been shortened by the notorious rejection by the Irish Government of his so-called Geneva Window, which had been commissioned as a gift to the International Labour Office in Geneva and was intended as a tribute to the leading Irish writers of the time. At a late hour, the politicians or civil servants took fright at the inclusion of a semi-nude dancer in the section illustrating Liam O'Flaherty's *Mr Gilhooley* – which indeed seems to belong to Wilde's *Salomé* rather than to O'Flaherty's relatively primitive emotional world. Instead the work was returned to its creator, in one of the most malodorous and depressing episodes of Irish censorship, and remained for years in the hands of his widow. At least Clarke, before dying at forty-one, had managed to complete his remarkable 'Resurrection' for Newport in County Mayo, which some good judges regard as his masterpiece. By contrast, the gifted Henry Healy did not live to complete his series of seven windows for Clongowes Wood College; he had finished only three of them when he died in 1941, and the series was completed by Evie Hone.

Hone herself had come relatively late to stained glass, after apparently settling into a career as an abstract painter (she had exhibited with the Abstraction-Creation group in Paris, and was also for a time a member of the Seven and Five group in London which included Ben Nicholson and David Jones). She made her first glass panels at Wilhelmina Geddes's kiln in London in 1933, and a year later joined An Túr Gloine, the famous co-operative workshop created mainly by Sarah Purser. Her fame began with the commission of the window 'My Four Green Fields' for the Irish Pavilion at the New York World Fair in 1937, designed by the young architect Michael Scott. After that her output was steady and commissions came from overseas as well as home, in spite of the fact that she had suffered from polio and arthritis from her schooldays and was in constant pain and discomfort. When An Túr Gloine dissolved itself in 1944, she opened her own studio in Rathfarnham and from there became virtually a national institution, respected as much for her nobility of character as for her art. Evie Hone had become a Catholic in 1937, and a revival of religious art was always on her mind; she was awed by the stained glass at Chartres Cathedral and greatly admired the paintings of Rouault. Both influences can be seen in her great five-light window for St Michael's Church at Highgate in London, though it has been rather overshadowed by her East Window in Eton College Chapel. Her own favourite among her works is said to have been her four windows in the Church of the Immaculate Conception at Kingscourt in County Cavan, which surprisingly few people appear to have visited. A large memorial exhibition was mounted at University College Dublin in 1958.

In architecture, Ireland did not produce a modernist school to equal Aalto and Saarinen in Finland, any more than it produced a Sibelius or even a Tubin in music. Though the Catholic Church had patronised the leading stained-glass artists, it was rather slow to patronise modern architects, and an eclectic historicism – not to say pastiche – dominated most church buildings in the years between the two world wars. The Church of Christ the King at Turner's Cross on the outskirts of Cork city, built in 1927-31, was in fact designed by an American, Francis Barry Byrne, who had studied under Frank Lloyd Wright; in any case, this remained a rather isolated case, though it caused some excitement at the time. It was not until the Sixties that a genuinely original style of church architecture emerged in such buildings as Liam McCormick's circular Church of St Aengus at Burt, in County Donegal.

Secular architecture was rather more advanced, and though Desmond FitzGerald's Airport Terminal Building at Collinstown in County Dublin (now Dublin Airport) is scarcely a masterpiece, for its time it was a considerable act of faith. FitzGerald, who had left college only a few years earlier, headed a team of young architects under the Board of Works in the late Thirties, and the building was begun in 1939 and finished in 1941. Though today it looks like a good many other buildings of its period scattered all over the world, it was a definite breakthrough considering the conservative official taste of the era. There were, however, relatively few similar public commissions until Michael Scott – who had designed the Irish Pavilion at New York in 1937 and had also created the Gate Theatre for Mac Liammóir and Edwards, as well as designing Portlaoise Hospital in the mid-Thirties – was given the task of designing the Central Bus Station in Dublin in 1944.[7] Called Busáras by virtually everyone in Dublin today, it was begun in 1944, but the Government then changed its mind and decided to convert it into a labour exchange. Later it went back to its original plan, and Busáras finally became operative in 1953. When it opened, close to Gandon's Custom House, one Dublin wit is said to have remarked: 'C'est magnifique, mais c'est ne pas la gare!'

To a great extent Busáras brought to Dublin the international style of Le Corbusier as well as that of the Bauhaus and Mies van der Rohe, with its concrete box-frame construction, large areas of double glazing, and use of inner space. As such it was a pioneering achievement and it has had a large progeny, much of it undistinguished. Scott was more fortunate in his career than the Australian-born Raymond McGrath, who had won a considerable reputation as a writer, theorist and designer, as well as for his work as an architect, before he came to Ireland in 1940. He became principal architect to the Board of Works in 1948, but much or most of his energies went on restoring or renovating State buildings, including Dublin Castle and Áras an Uachtaráin (formerly the Vice-Regal Lodge) in the Phoenix Park. There is a ground-bass of disappointment and even frustration underlying his long years in Ireland; his design for the JFK Memorial Hall in Dublin was never built, while his RHA Gallagher Gallery in Ely Place was left an unfinished shell for years when the funds ran out and was not completed until well after his death in 1977. Raymond McGrath was a major architect, but an unlucky one.[8]

Chapter 19

MUSICAL LIFE AND LIVES

It seems to be generally agreed that Ireland has not produced a great twentieth-century composer in the European sense, or even in the 'national' sense that Smetana, Kodály, Suk, Moniuszko and other Central and Eastern European composers of the late nineteenth and early twentieth centuries are great to their fellow-countrymen, if not necessarily to the world at large. This may be a case of arrested development; or it may be that, like so many other native traditions, Irish music was wrenched from its natural base two centuries ago and has not fully found itself since; or it may be simply the fact that great musicians do not appear to order. With all respect to such vigorous and versatile musicians as Hamilton Harty (whose folksy scherzo from his *Irish Symphony*, rather incongruously, was for years heard in thousands of households as the signature tune for the long-running Radio Éireann serial 'The Kennedys of Castlerosse'), the Literary Revival never found its parallel composer in the sense that Jack Yeats is its equivalent in painting. Or if it did, it was not in any Irish-born composer but in English musicians with a deep engagement to Irish culture – a remarkable feature of the period which this chapter deals with.

One of the main attractions to them was undoubtedly the poetry of Yeats, which again and again has proved a magnet for musicians – although Yeats himself, notoriously, was tone-deaf and indifferent to music. The most eminent example of this is the haunting setting of a cycle of early poems from 'The Wind in the Reeds' by the tragic Peter Warlock (Philip Heseltine, 1894-1930) entitled *The Curlew* – an astonishing achievement from a man in his early twenties, though Heseltine was nothing if not precocious. Warlock-Heseltine, however, did not limit himself to admiring Irish culture from a distance. He spent some time in Ireland in 1917 and 1918, and even learned Irish (he had previously learned Cornish) well enough to write it as well as speak it. According to his first biographer and fellow-musician, Cecil Gray, he achieved this in a mere two months spent on the Aran Islands and in Achill.[1]

In what must have been one of the strangest evenings in the Abbey Theatre's history, Warlock lectured there on 'What Music Is', wearing a blue African medicine-man's robe and 'a large and unruly beard' which he seems to have grown specially for the occasion. His lecture was long, erudite and strange, covering the whole theory and practice of music from the tenth century to the twentieth. This was succeeded by a group of traditional Irish folksongs; then another singer sang songs by Moussorgsky, Delius, Schubert, and Warlock's admired friend and teacher, Bernard van Dieren. After that, Warlock himself played some Bartòk on the piano, and another pianist played music by Chopin and Scriabin. During this exotic entertainment, the stage was lit with dim lights and amber top-lights (no footlights) while the auditorium was in total darkness. To his friend Gray back in London, Warlock wrote: 'Some four hundred persons listened with respect and – as I discovered from certain questions put to me at the close – scarcely a grain of understanding.'[2]

Warlock, who had a fine critical intellect and a natural insight into all the arts, met Yeats in person and talked to him about an embryo literary work which obviously later became A Vision. Unlike so many intelligent but culturally conditioned Englishmen, who have usually found Yeats's personal mythology spurious or at least dubious, Warlock understood the deep roots of the poet's symbolism and defended it eloquently in his letters. He also wrote to Gray with excitement about his discovery of the paintings of Yeats's brother Jack, 'at once real and utterly fantastic'. But above all, he thought that Ireland was 'rife for music; in utter contradistinction to England, it is spiritually alive . . . You feel this undercurrent from the first moment when one is struck by its intense foreignness to England.'[3] He also thought that 'Irish music has not emerged from the melodic stage' and noted, with the exception of 'the imbecile reels and jigs', a fundamental analogy between Ireland and the East.

Since Warlock gassed himself in the year at which this book opens,[4] he does not strictly belong here, but his case is a unique one and he anticipated much of what came later. His innate empathy with Ireland and things Irish are unquestionable. Certainly The Curlew has a special place among the many settings of Yeats by various composers, and since Warlock was unhappy in his marriage and unlucky in his love affairs, his own experiences may have given it extra poignance. By contrast, Ralph Vaughan-Williams's 1931 opera based on Synge's Riders to the Sea seems to have dropped out of the repertory, though the critic Scott Goddard thought it his 'finest stage work and his least known'.[5]

When a memorial concert for Peter Warlock was given at the Wigmore Hall in London in February 1931, the conductor was the composer Constant Lambert (whose life was only marginally less tragic than Warlock's) and at the piano was an older composer, Arnold Bax. Bax's links with Ireland were far more extensive than those of Warlock/Heseltine, and lasted much longer. In fact, they only ended with his sudden death in Cork in 1953, aged seventy – nearly twice the lifespan of the younger man. Bax's love affair with Ireland had begun in 1902, when as a nineteen-year-old student of the Royal College of Music he read Yeats's 'The Wanderings of

Usheen' and was conquered. In his own words, 'in a moment the Celt within me stood revealed'.[6] In 'great spiritual excitement' Bax visited Ireland, going to remote Glencolumbkille in County Donegal which became a favourite retreat; as late as 1930 he wrote that life there had hardly changed in 100 years and of its 'gentle and innocent people – a great privilege, they regard me as one of their own'.

In Dublin Bax became a friend and protégé of AE and was deeply moved by the 1916 Rising, several of whose dramatis personae were known to him personally. He wrote poetry and short stories under the name 'Dermot O'Byrne' which are no better or worse than those by any of two dozen other epigones of the Celtic Twilight. But far more important creatively than his encounter with Irish literature is his encounter with Irish music; he wrote that of all countries in the world, Ireland possessed the most beautiful and varied folk music. Though he had (in spite of what is often claimed) at least some Celtic blood, Bax's ancestry was mainly English Quaker and his background was prosperous and cultured upper-middle-class – Clifford Bax, the poet and playwright, was his brother. His powerful and almost lifelong pull to Ireland appears to have been a mental and emotional affinity rather than an atavistic call of the blood. It was, to an extent, generically Celtic rather than exclusively Irish, since he was equally drawn to Scotland and wrote some of his finest orchestral works there; but the fact remains that Ireland had a unique and central role in his life as well as in his music. He did not try to become an Irish composer, and as his commentators have pointed out, his influences are Russian and German and Scandinavian as well as Celtic; neither was he ever a folk composer in the sense so common early in the century. The Irish music critic Charles Acton has argued persuasively that Bax always remained, in essence, an English composer. Nevertheless, in view of how much he owed spiritually both to Yeats and AE, as well as to the Irish landscape and Irish legend, it is hardly an exaggeration to call him the real musician of the Irish Renaissance, and to a considerable extent his imagination was haunted by the same themes and obsessions as its leading writers.

That first reading of 'The Wanderings of Usheen' bore fruit in the early tone poem *In the Faery Hills*, which is based on an episode in Yeats's poem and was Bax's first orchestral work to win him some recognition. Celtic legend was also the inspiration of a slightly later tone poem *The Garden of Fand* while there was also an abortive attempt to write an opera on the Deirdre story. He spent his honeymoon in Ireland and even – this was still before the first World War – took a house in Rathgar, where AE was a near-neighbour. Both of Bax's children were born in Rathgar; his son Dermot Colum and his daughter Maeve Astrid. He and his wife Elsita became close to Padraic and Mary Colum, soon to depart for New York – and stay there – and Bax set poems by Colum to music as well as works by Joseph Campbell and Synge.

However, Bax's marriage broke up through his involvement with the pianist Harriet Cohen ('Tania'), the *femme fatale* of his life and a source both of ecstasy and misery. The emotional turmoil in which this engulfed him, combined with 'The

Troubles' in Ireland, is reflected in the angry and violent music of his *First* and *Second* Symphonies, in which one movement in particular has been linked with the death of Michael Collins. On a more friendly note, in 1927 he began his lifelong friendship with Aloys G. Fleischmann and his wife Tilly, and his lifelong links with Cork. Invited by the committee of the local Father Matthew *Feis* to act as an adjudicator, he came three years in a row and from then on visited the Fleischmann family every year, except for the wartime period of 1939-46. He became an external examiner for the Department of Music in University College Dublin, and it was in that capacity that he came on his last visit to Ireland in 1953 (in letters to friends, he admitted that he sometimes found the examinations rather a boring chore; Bax had no interest in teaching).

It is true that Harriet Cohen, in her autobiography, claimed that with the 1930 *Winter Legends* Bax largely broke with things Celtic and moved imaginatively to Northern Europe; she even quotes him as saying 'I have gone Northern.' One of the forces behind this was almost certainly his encounter with the music of Sibelius, whom he visited with Harriet Cohen in Finland in 1932 and whose *Tapiola* had made him weep when he heard it in London in 1928. However, the opening of his *Fifth Symphony* has been linked by one of Bax's biographers, Lewis Foreman,[7] with the composer's description of suddenly seeing the sea from the summit of Slieve League, one of his favoured places in the West of Ireland. And in 1932 he was asked by his friend Herbert Hughes to contribute to a project called 'The Joyce Book', aimed at helping James Joyce who had recently gone through rough times financially. Designed by the musicologist Hubert Foss, it was an elaborate affair bound in handwoven silk, and printed in a numbered and limited edition; Augustus John contributed a drawing of Joyce as a frontispiece, there were contributions by James Stephens, Padraic Colum and Arthur Symons, and then settings by different composers of the thirteen poems from *Pomes Pennyeach*. Besides Bax, the composers involved were E. J. Moeran, Albert Roussel, Hughes himself, John Ireland, Roger Sessions, Arthur Bliss, Herbert Howells, George Antheil, Edgardo Carducci, Eugene Goossens, C. W. Orr and Bernard van Dieren.[8]

After the war Bax resumed his visits to Ireland and in 1947 was conferred with an honorary degree from the National University in Dublin, an honour which, in his own words, made him feel 'that I am taking an authentic place again in the cultural life of this beloved land'. He shared it with Jack B. Yeats, whose paintings he admired, and 'a Celtic professor', all of them wearing red robes with hoods and velveteen hats; the parchments were handed to them by the Taoiseach, Mr de Valera, by whom Bax was 'very impressed' personally. Later he attended rehearsals of two of his tone poems, *Tintagel* and *In the Faery Hills*, by the recently formed Radio Symphony Orchestra. All in all, this was one of the happiest weeks of his life and he wrote a warm letter of appreciation which appeared in *The Irish Times*.[9] Pointing out that 'From earliest youth Éire has been my Land of Heart's Desire', he went on to pay tribute to the musicianship of Arthur Duff and to the Irish pianist

Charles Lynch, who had 'played one of my pianoforte pieces with a mastery that can only enhance his fame'.

This letter has a certain elegiac tone, since in fact Bax's great creative years were already behind him and in the last five years of his life he wrote little of importance. He seems to have drunk fairly heavily in his last years and to have aged rapidly, feeling increasingly estranged from his milieu and spending most of his time in a Sussex village. His appointment as Master of the King's Musick – which in a few years became the Queen's Musick when Elizabeth II succeeded George VI to the throne – took up a lot of his time and energies, so that he spoke to his friends about retiring from the post and going to live in Cork. (He ruled out Dublin because it was 'becoming too cosmopolitan'.) Bax did not live long enough to do so, dying in Cork in October 1953, a few hours after watching a spectacular sunset off the Old Head of Kinsale. Fittingly enough, the last time he heard his own music had been in Dublin a few days earlier, when the RÉ Symphony Orchestra (as it had become) played a Bax evening including *The Garden of Fand* and the *Concertante for Piano Left Hand*, with Harriet Cohen playing the solo part. His funeral to St Finbarr's Cemetery in Cork was a major event, followed by many notables, academics and musicians, and among the mourners were Daniel Corkery (a warm admirer of Bax's music) and the sculptor Seamus Murphy. Some months later a Bax Memorial Room was established in University College Cork, and was opened officially by Bax's octogenarian friend and colleague, Sir Ralph Vaughan Williams.

From the early 1930s, Bax had formed the habit of staying for periods at the Lansdowne Arms hotel in Kenmare, County Kerry, with his close friend the composer E. J. Moeran. Moeran (whose first name was Ernest, but was always called Jack by his friends) has already been mentioned in connection with the Joyce settings to which Bax contributed, but he had by then composed the striking *Seven Poems of James Joyce* (1929). Moeran was the son of an English father and an Irish mother. He had served as a young officer in the first World War, suffering a head wound 'to the after-effects of which may perhaps be attributed a certain instability in his character later on', as Bax wrote after his friend's death. Moeran was a heavy drinker for most of his life, but especially when he shared a cottage in a Kentish village with Philip Heseltine in the 1920s – a wild, bohemian interlude in the lives of both men. Like Heseltine/Warlock, and like their younger friend Constant Lambert, Moeran was an emotional, hypersensitive, erudite man, tending to alternate between exuberance and withdrawal. He was as strongly drawn to Ireland, and Irish culture, as Bax was, and at a time when the *sean-nós* form of Irish singing was little regarded, Moeran encouraged old folk musicians to sing or perform for him and wrote down in notation what he had heard. He was, in fact, an expert on folk song and made a collection of folk-tunes.

The son of a clergyman, Moeran had spent his youth in Norwich, where presumably he got his feeling for nature; of his *Symphony in G Minor* he wrote: 'The material of the second movement was conceived around the sand-dunes and marshes of East Norfolk.' That, however, does not alter the fact that, as he also wrote, the greater part of this symphony was written (in 1934-97) 'among the mountains and seaboard of County Kerry' and that the work 'may be said to owe its inspiration to the natural surroundings in which it was planned and written'. Though the influence of Sibelius is plain enough and has been duly noted by numerous critics, this work is one of the finest British symphonies of its time, even if Moeran was scarcely a born symphonist (as Bax undoubtedly was). He is probably best in his songs and shorter pieces, including the orchestral work *Lonely Waters*, and in his choral music. Bax also greatly admired his *Violin Concerto*, and the sympathetic friendship between the two musicians makes a welcome contrast to the bitchiness and envy so common among creative artists. Those long spells spent together in Kenmare encompassed much hard work, high spirits and interchange of ideas; but they also included a good deal of hard drinking, and with both of them in later life the drinking tended to become even harder. Just how large a part it played in Moeran's tragic death in 1950 off Kenmare pier remains a mystery. There are conflicting reports about it; some local people maintained that he was blown into the sea by a sudden gust of wind, others that he had drunk a little too much and missed his footing while strolling on the pier to clear his head, while others again have hinted at suicide on some sudden, dark impulse. Moeran as a man was much loved, by fellow-musicians and Irish friends alike, and I myself heard people in Dublin literary circles talk about him affectionately long after his death.

While Bax's pull to Ireland was imaginative and emotional rather than racial, Moeran's was almost certainly the latter. The critic J. A. Westrup, discussing the 'unmistakably Irish' character of many of his musical themes, remarked: 'Such a character might be assumed. In the case of Bax it is the result of residence in Ireland and a curiously sympathetic understanding of her traditions and culture. With Moeran we may safely attribute it to Irish ancestry, even though his birth and upbringing were English.'[10] Which in turn raises the question of how far either of them validly belongs here in a chapter which is, after all, at least nominally about Irish music. Both were not only English-born but English-trained, and we do not consider Delius a French composer because he settled in Grez-sur-Loing. The answer is that if Irish-born writers such as Louis MacNeice or Elizabeth Bowen are so often enrolled as honorary English ones, on the strength of their spending so much of their active careers in England, then surely two English-born composers can at least be partly annexed to the country whose culture, scenery, people and traditions they virtually made their own – and in which they died.

Of the native-born Irish composers of their generation or a little younger, Bax's friend Arthur Duff already seems to be more than half-forgotten, although his *Irish Suite for Strings* and *Echoes of Georgian Dublin* might still make attractive concert pieces. A cultured, witty and versatile man, he also wrote incidental music for many plays at the Abbey and Gate Theatres and even had a play of his own, *Cadenza*, produced at the Gate. John F. Larchet was probably more influential as a teacher than as a composer, especially in his role as Professor of Music in University College Dublin, from 1921 to 1958 – a long span. He was also Professor of Music at the Royal Irish Academy of Music, where he trained a whole generation of Irish composers. Frederick May (1911-1985) is a tragic figure – a highly strung homosexual at a time when homosexuality was still, publicly and privately, regarded as either a vice or an aberration; an alcoholic, a misfit, but a musician of great though only partly fulfilled talent. His *String Quartet in C Minor* has become a recognised and much-loved classic (when it was recorded by Claddagh Records some years ago, the recording carried an enthusiastic sleeve-note by the writer James Plunkett, who is an amateur violinist of talent). Some of his songs, and perhaps the tone-poem *Sunlight and Shadow*, also deserve resurrection. May had a thoroughly cosmopolitan background and training, first under Vaughan Williams in England and later under Egon Wellesz in Vienna. The prolific, versatile Brian Boydell (born 1917) is still active at the time of writing and has had a long and honourable career as Professor of Music in Trinity College, Dublin. In the opinion of the critic Richard Pine, his *Violin Concerto* of 1953 is arguably the most important work of this century after May's *String Quartet*. A. J. (Archie) Potter, born a year later than Boydell, was another Vaughan Williams pupil whose output ran from orchestral pieces to composing an opera for television to a libretto written by Donagh MacDonagh. Very much a Dublin figure of his epoch, he was known personally for his caustic wit, his conviviality, and the practised ease with which he sank a pint of beer; but professional musicians respected him (particularly for his knowledge of orchestration) and his opinions, which he was never backward in expressing.[11]

The career of Seán Ó Riada, which was intense, highly controversial, but tragically short, only marginally belongs here since the period of his greatest fame and activity was in the 1960s. Yet the score to the Gael Linn film *Mise Éire* dates from 1959, and it was prodigiously successful at the time, even if Ó Riada later found its popularity something of a millstone in terms of getting his more substantial works accepted. Some of his songs and orchestral pieces were written before he was thirty (Ó Riada was born in 1931) and he was prophetic in several senses, since his setting up of the group he called Ceoltóirí Chualann virtually triggered off at least one aspect of the folk revival which raged through the Sixties and went on well after Ó Riada's premature death at forty. And it was not a folk-music revival only, since he was a key figure in what was, in effect, a miniature Celtic Renaissance that began in the 1950s and penetrated into many fields including film, literature, journalism and even ballet. It would not be an exaggeration to say that Ó Riada largely transformed public perception of what Irish music was, since he killed off the old Clandillon-style céilí band which had been omnipresent since the 1920s.

I t was recognised from early on in the Irish State that Radio Éireann carried a special responsibility for bringing music to the Irish public. The BBC had blazed the trail, and the BBC Symphony Orchestra was for a long time the best in the British Isles, which musicians as eminent as Toscanini were happy to conduct in a guest capacity. Originally, Radio Éireann's 'Station Orchestra' was small and had to be augmented when it gave anything approaching a symphony concert. Its numbers were raised to 24 in 1936, then a little later to 28, but public concerts had to be discontinued through lack of support – a poor comment on cultural Dublin. However, a series of four concerts promoted at the Gaiety Theatre brought in three notable English musicians as guest conductors – Sir Adrian Boult, Frank Bridge the composer and teacher of Benjamin Britten, and the multi-gifted Constant Lambert. The fourth concert was conducted by Professor Aloys Fleischmann from Cork. The programmes included Frederick May's *Spring Nocturne* and Moeran's *Second Rhapsody*, while Charles Lynch – the only Irish pianist of the era to win an international reputation – was the soloist in Elizabeth Maconchy's *Piano Concerto*. These events were well publicised and most of the Irish Cabinet attended each performance. In 1940 Sir Hamilton Harty conducted what was intended to be the first of another series, but the war put a stop to that.

In view of the present-day tendency to regard the Irish Civil Service, and officialdom generally, as philistine and tied in by Green Tape, it should be recorded that there was always a core of men in high positions who were very much the opposite of this stereotype. For instance, P. J. (Paddy) Little, who as Minister for Posts and Telegraphs ruled RÉ as part of his fief, was an enthusiast for classical music who wanted a permanent national concert hall, and even a State opera house. The Rotunda in Dublin was considered for the role and there was even some talk of acquiring the Capitol Cinema, but wartime pressures and his own departure from office ended these projects. Dublin was not to get its concert hall for many years, when the Aula Maxima in the old UCD building in Earlsfort Terrace was converted into one; as for a State opera, it remains a chimaera, although Belfast has since built itself a fine opera house. Another high-ranking public servant who helped to 'push' music was León Ó Broin, secretary to the Department of Posts and Telegraphs from 1948, for many years *eminence grise* of Radio Éireann, and a Gaelic scholar and author of various biographies. His interests ran to folk music as well as classical, and his influence can be felt behind the folk-music revival of the 1950s which included men such as Ciarán Mac Mathúna and Seán Mac Réamoinn.

Another step forward, during the war years, was the founding of Cór Radio Éireann with 24 trained singers. Meanwhile symphony concerts went on and one concert, given in the Round Room of the Mansion House with Sir Adrian Boult again the guest conductor, seems to have filled the 800 seats. Moura Lympany, the English pianist who was then at the peak of her powers, played at one of these events, and Jack Moeran came expressly to rehearse Nancy Lord in his own *Violin Concerto*. However, it was not until the immediate postwar years that the whole issue of a symphony orchestra was at last taken in hand and when the French musician Jean Martinon conducted a concert at UCD in 1946, attended by Seán T. O'Kelly as President, it was taken as a special occasion. The following year Michael Bowles, who had a long association with RÉ, was sent to the Continent on leave of absence for two years, to recruit orchestral musicians. Bowles resigned when he did not get the job of principal conductor, which went instead to Martinon, with the orchestra now raised from 40 players to 62. The visiting conductors whom it played under included Hans Schmidt-Isserstedt from Hamburg, Norman del Mar from Britain, Jean Fournet from France, and Sixten Eckerberg from Scandinavia. In 1955 the RÉSO got its first permanent conductor in Milan Horvat, later succeeded by Tibor Paul. Meanwhile the Radio Éireann Light Orchestra, while no heavyweight institution as its name suggests, gave good and long service, especially under the baton of Dermot O'Hara. In fact, if it is considered that able musicians such as Ó Riada, Gerald Victory and Éamonn Ó Gallchóbhair all had a close association with the Henry Street studios, it should probably rank in retrospect as Irish broadcasting's golden age of music.

While there was still no proper or even reasonably adequate concert hall, the Phoenix Hall in Exchequer Street was used as a stopgap, though it seated no more than 400 people. Here the Radio Éireann Symphony Orchestra – as it was now called – played twice a week for most of the year, and with a decent, though unchallenging repertoire (I was at many of these concerts, held on Tuesdays and Fridays, during my twenties). Admission was free, though tickets could be obtained in advance by those who took the trouble. There were also concerts given in the Gaiety and the Theatre Royal, and among the soloists whom I heard at these during the 1950s was the great Lisztian pianist Louis Kentner and the oboist Leon Goossens. (I also remember seeing, at the Theatre Royal in 1959, the great dancer Antonio.)

In any case, Dublin had a long history – in spite of its chronic lack of really suitable halls even for recitalists – of playing host to visiting singers, instrumentalists and performers. Obviously this was disrupted by the war years, but it was soon resumed, and included some world-famous orchestras under celebrity conductors. A few years ago the much-respected and long-serving music critic of *The Irish Times*, Charles Acton, published a selection of his reviews from a period of thirty years, beginning in 1955.[12] Of necessity, this gives only the merest selection from the thousands of notices he wrote, but the five years from 1955 to 1960 include a Segovia guitar recital at the Theatre Royal, the Boston Symphony Orchestra (which under Koussevitzky had been one of the world's finest) under Charles Munch and proving a major disappointment, as had the BBC Symphony Orchestra under Sir Malcolm Sargent a few weeks previously, Liberace at the

Theatre Royal (!), the Essen Opera's production of *Die Walküre* at the Gaiety, Bill Haley and his Comets at the Theatre Royal (in March 1957, a performance which virtually launched rock-n-roll in Ireland), the Bamberg Symphony Orchestra at the Theatre Royal, a Yehudi Menuhin concert in the same venue, a memorable performance of Elgar's *Gerontius*, again in the Theatre Royal, and Isaac Stern in 1960 in the same theatre. All of which at least goes some way towards upsetting the view of the entire decade as economically depressed and culturally impoverished. Dublin also, at this period, had a number of excellent record shops, including the long-vanished Mays of Stephen's Green which also kept several shelves of recent musical literature on view.

As I am neither a musician nor a period historian, this chapter must pass over such admirable groups as the Dublin Orchestral Players, the Culwick Choral Society, the Dublin String Orchestra founded by Terry O'Connor who had once been the leader of the RÉ Station Orchestra, and various others. Though Dublin musical life was, on the whole, conservative, it was not hidebound and to call it provincial only applies with any accuracy if it is compared with that of New York or London or Paris. Radio Éireann could scarcely compare with the resources and manpower of Broadcasting House in London, and undoubtedly there were often slipshod performances and a degree of semi-amateurism; against that, there were also examples of native flair and even of brilliance, as well as selfless and devoted hard work. An interesting footnote, incidentally, is the fact that near the end of the war years RÉ finally relaxed its official hostility to jazz, which had been derided as 'jungle music' by purists and conservatives, most of whom knew very little about it and often confused it with swing or even with the run-of-the-mill, commercial products of Tin Pan Alley. Amends were made when Brian Boydell – a very gifted broadcaster, among his other talents – gave a series of illustrated talks entitled 'In Search of Jazz'.

Chapter 20

THE FIFTIES

The Fifties were in every way a watershed, in which an entire epoch ended and the modern one emerged. This is not, perhaps, fully understood yet, because the Sixties – in retrospect, a less gifted, less substantial age – have claimed much of the credit for Ireland's supposed quantum leap in to modernity. In the latter decade censorship finally had its teeth pulled, sexual permissiveness was upon us, 'internationalism' was officially embraced, and in every field a new, emancipated generation emerged. So the semi-official version goes. But things simply do not change overnight like that, and what happened in the Sixties was largely the culmination of a process which had begun well before that. As in Britain and other countries, the Sixties – so outwardly colourful and challenging, yet in many ways meretricious and opportunistic – have taken credit for more than they achieved in reality. Most of the battles had already been fought, stubbornly, bloodily and over a long period, and the walls and bastions of conservatism had been steadily mined from underneath, so that in the end they collapsed with a suddenness which surprised most people, but which in retrospect was quite inevitable.

There was, unquestionably, a great deal of unrest, disillusion and frustration during the decade, and these were felt in a great many fields. It was like the collision of hot and cold air currents, as the realities of life in post-war Europe increasingly intruded into a society where many people still clung to what seemed to them a safe, settled, familiar world in which the old certainties (or were they ever that in reality?) functioned as a kind of social and ideological insurance policy. In politics, the age of de Valera had plainly come to an end, and in 1959 he retired (there is no other word for it) to the Presidency, leaving Lemass as his obvious successor. This was a symbolical happening as well as a historical one, since it marked the close of an entire cycle of Irish history; and Dev's last years in power were not happy ones. The grim figures for unemployment and emigration swelled in the mid-decade, so that people who remembered the Economic War, wartime rationing and postwar austerity were confirmed in their pessimistic fatalism: 'we'll never stand on our own feet!'

The Church, apart from being almost insanely obsessed with international Communism which was never even a shadow-threat in Ireland, had greatly discredited itself in the Mother and Child political controversy of 1951, during which it appeared blatantly concerned more with halting any attempt at socialised medicine, than with social equity or justice. (This inevitably drew some embittered comparisons with Britain, where the Welfare State first envisaged by Lord Beveridge and others was proving not only workable, but successful.) Archbishop McQuaid, Bishop Browne of Galway and other leading churchmen had demonstrated that increasingly they faced backwards rather than moving pragmatically with the times, and there were some ugly attempts to give back book censorship something like its old power.[1] In 1955 a quasi-official visit to the Soviet Union by a number of Irish trade unionists, writers and intellectuals (they included the novelist James Plunkett and the poet-critic Anthony Cronin[2]) provoked strong press reactions and a virtual smear campaign from the Catholic *Standard*. Though this malodorous incident did little lasting harm, the careers of a number of people suffered for a time, and their families endured some unpleasant exposure.

All of this certainly seemed to many open-minded people to indicate an essential spirit of retrogression, rather than a forward-looking or even realistic recognition that the world had changed greatly since the war and was still changing fast. However, it was really almost the last great counter-offensive of the old guard and the obscurantists, whose days in almost every area were now numbered. In the religious field, the election of Pope John XXIII in 1957 signalled the start of a new era of ecumenism, while the new Protestant Archbishop of Dublin, Dr George Otto Simms, showed himself an adroit, humane builder of bridges – in fact, it would be no exaggeration to call him the greatest Irish churchman of his generation, and possibly the greatest since the foundation of the State. And some Catholic clerics were also prominent in calling for a re-examination of the education system, opening the way for its major overhaul and expansion in the Sixties.[3]

In 1958 the Programme for Economic Expansion, sometimes called the Whitaker Report, laid the grounds for the policies which Lemass pursued in his too-short period in office. Other major innovations of the decade were the founding of the Agricultural Institute which revolutionised Irish farming research, and the setting up of the Voluntary Health Insurance Organisation, to mention only two of many. Meanwhile, Ireland entered the era of jet flight, which again had a symbolic aspect as well as a highly practical one. It was, in short, a decade of remarkable changes as well as rearguard actions by the ultra-conservatives. For example, the last Irish hanging took place in 1954, of a young Limerick man who had raped and killed a nurse; after that the death penalty was *de facto* abolished. (In England, by comparison, hangings went on well into the decade, and as late as 1960 James Hanratty was hanged for a murder which it is now reasonably certain he did not commit.) These developments do not, obviously, belong in any real sense to the cultural field, but they are quoted here as examples of how the whole complexion of life had altered.

The Tóstal, a kind of cultural festival which was bigger in aspiration than in achievement, is now almost forgotten – though one oddity or public folly (using the word in the architectural sense) associated with it was the atrocious 'Bowl of Light' built on O'Connell Bridge, and later demolished after sustained sniping from the Dublin intelligentsia and from many ordinary citizens. Arland Ussher, in a letter to *The Irish Times*, said it was better suited to Coney Island than to Dublin, while Myles na Gopaleen called it The Tomb of the Unknown Gurrier, a witticism which gained considerable currency. Other festivals, however, proved more lasting including the Wexford Opera Festival launched in 1951, the Cork Film Festival launched in 1956 and, above all, the Dublin Theatre Festival, launched in 1957.

In 1955, Cyril Cusack courageously presented a new O'Casey play, *The Bishop's Bonfire*, a highly uneven and rather confused work whose anti-clerical sentiments caused some trouble on the opening night. It was, however, no more than a storm in a pint glass, and both O'Casey's attackers and his defenders – including Cusack himself, who spoke well and wittily from the stage at the end – seemed to be enacting their own drama or farce of another age. If O'Casey's vision of his homeland had come by then to sound almost surrealistically out of date, the attitudes of those who bayed at him as ungodly and atheistic belonged to the age of Matt Talbot.

The great literary magazines were vanishing, and the death of Seumas O'Sullivan marked not only the demise of the *Dublin Magazine* but the end of a whole chapter stretching back to Edwardian days and the epoch of Moore and AE. Of the old generation, Colum came occasionally to Dublin from New York, and Corkery was for a time in the Irish Senate, but they were survivors rather than active forces, and the Twilight itself seemed misty and far away. Joyce was the writer most quoted by the avant-garde, although the beginnings of a Beckett cult began to appear after the performance of *Waiting for Godot* at the Pike in 1955.

It may have been partially the demise of the literary magazines which made Irish writers look abroad for new outlets, but increasingly the American literary market was the one which counted. In particular, the *New Yorker* magazine since the late 1940s had shown itself well disposed to Irish short-story writers, and though O'Connor and O'Faolain had been early in the American field, a new, largely post-war generation which included Benedict Kiely, Mary Lavin and several others soon established a firm American readership. The poets, too, looked more and more to America, though Auden – by then, in any case, heavily Americanised – had been probably the major influence of the late 1940s and he continued to be a potent voice and example well into the Sixties. Anthony Cronin and John Montague openly proclaimed him as their master, or at least one of their masters, while the earlier work of Thomas Kinsella showed his fingerprints too. The decade had also seen a major rebirth of interest in Ezra Pound, who was becoming intellectually respectable again after his wartime infatuation with Mussolini, and this too spread to Dublin – Donald Davie, the English poet-critic, was for a time a lecturer in Trinity and a few years later was to write an important book on Pound. Denis Donoghue, the leading figure in a new generation of Irish literary critics, was also strongly committed to American writing and championed the cause of Wallace Stevens in particular – though it is difficult to trace any obvious influence by Stevens on Irish verse. Robert Frost, now a grand old man of American literature, was also respected, and in 1957 he visited Dublin (for the second time) and was given an honorary degree by the NUI. Younger American poets were increasingly read too, including Robert Lowell and Richard Wilbur, though Sylvia Plath was very little known in Ireland before the Sixties.

The ascendancy of Auden's verse over a whole generation of Irish poets is something which future critics and commentators may find it slightly hard to understand. It is even difficult to account for it today, when Auden's reputation is seemingly in eclipse and MacNeice's is correspondingly rising. In MacNeice, one would have thought, the modernising postwar generation had a perfect model, ready-made and at hand, a writer who was both Irish and cosmopolitan, lyrical and complex – in short, a genuine and major Modernist. Yet Auden obviously offered something which the times needed – a specific new tone of voice, colloquial yet distanced, self-confident, streetwise, ironic, sophisticated, Big-City, with a wide range of intellectual and topical references. Even Patrick Kavanagh read and studied him, prompted by his young followers who included Cronin, John Jordan and the painter Patrick Swift.[4] In a decade when so many writers wanted to wipe the cow-dung off their shoes and the holy water from their brows, he seemed the perfect antidote. The novelist John Updike has remarked on the 'exaggerated urbanism' of a whole generation of American writers and artists, many of whom were from rural or small-town backgrounds, but who were consumed by the same megalopolitan obsession. (One might even say that it applies to Ezra Pound, from Idaho.)

It was all very different from the Thirties and Forties, when European writers such as Rilke, Lorca and Rimbaud had all been dominant influences on Irish poets, Denis Devlin had translated Char and Eluard, and even the poetry of Akhmatova had been translated by Blanaid Salkeld. Increasingly, Irish culture faced westward rather than towards the Continent, while American writers, stage and screen actors such as Burgess Meredith, folk singers such as Burl Ives, and leading journalists were regular visitors, usually via the recently created Shannon Airport; in turn, the actress Siobhán McKenna became a celebrity in New York, and slightly later Brendan Behan enjoyed a personal vogue there. The couturier Sybil Connolly pioneered a fashion for quality Irish clothes. To jumble these disparate names together may seem facile or trivial, yet in their various ways they were all representative of a changing society and outlook in which most areas of activity were affected. There was a new craving for things which were chic, cosmopolitan, knowing, and had 'style', an urge to get away from what were viewed as the backwardness and homespun simplicities of Irish life. Even Austin Clarke, once reckoned as the most intrinsically Gaelic and bardic poet of the generation after Yeats, seemed to have caught the Transatlantic fever in some of his later poetry – or was it simply that his own development had drawn him on a parallel course with contemporary American verse? He, too, had read Pound's *Cantos* carefully,[5] though in any case Pound had been well known to Irish poets since the Thirties. Thanks largely to his modernist rejuvenation, Clarke was soon adopted by the younger poets associated with Liam Miller's Dolmen Press as a kind of icon and elder statesman, and he published busily in his old age.

By comparison, Patrick Kavanagh went rather into eclipse in the decade, in spite of the short-lived, idiosyncratic newspaper which he launched with his brother Peter, *Kavanagh's Weekly*. It was typical Kavanagh, a strange mixture of pub garrulity and topical comment, shrewd analysis, coat-trailing and dogmatising – in short, very like his conversation to his own faithful circle in McDaid's pub. In the eyes of many people, he had seemed to reach an impasse as a writer after *The Great Hunger* and the novel *Tarry Flynn*, both published in the 1940s; he still kept a close following, a kind of Praetorian Guard who stood watch and resented any slight to their leader, but much or most of his late poetry seemed a falling-off, and there were even people who thought he had degenerated into a pub character, one of Dublin's uncounted literary hangers-on and has-beens. His 1954 libel action against the *Leader* magazine, which had published an offensive article about him, made headlines almost daily for week after week in *The Irish Times*, and Kavanagh, who had an exhibitionistic streak like most writers and felt ignored by the greater public, enjoyed his hour in the limelight as he postured in the witness box, played the pundit and argued with the counsel for the defence, John A. Costello – who was shortly to become Taoiseach for a second term, but in the interim had reverted to his old profession, the law.[6] In some ways it was like a homespun, provincial repeat of the Wilde trial sixty years earlier, and the result was much the same: once again it was the writer who lost, having managed to antagonise the jury by his bluster. Subsequently Kavanagh appealed against the verdict and this time got a suitable settlement, which he should have got in the first place since the article – probably intended merely to be provocative – was wounding, tasteless and ultra-personal.[7] Dublin, as usual, enjoyed it all with malicious relish as a kind of highbrow spectator sport; but for some of the intelligentsia, the whole affair left a bitter taste. A leading writer, so his followers and admirers felt, had been skilfully made look a mere provincial gasbag or comic turn in the witness box by an experienced lawyer-politician who had fed him precisely the right length of rope, and was then brought down and humiliated by a jury of philistines who resented what they saw as arrogance.

The great literary magazines were all dead or dying, and they were not replaced. The death of Bertie Smyllie of *The Irish Times* in 1954 was another landmark, although Myles na Gopaleen's 'Cruiskeen Lawn' column continued to appear intermittently until well in to the following decade. Though the national newspapers tried to offer outlets for writers, there was now a vacuum in terms of cultural/intellectual journals, which was increasingly filled by English ones ranging from the weekly *New Statesman* to the short-lived periodical *Encounter*. However, in face of much public abuse or apathy, Radio Éireann performed sterling work in many fields – arguably these were its golden years, just as they were golden years in British broadcasting, and television had not come yet to push it firmly into a secondary role. Writer-intellectuals such as Roibeárd Ó Faracháin, Mervyn Wall, Francis MacManus, James Plunkett, Micheál Ó hAodha ensured a high level of serious content, in spite of low budgets and civil service green tape.

One of the most important achievements of all was by the historians, many of whom were in fact practising 'revisionists' before the term became current. Arguably, this intellectual process was an old one, and O'Faolain's biography *The Great O'Neill*, while popular rather than scholarly, broke moulds in showing O'Neill warts and all, instead of the pasteboard patriot of most school histories or historical novels such as Maurice Walsh's *Blackcock's Feather* (which, incidentally, had been on primary-school courses). Robin Dudley Edwards, Desmond Williams, Conor Cruise O'Brien, were only a few of the new generation who challenged the old romantic-nationalist conception of history – which was still prevalent in many countries even after the second World War – and insisted that careful research, including economic facts, must come first, and well before opinions and personal interpretation. Events such as the Famine, which were part of popular mythology, were looked at afresh not from the viewpoint of political propaganda or moral denunciation, but with rigorous, impartial scholarship. It was plain that the nationalist simplicities which schoolchildren had been taught for thirty years would no longer serve. There was even a new tendency to look at areas of Irish history – the Civil War, for instance – which hitherto had been under ban, or where the facts were hard to obtain and assess properly.[8]

Yet many still remember the Fifties as a grim, grey, rather bitter decade, which no doubt in some respects they were. Internationally the Cold War had reached a stage of permafrost, and the mushroom-shadow of the Atomic Bomb hung over Europe, though there was still real faith in the capacity of the United Nations to maintain an international balance of power. Money was short, so too were jobs, and writers and artists in particular were badly paid; it was a period when many of them had to take casual employment of all kinds to tide them over until better times, and a number emigrated temporarily to London. Drink was one of the few things which were relatively cheap, and so the literary pubs both in Dublin and Soho, like the cafés in Paris, became more than ever the meeting-places of the disgruntled, displaced intelligentsia. Beckett's *Waiting for Godot* came just at the right time to catch the curiously low-toned emotional colouring of the period – verging on depressiveness – which is also part of the character of Louis le Brocquy's paintings. These grey half-tones and shadows often suggest a low vitality. Yet underneath it all there was in fact a considerable life force, just as the shabby streets and seedy pubs of Soho were the stamping-ground for Francis Bacon, David Wright, Lucien Freud and others who now rank as major figures. (Wright and Freud, incidentally, were frequent visitors to Dublin.) Those who are still sceptical of the energy and creativity of the decade might ponder over the following dates and events:

1950. Padraic Fallon's poetic play *Diarmuid and Gráinne* is broadcast from Radio Éireann. The RÉ switchboard is blocked for hours afterwards with congratulatory calls from listeners.

1951. Wexford Opera Festival is founded, with Dr Tom Walsh as its first chairman.

1951. Fire destroys much of the Abbey Theatre and the company moves temporarily to the old Queen's Theatre (now demolished).

1951. The resignation of Dr Noel Browne as Minister for Health in the Inter-Party Government, after his Mother and Child Scheme had antagonised both the Catholic hierarchy and Cabinet colleagues, triggers off a major political controversy. In his 'Cruiskeen Lawn' column in *The Irish Times*, Myles na Gopaleen joins battle with Dr Alfred O'Rahilly, writing in *The Standard*.

1951. Professor Ernest Walton of TCD wins the Nobel Prize for Physics, along with Sir John Cockroft of the UK. He is the first Irishman to be so honoured, and to date he remains the last.

1951. Comhaltas Ceoltóirí Éireannn founded to foster Irish traditional music.

1951. Liam Miller founds Dolmen Press.

1952. Publication of *Eireaball Spideóige* by Seán Ó Ríordáin, marking a new epoch of writing in Gaelic.

1952. *Kavanagh's Weekly* is launched and runs for thirteen issues before folding.

1952. The painters Nano Reid and Norah McGuinness represent Ireland at the Venice Biennale.

1952. Exhibition of paintings by Patrick Swift at the Victor Waddington Gallery in Dublin. Swift leaves shortly afterwards for London.

1952. Maurice Craig publishes *Dublin 1660-1860*, which rapidly establishes itself as a classic of its kind.

1953. Government committee set up to investigate the implications of an Irish television service.

1953. Publication of *Dúil*, a collection of Liam O'Flaherty's short stories in Irish.

1953. Radio Éireann broadcasts Padraic Fallon's play *The Vision of Mac Conglinne*.

1953. Michael Scott's design for Busáras, on the Dublin quays, is one of the first Modernist buildings in Ireland.

1953. New World Writing, a paperback series published internationally from New York, carries the work of ten Irish poets. They are Denis Devlin, Patrick MacDonogh, Austin Clarke, Patrick Kavanagh, Padraic Fallon, Robert Farren, Donagh MacDonagh, Robert Greacen, Roy McFadden, Anthony Cronin.

1954. Brendan Behan's *The Quare Fellow* gets its first performance at the Pike Theatre in Dublin, and shortly after has a six-month run in London.

1955. Publication of James Plunkett's collection of stories with a Dublin setting, *The Trusting and the Maimed*.

1955. Austin Clarke breaks a long silence as poet with *Ancient Lights*.

1955. Seán O'Casey's *The Bishop's Bonfire* is produced by Cyril Cusack at the Gaiety Theatre in Dublin.

1955. Ritchie Hendriks Gallery opens in St Stephen's Green, Dublin. Patrick Collins and George Campbell are among the Irish painters regularly exhibited; later, numerous artists from overseas are also shown.

1956. Seán O'Faolain becomes first chairman of the Arts Council of Ireland.

1956. Beckett's *Waiting for Godot* performed at the Pike Theatre in Dublin, not long after its English premiere.

1956. Cork Film Festival launched.

1957. Bill Haley and his Comets perform rock-n-roll music at the Theatre Royal in Dublin. Mass reaction of young people shows that a new era in popular music has spread to Ireland.

1957. Dublin Theatre Festival launched under the chairmanship of Brendan Smith.

1957. Publication of *Parnell and his Party* by Conor Cruise O'Brien.

1958. Publication of Behan's *Borstal Boy*.

1958. O'Casey withdraws his play *The Drums of Father Ned* from the Dublin Theatre Festival programme, alleging clerical interference. As a result, the festival is cancelled.

1958. Publication by Dolmen Press of *Another September*, poems by Thomas Kinsella.

1958. Publication of *One Landscape Still*, poems by Patrick MacDonogh.

1959. De Valera retires as Taoiseach and becomes President. His successor, Seán Lemass, proposes a custom union between the Republic and Northern Ireland; there is no response from Belfast. In the same year, Ireland applies to the Commission of the European Community in Brussels for permission to open diplomatic relations with the EC.

1959. Publication of *The Oxford Book of Irish Verse* edited by Donagh MacDonagh and Lennox Robinson.

1959. Publication of Tomás de Bhaldraithe's *English-Irish Dictionary*, a landmark in Irish scholarship.

1959. James White, previously known chiefly as an art critic, takes over in the Municipal Gallery of Modern Art in Dublin, which he quickly rejuvenates.

1959. Eugene O'Neill's *Long Day's Journey into Night* is performed by the Abbey Theatre (then still housed temporarily in the Queen's Theatre) and is a major success with critics and audiences.

1959. George Morrison makes the film *Mise Éire* for the Irish language body Gael-Linn, with music by Seán Ó Riada.

1959. Gabriel Marcel, the French philosopher and dramatist, lectures in Dublin as part of a series organised by the Arts Council.

1959. Terence de Vere White publishes *A Fretful Midge*, which rapidly establishes itself as a minor classic of autobiography.

1960. Publication of Patrick Kavanagh's book of poems *Come Dance with Kitty Stobling*, which brings a revival of his reputation.

1960. The Irish Exhibition of Living Art hangs a selection of contemporary English painting in its annual show at the National College of Art in Kildare Street, Dublin. Important works by Ben Nicholson and Peter Lanyon are included.

1960. Georges Rouault's 'Miserere' series is shown at the Building Centre in Dublin. In the same year, the newly-formed Independent Artists mount their first group exhibition there.

1960. Beckett's one-man play *Krapp's Last Tape* is performed by Cyril Cusack at the Abbey.

1960. Frank O'Connor returns to Ireland after years of lecturing in America.

A glance at this (necessarily truncated) list will show that it contains a number of events which were, in themselves, historical landmarks and led directly to the very different Ireland of the past thirty years. In particular, the prolonged, bitter battles of words which followed Noel Browne's resignation in 1951 marked a turning point in public attitudes to the Church.[9] Browne was a doctor and that rather rare thing for the time, a Trinity Catholic, known publicly for his virtual obsession with TB, from which he himself had once suffered. As Minister for Health he did much to fight the disease and gained a strong popular following, which saw him as the Poor Man's (and Poor Woman's) friend and the people's special doctor/politician. He entered the first Inter-Party Government while a member of Clann na Poblachta, originally a kind of neo-republican party led by Seán MacBride. There is little doubt that his dispute with the hierarchy was poorly and tactlessly handled, but the indications are that his own party chief (then Minister for External Affairs) intrigued against him; the behaviour of the Taoiseach, Costello, was also devious or at least questionable, and it was plain that Fine Gael did not relish a fight with the bishops. So Browne fell – he was never a team player in any case, as the rest of his maverick political career was to show. MacBride, now his confirmed enemy, soon fell too and quickly faded out of Irish political life, though later he deservedly made an international name through his work as head of Amnesty International.

Somehow, however, the affair did not rest there. A latent anti-clericalism began to show itself both publicly and privately, partly because the bishops had adopted a reactionary stance towards any hint of state or socialised medicine, and partly because Browne was perceived by many, quite ordinary people as a decent man who had been done down by the clergy and the politicians (and of course the wealthy doctors) acting in unison. The hierarchy, headed by McQuaid and using as their official spokesman the insufferably self-satisfied Dr James Staunton, Bishop of

Ferns,[10] did not concede an inch to criticism and indeed seemed outraged at public reaction. While *The Irish Times* correspondence columns predictably echoed with sounds of verbal battle, Professor Alfred O'Rahilly pontificated in *The Standard* with a typical mixture of spleen and condescension and was taken head-on by Myles na Gopaleen in his 'Cruiskeen Lawn' column. O'Rahilly treated his opponent as a hack journalist who was unworthy to face him, while Myles in turn succeeded, with a quicker wit and much greater verbal agility, in making him look and sound ridiculous.

It could scarcely have happened ten or even five years earlier – the bishops facing open criticism even from their own side of the fence, and Dr O'Rahilly, widely regarded as the intellectual and academic heavyweight of the Catholic Right, being mocked in public by a mere columnist.[11] The scales began to fall from many eyes. Even good Catholics realised that the hierarchy had overreached itself by interfering in the area of public health, which was not its domain, while Dr O'Rahilly, for years respected and rather feared, suddenly began to look anachronistic, reactionary, perhaps even a pontificating old ass. From that day – though as I have said, the fact is not yet fully recognised – the power and authority of the Catholic hierarchy began to decline, until it reached its present nadir. A haemorrhage had developed from which it continued to bleed, silently and steadily, and in retrospect Maynooth has never quite recovered from the blood-loss. Predictably, few of the intellectuals mourned its slow decline in power and prestige; too many of them had old sores that still smarted.

The burning down of the old Abbey Theatre building was also a landmark, though of a very different kind, and the Babylonian Captivity of the company in the large but shabby Queen's Theatre nearby was not one of its brighter chapters. Though Ernest Blythe retained considerable power, new theatrical groups were emerging including the Globe Theatre Company and, typically, the Abbey reacted too slowly and too late to the emergence of Beckett and Behan. At the Gate, Mac Liammóir and Edwards were both ageing men with no real successors, and their favourite playwright, Denis Johnston, was in America; in any case, the emergence of Beckett took away much of his gloss as the leading avant-garde Irish dramatist. A vacuum was gradually opening up, but it was not until the Sixties that it was filled by a new generation of dramatists who included Brian Friel, Tom Murphy, Sam Thompson, Hugh Leonard *et alii*, as well as a new wave of actors and producers.

Censorship was visibly ebbing by the end of the decade, and a few years later it made virtually its last stand with the banning of novels by John McGahern, Edna O'Brien and certain others. It was no secret that Irish Governments increasingly found the Censorship Board an embarrassment, particularly at a time when official policy was to sell Ireland abroad as a progressive, rapidly developing country. After its conduct in the early years of the decade had approached lunacy, attempts were made to tone it down at least, and to move the genuinely die-hard censors into the background.[12] However, it was not until 1967 that the ghost was finally laid, and even then there were occasional squalls of reaction, though growing steadily weaker. In the visual arts, a hectic controversy about Henry Moore's bronze 'Reclining Figure' ended in its official purchase by the Dublin Municipal Gallery of Modern Art – a thumb in the eye for the academic artists who had regarded it with horror. At the National College of Art and Design, however, a reactionary teaching regime continued in power until the late 1960s.

P erhaps the developments outlined will make some people realise the complexities and conflicts of the decade and will convey the overall message that Irish society and culture did not, in effect, go into retrogression for an entire generation. A fairer and more positive interpretation is that there were nearly always opposing philosophies and mutually irreconcilable mentalities locked together in argument and counter-argument, each virtually making a point of misinterpreting or seeing the worst in the other. The facts also suggest that the degree of continuity between past and present is far greater than is habitually believed, and that many of these arguments and attitudes are cyclic in Irish life and may appear again quite soon, though with a different emphasis or wearing different uniforms. Today, we owe very much more to pre-Sixties Ireland than we like to admit. The generation gap, however, is great, and is not confined to Ireland by any means – far greater, say, than that between the Fifties and the Forties, or even the Thirties. (On the other hand, the Twenties and the Sixties have a remarkable amount in common.) Between those who inherited the values of the Permissive Age and those who grew to maturity before it, there is an almost unbridgeable space, mentally and emotionally. As Philip Larkin wrote:

> Sexual intercourse began
> In nineteen sixty-three
> (Which was rather late for me)
> Between the end of the Chatterley ban
> And the Beatles' first LP.[13]

The Sixties, a noisy, high-spirited, exhibitionistic and relatively monied decade, of course marked the emergence of a wholly new outlook and new values. Yet seen in retrospect, too many of its most typical products and personalities were careerists lacking in weight or seriousness; and so much so-called liberation was little more than media babble, or self-advertisement, or even sheer commercial exploitation. Much of its flaunted sophistication, too, was little more than a fashionable pose, sometimes hiding intellectual naïveté and even a quite surprising degree of cultural ignorance. Certainly it is a brittle stick with which to beat the preceding decade, whose typical personalities had a far harder fight and faced greater obstacles, and yet achieved much that was important, or even lasting.

Can we really afford to cock a snook at the past? Are our present cultural achievements really so outstanding, then, even if we do have a Nobel Prize winner in Seamus Heaney? (His career, in any case, owes little to Dublin or the Republic in general, since much or most of it has been conducted in England and America.) Do we have a Jack Yeats among us today, and can literary Dublin genuinely compare with the days of Myles, Kavanagh, Behan and the rest? True, recent decades have produced a wave of Irish film talent, something which never existed before; musical life is vibrant; the visual arts are probably healthier than they ever have been, at least in terms of public interest and state support. But the wave of so-called internationalism has washed away much of the legacy of the Literary Revival and the entire national revival of which it was part. No doubt, as I said in the opening chapter, it was an overdue reaction but it went too far and the pendulum, in swinging so violently, has become jammed and cannot resume its normal rhythm. The result is, quite unavoidably, a loss of cultural identity and self-definition, particularly in the literary field. Behind its present economic prosperity and almost manic self-confidence, Ireland is now in certain respects a curiously confused and riven country, psychologically ill at ease with itself. Very often, the ultimately unavoidable questions of where it is going, and what it aspires to be, are shelved in a hectic swirl of pseudo-modernity. Almost any normal, un-ideological expression of nationality is pounced upon as regressive nationalism, prosperity is confused with mental maturity, and – saddest of all – dismissive ignorance of the past is confused with liberation from it. The long-drawn crisis of Northern Ireland has provoked some strange and atavistic reactions in the Republic, raising doubts concerning the quality of its self-styled liberalism and degree of self-knowledge.

The oddity, the crankery and the ingrown quality which are an essential aspect of the decades this book is about must seem virtually incomprehensible to young people today, and even to many middle-aged people who can barely remember them. It must seem as if they were contemplating not only another era, but almost another country and race. I have repeatedly rejected the myth of isolationism, but there is no doubt at all that Ireland was an insular country in several senses besides the baldly geographic one. It was European certainly, but not European in the sense that the Continental nations of the time were, even the Scandinavian ones (though descriptions of Spain in the Thirties suggest much in common with Ireland, and so do descriptions of Poland before the second World War). Ireland was 'different', as many visitors agreed, without necessarily intending it as either praise or blame. The quality of 'Irishness' was unmistakable, so much so that some felt it to be claustrophobic and even repellent, while others romanticised it as an escape from the pressures of modernity.[14] Partly, of course, this was due to the national religiosity, equally off-putting to liberal-Protestant Anglo-Saxons and to secularised, often anti-clerical continentals, though fascinating to a Catholic writer such as

Heinrich Böll as late as the Fifties.[15] John Montague quotes Auden – who had never been to Ireland and didn't want to go there – saying in a conversation that Ireland seemed to him 'remote' and 'mad'. A Jewish intellectual, who taught in one of the Irish universities for a time during the early Sixties, even told me that Ireland to him was a nineteenth-century country.

What is overlooked today is that this national oddity, ingrown-ness and tendency towards self-contemplation may have had their positive sides – that they may even be linked umbilically and organically to the achievements of Irish writers and artists. Certainly they seem inseparable from the greatness of Jack Yeats as a painter; he made almost a cult of ignoring international Modernism as much as he could and avoided exhibitions as a general rule. Yet Yeats was in himself acutely modern, a recognisable product of the mid-twentieth-century *Zeitgeist*. He did not feel the need to travel much abroad, or to compare his style with that of others, in order to realise his gifts fully. He was, if you like, a deliberate and self-conscious isolationist, but in a positive sense and not a negative one – certainly not an ignorant one. Quite simply, he found Ireland in itself was enough for him, a challenge which he felt compelled to face, and he needed no other subject matter or stimulus to make him paint. Or, on another plane, take Myles na Gopaleen/Flann O'Brien, who found virtually all his material within a radius of a few miles. It may have been a case of love-hate, yet if he had been transported to another country his talent probably would have withered away inside a few years, or at the very least would have lost its centre of gravity. Myles was as much part of Dublin as Karl Kraus was of Vienna. Probably, in any case, he needed the stimulus of hate or irritation as much as love, and there is no particular proof that he envied Joyce his exile. Like Akhmatova or Pasternak in Russia, these men were tied umbilically to their own country and felt that it needed them in turn.

The Irish writer and Irish artist of a generation ago were mainly inspired by the country's unique landscape, by the living actuality of the past, by mythology, by the folk vitality which still existed then, by the closeness of family and clan life, by ancestral tradition and its clash with modernity, by religion and its tensions, by the often desolate poetry of small, anonymous lives. It goes without saying that most of these themes or preoccupations are devalued today, sometimes by a lax indifference and sometimes by outright hostility. Our age is predominantly abstract and cosmopolitan, technological, irreligious and anti-mystical, urban rather than rural, rationalist rather than intuitive or ritualistic, theoretic and programmatic rather than organic, dominated by mass media and mass consumerism, not so much a Global Village as a Global Suburb. No doubt there will be a swing against these values – in fact, it is already manifesting itself in such phenomena as the New Age religiosity, though that appears to have no deeper foundations than the Beats or Hippies of a few decades ago.

Far too much was made, several decades ago, of Ireland's uniqueness – a veritable mystique which has recoiled on its inventors, who have since been accused of more or less glamorising backwardness and obscurantism.[16] In fact, a brief scan of Irish history in this century reveals many parallels with other European nations, even in 1916; Pearse curiously resembles Karl Liebknecht, just as his followers resemble the Spartacists of 1918-19. De Valera combines certain traits of President Masaryk of Czechoslovakia, General Smuts of South Africa, and President Salazar of Portugal, while the popular unrest of the years just before he came to power resembled the agrarian unrest in contemporary Spain. Similarly, the Blueshirts and their more respectable allies had much in common with the Dolfuss regime in Austria. And there are/were a good many characteristics – good and bad – which Fianna Fáil shared with the Party Praesidium of the lately deceased Soviet Union; even the physical appearance and type of the politicians concerned was very similar. The red-faced, grey-haired, baggy-suited Fianna Fáiler of de Valera's age might almost have walked directly out of a Party office in Moscow or Leningrad.

In literature the parallels continue: for instance, the 'rural school' of Irish writing, at that time often talked and written about as though it was something unique to this country, closely resembled what was happening in the Scandinavian countries at the time[17] – though of course minus the Catholicism – and in various East European ones. The cult of the folksong pursued by F. R. Higgins and many others was a European phenomenon whose products ranged from pseudo-peasant pastiche to the sophisticated use of Andalusian song and folklore in Lorca's *Romancero Gitano*. (Its origins, in any case, go back to Herder in late eighteenth-century Germany.) Those who find something particularly risible in the preoccupation of Yeats and various of his successors with mythology, might reflect that this was a preoccupation shared by a huge number of writers all over Europe – including Rilke, Valéry, Cocteau, Mandelstam, and even Modernists such as Eliot and Pound.[18] Even Yeats's immersion in neo-Platonism, Rosicrucianism and hermetic lore generally is a characteristically twentieth-century motif and not – as his detractors have often claimed – a backward-looking or reactionary one. And though in art Jack Yeats remains a solitary figure, he still has something in common with Lovis Corinth in Germany and with Kokoschka (who admired him greatly) in Austria.

As I have already remarked, the stiffening literary censorship in Ireland was also shared by many or most other countries at the time, probably in reaction against Twenties permissiveness and in line with the new 'family' values propagated everywhere. (It could also, of course, be seen as a typically twentieth-century expression of mass-minded conformity, in contrast to the individualism of the nineteenth.) Even the Stalinist campaign against Russian writers shows some traces of the same origins. Similarly, the tendency towards a renewed cultural nationalism emerged in many places shortly before the second World War, and possibly reflected a general recoil before the economic tentacles of international capitalism and the ideological threat of international Marxism. It was strong even in America – *vide* the 'native American' school of painting which produced Grant Wood, Curry, Benton etc. – while in Russia there was a growing hostility against Western-influenced writers such as Pasternak, Mandelstam and Akhmatova and a strong stress on native peasant and proletarian virtues, though shorn of traditional religion.

In the Fifties, the battle between conservatism and renewal – which I have already compared to the meeting of hot and cold currents – was fought out virtually everywhere. In Russia it was codified in Khruschev's famous posthumous denunciation of Stalin; in America it produced a huge unrest among the young, typified by the Beat generation, Action Painting, drugs and sexual permissiveness; in Britain, it was symbolised by Churchill's retirement from active politics and marked a little later by the emergence of the Angry Young Men generation. France, like Britain in the Suez Canal venture of 1956, suffered imperial rebuffs in Indo-China and North Africa and an entire generation of squabbling politicians was swept aside by the return of de Gaulle. In reaction, a whole new, critically minded generation emerged. All this is to state the obvious and the known. Yet many other reactionary outcrops of the time are forgotten – for instance, who remembers the public attacks on modern art by Eisenhower and Khrushchev respectively? Who remembers Poujadisme in France? Even McCarthyism in America has become only a blurred memory. Yet all in their way were typical rearguard actions, often fought with the powerful backing of whatever Establishment was involved, and fought viciously too, but failing to stave off the march of events.

So Ireland, though more often than not without knowing it, was mostly in step with the times, in her own odd way and at her own peculiar gait. Facile labels such as reactionary, provincial, isolationist (again!) have only strictly limited relevance and are essentially as one-sided as the old 'Faith of our Fathers' crawthumpers with their simplistic shibboleths. The reality lies somewhere else, so it seems to me, in some ways cruder and rawer than these people liked to admit, and in other ways more subtle, complex and even contradictory. In some way or other, Ireland produced her own 'modernism'; the mid-twentieth-century *Zeitgeist* may have been more varied and unpredictable than the current Anglo-American aesthetic allows or recognises. Under the rather shabby, dun-coloured outward envelope of the years I have described there was a surprising pulse of vitality and creativity, much of which met with little or no financial reward and in some cases functioned only for a small audience or readership. There was also a surprising intelligence, of a very native kind which – it is not too fanciful to say it – runs right back to the writings of the Bardic poets. It was not a Golden Age, yet it has its own seam or seams of gold which in places are silted over and may need time and sympathetic care to follow or track down; but it will be worth it.

REFERENCES

CHAPTER 1 (PAGES 1-17)

1. *Elizabeth Bowen*, Victoria Glendinning (Weidenfield & Nicholson, 1977).
2. *John Betjeman Letters, vol 1 1926-51*, Candida Lycett Green, ed (Methuen, 1994).
3. See *Irish Diplomacy at the United Nations, 1945-1965*, Joseph Morrison Skelly (Irish Academic Press, 1997) and review in *The Irish Times* by Tadhg O'Sullivan, 9 August 1997.
4. *Nationalism and Independence*, Nicholas Mansergh (Cork University Press, 1997).
5. 'The Ambivalence of de Valera', Tom Garvin, *The Irish Times*, 9 April 1998.
6. Cf. *The Story of Ireland* and *West Briton* by Brian Inglis (Faber and Faber, 1956 and 1966 respectively).
7. This could lead to risible results as when the magazines *Crime* and *Crime Detective* were banned on the grounds that they devoted too much space to 'matters relating to crime'.
8. See Seán O'Faolain's autobiography, *Vive-moi!* (Sinclair/Stevenson, 1963).
9. For a discussion of MacNeice's essential Irishness, see 'Ireland and the Poetry of Louis MacNeice', Eamon Grennan, *Studies, Summer/Autumn, 1981* and *Journalism*, Derek Mahon (Gallery Books, 1996).
10. *Einstein, A Life*, Denis Brian (John Wiley & Sons, 1996).
11. *The New Ireland*, J. B. Morton (Paladin, 1935).
12. *On Irish Themes*, James T. Farrell (University of Pennsylvania Press, 1982).
13. *Autobiographies*, R. S. Thomas (Dent, 1997).
14. *Antonin Artaud, Blows and Bombs*, Stephen Barber (Faber & Faber, 1993).

CHAPTER 2 (PAGES 19-26)

1. *Unfinished Business*, Liam de Paor (Hutchinson Radius, 1990), p.48.
2. *The Years of the Great Test 1926-39*, Francis MacManus, ed (Mercier Press, 1967), p.176.
3. *Portrait of Europe*, Salvador de Madariaga (Hollis & Carter, 1967), p.176.
4. An outstanding example of this is George Fitzmaurice's early play *The Moonlighter*.
5. 'The Ambivalence of de Valera', Tom Garvin, *The Irish Times*, 9 April 1998.
6. *I went to Russia*, Liam O'Flaherty (Jonathan Cape, 1931).
7. Brendan Behan was particularly given to this, yet he liked the English and was entirely at home in Britain. The songs of his uncle, Peadar Kearney, are full of it.

CHAPTER 3 (PAGES 27-37)

1. *Ireland: 1828-1923, From Ascendancy to Democracy*, D. George Boyce (Blackwell Publishers, 1992), p.3.
2. *The Dual Tradition*, Thomas Kinsella (Carcanet, 1995).

3. *The Portable Malcolm Cowley*, Donald W. Faulkner, ed (Penguin, 1990). See essay 'The Revolt against Gentility', pp190-196.
4. *All Cultivated People*, Patricia Boylan (Colin Smythe Ltd, 1988).
5. *Unfinished Business*, Liam de Paor (Hutchinson Radius, 1990).
6. *West Briton*, Brian Inglis (Faber and Faber, 1966).
7. *The Years of the Great Test 1926-39*, Francis MacManus, ed (Mercier Press, 1967); F. S. L. Lyons in 'The Minority Problem in the 26 Counties', writes '. . . Whenever the British team won the Aga Khan Cup at the Horse Show, this was the signal for an almost hysterical rendering of *God Save the King*, which indeed, some at least of the minority never ceased to regard as the National Anthem.'
8. Quoted from *Selected Literary Criticism of Louis MacNeice*, Alan Heuser, ed (Clarendon Press, 1987), p.118.
9. A more flattering picture of Murphy emerges in the recent booklet *William Martin Murphy*, Thomas Morrissey SJ (Historical Association of Ireland, 1997).
10. The poet Padraic Colum, in his later years, sharply denounced the decline of public speaking in Ireland over his lifetime.
11. The 'dole' was introduced in 1933 and widows' pensions two years later.
12. See the disillusioned tone of O'Faolain's articles on de Valera in *The Bell*.

CHAPTER 4 (PAGES 39-57)

1. *Missing Persons: An Autobiography*, E. R. Dodds (Clarendon Press, 1997).
2. *The Yeats I Knew*, Francis MacManus, ed (RTÉ/Mercier Press, 1951).
3. See Frank O'Connor's autobiographical *My Father's Son* (Macmillan, 1967). When I spoke once to the poet Roibeárd Ó Faracháin about O'Connor's claims to have been intimate with Yeats, he told me that, to his personal knowledge, the two men met at most a dozen times.
4. The writer V. S. Pritchett was struck by Yeats's birdlike appearance when he called on him in Dublin in the 1930s.
5. See MacDiarmid's autobiography, *Lucky Poet*.
6. *Imagination of the Heart; The Life of Walter de La Mare*, Theresa Whistler (Duckworth, 1993), pp 209-211.
7. See *Rabindranath Tagore: A Biography*, Khrishna Kripalani (Oxford University Press, 1962).
8. *The Yeats I Knew*, Francis MacManus, ed, op.cit.
9. *The Poetry of W. B. Yeats*, Louis MacNeice (Oxford University Press, 1940).
10. *After the Irish Renaissance*, Robert Hogan (Macmillan, 1968).
11. Cf. *Yeats, Selected Criticism*, A. Norman Jeffares, ed (Macmillan, 1964).
12. 'Yeats and the Stage', Padraic Fallon, *The Irish Times*, 26 January 1963.
13. *Winter Pollen: Occasional Prose*, Ted Hughes, William Scammell, ed (Faber & Faber, 1994).
14. *W. B. Yeats: Man and Poet*, A. Norman Jeffares (Routledge and Kegan Paul, 1949; new edn, Gill and Macmillan, 1996).
15. *Scattering Branches*, F. R. Higgins (Macmillan, 1940), p.154.
16. *Agenda, Irish Poetry*, Double Issue, Patricia McCarthy, ed (Vol 33, 1996).

17. Yeats's epitaph ending '. . . *Horseman pass by*' was apparently written as a reaction to some of Rilke's pronouncements which he had been reading. See Yeats's own letters.
18. *The Irish Times* in particular carried a large and authoritative supplement on the poet.
19. *The Collected Poems of W. B. Yeats* (Macmillan, 1937), p.388.
20. *The Redress of Poetry*, Seamus Heaney (Faber & Faber, 1995) and *Preoccupations: Selected Prose 1968-1978*, Seamus Heaney (Faber & Faber, 1980).

CHAPTER 5 (PAGES 59-71)

1. In Joyce's case, Sylvia Beach, Carola Giedion-Welcker and Harriet Weaver, among others; in Wagner's case his second wife Cosima, Mathilde Wesendonck, Mathilde von Maysenbug and many more.
2. *Heritage Now*, Anthony Cronin (Brandon Books, 1982).
3. *The Portable Malcolm Cowley*, Donald W. Faulkner, ed (Penguin, 1990), p.49.
4. ibid, p.52.
5. *James Joyce*, Richard Ellmann (Oxford University Publications, 1959, revised edition 1982).
6. *Conversations with James Joyce*, Arthur Power (Millington, 1974), p.50.
7. In *Our Friend James Joyce* written jointly with her husband, Mary Colum suggests that Joyce did not, in fact, take Dujardin very seriously.
8. *Conversations with Joyce*, Arthur Power, op. cit, p.43.
9. *Stella Steyn*, Memoir and catalogue, S. B. Kennedy, ed (Gorry Gallery, 1995).
10. The adjective 'Celtic' has fallen into disfavour through overuse or abuse. However, no one appears to have suggested a useful alternative. Since there are Celtic languages and Celtic races, the word seems to me as legitimate as the adjective 'Latin' when applied to the Italian, Spanish and French nations.
11. *Conversations with Joyce*, Arthur Power, op cit, pp91-93.
12. *James Joyce, Portraits of the Artist in Exile*, Willard Potts, ed (Wolfhound Press and Washington University Press, 1979).
13. *A Penny in the Clouds*, Austin Clarke (Routledge & Keegan Paul, 1968).
14. *James Joyce,* Willard Potts, op. cit, p.223.
15. ibid., p.28.
16. ibid, p.240.
17. ibid, p.270.
18. Siobhán McKenna's recording of Molly Bloom's soliloquy enjoyed a considerable vogue in Dublin in the later 1950s. At one stage, it seemed impossible to attend any party or gathering without being obliged to listen to it.
19. This is largely the approach taken in *The Face and Mind of Ireland*, Arland Ussher (Victor Gollancz Ltd, 1949).

CHAPTER 6 (PAGES 73-93)

1. *Novels and Novelists*, Katherine Mansfield (Alfred A. Knopf, 1930), pp243-45.
2. *The Death of the Moth*, Virginia Woolf (Hogarth Press, 1942, republished Penguin, 1961), pp136, 138.
3. *George Moore: A Reconsideration*, Malcolm Brown (University of Washington Press, 1955).

4. *George Moore on Parnassus*, Helmut E. Gerber, ed (Associated University Presses, 1988).
5. *Imagination of the Heart: The Life of Walter de La Mare*, Theresa Whistler (Duckworth, 1933), pp330-331.
6. *Epitaph on George Moore*, Charles Morgan (Macmillan, 1935), pp36-39.
7. *George Moore*, Malcolm Brown, op. cit.
8. *The Masterpiece and the Man*, Monk Gibbon (Hart-Davis, 1959).
9. *The Poetry of W. B. Yeats*, Louis MacNeice (Oxford University Press, 1940).
10. See Anthony Cronin's *Heritage Now* (Brandon Books, 1982), pp69-74.
11. *A Penny in the Clouds*, Austin Clarke (Routledge & Kegan Paul, 1968).
12. *Irish Statesman*, 3 November, 1923.
13. *Horace Plunkett: Co-operation on Politics, an Irish Biography*, Trevor West (Colin Smythe Ltd, 1986).
14. *Helen Waddell, A Biography*, Dame Felicitas Corrigan (Victor Gollancz, 1986).
15. ibid, p.280.
16. ibid.
17. The complex relationship between the two men is discussed in *Yeats and AE*, Peter Kuch (Colin Smythe, 1986).
18. *A Penny in the Clouds*, Austin Clarke, op. cit.
19. Conversation with my father.
20. 'The Practical Mystic, AE Glimpsed through his Letters', Padraic Fallon, *The Irish Times*, 14 December 1961.
21. *The Course of Irish Verse*, Roibeárd Ó Faracháin (Sheed and Ward, 1948).
22. See *My Father's Son*, Frank O'Connor (Macmillan, 1968).
23. *Bernard Shaw*, Michael Holroyd (Chatto & Windus, 1988; reprinted Penguin, 1990-93; 1997 one-volume edition).
24. *British Dramatists*, Graham Greene (Collins, 1942; republished Prion 1996), pp76-79.
25. *The Matter with Ireland*, Dan H. Laurence and David H. Greene, eds (Hill and Wang, 1962).
26. *G. B. Shaw*, John O'Donovan (Gill & Macmillan, 1983).
27. *Shaw and Religion*, Charles E. Berst, ed (Pennsylvania State University Press, 1981).

CHAPTER 7 (PAGES 95-106)

1. *A Literary History of Ireland*, Douglas Hyde (Unwin, 1899; rev. edn Brian Ó Cúin, Ernest Benn, 1967).
2. *The Course of Irish Verse*, Roibeárd Ó Faracháin (Sheed and Ward, 1948).
3. Colum was born in 1881, Corkery in 1878, Fitzmaurice in 1877, and T. C. Murray in 1873.
4. *George William Russell (AE): Selections from the Contributions to the Irish Homestead*, vol 11, Henry Summerfield, ed (Humanities Press, 1978), p.861.
5. Eavan Boland's interview with Padraic Colum, *The Irish Times*, 1981.
6. 'Gloom without Sunshine: The Reception of T. C. Murray in America 1911-1938', Albert J. de Giacomo, in *Éire/Ireland* (Fomhair 1995).
7. *The Irish Drama*, Andrew E. Malone (Constable, 1929), pp185, 194.
8. *Synge and Anglo-Irish Literature,* Daniel Corkery (Cork University Press and Longman Green, 1931).

9. *Dublin Magazine*, June/March 1932.
10. See Kinsella's *The Dual Tradition* (Carcanet, 1995).
11. See *Theatre in Ireland*, Micheál Ó hAodha (Basil Blackwell, 1974).
12. *Dublin Magazine*, January 1940.

CHAPTER 8 (PAGES 107-122)

1. *The Course of Irish Verse*, Roibeárd Ó Faracháin (Sheed and Ward, 1948).
2. A volume of translations from Lorca by A. C. Lloyd, entitled *Death of a Bullfighter and Other Poems*, circulated in Dublin during the late 1930s. Rilke was largely known through the translation of J. B. Leishman.
3. *The Penguin Book of Nineties Verse*, John Betjeman, ed (London, 1978).
4. See Frank O'Connor's tribute in *The Bell*, February 1941.
5. See the essay, 'The Gallivanting Poet' in *Irish Writing*, November 1947 and the essay in *The Bell* the following month entitled 'Coloured Balloons'.
6. *Vive-Moi!*, Seán O'Faolain (Sinclair/Stevenson, 1963).
7. See *The Letters of Dylan Thomas*, Constantine Fitzgibbon, ed (Dent, 1966), p.233.
8. *The Collected Poems of Louis MacNeice*, E. R. Dodds, ed (Faber and Faber, 1966), p.405.
9. 'The Poetry of F. R. Higgins', Padraic Fallon, *The Irish Times*, 'Reassessments' series, 1972.
10. *The Celtic Renaissance*, Richard Fallis (Syracuse University Press, 1977).
11. *The Course of Irish Verse*, Roibeárd Ó Faracháin, op.cit.
12. *Nationalism in Modern Anglo-Irish Poetry*, Richard Loftus (University of Wisconsin Press, 1964).
13. *Modern Irish Fiction: A Critique*, Benedict Kiely (Golden Eagle Books, 1950).
14. *These the Companions*, Donald Davie (Cambridge University Press, 1982), pp88-91.
15. *The Poetry of W. B. Yeats*, Louis MacNeice (Oxford University Press, 1940).
16. *Journal of Irish Literature*, September 1979.
17. *Joseph Campbell: Poet and Nationalist 1879-1944*, Norah Saunders and A. A. Kelly (Wolfhound Press, 1988).
18. *Padraic Fallon, Collected Poems*, Brian Fallon, ed (Carcanet Press and Gallery Books, 1990).

CHAPTER 9 (PAGES 123-132)

1. General Boulanger ended by shooting himself on his mistress's grave after a planned *coup d'état* had been aborted.
2. See Connolly's *Unquiet Grave* (Hamish Hamilton, 1945).
3. *Poems from Ireland*, Donagh MacDonagh, ed (Irish Times Publication, 1944).
4. *Damned to Fame: The Life of Samuel Beckett*, James Knowlson (Bloomsbury, 1996). Francis Stuart also lived in Paris in 1950-51, where he was reunited with his (second) wife, Medeleine.
5. The *Dublin Magazine*, Seumas O'Sullivan, ed April-June 1956.
6. *The Bell*, January 1952.

CHAPTER 10 (PAGES 133-147)

1. The Dublin Drama League was active for ten years. During this time it produced plays by Chekhov, Cocteau, d'Annunzio, O'Neill, Pirandello and Strindberg.

2. See Denis Johnston's somewhat ironical account in *The O'Casey Enigma*, Micheál Ó hAodha, ed (Mercier Press, 1980).
3. *Twentieth-century Irish Drama*, Christopher Murray (Manchester University Press, 1997), p.121.
4. O'Connor seems not to have forgiven Higgins for this and other slights. His portrait of him in the second volume of his autobiography is almost belittling.
5. *After the Irish Renaissance*, Robert Hogan (Macmillan, 1968), pp6-7.
6. O'Casey in his letters complains about the negative attitude of several Irish writers including O'Faolain and M. J. McManus.
7. *The Star Turns Red* (1940) disappointed even his leading admirers. George Jean Nathan remarked that Communism had adversely affected O'Casey as a dramatic artist.
8. *The Green Cow: Selected Writings of Seán O'Casey* (George Braziller, 1956; repub Virgin Books, 1994).
9. Byrne, a barrister, had been jailed for IRA involvement in 1940, but was released after a hunger strike. He died in 1968.
10. *Poetry Magazine*, January 1952.
11. Two policemen who attended the performance, regarded as obscure the incident in which a contraceptive is dropped on the stage.
12. There are numerous references to Mac Liammóir in Noel Coward's *Diaries* (Papermac, 1983).
13. Quoted in R. Hogan's *After the Irish Renaissance*, op. cit., pp112-113.
14. See his book *Put Money in thy Purse* published by Methuen in 1952, with a foreword by Orson Welles; reissued as a paperback by Virgin Books, 1994.
15. *The Mantle of Harlequin*, Hilton Edwards (Progress House, 1958).
16. *The Boys*, Christopher Fitz-Simon (Nick Hern Books, 1994).
17. See note 14.
18. The distinguished radio, television and stage director, Michael Garvey, has told me that when he came to Dublin from University College Galway in the 1950s he was dismayed by the generally low level of stage production. In his opinion, much of the best and most imaginative production at the time was on radio.
19. *Eugene O'Neill in Ireland*, Edward L. O'Shaughnessy (Greenwood Press, 1988).
20. *The Irish Monthly*, January 1942.
21. Ó hAodha's *Plays and Places* devotes a chapter to these works. Part of *Diarmuid and Gráinne* appears in the *Dublin Magazine*, shortly after its production, and the *Vision of Mac Conglinne* has been published in America. A selection of these plays is expected to appear in the near future.

CHAPTER 11 (PAGES 149-157)

1. *Self-Portrait*, Patrick Kavanagh (Dolmen Press, 1962).
2. Related to me by an onlooker.
3. *Head or Harp?*, Lionel Fleming (Barrie and Rockliff, 1965).
4. A distorted version of this appears in *Irish Literary Portraits*, by W. R. Rodgers (BBC, 1972).
5. See Anthony Cronin's *Dead as Doornails* (Dolmen Press, 1975).
6. *Horizon Magazine, Special Irish Number*, 1942.

7. *Mind You, I've Said Nothing!*, Honor Tracy (Methuen, 1953; Penguin, 1961), p.68.
8. ibid, p.72.
9. ibid, p.72.
10. ibid, p.72.

CHAPTER 12 (PAGES 159-171)

1. *Vide* his letters from this period. It has also been suggested, probably with little foundation, that he needed Gaelic in order to read intercepted IRA correspondence.
2. *An Béal Bocht*, Myles na Gopaleen (National Press, 1941). The English translation by Patrick C. Power was published in 1964 under the title *The Poor Mouth*.
3. Quoted in *Recollections of Wittgenstein*, Rush Rhees, ed (Oxford University Press, 1984), pp137-38.
4. Quoted by Seán Ó Catháin in *The Years of the Great Test 1926-39* (Mercier Press, 1967).
5. *Writing in Irish Today*, David Greene (Mercier Press, 1972).
6. *W. B. Yeats: Selected Criticism*, A. Norman Jeffares, ed (Macmillan, 1964), pp270-272.
7. *Writing in Irish Today*, David Greene, op. cit.
8. ibid.
9. See the *New Oxford Book of Irish Verse*, chosen and edited by Thomas Kinsella (Oxford University Press, 1986).
10. Written in 1948 while Behan was a prisoner in Mountjoy Jail.
11. *Nuabhéarsaíocht 1939-1949*, Seán Ó Tuama, ed (Sáirséal agus Dill, 1950).
12. *The Gaelic League Idea*, Seán Ó Tuama, ed (Mercier Press, 1972).

CHAPTER 13 (PAGES 173-182)

1. See *Twilight of the Ascendancy*, Mark Bence-Jones (Constable, 1987; paperback edition 1993). For a wider context see David Cannadine's masterly study, *The Decline and Fall of the British Aristocracy* (Yale University Press, 1990).
2. *Cyril Connolly*, Clive Fisher (Macmillan, 1995), p.368.
3. *The Story of Ireland*, and *West Briton*, Brian Inglis (Faber and Faber, 1956 and 1966 respectively).
4. As late as the 1960s, Terence de Vere White received a number of angry or abusive letters from Protestant readers of *The Irish Times* who resented some mildly critical remarks he had made about Churchill's style of oratory.
5. *The Face and Mind of Ireland*, Arland Ussher (Victor Gollancz, 1949).
6. I first found their works as a teenager in the Wexford County Library. The dates stamped on them indicated they had been in constant use.
7. See *The Living Novel*, V. S. Pritchett (London, 1947).
8. *Bowen's Court*, Elizabeth Bowen (Gollancz 1942; reissued by Collins Press, 1998).
9. The home was demolished shortly after Elizabeth Bowen had sold it – apparently in the belief that otherwise it would be preserved.
10. See *British Aristocracy*, Cannadine, op. cit.
11. Including the role in resolving the long impasse over the Lane pictures.
12. *New Irish Poets*, Devin A. Garrity (Devin-Adair, 1948).
13. *The Years of the Great Test 1926-39*, Francis MacManus, ed (Mercier Press, 1967), p.97.
14. ibid. p.99.
15. *These the Companions*, Donald Davie (Cambridge University Press, 1982), p.98.

16. *The Recollections of Wittgenstein*, Rush Rees, ed (Oxford University Press, 1984), p.137.
17. Binchy was for a time Irish Minister Plenipotentiary to Germany. Later he was Senior Professor at the School of Celtic Studies in Dublin. His life's work was a study of Irish Law.
18. Now the National Concert Hall. This is the building which appears in Joyce's *Portrait of the Artist as a Young Man*.
19. She was one of the earliest Irish admirers of Lorca whom she wrote about in the *Dublin Magazine*.
20. Today there is a theatre named after him in the Arts Block of Trinity College Dublin.

CHAPTER 14 (PAGES 183-199)

1. *Ireland*, Camille Bourniquel (Vista Books, Longacres Press, 1960), p.134.
2. 'The Great Hunger' from *Patrick Kavanagh: Collected Poems* (Martin Brian and O'Keefe, 1972), p.42.
3. *Twentieth-Century Ireland: Nation and State*, Dermot Keogh (Gill and Macmillan, 1994).
4. *The Irish Catholic Experience*, Patrick Corish (Gill and Macmillan, 1985).
5. A copy of this pamphlet can be read in the National Library.
6. *De Valera's Constitution and Ours*, Brian Farrell, ed (Gill and Macmillan for RTÉ, 1988).
7. Yeats visited several Irish schools in 1926. He wrote, 'Teacher after teacher in Ireland has said to me that the young people are anarchic and violent . . . they respect nothing . . . the proper remedy is the teaching of religion.' ('The Child and the State', published in the *Irish Statesman*, December 1925).
8. See *The Irish and Catholic Power*, Paul Blanshard (Beacon Press, 1953).
9. There is always a danger of simplifying a complex issue in these terms. For a detailed study, see *Church and State in Modern Ireland 1923-1970*, J. H. Whyte (Gill and Macmillan, 1971; republished as *Church and State in Modern Ireland 1923-1979*, 1980).
10. One anti-clerical French government had even proposed closing the cathedrals to worshippers and converting them to purely civic uses. Proust's essay, *A Massacre of Churches*, was written as a challenge to this.
11. When O'Faolain was appointed first chairman of the Irish Arts Council, Archbishop McQuaid of Dublin intrigued to have him replaced by Thomas Bodkin. Bodkin was offered the post by the then Taoiseach, J. A. Costello, but to his credit refused. See *Seán O'Faolain: A Life*, by Maurice Harmon (Constable, 1994), pp208-209.
12. *Seán O'Faolain*, Maurice Harmon, op. cit.
13. Ó Faracháin was under pressure to banish Plunkett from Radio Éireann, but instead managed to move him sideways. Lennox Robinson, another of the Irish visitors to Russia, lost his regular column in the *Irish Press*, but as a consolation prize his articles were collected and published in book form under the title *I Sometimes Think* (Talbot Press, 1956).
14. The Cork writer Robert Gibbings, author of *Lovely is the Lee* and other books, was a close associate of Gill. See *Eric Gill*, Fiona MacCarthy (Faber and Faber, 1990).
15. *A Priest in Changing Times*, Michael O'Carroll CSSp (Columbia Press, 1998).
16. *Collected Poems of Austin Clarke*, Liam Miller, ed (Dolmen Press and Oxford University Press, 1974).
17. *The Letters of Brendan Behan*, E. H. Mikhail, ed (Macmillan, 1992, p.45).

18. Curiously enough, Irish illegitimate births seemed to have increased during the forties.
19. 'A Hand of Snapshots' from *The Collected Poems of Louis MacNeice*, E. R. Dodds, ed (Faber and Faber, 1972), p.450.
20. See *G. K. Chesterton*, by Michael Ffinch (Wiedenfeld & Nicholson, 1986), pp329-330. Chesterton himself describes the occasion in his book *Christendom in Dublin* (1932).
21. *The Death of Religious Life?*, Tony Flannery CSsR (Columbia Press, 1997).
22. See several of his pronouncements in *Kavanagh's Weekly*.

CHAPTER 15 (PAGES 201-210)

1. *Signe Toksvig's Irish Diaries, 1926-1936*, Lis Pihl, ed (Lilliput Press, 1994).
2. *D. P. Moran*, Patrick Maume (Historical Association of Ireland/Dundalgan Press Ltd, 1995).
3. *The Face and Mind of Ireland*, Arland Ussher (Victor Gollancz, 1949), pp99-100.
4. *Censored*, T. D. Mathews (Chatto & Windus, 1994).
5. *One Way of Love*, Gamel Woolsey (Virago Press, 1987).
6. *Patrick White, A Life*, David Marr (Jonathan Cape, 1991; Vintage, 1992).
7. *Raising Kane and Other Essays*, Pauline Kael (Marion Boyars Ltd, 1996), pp25-26.
8. *A Life at the Centre*, Roy Jenkins (Macmillan, 1991).

CHAPTER 16 (PAGES 211-223)

1. *Nationalism and Independence*, Nicholas Mansergh (Cork University Press, 1997). Mansergh repeatedly mentions de Valera's 'academic cast of mind' as well as his pragmatic qualities.
2. *H.G.: The History of Mr Wells*, Michael Foot (Doubleday, 1995), p.284.
3. For a spirited defence of de Valera in this context, see J. B. Morton's *The New Ireland*, (Paladin, 1935).
4. It is sometimes forgotten that New England patricians of the time received an upbringing which corresponded closely to the English public school one.
5. *Victors, Beware!*, Salvador de Madariaga (Jonathan Cape, 1946), pp135-142.
6. *The Matter with Ireland*, Dan H. Laurence and David H. Greene, eds (Hill and Wang, 1962).
7. *They Go, The Irish – A Miscellany of War-time Writing*, compiled by Leslie Daiken (Nicholson & Watson, 1944).
8. *Neutral Ireland and the Third Reich*, John P. Duggan, foreword by Douglas Gageby (Gill and Macmillan, 1985; paperback, Lilliput Press, 1989).
9. ibid.
10. *Irish Studies 5. Ireland and Britain since 1922*, P. J. Drudy, ed (Cambridge University Press, 1986).
11. *One Hundred Years of Socialism*, Donald Sassoon (Fontana Press, 1997).
12. *The Face and Mind of Ireland*, Arland Ussher (Victor Gollancz, 1949), p.70.
13. See *The Collected Poems of Louis MacNeice*, E. R. Dodds, ed (Faber and Faber, 1979). Poem cited written September 1942. See also poem, 'Convoy', written some months later.
14. These difficulties arose mainly out of her early, unsuccessful marriage to a Dutch citizen.
15. See Dr Nicholas Mansergh's essay, 'Ireland: External Relations 1926-39', included in *The Years of the Great Test 1926-39*, Francis MacManus, ed (Mercier Press, 1967).

16. *Horizon* magazine, January 1942.
17. *Harold Nicholson: Diaries and Letters 1930-1964* (condensed edn, Flamingo, 1996), pp227-228.
18. *Robert Graves, Life on the Edge*, Miranda Seymour (Doubleday, 1995).
19. See Thomas's now canonical history, *The Spanish Civil War* (Hamish Hamilton, revd, 1977), pp592, 768, 979.
20. ibid.
21. Reprinted recently in the *Penguin Book of Spanish Civil War Verse* (London, 1996).
22. *Charlie Donnelly, The Life and Poems*, Joseph Donnelly (The Dedalus Press, 1987).
23. Later president of Israel.
24. Since this chapter was written, an authoritative new study has been published by Dr Dermot Keogh, *Jews in Twentieth Century Ireland* (Cork University Press, 1998).
25. The obvious exception was the Limerick pogrom at the beginning of the century.

CHAPTER 17 (PAGES 225-235)

1. Gallagher was the author of a fine republican jail journal, *Days of Fear* (John Murray, 1928).
2. He also wrote a rather partisan book on de Valera.
3. Patrick Campbell's pen portrait catches the man best of all.
4. *Brendan Behan, A Life*, Michael O'Sullivan (Blackwater Press, 1997).
5. See article by Lt Gen. M. J. Costello, 'Let us Have the Truth', in *The Irish Times* of 8 May 1985.
6. See Maurice Gorham's *40 Years of Irish Broadcasting* (Dublin, 1967), an official history of Radio Éireann from its inception.
7. *An Index of Contributors* was compiled and published by Rudi Hozapfel in 1960.
8. See Cronin's satirical novel, *The Life of Reilly* (Secker and Warburg, 1964).
9. *The Bell*, May 1945.

CHAPTER 18 (PAGES 237-246)

1. A sculpture by him was in the collection of the Hugh Lane Municipal Gallery of Modern Art, but I have never seen it on exhibition.
2. O'Brien had been PRHA since 1910.
3. *Irish Art and Modernism 1880-1950*, S. B. Kennedy (Institute of Irish Studies, Queen's University, 1991).
4. Kokoschka had visited Ireland in the late 1920s, and may have seen paintings by Yeats at that time. Claims that the two men met on a number of occasions have yet to be documented.
5. See *Jack B Yeats*, Hilary Pyle (André Deutsch, 1989). At the time of writing, Bruce Arnold's biography has not yet appeared in print.
6. At his London gallery in Cork Street, Waddington was largely responsible for bringing the abstract pictures of the St Ives School before the public. His sons have since followed in his footsteps.
7. See *Michael Scott, Architect: Conversations with Dorothy Walker* (Gandon Editions, 1994)
8. See *God's Architect: A Life of Raymond McGrath*, Donal O'Donovan (Kilbride Books, 1995).

CHAPTER 19 (PAGES 247-256)

1. See Gray's biography, *Peter Warlock* (Jonathan Cape, 1934).
2. ibid.
3. ibid.
4. His death was generally taken as suicide, though the jury returned an open verdict.
5. *The British Music of Our Time*, A. L. Bacharach, ed (Penguin, 1951).
6. See Bax's autobiography, *Farewell my Youth* (Longman Green, 1943).
7. *Bax, A Composer and his Times*, Lewis Foreman (Scolar Press, London and Berkeley, 1983). Also, a biography, *Arnold Bax*, Colin Scott-Sutherland, had appeared earlier (Dent, 1973).
8. Richard Ellmann in his biography of Joyce relegates this episode to a footnote.
9. *The Irish Times*, 16 July 1947.
10. *British Music of Our Time*, A. L. Bacharach, op. cit.
11. See *Four Centuries of Music in Ireland*, Brian Boydell, ed (BBC, 1979) and *Music in Ireland 1848-1998*, Richard Pine, ed (Mercier Press, 1998).
12. *Acton's Music: Reviews 1955-1985*, Charles Acton (Kilbride Books, 1996).

CHAPTER 20 (PAGES 257-271)

1. In *Seán O'Faolain: A Life*, Maurice Harmon (Constable, 1994), dealing with the years 1953-1957 speaks of the energetic campaign of Archbishop McQuaid in this field. 'During this period the Archbishop, backed by the hierarchy, had spearheaded what the Government recognised as an orchestrated attack on "immoral" literature. Many Catholic lay organisations engaged in a campaign of letter-writing to the Taoiseach', pp209-210.
2. Cronin expressed his disillusionment with Russia in a number of articles published in *The Irish Times*.
3. Notably Dr Peter Birch, later Bishop of Ossory and at that time a theologian in Maynooth.
4. According to one account, it was actually Swift who thrust a volume of Auden's poetry into Kavanagh's hands in McDaid's pub. See *PS . . . of course, Patrick Swift 1927-1983*, Veronica Jane O'Mara, ed (Gandon Books, 1993).
5. I was present once when he discussed the *Cantos* at length with a fellow poet.
6. For an account of this trial, see Anthony Cronin's *Dead as Doornails*.
7. *The Leader* at this time was associated with a group of ambitious young historians, including the late Desmond Williams. The article probably originated from one of this group, and was almost certainly motivated by mischief rather than malice.
8. See *The Making of Modern Irish History*, D. George Boyce and Alan O'Day, eds (Routledge, 1996).
9. At the time of writing, John Cooney's life of Dr McQuaid has not yet appeared in print. However, excerpts carried by *The Irish Times* confirm my previous conviction that the hierarchy was activated primarily by fear of socialism. John Cooney also agrees with my analysis that the decline in the Church's power in Ireland ultimately dates from this incident.
10. At secondary school in Wexford, I saw a good deal of this prelate and grew to dislike him intensely.

11. Dr O'Rahilly was ordained a priest not long afterwards. To do him justice, he had been an able president of University College Cork.
12. Notably Dr Pigott, former chairman of the Censorship Board.
13. 'Annus Mirabilis' from *Philip Larkin: Collected Poems* (Faber and Faber, 1990), p.167.
14. Roger Chauviré's excellent little *History of Ireland* (Clonmore & Reynolds, 1952) does occasionally err in this direction.
15. See his *Irisches Tagebuch*, which records his years of residence in the West of Ireland. English translation as *Irish Journal* (Secker and Warburg, 1963).
16. Russian writers such as Pasternak have repudiated this approach towards their country as a romantic distortion.
17. The case of Karlfeldt in Sweden is the most eminent. He wrote about his own rural region, but his tone and outlook are extremely modern.
18. *The Waste Land* of Eliot is largely built on a ground-bass of myth. Even Pound's *Cantos* contain many mythic resonances.

BIBLIOGRAPHY

GENERAL AND CULTURAL

ADAMS, Michael, *Censorship: The Irish Experience* (Dublin: Sceptre Books 1968)

BÖLL, Heinrich, *Irish Journal* (London: Martin Secker & Warburg 1983)

BOYLAN, Henry, *A Dictionary of Irish Biography*, 3rd ed. (Dublin: Gill & Macmillan 1998)

BROWN, Terence, *Ireland: A Social and Cultural History 1922-1985* (London: Fontana Press 1981)

BROWN, Terence, *Ireland's Literature: Selected Essays* (Dublin: Lilliput Press/New Jersey: Barnes & Noble Inc. 1988)

BUTLER, Hubert, *Escape from the Anthill* (Dublin: Lilliput Press 1985)

CAHALAN, James M., *Modern Irish Literature and Culture: A Chronology* (New York: G. K. Hall & Co. 1993)

CORCORAN, Neil, *After Yeats and Joyce: Reading Modern Irish Literature* (Oxford University Press 1977)

CRAIG, Patricia (ed.), *The Oxford Book of Ireland* (Oxford University Press 1998)

DAMES, Michael, *Mythic Ireland* (Thames & Hudson 1992; rev. paperback ed. 1996)

DEANE, Seamus (ed.), *The Field Day Anthology of Irish Writing*, 3 vols (Derry: Field Day Publications 1991)

DE MADARIAGA, Salvador, *Portrait of Europe* (London: Hollis & Carter 1967)

DE PAOR, Liam, *Unfinished Business: Ireland Today and Tomorrow* (London: Hutchinson 1990)

EVANS, E. Estyn, *The Personality of Ireland* (Dublin: Lilliput Press 1992)

EVANS, E. Estyn, *Ireland and the Atlantic Heritage: Selected Writings* (Dublin: Lilliput Press 1995)

FLYNN, Dennis (ed.), *On Irish Themes* by James T. Farrell (Philadelphia: University of Pennsylvania Press 1982)

GONZALEZ, Alexander G. (ed.), *Modern Irish Writers: A Bio-critical Sourcebook* (London: Aldwych Press 1977)

GROSS, John (ed.), *The Modern Movement* (London: The Harvill Press 1992)

HARMON, Maurice, *Anglo-Irish Literature and its Backgrounds: An Irish Studies Handbook* (Dublin: Wolfhound Press 1977)

HAYLEY, Barbara and Enda McKay, *Three Hundred Years of Irish Periodicals* (Dublin: Lilliput Press 1987)

HEANEY, Seamus, *Preoccupations: Selected Prose 1968-1978* (London: Faber & Faber 1980)

HEANEY, Seamus, *The Government of the Tongue* (London: Faber & Faber 1988)

HOGAN, Robert (ed.), *Dictionary of Irish Literature*, 2 vols, rev. and expanded ed. (London: Aldwych Press 1996)

HUGHES, Ted, *Winter Pollen: Occasional Prose* (London: Faber & Faber 1994)

IRELAND, Denis, *From the Irish Shore* (London: Rich & Cowan 1936)

KIBERD, Declan, *Inventing Ireland: The Literature of the Modern Nation* (London: Jonathan Cape 1995)

LANE, Denis and Carol McCrory Lane (eds), *Modern Irish Literature: A Library of Literary Criticism* (New York: Ungar 1988)

LEE, Joseph and Gearóid Ó Tuathaigh, *The Age of de Valera* (Dublin: Ward River Press/RTÉ 1982)

LYONS, F. S. L., *Culture and Anarchy in Ireland, 1890-1939* (Oxford: Clarendon Press 1979)

McDIARMID, Lucy and Maureen Waters (eds), *Lady Gregory: Selected Writings* (Harmondsworth: Penguin 1995)

MACMANUS, Francis (ed.), *The Years of the Great Test* (Cork: Mercier Press/RTÉ 1967)

MANNIN, Ethel, *Connemara Journal* (London: Westhouse 1947)

O'BRIEN, Conor Cruise (ed.), *The Shaping of Modern Ireland* (London: Routledge 1960)

O'BRIEN, Conor Cruise, *States of Ireland* (London: Hutchinson 1972)

O'BRIEN, Kate, *My Ireland* (London: B. T. Batsford 1962)

O'FAOLAIN, Seán, *The Irish* (Harmondsworth: Pelican 1947)

ORTEGA Y GASSET, José, *The Revolt of the Masses*, English translation (New York: Norton 1932)

PRINCESS GRACE IRISH LIBRARY (ed.), *Irishness in a Changing Society* (Gerrards Cross: Colin Smythe 1988)

STOREY, Mark, *Poetry and Ireland since 1800: A Source Book* (London: Routledge 1988)

TAYLOR, Geoffrey, *The Emerald Isle* (London: Evans 1952)

USSHER, Arland, *The Face and Mind of Ireland* (London: Victor Gollancz 1949)

WELCH, Robert (ed.), *The Oxford Companion to Irish Literature* (Oxford: Clarendon Press 1996)

WILSON, Edmund, *Axel's Castle* (New York: Scribners 1931)

BIOGRAPHY, MEMOIRS, LETTERS

ALDRICH, Keith, *W. B. Yeats: The Man and the Milieu* (London: John Murray 1997)

CLARKE, Austin, *A Penny in the Clouds* (London: Routledge and Kegan Paul 1968)

COOTE, Stephen, *W. B. Yeats: A Life* (London: Hodder & Stoughton 1997)

CRONIN, Anthony, *Dead As Doornails* (Dublin: Dolmen Press 1975)

CRONIN, Anthony, *No Laughing Matter: The Life and Times of Flann O'Brien* (London: Grafton Books 1989)

DAVIE, Donald, *These the Companions* (Cambridge University Press 1982)

DUNLEAVY, Janet Eagleson and Gareth Dunleavy, *Douglas Hyde: A Maker of Modern Ireland* (Berkeley: University of California Press 1991)

EGLINTON, John, *A Memoir of AE* (London: Macmillan 1937)

ELBORN, Geoffrey, *Francis Stuart: A Life* (Dublin: Raven Arts Press 1990)

ELLMAN, Louis, *Yeats: The Man and the Masks*, 1948, rev. ed. (Oxford University Press 1979)

ELLMANN, Richard, *James Joyce* (London: 1959; rev. ed. Oxford University Press 1982)

FINCH, Michael, *G. K. Chesterton* (London: Weidenfeld and Nicolson 1986)

FISHER, Clive, *Cyril Connolly: A Nostalgic Life* (London: Macmillan 1995)

GERBER, Helmut E., (ed.), *George Moore on Parnassus: Letters 1900-1933* (London: Associated University Presses 1988)

GLENDINNING, Victoria, *Elizabeth Bowen* (London: Weidenfeld and Nicolson 1977)

GOGARTY, Oliver St John, *It Isn't This Time of Year At All!* (London: MacGibbon & Kee 1954)

GREEN, Candida Lycett, *John Betjeman: Letters, Volume One: 1926 to 1951* (London: Methuen 1994)

HARMON, Maurice, *Seán O'Faolain: A Life* (London: Constable 1995)

HOLROYD, Michael, *Augustus John*, rev. ed. (Harmondsworth: Penguin 1976)

HOLROYD, Michael, *Bernard Shaw*, 1-volume definitive ed. (London: Chatto & Windus 1997)

HONE, Joseph, *The Life of George Moore* (London: Faber & Faber 1936)

HONE, Joseph, *W. B. Yeats: Man and Poet* (London 1949; reprinted Harmondsworth: Penguin 1971)

JEFFARES, A. Norman, *W. B. Yeats: Man and Poet* (London: Routledge and Kegan Paul 1949; rev. ed. Dublin: Gill & Macmillan 1996)

KELLY, A. A. (ed.), *The Collected Letters of Liam O'Flaherty* (Dublin: Wolfhound Press 1994)

KNOWLSON, James, *Damned to Fame: The Life of Samuel Beckett* (London: Bloomsbury 1996)

KOHFELDT, Mary Lou, *Lady Gregory: The Woman Behind the Irish Renaissance* (London: André Deutsch 1985)

KRAUSE, David (ed.), *The Letters of Seán O'Casey*, 4 vols (New York: Macmillan 1975-1992)

KUCH, Peter, *Yeats and AE: The Antagonism that Unites Old Friends* (Gerrards Cross: Colin Smythe 1986)

LEWIS, Giffard, *The Yeats Sisters and the Cuala* (Dublin: Irish Academic Press 1994)

MAC LIAMMÓIR, Micheál, *All For Hecuba* (London: Methuen 1946)

MACNEICE, Louis, *The Strings are False* (London: Faber & Faber 1965)

MIKHAIL, E. H. (ed.), *The Letters of Brendan Behan* (London: Macmillan 1992)

MONK, Ray, *Ludwig Wittgenstein* (London: Jonathan Cape 1990)

O'CASEY, Seán, *Autobiographies* (London: Macmillan 1963)

O'CONNOR, Frank, *An Only Child* (London: Macmillan 1962)

O'CONNOR, Frank, *My Father's Son* (London: Macmillan 1968)

O'CONNOR, Garry, *Seán O'Casey: A Life* (London: Hodder & Stoughton 1988)

O'CONNOR, Ulick, *Oliver St John Gogarty* (London: Jonathan Cape 1964)

O'FAOLAIN, Seán, *Vive Moi! An Autobiography* (London: Sinclair-Stevenson 1963)

O'SULLIVAN, Michael, *Brendan Behan: A Life* (Dublin: Blackwater Press 1998)

PIHL, Lis (ed.), *Signe Toksvig's Irish Diaries 1926-1937* (Dublin: Lilliput Press 1994)

POTTS, Willard (ed.), *James Joyce: Portraits of the Artist in Exile* (Dublin: Wolfhound Press, and Seattle: Washington University Press, 1979)

POWER, Arthur, *Conversations with James Joyce* (London: Millington 1974)

PYLE, Hilary, *Jack B. Yeats: A Biography* (London: André Deutsch 1989)

QUINN, Antoinette, *Patrick Kavanagh: Born-again Romantic* (Dublin: Gill & Macmillan 1991)

QUINN, John (ed.), *A Portrait of the Artist as a Young Girl* (London: Methuen 1986)

ROBINSON, Lennox, *Curtain Up: An Autobiography* (London: Michael Joseph 1942)

SAUNDERS, Norah and A. A. Kelly, *Joseph Campbell: Poet and Nationalist* (Dublin: Wolfhound Press 1988)

SEYMOUR, Miranda, *Robert Graves: Life on the Edge* (London and New York: Doubleday 1995)

SMITH, Constance Babington, *John Masefield* (Oxford University Press 1978)

STALLWORTHY, Jon, *Louis MacNeice* (London: Faber & Faber 1995)

STOCK, Noel, *The Life of Ezra Pound*, Pelican Biographies (Harmondsworth: Penguin 1974)

SUMMERFIELD, Henry, *That Myriad-minded Man: A Biography of G. W. Russell-AE* (Gerrards Cross: Colin Smythe 1975)

WHISTLER, Theresa, *Imagination of the Heart: The Life of Walter de la Mare* (London: Gerald Duckworth 1993)

WHITE, Terence de Vere, *A Fretful Midge* (London: Routledge and Kegan Paul 1959)

YEATS, W. B., *Dramatis Personae* (London: Macmillan 1935)

HISTORICAL

BOYCE, D. George and Alan O'Day (eds), *The Making of Modern Irish History* (London: Routledge 1996)

CHUBB, Basil, *The Government and Politics of Ireland* (London: Longman 1970)

CONNOLLY, S. J. (ed.), *The Oxford Companion to Irish History* (Oxford University Press 1998)

COOGAN, Tim Pat, *De Valera: Long Fellow, Long Shadow* (London: Hutchinson 1993)

DRUDY, P. G. (ed.), *Ireland and Britain since 1922*, Irish Studies 5 (Cambridge University Press 1986)

DUGGAN, John P., *Neutral Ireland and the Third Reich* (Dublin: Gill & Macmillan 1989)

DWYER, T. Ryle, *De Valera: The Man and the Myths* (Dublin: Poolbeg Press 1991)

EDWARDS, R. Dudley, *A New History of Ireland* (Dublin: Gill & Macmillan 1972)

ENGLISH, Richard and Graham Walter (eds), *Unionism in Modern Ireland* (Dublin: Gill & Macmillan 1996)

FARRELL, Brian (ed.), *De Valera's Constitution and Ours*, Thomas Davis Lectures (Dublin: Gill & Macmillan/RTÉ 1988)

FISK, Robert, *In Time of War: Ireland, Ulster and the Price of Neutrality 1939-45* (London: André Deutsch 1983)

FITZPATRICK, David, *The Two Irelands 1912-1939* (Oxford University Press 1998)

FOSTER, Roy, *Modern Ireland 1600-1972* (London: Allen Lane 1988)

GRAY, Tony, *The Lost Years: The Emergency in Ireland 1939-45* (London: Little, Brown & Co. 1997)

HEDERMAN, Miriam, *The Road to Europe* (Dublin: Institute of Public Administration 1983)

KEOGH, Dermot, *Jews in Twentieth-century Ireland* (Cork University Press 1998)

KEOGH, Dermot, *Twentieth-century Ireland: Nation and State* (Dublin: Gill & Macmillan 1994)

LONGFORD, Earl of and Thomas P. O'Neill, *Eamon de Valera* (London: Hutchinson 1970)

LEE, J. J., *Ireland 1912-1985: Politics and Society* (Cambridge University Press 1989)

LYONS, F. S. L., *Ireland Since the Famine*, rev. ed. (London: Weidenfeld & Nicolson 1973)

MACDONAGH, Oliver, *States of Mind: Two Centuries of Anglo-Irish Conflict* (London: Allen & Unwin 1983)

MCLOUGHLIN, Michael, *Great Irish Speeches of the Twentieth Century* (Dublin: Poolbeg Press 1966)

MANSERGH, Nicholas, *Nationalism and Independence* (Cork University Press 1997)

MURPHY, John A., *Ireland in the Twentieth Century* (Dublin: Gill & Macmillan 1975)

SLOAN, G. R., *The Geopolitics of Anglo-Irish Relations in the 20th Century* (Leicester University Press 1977)

STEPHAN, Enno, *Spies in Ireland* (London: Macdonald 1963)

WOLFSON, Robert, *Years of Change: European History 1890-1945* (London: Edward Arnold 1978)

CRITICISM AND MONOGRAPHS

AYLING, Ronald (ed.), *Seán O'Casey: Modern Judgments* (London: Macmillan 1969)

BERST, Charles E., *Shaw and Religion* (Pennsylvania State University Press 1981)

BURGESS, Anthony, *Here Comes Everybody: An Introduction to James Joyce for the Ordinary Reader* (London: Faber & Faber 1965)

CLARKE, Austin, *Poetry in Modern Ireland* (Dublin: Cultural Relations Committee 1961)

CLUNE, Anne and Tess Hurson, *Conjuring Complexities: Essays on Flann O'Brien* (Institute of Irish Studies, Queen's University of Belfast 1997)

CORKERY, Daniel, *Synge and Anglo-Irish Literature* (Cork University Press 1931)

CRAIG, Patricia, *Elizabeth Bowen* (Harmondsworth: Penguin 1986)

CRONIN, Anthony, *Heritage Now: Irish Literature in the English Language* (Dingle, Co. Kerry: Brandon Books 1982)

CRONIN, John, *Irish Fiction 1900-1940* (Belfast: Appletree Press 1992)

CULLINGFORD, Elizabeth, *Yeats, Ireland and Fascism* (Dublin: Gill & Macmillan 1981)

DONOGHUE, Dennis, *Yeats* (London: Fontana/Collins 1971)

GRENE, Nicholas, *Bernard Shaw: A Critical View* (London: Macmillan 1984)

HARMON, Maurice, *Seán O'Faolain: A Critical Introduction* (Dublin: Wolfhound Press 1984)

HEANEY, Seamus, *The Redress of Poetry: Oxford Lectures* (London: Faber & Faber 1995)

HEUSER, Alan (ed.), *Selected Literary Criticism of Louis MacNeice* (Oxford: Clarendon Press 1987)

JEFFARES, A. Norman (ed.), *Yeats: Selected Criticism* (London: Macmillan 1964)

JOHNSTON, Rory (ed.), *Orders and Desecrations: The Life of the Playwright Denis Johnston* (Dublin: Lilliput Press 1992)

KENNER, Hugh, *Dublin's Joyce* (London: Chatto & Windus 1955)

KINSELLA, Thomas, *The Dual Tradition* (Manchester: Carcanet Press 1995)

LONGLEY, Edna, *Louis MacNeice: A Study* (London: Faber & Faber 1989)

MARTIN, Augustine, *Yeats* (Gerrards Cross: Colin Smythe 1990)

MATTHEWS, James H., *Frank O'Connor* (London: Associated University Presses 1976)

MERCIER, Vivian, *Beckett/Beckett* (London: Souvenir Press 1990)

MERCIER, Vivian, *The Irish Comic Tradition* (Oxford: Clarendon Press 1962)

MILLER, Liam, *The Noble Drama of W. B. Yeats* (Dublin: Dolmen Press 1977)

NOLAN, Emer, *James Joyce and Nationalism* (London: Routledge 1994)

O'BRIEN, Patrick (ed.), *Erect Me a Monument of Broken Wings: An Anthology of Writings by and on Padraic Fallon* (Athenry, Co. Galway: V. P. Shield 1992)

O'CASEY, Seán, *The Green Crow: Selected Writings of Seán O'Casey* (New York: George Braziller 1956; repub. London: Virgin Books 1994)

Ó FARACHÁIN, Roibeárd, *The Course of Irish Verse* (London: Sheed & Ward 1948)

Ó hAODHA, Micheál (ed.), *The O'Casey Enigma*, Thomas Davis Lectures (Cork: Mercier Press/RTÉ 1980)

SAUL, George Brandon, *Daniel Corkery* (Pennsylvania: Bucknell University Press 1973)

SHEERAN, Patrick, *The Novels of Liam O'Flaherty* (Dublin: Wolfhound Press 1976)

TAPPING, Craig, *Austin Clarke* (Dublin: Academy Press 1981)

THEATRE

DOYLE, Paul A., *Paul Vincent Carroll* (Pennsylvania: Bucknell University Press 1971)

EDWARDS, Hilton, *The Mantle of Harlequin* (Dublin: Progress House 1954)

ELLIS-FERMOR, Una, *The Irish Dramatic Movement* (London: Methuen 1954)

FITZ-SIMON, Christopher, *The Boys: A Double Biography* [of Micheál Mac Liammóir and Hilton Edwards] (Dublin: Gill & Macmillan 1994)

HOGAN, Robert, *After the Irish Renaissance* (London: Macmillan 1968)

HUNT, Hugh, *The Abbey: Ireland's National Theatre 1904-1979* (Dublin: Gill & Macmillan 1979)

MAC LIAMMÓIR, Micheál, *Theatre in Ireland* (Dublin: Cultural Relations Committee of Ireland 1964)

MAXWELL, D. E. S., *A Critical History of Modern Irish Drama 1891-1980* (Cambridge University Press 1981)

MURRAY, Christopher, *Twentieth-century Irish Drama* (Manchester University Press 1997)

Ó HAODHA, Micheál, *Theatre in Ireland* (Oxford: Basil Blackwell 1990)

Ó HAODHA, Micheál, *Plays and Places*, (Dublin: Progress House 1961)

ROBINSON, Lennox, *Ireland's Abbey Theatre: A History 1899-1951* (London: Sidgwick & Jackson 1951)

SHAUGHNESSY, Edward L., *Eugene O'Neill in Ireland: The Critical Reception* (Connecticut: Greenwood Press 1988)

SWIFT, Carolyn, *Stage by Stage* (Dublin: Poolbeg Press 1985)

RELIGION

BLANSHARD, Paul, *The Irish and Catholic Power* (Boston: The Beacon Press 1953)

CORISH, Patrick, *The Irish Catholic Experience: A Historical Survey* (Dublin: Gill & Macmillan 1985)

ELLIS, Ian, *Vision and Reality: A Survey of Twentieth-century Irish Inter-Church Relations* (Queen's University of Belfast, 1992)

FLANNERY, Tony, CSsR, *The Death of Religious Life?* (Dublin: Columba Press 1997)

MEIGS, Samantha A., *The Reformations in Ireland* (Dublin: Gill & Macmillan 1997)

NEWMAN, Jeremiah, *The State of Ireland* (Dublin: Four Courts Press 1977)

O'BRIEN, Conor Cruise [using pseudonym 'Donat O'Donnell'], *Maria Cross: Imaginative Patterns in a Group of Modern Catholic Writers* (London: Chatto & Windus 1952)

O'CARROLL, Michael, CSSp, *A Priest in Changing Times* (Dublin: Columba Press 1998)

O'SULLIVAN, Patrick (ed.), *The Irish World Wide. Volume 5: Religion and Identity* (Leicester University Press 1996)

WHITE, John H., *Church and State in Modern Ireland 1923-1979* (Dublin: Gill & Macmillan 1980)

WHITE, W. J., *Minority Report: The Protestant Community in the Irish Republic* (Dublin: Gill & Macmillan 1975)

WHITEHOUSE, J. C. (ed.), *Catholics on Literature* (Dublin: Four Courts Press 1997)

THE IRISH LANGUAGE

CORKERY, Daniel, *The Fortunes of the Irish Language* (Cork: Mercier Press 1954)

FLOWER, Robin, *The Irish Tradition* (Oxford: Clarendon Press 1947, republ. 1978)

GREENE, David, *Writing in Irish Today* (Cultural Relations Committee of Ireland/Cork: Mercier Press 1972)

MHAC AN TSAOÍ, Máire, *Margadh na Saoire* (Dublin: Sairséal agus Dill 1956)

NA GCOPALEEN, Myles, *An Béal Bocht* (Dublin: An Press Náisiúnta 1941, republ. Dublin: Dolmen Press 1964); English translation as *The Poor Mouth* (Dublin: Dolmen Press 1964)

Ó CADHAIN, Mairtín, *Cré na Cille* (Dublin: Sairséal agus Dill 1948)

Ó COILEÁIN, Seán, *Seán Ó Riordáin: Beatha agus Saothar* (Dublin: An Clóchomar 1982)

Ó COILEÁIN, Seán, *Scríbhneoirí na Gaeilge 1945-1995* (Dublin: Comhar 1995)

Ó CUIV, Brian (ed.), *A View of the Irish Language* (Dublin: Stationery Office 1969)

Ó DIREÁIN, Mairtín, *Rogha Dánta* (Dublin: Sairséal agus Dill 1949)

Ó RIORDÁIN, Seán, *Eireaball Spideóige* (Dublin: Sairséal agus Dill 1952)

Ó SUILLEABHÁIN, Muiris, *Fiche Bliain ag Fás* (Dublin: Talbot Press 1933); English translation as *Twenty Years A-Growing* by George Thomson and Moya Llewellyn Davies (London: Chatto & Windus 1933)

Ó TUAMA, Seán (selection and introduction by), *Nuabhéarsaíocht* (Dublin: Sairséal agus Dill 1950)

Ó TUAMA, Seán (ed.), *The Gaelic League Idea* (Cork: Mercier Press 1972)

SAYERS, Peig, *An Old Woman's Reflections*, transl. by Seamus Ennis (Oxford University Press 1962)

ANGLO-IRISH THEMES

BECKETT, J. C., *The Anglo-Irish Tradition* (London: 1976)

BENCE-JONES, Mark, *Twilight of the Ascendancy* (London: Constable 1987)

BENCE-JONES, Mark, *Life in the Irish Country House* (London: Constable 1996)

BOWEN, Elizabeth, *Collected Impressions* (London: Longmans Green 1950)

BOWEN, Elizabeth, *Bowen's Court* (London: Victor Gollancz 1942; republ. Cork: Collins Press 1998)

CANNADINE, David, *The Decline and Fall of the British Aristocracy* (Massachusetts: Yale University Press 1990)

FINGAL, Countess of, *Seventy Years Young: Memories of Elizabeth, Countess of Fingal* (London: Collins 1937; republ. Dublin: Lilliput Press 1991)

GOFF, Annabel, *Walled Gardens: Scenes from an Anglo-Irish Childhood* (London: Barrie & Jenkins 1990)

LEWIS, Gifford, *Somerville and Ross: The World of the Irish R. M.* (London: Viking 1985)

MCCORMACK, W. V., *Ascendancy and Tradition in Anglo-Irish Literary History 1789-1939* (Oxford University Press 1985)

WHITE, Terence de Vere, *The Anglo-Irish* (London: Victor Gollancz 1972)

ART AND ARCHITECTURE

ARNOLD, Bruce, *Mainie Jellett and the Modern Movement in Ireland* (Massachusetts: Yale University Press 1991)

ARNOLD, Bruce, *A Concise History of Irish Art* (London: Thames & Hudson rev. ed. 1977)

BECKER, Annette, John Olley and Wilfried Wang (eds), *20th-century Architecture: Ireland* (Munich/New York: Prestel 1997)

BOWE, Nicola Gordon, *The Life and Work of Harry Clarke* (Dublin: Irish Academic Press 1989)

DANAHER, Kevin, *Ireland's Vernacular Architecture* (Cultural Relations Committee of Ireland/Cork: Mercier Press 1975)

FALLON, Brian, *Irish Art 1830 to 1990* (Belfast: Appletree Press 1994)

HENRY, Paul, *An Irish Portrait* (London: B. T. Batsford 1951)

KENNEDY, S. B., *Irish Art and Modernism* (Institute of Irish Studies, Queen's University of Belfast 1991)

LYNCH, Brian (ed.), *Tony O'Malley* (London: Scolar Press and Kilkenny: Butler Gallery 1996)

MALLON, Declan, *Nano Reid* (Drogheda, Co. Louth: Sunnyside Publications 1994)

Michael Scott, Works 10 (Kinsale, Co. Cork: Gandon Editions 1993)

MURPHY, Seamus, *Stone Mad* (London: Routledge and Kegan Paul 1966)

O'DONOVAN, Donal, *God's Architect: A Life of Raymond McGrath* (Bray, Co. Wicklow: Kilbride Books 1995)

O'MEARA, Veronica Jane (ed.), *PS . . . Of Course: Patrick Swift 1927-1983* (Kinsale, Co. Cork: Gandon Books 1993)

PENROSE, Roland (introduction by), *MacWilliam* (London: Alec Tiranti 1964)

PYLE, Hilary, *Jack B. Yeats: A Catalogue Raisonnée of the Oil Paintings*, 3 vols (London: André Deutsch 1992)

SHAFFREY, Patrick and Maura, *Buildings of Irish Towns* (Dublin: O'Brien Press 1983)

SNODDY, Theo, *Dictionary of Irish Artists, 20th Century* (Dublin: Wolfhound Press 1996)

TOOBY, Michael and Simon Morley, *William Scott* (London: Merrell Holbexton, and Dublin: Irish Museum of Modern Art 1998)

TURPIN, John, *A School of Art in Dublin since the Eighteenth Century* (Dublin: Gill & Macmillan 1995)

WALKER, Dorothy, *Modern Art in Ireland* (Dublin: Lilliput Press 1997)

WALKER, Dorothy, *Louis le Brocquy* (Dublin: Ward River Press 1981)

WHITE, James, *Gerard Dillon* (Dublin: Wolfhound Press 1994)

WHITE, James and Michael Wynne, *Irish Stained Glass* (Dublin: 1963)

NOTES ON THE TEXTS DISCUSSED

Because Yeats, Joyce and various other leading Irish writers are nowadays so widely available, and sometimes in so many formats, it seems redundant and even silly to list them here at length. For Yeats, I have relied on *Yeats's Poems*, edited and annotated by A. Norman Jeffares, with an appendix by Warwick Gould (London: Papermac 1989). The current debates over Joyce's texts are an area into which I do not propose to enter, nor do I have the necessary scholarship to do so.

Although George Moore's novels have been slowly reappearing in print, this is largely confined to his earlier books, while much of his late fiction is virtually unobtainable. The works of AE are almost wholly out of print. So too are the poems of Seumas O'Sullivan. The Cuala Press editions of F. R. Higgins are collectors' items; however, Dardis Clarke has courageously printed a selection of his work, *F. R. Higgins: The 39 Poems* (Dublin: Bridge Press 1992). Since Patrick MacDonagh's *One Landscape Still* appeared in 1958, there has been no further edition of his poetry, but there are hopes that the Gallery Press will bring out a new edition shortly. *The Collected Poems* of my father, Padraic Fallon, appeared in 1990 in an edition published jointly by the Carcanet Press in Manchester and the Gallery Press in Dublin. The poems of Austin Clarke and Patrick Kavanagh are readily available, and the Dolmen Press has reprinted Clarke's novels. Flann O'Brien/Myles na Gopaleen can now be bought in any bookstore.

The Complete Plays of Seán O'Casey were collected by David Krause into five volumes in 1985; Krause also edited the collected letters. Samuel Beckett's plays, major and minor, are available from Faber & Faber. There appears, as yet, to be no coherent or authoritative edition of the collected writings of Brendan Behan – plays, stories, verse, journalism. For the moment, at least, he has to be read piecemeal. The works of many other Irish playwrights of the last sixty years are still relatively difficult of access.

The Wolfhound Press in Dublin has been responsible for bringing back into print the corpus of Liam O'Flaherty's fiction, though some of his other books are hard to find outside libraries. Seán O'Faolain and Frank O'Connor are both well represented in contemporary lists, and the novels of Benedict Kiely have recently been republished in paperback format, as well as his pioneering study of William Carleton, *Poor Scholar* (1947). Virago Press has reprinted the early novels of Molly Keane, most of them published under the alias of M. J. Farrell, and various works by Kate O'Brien. The works of Elizabeth Bowen are available in Penguin Books and elsewhere.

INDEX